Hellenic Studies 46

EVE OF THE FESTIVAL

Recent Titles in the Hellenic Studies Series

http://chs.harvard.edu/publications

EVE OF THE FESTIVAL
Making Myth in *Odyssey* 19

Olga Levaniouk

CENTER FOR HELLENIC STUDIES
Trustees for Harvard University
Washington, D.C.
Distributed by Harvard University Press
Cambridge, Massachusetts, and London, England
2011

Eve of the Festival: Making Myth in *Odyssey* 19 by Olga Levaniouk
Copyright © 2011 Center for Hellenic Studies, Trustees for Harvard University
All Rights Reserved.
Published by Center for Hellenic Studies, Trustees for Harvard University, Washington, DC.
Distributed by Harvard University Press, Cambridge, Massachusetts, and
    London, England
Printed in Ann Arbor, MI by Edwards Brothers, Inc.

LIBRARY OF CONGRESS CATALOGING-IN-PUBLICATION DATA:
Levaniouk, Olga, 1971-
 Eve of the festival : making myth in Odyssey 19 / by Olga Levaniouk.
    p. cm. -- (Hellenic studies ; 46)
 Includes bibliographical references and index.
 ISBN 978-0-674-05335-9 (alk. paper)
1. Homer. Odyssey. Book 19. 2. Myth in literature. 3. Penelope (Greek mythology) in
literature. 4. Odysseus (Greek mythology) in literature. 5. Epic poetry, Greek--History and
criticism. I. Title. II. Series.
  PA4168.A19L48 2010
  883'.01--dc22

                                                                    2010023638

To the memory of my grandparents,
Maria and Mendel

ACKNOWLEDGMENTS

IT IS MY PLEASURE TO THANK THE MANY PEOPLE who contributed to this book. I owe my first and deepest thanks to Gregory Nagy, who was my thesis director and has been a source of inspiration, a mentor, and a friend ever since. Though my interest in Homer is older, I was drawn to Homeric Studies by the magnetic power of Greg's work. It opened my eyes to what scholarship could do, and the transformative force of that discovery remains fresh in my memory. It is my great luck to have later become Greg's student and then colleague, and to experience first-hand his life-affirming generosity with ideas and time. On this occasion, I thank him especially for reading an earlier version of this book and giving me crucial comments. My references to Greg's work will make his scholarly influence clear, but my debt to him is more profound than can be acknowledged in footnotes.

A fellowship from the Loeb Library Foundation in 2005 gave me time to imagine the overall shape of the book so that writing could begin in earnest. The Department of Classics at the University of Washington has been a wonderfully collegial and supportive place to work. I am grateful in particular to Stephen Hinds, Jim Clauss, Alain Gowing, Catherine Connors, and Ruby Blondell for their feedback and encouragement.

Calvert Watkins and Gloria Ferrari read my dissertation on local traditions in the *Odyssey*, from which parts of this book originate. Their instruction was of great help at that now distant stage, and they continue to guide my steps indirectly through the example of their scholarship. Chapter 17 began its life as an essay for a collection, *Nine Essays on Homer*, and I am indebted to all participants in that project (Miriam Carlisle, Brian Breed, Mary Ebbott, Andrea Kouklanakis, Fred Naiden, Corinne Pache, John Watrous) for their critiques and editorial help. Albert Henrichs' recommendations were instrumental in the shaping of Chapter 2 in its earlier instantiation as an article (Levaniouk 2000a). Parts of Chapters 12 and 16 were presented at the conference "Penelope's Revenge," held in Calgary in 2004, and much improved by reactions I received there, especially those of Reyes Bertolín-Cebrián,

Pura Nieto-Hernández, David Konstan, and Ingrid Holmberg. This book benefited from the many stimulating conversations I had with Natasha Bershadsky and from her masterful stylistic advice. Anita Nikkanen read this book in its preliminary shape and sent me a multitude of useful suggestions and corrections. Jill Curry Robbins shepherded the manuscript through the editorial process with understanding, efficiency and expertise. Irene Convey formatted and proofread the text. Special thanks are due to Leonard Muellner for countless good deeds ranging from professional counsel to help with computers, for his graceful realism and immense forbearance during the years of my work on this book, and for his remarkable scholarship.

Finally, this book would never have been written without my family. I am endlessly grateful to my parents for their patience and also for their impatience, for babysitting and practical help, but most of all for their encouragement and moral support. I thank my aunt, Irina Petrovna Levaniouk, for introducing me to the epic of Alpamysh. I am grateful to my son Tosha for being born between part one and part two and making me see that I must finish the manuscript. And I am grateful to my husband and colleague, Alex Hollmann, for being my first reader, for offering countless comments and saving me from numerous mistakes, and for never refusing to re-read a section, even when I myself could no longer bear to do so. I owe a great deal to his critical judgment and sage advice. Needless to say, any mistakes and infelicities remaining are my own.

CONTENTS

INTRODUCTION

T HIS BOOK IS ABOUT THE POETICS OF MYTH in a single Homeric conversation, the dialogue between Penelope and Odysseus in *Odyssey* 19, their first, longest, and most enigmatic exchange of words. My interest in the way myth functions in oral poetry precedes my interest in the dialogue and goes beyond it, but making general theoretical claims on the subject is not the primary goal of the current work. Rather, this is an applied endeavor, an attempt not only to illustrate the workings of myth in Homer, but also to study a particular episode through a mythological lens and to gain interpretive ground in this way.

The scene I have chosen for my test case has received its share of scholarly attention and has been viewed as everything from a compositional low point to a masterpiece of indeterminacy.[1] Interpretations have changed dramatically over the last hundred years, and in my opinion much for the better, so that at the moment the treatment of dialogue constitutes a good example of advances in Homeric scholarship. The study of Homeric genres of discourse, voices, conversational patterns, and properties of spoken word has been something of a growth industry in recent decades, with the result that the old subject of "speeches" in Homer has emerged in a completely new light.[2] Questions of

---

[1] Dissatisfaction with the composition of Book 19 was prevalent at the end of nineteenth and the beginning of the twentieth centuries. The dialogue scene was criticized by Wilamowitz (1884:61–63), von Mühl (RE Supplement VII col. 750 lines 23–38), and Schwartz (1924:110). Woodhouse expresses a typical opinion when he writes,"the poet's construction hereabouts resembles some ramshackle engine" (1930:88), (further references and discussion in Harsh 1950). Harsh attempted to resolve the difficulties and uncover the coherence of the scene by arguing that Penelope recognizes Odysseus during the dialogue. His argument has not enjoyed much scholarly acceptance, though it is followed, up to a point, by Winkler (1990:155, 160), who, however, rejects the term "recognition" and labels Harsh's suggestion as "certainly untenable" in its "literal form." Other attempts to resolve the compositional difficulties of Book 19 include, e.g., Whitman 1958:303–304, Amory 1963, Austin 1975, Russo 1982. The focus in recent years has shifted from attempts to impart consistency to this part of the *Odyssey* toward an appreciation of inconsistency in its own right. See especially Murnaghan 1987, Katz 1991, Felson 1994, Doherty 1995, Peradotto 2002.

[2] The fundamental works are Martin 1989 and Bakker 1997; recent studies include Beck 2005 and Minchin 2007, both with abundant bibliographies.

disguise, identity, recognition, coded speech, knowledge, and ignorance have also been at the center of Odyssean studies.[3] As one of the longest sustained conversations in Homer, especially interesting for its interlocutors of different genders, the dialogue has become a battleground and a test case for these scholarly trends. More than that, the scene in Book 19 is also arguably the moment of Penelope's most crucial decision in the poem, and accordingly has attracted the attention of scholars interested in questions of agency in general and female agency in particular.[4] Important work on gender and gendered poetics in the *Odyssey* has also focused on the dialogue, not surprisingly, since this is the scene where Penelope says more about herself than anywhere else.[5] In short, there is no shortage of excellent and compelling scholarship on the very scene I propose to discuss, and I can make no pretences here about correcting past wrongs or restoring an overlooked subject to its proper place under the sun. The dialogue has not, to my knowledge, been analyzed from the particular angle I adopt, but this only partly justifies my decision to focus on this well-studied scene. Primarily I venture to write about it because, for all the unquestionable scholarly advances, the episode remains among the most mysterious in the *Odyssey,* its mysteries perhaps deepened rather than resolved by recent scholarship.

Several factors make the interpretation of the dialogue so complicated. For one thing, Penelope and Odysseus do not speak plainly, but in hints, coded messages, and multi-layered statements, Odysseus' physical disguise as a beggar being only one of many levels of concealment and revelation that come into play as the couple talk. Introducing the stranger, Eumaeus prepares Penelope for someone who speaks like a poet, a master of words, a person whose power of speech is enchanting (*Odyssey* 17.518–521). For his part, Odysseus observes Penelope with the suitors and concludes that she says one thing but hides another meaning underneath, and that she too has the power to charm with words (*Odyssey* 18.281–283). When the two meet, they put their impressive powers of verbal art to full use, engaging in an exchange of performances, in fact a dialogue in performances, where each interlocutor is fully able to appreciate the other's skills. Indirect, allusive, enigmatic, powerful, and manipulative discourse is omnipresent in the scene. In my opinion, the dialogue in *Odyssey* 19 can even be seen as a performative *agon*, and one of

---

[3] Murnaghan 1987, Peradotto 1990, Felson 1994, Papadopoulou-Belmehdi 1994, Doherty 1995, Ahl and Roisman 1996, to name just a few book-length studies.

[4] Most notably Foley 1995 and 2001, Marquardt 1985.

[5] Works cited in the two previous notes fit into this category as well; important recent contributions include Clayton 2004 and Minchin 2007.

the most sophisticated examples of such agonistic exchanges that have come down to us from antiquity. All of this is what makes the dialogue so interesting but it also makes for a difficult task for a modern, or for that matter ancient, interpreter. No doubt the scene, full of hints and riddles as it is, was meant to entertain by exercising the detective faculties even of the ancient audiences, but modern scholars are at a particular disadvantage, being outsiders who do not speak the language, literally and metaphorically.

In the case of *Odyssey* 19, our plight is aggravated by what has been called "the Penelope question," the question whether or not Penelope recognizes Odysseus at this stage.[6] This has been one of the most debated problems in Odyssean studies, with battle lines firmly drawn and copious argumentation presented on both sides.[7] I attempt to keep this question somewhat in the background, in the hopes of preventing it from overshadowing the rest of the argument, though I do, of course, make my answer to it clear. My reluctance to engage with the "Penelope question" more fully is motivated by the realization that no argument on this subject is likely to change many minds, a conclusion that can be safely drawn from recent scholarship. There is an inevitable element of subjectivity in each scholar's answer to the question, as all such answers involve some reasoning based on what Penelope is or is not likely to do or say, and on what does and does not make sense.

And yet there is in the end no avoiding of the troublesome Penelope question, at least not entirely, since Penelope's utterances and her actions may be taken in widely different ways depending on whether she speaks to a complete stranger or to someone whom she at least suspects of being her husband. When I suggest my own interpretation of the dialogue, therefore, and argue as part of it that in Book 19 Penelope does indeed think that the beggar is Odysseus, I am far from imagining that I have found the "right" way to understand the episode. Rather, my secondary claim is that such an interpretation is indeed possible (contrary to the prevalent scholarly opinion), is not contradicted by anything in the poem, and is internally logical. In my opinion, the opposite assumption, that Penelope has no inkling about the identity of her guest, is, on the contrary, less logical and less internally consistent (though it may still be more appealing to some audiences of the poem, for reasons of their own). My main claim, however, and the one that I find more

---

[6] See Doherty 1995 for a useful survey of critical literature on the "Penelope question" (her term).

[7] See note 1; recent studies that argue against recognition include Foley 2001 and Heitman 2005. To my mind, the most profitable recent reconsideration and reformulation of the question (in terms that remove the question of Penelope's psychology) is Scodel 2001.

interesting, is that there are layers and levels of meaning in the *Odyssey* that are fully activated only if Penelope is granted insight into the beggar's identity, and, further, that these layers of meaning are present not only in Penelope's own words but also in those of Odysseus. The last point raises the stakes of the Penelope question since it becomes also an Odysseus question, and at the same time leads me to shun the notion of recognition, even if I find it hard to avoid using this term completely.

The problem I see with the word "recognition" is that it invites the notion that Penelope is the only actor involved, that the question of recognition is a matter of her doing or failing to do something. The dialogue and the recognition can then be seen as separate matters: in the course of their conversation Penelope either does or does not recognize Odysseus, but that has little to do, at least initially, with the conversation itself. My view, in contrast, is that what is at stake is the question not of recognition but of communication, with both parties equally involved in the process. Odysseus makes a veiled claim to his identity, which Penelope understands and acknowledges, whether or not she actually recognizes (or believes) him, and her understanding is, in turn, conveyed to Odysseus, who, for his part, understands the message and lets Penelope know that he does so.

At all stages of the conversation, myth is involved in communication, through use as an *exemplum*, allusion, evocation, or appeal to myth-making patterns. As Martin has demonstrated, the word *muthos* in its Homeric usage actually applies to speech acts such as boasts, prophecies, prayers, etc., and its later extension to "imaginative traditional narratives" may in fact be traced to an earlier stage in which the authoritative speech acts it designated would often be enhanced by the traditional narratives. As Martin explains, "The best *muthoi* in the original sense would naturally involve the most powerful images, often resorting to genealogical recitation and claims about past status. It is only when such rhetoric is cut loose from its context of political antagonism that it takes on the appearance of harmless and pleasant fiction."[8] Neither the myths nor even the mythological allusions in the dialogue between Penelope and Odysseus fall into the category of "harmless and pleasant fiction," for they are at least in part agonistic and constitute part of vitally important negotiations between the two parties. Both Odysseus and Penelope are masters of *muthoi* and consequently of myth and mythological allusion, the virtuoso use of which is as much a part of their dialogue as are various linguistic codes and conventions.

---

[8] Martin 1989:54–55.

In trying to understand both the mechanics and meaning of their myth-making, I take my inspiration from the work of Slatkin, who observes that by oblique reference to myth the poet "incorporates into this narrative another discourse, one that makes its appearance on the surface of the poem though oblique references, ellipses, or digressions, evoking for his audience themes that orient or supplement the events of the poem in particular ways."[9] All poetry, and indeed all speech, has a connotative as well as denotative level, and all speech is to some extent elliptical and allusive. I follow Slatkin, however, in asserting that oral traditional poetry, such as the *Odyssey*, is elliptical and allusive in a special way and to an extraordinarily high degree. As Lord observed, phrases in Homeric poetry "resound with overtones from the dim past whence they came," a feature that distinguishes it from most kinds of written composition.[10] Complex interconnections, intricate correlations, and most of all the resonant power of themes and phraseology are a mark of a long and developed tradition of oral poetry such as the Homeric one.[11] Mythological evocation is only one of many kinds of allusion, digression, and ellipsis that are present in the *Odyssey*, but it is a very pervasive one, and excluding it from analysis of the scene would amount to a flattening of the dialogue. I see my attempts to analyze this register of *Odyssey* 19 as a contribution to the study of specifically oral poetics.[12]

I take this position in full awareness of the fact that oral poetics is not a clear-cut category and that it may not be possible to define it in a simple way. For example, listing features that are only found in oral poetry and never in written or vice versa may be a doomed undertaking. Each individual feature, such as formulaic nature or tendency towards ring composition, may be present in both written and oral poetry, but it will not be present to the same extent. When many such quantitative differences are combined the result is a noticeable difference between oral and written poetics, even in the absence of

---

[9] Slatkin 1991:xv–xvi.

[10] Lord 1960:65

[11] See, e.g., Foley 1999:23–34 for a discussion of this quality of Homeric poetry, and see further below.

[12] Notopoulos (1949) introduced the notion that an "oral aesthetic" was a subject to be pursued by the Homeric scholarship. I prefer to think of oral poetics, however, rather than aesthetics, though there is presumably an overlap. The connotative aspect of oral Homeric poetry emerges clearly in studies such as Nagy 1979, Muellner 1976 and 1996, Slatkin 1986 and 1991, Lowenstam 1981 and 1993, and Nagler 1974. Foley has coined the term "traditional referentiality," and has consistently championed this aspect of Homeric poetry in his work (see especially Foley 1991 and 1999). The term has entered into common usage as the phenomenon has gained recognition (see, e.g. Danek 2002).

a clear boundary line. It is perhaps this impossibility of an easy definition that leads some scholars to question oral poetics as a legitimate object of study. Cairns, for example, states plainly that "no such thing is necessary" and that "the onus is now on oralists to demonstrate that there is any significant way in which the status of the *Iliad* as an oral-derived text precludes the application of familiar interpretive strategies."[13] My answer to this is that we should expect to find some overlap between oral and written poetry, and that it is, of course, manifestly possible to analyze Homeric poetry as if it were a written text, but that this is not a good criterion for rejecting the notion of oral poetics. The point is not that the "application of familiar interpretive strategies" is precluded, but rather that it is insufficient: it misses something because such interpretive strategies tend to be blind to certain essential aspects of Homeric poetry.

Oral poetry is referential and self-referential in a distinct way, as formulated by Nagy, following Lord: "From the standpoint of oral poetics, each occurrence of a theme (on the level of content) or of a formula (on the level of form) in a given composition-in-performance refers not only to its immediate context but also to all other analogous contexts remembered by the performer or by any member of the audience."[14] This, I think, applies to evocation of myths as much as it does to formulas: each occurrence of a particular mythic pattern or element has the potential to activate a larger set of contexts associated with this pattern or element in the totality of tradition. Oral tradition is not a text or a collection of texts, but a system of human behavior, and the properties of mythological evocation in the *Odyssey* stem in part from this factor.[15] Nagy adduces as an analogy the linguistic distinction between *langue* and *parole* as formulated by Ferdinand de Saussure.[16] There is a two-way relationship between the system and its instantiations, tradition and performance, and *langue* and *parole*. Elements can become metonymically connected because of co-occurrence and the connection itself then becomes part of the *langue*, available for its speakers to use. The phenomenon of traditional referentiality, or meaning through reference, is therefore by its nature diachronic,

---

[13] Cairns 2001:53. The opinion that the *Iliad* and the *Odyssey* were composed with the aid of writing and should be analyzed exclusively as written text is expressed in strong terms by West 2001a, 2001b, and 2003.

[14] Nagy 1996a:50.

[15] See Nagy 1979:xiv–xv on Homeric poetry as a system.

[16] Nagy 1996a:1.

dependent on the evolution of the tradition in the process of continuous re-performance.[17]

Just as certain words are synonymous in a language, so certain myths and mythological patterns are synonymous in the system that is the mythological corpus. The synonyms can be combined to reinforce meaning: one may bring others to mind. Yet equally essential are the distinctions between them, the choice of one over the other. This results, in effect, in an additional register of discourse achieved through myth, a register that is both very nuanced and very frequently engaged in Homer, but that is not always obvious. As Slatkin puts it, talking about the mythological corpus: "The poet inherits as his repertory a system, extensive and flexible, whose components are familiar, in their manifold variant form, to his listeners. For an audience that knows the mythological range of each character, divine or human – not only through this epic song, but through other songs, epic or non-epic – the poet does not spell out the myth in its entirety but locates a character within through allusion or oblique reference."[18] As Foley points out, this principle "enables a highly economical discourse among insiders" while often leaving the outsiders in the dark, or at least sensitive only to the more overt parts of the performance.[19]

Though I do not eschew the word completely (in the absence of a ready substitute), I have reservations regarding the term "allusion." Among other things, it invites the assumption that some particular text is being alluded to, which is not the case in an oral tradition. For the purposes of this study "allusion" should be understood to refer to a specifically oral phenomenon, which has as its target not a text but rather, to come back to Nagy's formulation, "contexts remembered by the performer or by any member of the audience." This does, of course, mean that the same allusion in the same performance could point to different targets for different listeners, and yet that would not, in my opinion, impede communication between the poet and his audience. My working assumption is that when Homeric poetry alludes to a myth it alludes in effect to something in the system, in the *langue*, of the tradition that is familiar to most of the audience. Each particular member might know this part of the *langue* through different experiences on the level of *parole*, primarily different poetic performances, but also any other ways of learning

---

[17] I refer here to Nagy's evolutionary model for the creation of Homeric poetry, according to which the poems we know as the *Iliad* and the *Odyssey* underwent a period of progressive fixation and achieved a relatively stable form well before written texts came to play any role in their perpetuation. See Nagy 1979:xiv–xvii and Nagy1996b.29–63.

[18] Slatkin 1991:xv.

[19] Foley 1999:27

myths. As long as the *langue* of tradition persists, however, the communication can continue, even if, as with any language, the language of myth could never be exactly the same in two different heads.

In trying to reflect the variable nature of the target of allusions in oral poetry I also use a synonymous term, "evocation." This word conveys the sense of activating notions and associations, of bringing to mind stories, characters, words, and actions that are not explicitly identified in the poem, but without necessarily presupposing any particular textual point of reference. Essentially the same phenomenon has been also called "resonance," a term Graziosi and Haubold define as a Homeric "ability to evoke a web of associations and implications by referring to the wider epic tradition."[20]

The difference between evocation and resonance, in turn, points to another thorny question in oral poetics, namely whether we are dealing with conscious artistic choices or with effects of the system that are independent of the poet. "Evocation" seems to presuppose a poetic design, while "resonance" leaves the question open. In oral poetry, where there is no single poet to reckon with, the strict distinction between design and its absence is neither possible nor desirable. We have no reason to doubt that the practitioners of this poetry were aware of the evocative powers of their words, and therefore there is no reason to deny them artistic intent in harnessing this power. It is the factor of tradition, however, that allows the poet to make such choices and to create the kind of resonant poetry that can be found in the *Iliad* and the *Odyssey*.[21]

Another thorny question in oral poetics that pertains especially to the study of associative meaning is the question of the audience and its ability or desire to notice it. Any work on allusion and resonance is open to questioning on the grounds that the poets and their audiences would not have been familiar with some specific myth involved. To this my reply is that I do not claim that all were familiar with a given myth, but that some may have been, and that is sufficient for the validity of the allusion. Moreover, since the allusions in question are not to particular texts but to multiform elements of a living oral tradition, it is not necessary to assume that the audiences knew precisely the versions of the myth familiar to us. The "analogous contexts" available to any given audience or any giver performer were in all likelihood different from the analogous context available to us. As long as all these contexts are still analogous, however, they are part of the same metonymical

---

[20] Graziosi and Haubold 2005:9.
[21] See Kelly 2007:5–6 for a discussion of this question.

system that is operative in the *Odyssey* and are essential for it. The resonances are there, in other words, to be felt, and no doubt some of them were felt most of the time, while others might have been accessible only to particular audiences.[22]

By the same token, my claim that Homeric poetry is aware of mythological variation and uses it creatively does not depend on the assumption that all Homeric audiences knew all the relevant versions of a given myth. The poets may select one version over another and gain additional meaning by doing so, but in most cases the audience familiar with any version of the myth will still be able to understand the reference on some level, and even an audience completely unfamiliar with the myth would not be entirely lost. Those in possession of the better-fitting version, however, or those more attuned to the mythological variation, will be in a position to appreciate the fuller effect of the utterance. There is no reason to endow any hypothetical ancient audience with an encyclopedic knowledge of myth, but there is every reason to think that ancient Greek audiences, for whom the differences, clashes, and modifications of multitudinous local myths were a lived reality, were much more attuned to the very phenomenon of mythological variation than modern scholars for whom panhellenic mythology as reflected in poetry is the main frame of reference.

With regard to the evocation of myth in *Odyssey* 19, I suggest not only that it is there, but also that the connotative level of discourse has a direct impact on its denotative level. In other words, if we miss the associative meanings activated by the use of myth, direct and indirect, and of mythological variation, then we miss not just some subtlety, some additional but non-essential flavor, but rather the actual meaning of the conversation. If that claim can be sustained, it in itself would constitute evidence for the existence of audiences who were well enough versed in poetry and myth to follow this mode of communication. A position very similar to mine has been recently articulated by Kelly, whose work, not coincidentally, is also centered on referentiality and based on the premise that the oral and traditional origins of our Homeric texts are deeply significant for the understanding of them. As Kelly puts it, the abilities of any particular listener do not constitute an "objection to be directed against the author's intention to generate that hypothetically maximum level

---

[22] See Kelly 2007:11–13 on the audience's familiarity with the poems and for the suggestion that the universalizing tendency of the Homeric poetry and its panhellenic status would lead to the expression of "the widest possible experience of epic language and world." See Scodel 2002, esp. 1–41 for extended discussion of these and other questions relating to the audiences of Homeric poetry.

of meaning." Further, Homeric epic may be especially prone to generating this "maximum level" of meaning since it is a panhellenic and universalizing genre aimed at the widest possible audience.[23]

We may not be able to get in touch with the reality of Homeric performances in antiquity, but we can try to get somewhat better in touch with those performances, explicitly or implicitly poetic, which are depicted within the *Odyssey* itself. Just as an oral poet uses myth in complex ways to achieve both immediate and far-reaching effects, so too do Penelope and Odysseus, and for them the factor of tradition is just as important. Like expert poets themselves, they use myths both directly and allusively, as main narratives and as *exempla*, in a way sensitive both to the moment and to the myth. As I examine these myths I observe that the way in which they fit into their context is so strikingly complex that virtually nothing appears to be *ad hoc*. I conclude that the myths in question are traditional not only in their content but even in their interactions with the context in which they are deployed, and that the fit between the myths and their context is itself a matter of tradition. By this I do not mean to say that Book 19 was re-performed for a long time with all its current elements in place and is free of innovations. Rather I suggest that expertly chosen elements, whenever they are introduced, instantly become deeply integrated into their Odyssean context because they bring with them sets of associations, of metonymies, which are congruent with those already activated in the poem. It may be, for example, that some myths alluded to in the *Odyssey* are innovations within the *Odyssey*, but drawn from traditional settings related or parallel to the poetic settings where they feature in Homer.[24] In keeping with my views regarding the oral character of Homeric poetry, I resist the notion of the uniqueness of our texts, and also the notion that there is only one way of achieving the remarkable degree of resonance, cohesion, and complexity that is observable in the *Odyssey*. I have little doubt that other elements could be substituted for some of our familiar text, including some of the mythological allusions, in such a way that the altered *Odyssey* would appear as equally well orchestrated as the one we know. The choices that are made in the *Odyssey*, however, have presumably withstood the test of time, and in that sense they

---

[23] Kelly 2007:12–13.

[24] See Nagy 1996b:113–146 on the traditional nature of Homeric mythological *exempla* and cf. the views exemplified by Wilcock 1964 and 1977, to which Nagy reacts. Lang (1983, esp. 149) offers a convincing argument against the notion of invention and drastic innovation in Homeric myths, showing that such invention would in fact deprive *paradeigmata* of their effectiveness. See also Scodel 2002:5–6 on the importance of context-bound remembering for the definition of tradition.

constitute excellent test cases for studying the intricacy of interactions between the myths and contexts in which they are told or alluded to.

My subject is not every kind of metonymy and resonance in *Odyssey* 19, but only evocation of myth. There is, however, no firm boundary between mythological and non-mythological evocation and consequently I have to admit to using the term "myth" in a rather vague and broad way and making arbitrary decisions regarding the inclusion or exclusion of particular parts of the dialogue. In my defense, I can only appeal to Aristotle, who advises, "to seek only so much precision in any subject as the nature of that subject affords."[25] Myth, of course, is notoriously impossible to define, or at least to define comprehensively, and perhaps a single definition is not necessary for my purposes.[26] It is, however, important to attempt to formulate what is at stake. Myth lends its power to many utterances of the dialogue, while mythic patterns contextualize it, and I suggest that some of the resulting effect depends not only on the content of myths but also on the very fact that they are myths rather than simply stories.

One way of defining a myth is to say that it is a narrative that is in some way authoritative and traditional for the group that perpetuates it, as distinct from a purely personal story, which does not have the same social value, be it true or fictitious.[27] Some of the myths I consider would easily fit this definition: these are narratives of the past that have become part of the canon, a common reference point for the society to whom they belonged. Other utterances look at first sight very much like personal stories. A case in point is Odysseus' Third Cretan Lie, in which he creates a fictitious identity for himself and tells Penelope an apparently equally fictitious story about Odysseus' visit to Crete. The story of Odysseus' visit to Crete on the way to Troy is not commonly regarded as a myth, yet by evoking myths and mythic patterns, it and other apparently personal and *ad hoc* stories can tap into the power, authority, and significance of myth *sensu stricto*. More importantly for my argument, this story is a myth from the internal standpoint of the *Odyssey*, a myth that is made by Odysseus, and whose making we can observe 'live' as Odysseus performs it.

Indeed, I would argue that the whole dialogue between Penelope and Odysseus may be seen as consisting of *muthoi* both in the Homeric sense of speech acts and in what seems to be the etymological meaning of the word

---

[25] *Nicomachean Ethics* 1094b.

[26] For some definitions and discussion of the question see Graf 1993.1–8, Edmunds 1990:1–20, Nagy 1990b:8 (discussed below), Burkert 1983:31–34, Pozzi and Wickersham 1991:1–10.

[27] Nagy 1990b:8.

muthos, namely 'special speech'.[28] I refer here to Nagy's comments regarding the distinction between unmarked everyday speech and the language of myth and ritual, which is marked: "In small-scale societies – rather than complex ones – we can observe most clearly the symbiosis of ritual and myth, how neither is to be derived from the other, and how the language of ritual and myth is marked, let us call it SONG, while everyday language, speech, is unmarked."[29] The dialogue between Penelope and Odysseus in Book 19 is non-everyday language in interesting and complex ways. There is an overlap between the language of ritual and myth as described by Nagy and the speech act, since both types of speech are indeed marked and both types depend on their occasion. This last factor is essential: the same words may constitute everyday speech in one setting but a myth in another setting. The details of Odysseus' costume, for example, may be every day speech in some context, but they are marked and special speech in the dialogue in Book 19.

Martin argues that Homeric poetry as a whole is a *muthos*, a grand speech-act, because it is inherently antagonistic, striving to overpower competing versions and probably created for poetic contest, thus being an act of powerful self-presentation on the part of its tradition and poets who perform it.[30] The totality of Homeric epic certainly fits Martin's definition of *muthos* within epic: "a speech-act indicating authority, performed at length, usually in public, with a focus on full attention to every detail."[31] But even more fundamentally, Homeric poetry is both myth and ritual, as Nagy has argued: "to perform this epic is to activate myth, and such activation is fundamentally a matter of ritual."[32] In the oral poetics of epic, composition interacts with performance in a way that parallels the interaction of myth and ritual, so that "the making of Homeric poetry is a matter of ritually performing the epic."[33] Its competitive nature is not the only reason to regard Homeric poetry as a whole as *muthos*, because composing such poetry in performance is always not only saying something but also doing something ritually.

Externally, then, all of Homer is marked speech, a speech-act, *muthos*. Internally, on the other hand, there are different degrees of markedness, and different ways of achieving it. Most obviously, Homeric poetry dramatizes the performance of *muthoi*, as, for example, when Phoenix performs the story

---

[28] Nagy 1990a:32.

[29] Nagy 1990a:31.

[30] Martin 1989:238–239.

[31] Martin 1989:12, Nagy 2007a:54.

[32] Nagy 2007a:53.

[33] Nagy 2007a:53, 54.

of Meleager or Odysseus performs his tales for the Phaeacians. Such overt dramatization of an actual performance is not, however, the only way of activating myth within the epic. I argue that a myth can be activated without being actually narrated: an evocation of a myth may trigger associations that ultimately depend on its meaning in local settings, where it is indeed special speech in Nagy's sense. Such associations may not be overt in Homer, but they can nevertheless be felt and used by poets and their audiences to create and understand poetry. In other words, Homeric poetry can evoke not only myths but also their various occasions, and such evocation taps into the power of myths as 'special speech'.

The ritual occasion for myth-making can also be created within the poem itself.[34] A case in point is the festival of Apollo in the *Odyssey* which occurs on the day on which Odysseus kills the suitors and fully returns to Ithaca and his position as king. The festival begins to exert its influence on the narrative long before it actually takes place: there are several mentions of its approach and Odysseus strikingly predicts that his own return will coincide with the festival. The day itself is marked by an assembly and a sacrifice in Apollo's sacred grove, followed by what seems to be a special meal in Odysseus's house, a feast that turns into a bow contest under Apollo's auspices and then into the slaughter of the suitors. The night of the same day sees the first performance of the *Odyssey* on Ithaca: Penelope tells her part of the story to Odysseus and Odysseus tells his adventures to Penelope all through the night (magically extended by Athena) until he is overcome with sleep. The *Odyssey* is famously self-conscious about its own poetics and the sliding, overlapping identities of its hero and the poetic voice. The mutual telling of the stories that concludes the festival day is a striking example of this self-referentiality, since in it the *Odyssey* dramatizes its own first performance and creates a very distinct occasion for it: the simultaneous completion of Apollo's festival and Odysseus' return. The stories, which on this occasion give pleasure to Odysseus and Penelope, are designated as *muthoi* (*Odyssey* 23.300), and arguably these stories are indeed not only 'authoritative statements' but also myths in the sense of 'special speech' uttered in a ritual setting, because on the poetic Ithaca created within the *Odyssey*, at the conclusion of its equally poetic festival of Apollo, the story of Odysseus' return is both a personal story and a central, reality-defining myth, and its performance a ritual act. To come back to Nagy's

---

[34] Cf. Bierl 2009, esp. 11–47 on the specifically ritual nature of comic choruses, not only as part of the festival of Dionysus, but also within the play, so that dramatic and ritual functions of the chorus are not easily separable.

formulation, Odysseus' composition-in-performance of his own tale for Penelope is a ritual act of activating a myth.[35]

I suggest that the same can be said about the dialogue between Penelope and Odysseus in Book 19, which takes place on the eve of the festival and which is also designated as *muthoi* (*Odyssey* 19.103). The eve of the festival is an occasion for preparation, both for the festival itself and for the concomitant return of Odysseus, which is on the verge of being accomplished. This is a special time much like the festival itself, a setting of heightened emotional state permeated by the anticipation of both the festival and of Odysseus' self-revelation. In this context the words exchanged by Odysseus and Penelope become "marked speech-acts associated with the special occasions of ritual and myth," to quote Nagy's words.[36]

The mythological allusions in the dialogue serve their purpose in the conversation, but I argue that they also interact with their setting, namely the eve of the festival and Odysseus' return. The dialogue between Penelope and Odysseus takes place in a special time and place, in the sphere of influence of Apollo's festival, and it both derives meaning from this circumstance and helps create the circumstance itself, its own poetic occasion. In the context of their setting, the apparently personal tales exchanged by Odysseus and Penelope are indeed 'special speech', and their performance within the poem is a ritual act. It is indeed this ritual act of performance that activates the myth of Apollo's festival in the *Odyssey* and makes the festival possible.

This is not to say, of course, that the dialogue constitutes, or includes, the myth of any actual festival of Apollo beyond the *Odyssey*, or that there is direct correspondence and complete inter-dependence between the festival and any myth narrated or evoked in the poem. It is entirely possible to imagine an *Odyssey* without any festival of Apollo at all, and in the *Odyssey* as we have it the nature of the festival remains relatively vague. Still, the festival of Apollo is a pivotal detail and in the *Odyssey* as we have it functions both as a poetic occasion and as a focal point for myth-making. To return again to Nagy's formulation, it is a question not of dependence, but of "symbiosis" of myth and ritual, in this case myth and ritual within the *Odyssey*.

Finding a correlation between Apollo's festival and the myths evoked in its proximity touches upon the question of connections between myth and ritual, a subject with a complicated scholarly history lasting now more than a century, so that the very phrase "myth and ritual" has become associated with

---

[35] Nagy 2007a:54
[36] Nagy 1990a:31.

theories and theorists no longer credible and with long decades of virulent polemics.[37] The older stages of the debate form a fascinating subject, which is, however, of little relevance to my work and accordingly needs no further mention here. For parts of my argument, however, I do rely heavily on the work of Burkert, which can be seen as a new way of tackling the old questions. Burkert rejects the notion that all myth originates in ritual or is associated with it, freely admitting that there are rites without myths and myths without rites and that the origins of either go too far back in time even to entertain the question of what came first. But at the same time, he does show, in my opinion, convincingly, that some myths and rituals do form a unity, a complex, that there are cases where myth is more or less explicitly associated with cultic activity, (most often, a festival), and where there is an observable correlation and parallelism between the myth and the ritual action.[38] I find this approach enlightening, and the notion that some myths and some rituals can be connected is important for my purposes. If myth can parallel ritual, then perhaps it can evoke ritual too (and ritual, in turn, can evoke myth), and in that case some of the *Odyssey*'s mythological allusions may acquire additional meaning through such evocation. If myth can, however complexly and loosely, be integrated into a festival, and if this connection between the myth and the festival is a part of the actual experience of Homeric poets and audiences, then the *Odyssey* can harness such experiences and evoke them in creating its allusive discourse under the aegis of Apollo's festival.

This is, of course, not achieved by directly reflecting any myth-ritual complex. Rather, precisely because the *Odyssey* is panhellenic, universalizing, and polyparadeigmatic it can mix and match myths in a way that transcends their local ritual connections, should there be any such, and perhaps even mix and match ritual echoes in the same way. The nature of Apollo's festival in the *Odyssey* is hinted at but not elaborated, and this may be a poetic strategy for ensuring the widest appeal and resonance for the festival without overburdening it with specifics. It seems to be a festival associated with seasonal change, certainly a beginning of a new period, and it also seems to be connected, in part, with the coming of age of a new generation. These two

---

[37] See Burkert 1983:29–34, and especially Versnel 1993:16–88.

[38] Burkert 1970, esp.1–2, Burkert 1983:29–34, Burkert 1966. Two of Burkert's many test cases have enjoyed particular success, convincing even some of the inveterate critics of any variety of myth-and-ritual approach (Kirk 1974:246): the Cecropides myth (Burkert 1966) and the myth of the Lemnian women in connection with the festival of Pyrphoria (Burkert 1970). The latter argument is important for my own, and remains in essence convincing (for a dissenting opinion, see Forsyth 1984).

aspects might have been combined in some actual festivals of Apollo, but it is unlikely that we are meant to think of any particular one. Some myths evoked in the *Odyssey* on this occasion may indeed have been associated with Apollo outside of Homer, or even correlate to a festival of the god, but such origins are not required for the myths to resonate with the festivals. The Odyssean choice of myths to allude to is neither simplistic nor random, and I come back here to Nagy's notion of "analogous context," which allows different myths from different places to form, within the *Odyssey*, a complex of their own.

Although my focus is on the working of mythological allusion in *Odyssey* 19 and not throughout the poem as a whole, it is, of course, impossible to isolate this crucial episode from its larger contexts, and consequently to isolate interpretation of myth within it from the interpretation of myth in the *Odyssey* as a whole. It so happens that the *Odyssey* has been something of a central text in the myth-and-ritual battles, with practically every school of thought seeing in it a perfect example of its own theories. As a result, the poem has been seen as reflecting multiple myth-ritual complexes, including first and foremost the two most prevalent ones: that of the dying and rising god, or king, at the New Year Festival, popular in the first half of the twentieth century and now discredited, and that of initiation, which, though arising earlier, enjoyed renewed popularity in the second half of the same century and still does today, in spite of some recent criticism. [39] This latter point is relevant to the current work, as I do appeal to the notion of "coming of age" and "transition" as part of my analysis. It is readily apparent that Van Gennep's tripartite initiation scheme, which is still the foundation for modern scholarship on the subject, mirrors in its basic outline the linear structure of countless quest narratives, including, for example, Russian fairy tales as analyzed by Propp.[40] The hero departs, undergoes trials, and returns. This is also, of course, the basic structure of Odysseus' adventures. In his extremely useful analysis of myth and ritual theories and their application to the *Odyssey*, Versnel sees the key to the *Odyssey*'s popularity in myth and ritual studies precisely in the fundamental and universal nature of its basic plot. The problem, as Versnel formulates it, is this: "How are we to explain that an '*Odyssey* pattern' shows itself in so many myths, fairy tales and stories, if we are not prepared

---

[39] The bibliography on the divine kingship and New Year complex in various religions is massive, beginning with the first two volumes of Fraser's *The Golden Bough* (1890) and Harrison's *Themis* (1912). For a historical survey and bibliography, see Versnel 1993:20–48. On initiation, see Versnel 1993:48–88, Padilla 1999, Dodd and Faraone 2003, and especially Graf 2003.

[40] Van Gennep 1977 (second edition of *The Rites of Passage*, originally published in French as *Les rites de passage* in 1909), Propp 1958 (translation of Propp 1928).

to trace this pattern invariably back either to the 'New Year complex' or to the 'initiation complex' or even to any ritual whatsoever?"[41] For an answer, Versnel turns to Burkert's theory that this tale's structure reflects a basic and ultimately biological "program of action."[42] The same explanation certainly cannot be applied to all myth, but Burkert makes a strong case for applying it to some, and also to some rites. The biology-derived program that, according to Versnel, underlies the *Odyssey*, is summarized by him in one verb: "to get," a program so basic that it is not even exclusively human. As Versnel puts it, "What the hero does in Propp's schema is essentially similar to what the rat does when – driven by hunger – it goes in search of prey and returns with the spoils, having escaped the street urchin's stones, the cat's jaws and envious fellow-rats."[43]

The next logical step is to suggest that both the New Year complex and the initiation complex go back to the same "most elementary and primordial scheme of (originally bio-sociological) functions," which is rehearsed in ritual and myth at points of crisis, such as the turning of the year, or a period of social transition.[44] Such a common origin would then explain both the fact that the proponents of the New Year and initiation theories often cite precisely the same evidence in support of their respective views, and also the fact that the *Odyssey* can be equally easily analyzed in terms of either scheme (or indeed of a number of other schemes, for example that of the shamanistic journey, which also involves the familiar sequence of separation, a period of marginality, and return).

Some of what I say may seem reminiscent of the "New Year complex" or the "initiatory complex" but this does not imply the application of any simplistic myth-and-ritual theory on my part. Although I do not see any connection between the *Odyssey* and Near Eastern New Year festivals, I do think that seasonal rhythm is present in the poem, and that Odysseus' return coincides with the end of one period and the beginning of another. By the same token, although there is nothing in the *Odyssey* that would fit a strict definition of an "initiation," there is much that undeniably has to do with transition from childhood to adulthood. The *Odyssey* is unlikely to derive from any single ritual or myth-and-ritual complex, but fundamental and pervasive patterns present in some rituals and some myth-ritual complexes are also present in the *Odyssey*, including those associated with coming of age, dissolution and

---

[41] Versnel 1993:73–74.
[42] See especially Burkert 1979, 1980, 1983.
[43] Versnel 1993:77.
[44] Versnel 1993:83.

restoration, perpetuation of family, and legitimation of (mythical) kingship. I think, further, that the *Odyssey* does not simply share some socio-biological origins with various mythic complexes, but also enters into contact with them. One of the things I hope my analysis illustrates is the way the *Odyssey* evokes different but mutually reinforcing mythological patterns to create what might be called a symphonic effect, with different themes creating a harmonious but complex whole and never converging into monotonous sound.

It is within this framework that I offer my observations regarding the solar themes in the *Odyssey*, observations that I feel require a special explanation in view of persistent scholarly aversion to solar mythology in the wake of Müller's excesses.[45] To make explicit what I hope will be obvious, I do not suggest that the *Odyssey* should be interpreted as a solar myth. But I do think the *Odyssey* evokes solar myths, and that this evocation is, within the *Odyssey*, a matter not only of poetic technique but also of ritual speech. The notion of the sun's disappearance and return parallels, of course, the basic initiatory scheme of separation and reintegration, as it does the "New Year" scheme of dissolution and restoration, and the basic pattern of departure and return that is undeniable in the *Odyssey*. And so it may come as no surprise that all these mythic complexes are alluded to in the poem. That this is done at all, however, is only a starting point. My interests lie in how it is done, and to what effect.

There is a great conceptual distance between observing the details of myth-making in a particular dialogue and seeking elemental foundations of myth and ritual that stretch back to the very origins of the human species. My aim here is the former rather than the latter, but at the same time I see this work as an attempt to combine two fields, poetics and mythology, to see myth not as something that underlies, but as something that constitutes the *Odyssey*, so that even the intricacies of the dialogue, or the ethics of Penelope's decision, cannot be analyzed without it. My goal, then, is to look at the dialogue in Book 19 through the lens of mythological evocation. Since Odysseus dominates the first part of the dialogue, I begin with the *muthoi* of Odysseus, focusing in particular on what is known as the Third Cretan Lie, and then move on to the second part of the dialogue, which is dominated by Penelope.

---

[45] Müller 1897. For a comprehensive recent discussion of Indo-European solar mythology, see West 2007:194–237. West (2007:237) concludes: "Müller's critics were right to castigate his excesses and those of the nature-myth school generally. But the reaction against that approach sometimes went too far. We have seen in this chapter that there was such a thing as solar mythology in Indo-European tradition, and a body of festive ritual associated with it."

PART ONE
ODYSSEUS

CHAPTER ONE

BEGINNING OF THE DIALOGUE
Setting up the Third Cretan Lie

THE DIALOGUE IN BOOK 19 STANDS OUT among the conversations in the *Odyssey* not only because of its length, but also because it is attempted, announced, and prepared so far in advance of the event. Not even the preliminaries of Odysseus' supplication of Arete, also a crucial and pre-arranged moment in the poem, can compare to the elaborateness and subtlety with which the audience is prepared to witness the first verbal exchange between Penelope and her husband. Penelope first attempts to have a conversation with the beggar in Book 17 and asks Eumaeus to bring him to her. Eumaeus reacts with some alarm, concerned about the effect the stranger's tales may have on his mistress. He compares the beggar's story-telling to the enchanting and captivating songs of an *aoidos* and even summarizes his stories for Penelope, including the claim that Odysseus is alive and now in Thesprotia, nearing home (*Odyssey* 17.512–527). This recap is perhaps a pre-emptive measure designed to give Penelope time to prepare for what is coming. Faced with Eumaeus' obvious reluctance, Penelope has to insist on her request and hint that she can make up her own mind about the stranger's report:

> τὸν δ' αὖτε προσέειπε περίφρων Πηνελόπεια·
> "ἔρχεο, δεῦρο κάλεσσον, ἵν' ἀντίον αὐτὸς ἐνίσπη.

> (*Odyssey* 17.528–529)

The circumspect Penelope responded to him:
"Come, call him here, so he can tell me himself."

There is no overt connection between this comment and what comes next. With apparent irony Penelope announces that in the meanwhile the suitors can continue to enjoy themselves at their feast, since it is not their own livelihood that they are consuming. This brings her to the absence of

Odysseus, defender of the household, and to her estimation of what would happen to her young wooers if he did come back:

εἰ δ' Ὀδυσεὺς ἔλθοι καὶ ἵκοιτ' ἐς πατρίδα γαῖαν,
αἶψά κε σὺν ᾧ παιδὶ βίας ἀποτείσεται ἀνδρῶν.

(Odyssey 17.539–540)

But should Odysseus come and return to his native land
together with his son he would make them pay for their
violence at once.

The beggar's hopeful report of Odysseus in Thesprotia is known to Penelope only at second hand and is *a priori* suspect, and yet somehow the very talk of this new visitor leads her to the thought of what might happen if Odysseus came back. Although elsewhere Penelope denies the possibility that her husband may still return, here her statement is an expression of potentiality, not a condition contrary to fact. What happens next is even more striking: Telemachus sneezes and the ever-pessimistic Penelope laughs and takes the sneeze as a good omen. This suddenly hopeful tone is again connected to the beggar's presence as Penelope, now for the third time, asks Eumaeus to bring the stranger to her:

ἔρχεό μοι, τὸν ξεῖνον ἐναντίον ὧδε κάλεσσον.
οὐχ ὁράᾳς, ὅ μοι υἱὸς ἐπέπταρε πᾶσιν ἔπεσσι;
τῷ κε καὶ οὐκ ἀτελὴς θάνατος μνηστῆρσι γένοιτο
πᾶσι μάλ', οὐδέ κέ τις θάνατον καὶ κῆρας ἀλύξει.

(Odyssey 17.544–547)

Go now and call the stranger to me.
Don't you see that my son sneezed at my words?
Therefore may death indeed come to the suitors,
all of them, and may not one escape death and fate.

Of course, Penelope laughs as she expresses this wish, and her laughter complicates the interpretation of her words. It certainly does not seem like the laughter of mirth. A wish for the suitors' death hardly seems to be a joke. Does the laughter mean that she is not in earnest? The laugh, whatever else it may mean, sets Penelope's remark apart from her usual tearful talk and attracts attention to it. At the same time, it seems to distance Penelope from her own words, and this means that there is something in them worth distancing, something potentially dangerous. It would be out of character for Penelope to put too much confidence in Telemachus' sneeze and it could be risky for her to express hope, since the suitors might notice and become suspicious. The laugh diffuses this danger and smoothes over the disparity between Penelope's habitual grief and her behavior in this scene. It offers Penelope the possibility of denying her own words and disguises the importance of what she says. But under the cover of laughter the possibility is raised that the stranger is telling the truth, that there may be some news of Odysseus.

It is hard to know who sees Penelope laughing: is it only Eumaeus, or also Telemachus and the suitors? This and other conversations on Ithaca are complicated by their crowded settings, with maids, the suitors, Telemachus, and above all Penelope herself listening, observing, and overhearing words not addressed directly to them. In any case, Telemachus' sneeze turns Penelope's words into an omen predicting Odysseus' return, and it is Penelope herself who interprets it this way. Even with the distancing laugh the fact that such an interpretation is uttered at all is remarkable, and it whets the audience's appetite for Penelope's conversation with the beggar.

Yet eager as the audience and Penelope herself may be to hear the beggar's tale, they all have to wait. Eumaeus does summon the stranger, but now it is the disguised Odysseus' turn to behave in an unexpected way. Claiming to be afraid of the arrogant suitors, he declines the interview for the moment and requests that Penelope wait until the evening when the suitors are gone. From the start he seems to be an unlikely beggar, a beggar who is invited by the mistress of the house to come and earn a reward of clothes for his report yet does not leap at the chance. Instead, he makes a further request, namely that Penelope seat him closer to the fire when they do talk. An advance request for a seating arrangement on the part of a beggar seems extraordinary. This is confirmed by the fact that Odysseus immediately camouflages his bold words by offering an ostensibly simple justification: he wants to sit closer to the fire because his clothes are so poor, as Eumaeus himself well knows (*Odyssey* 17.572–573). This is unlikely to be an honest desire for warmth, since later the beggar-Odysseus declines blankets and a warm bed offered to him (19.337–338) and he surely could ask Penelope herself for a place near the fire instead of doing so in advance. Poor clothes are a way of masking the actual goal of this seating request, which has to be concealed probably not so much from Eumaeus as from the suitors, who might overhear the conversation. Eumaeus completely understands what the beggar is doing and when he relates the message to Penelope, he interprets it as a request not for warmth but for privacy:

καὶ δὲ σοὶ ὧδ' αὐτῇ πολὺ κάλλιον, ὦ βασίλεια,
οἵην πρὸς ξεῖνον φάσθαι ἔπος ἠδ' ἐπακοῦσαι.

(*Odyssey* 17.583–584)

And for you too, o queen, it would be much better
to speak to a stranger and listen to him when you are alone.

Penelope's initial reaction upon seeing the swineherd come back without the stranger suggests that what Odysseus does here is unusual: as she puts it, 'a shy beggar is a poor one' (κακὸς δ' αἰδοῖος ἀλήτης, 17.579). Once Eumaeus relates Odysseus' request, however, Penelope remarks that, whoever he is, this stranger is intelligent (οὐκ ἄφρων ὁ ξεῖνος ὀΐεται, ὥς περ ἂν εἴη, 'The stranger is no fool about how things might be', 17.586). She has formed a first impression of her guest, and the upcoming interview has gained in importance by being postponed until it can be conducted in relative secrecy.

Book 18 intervenes, in which Penelope reveals her concern for the beggar when she reproaches Telemachus for being a poor host to him. In the same book, Odysseus observes Penelope appearing before the suitors, who are undone by desire as they look at her. When Eurymachus expresses his admiration, Penelope claims that her beauty and success perished when Odysseus left for Troy (the same words she uses later in her conversation with Odysseus himself), but also renews the suitors' hopes for marriage. She reminds them that Odysseus told her to take good care of the household, especially of his parents, and to remarry once Telemachus grows a beard. Significantly, she does not say when she plans to remarry, but only that it will happen, and that she is not being courted properly. In the past, she says, the suitors used to give gifts, not devour the property of others:

ἀλλὰ τόδ' αἰνὸν ἄχος κραδίην καὶ θυμὸν ἱκάνει·
μνηστήρων οὐχ ἥδε δίκη τὸ πάροιθε τέτυκτο,
οἵ τ' ἀγαθήν τε γυναῖκα καὶ ἀφνειοῖο θύγατρα
μνηστεύειν ἐθέλωσι καὶ ἀλλήλοισ' ἐρίσωσιν·
αὐτοὶ τοί γ' ἀπάγουσι βόας καὶ ἴφια μῆλα
κούρης δαῖτα φίλοισι, καὶ ἀγλαὰ δῶρα διδοῦσιν·
ἀλλ' οὐκ ἀλλότριον βίοτον νήποινον ἔδουσιν.

(*Odyssey* 18.274–280)

But this terrible distress comes to my heart:
this is not what the way of suitors used to be,
those who wish to woo a good woman, a wealthy man's
    daughter,

and compete with each other.
They themselves bring cattle and fat sheep
to feast the young woman's family, and give
glorious gifts:
they do not devour without recompense the
livelihood of others.

Penelope never speaks to the beggar, only to Telemachus and the suitors, but one wonders whether some of what she says might not actually aimed at him. Certainly he hears Penelope's long and impassioned reproach to Telemachus for not defending his guest (*Odyssey* 18.215–225). Penelope will express the same concerns directly to her guest in Book 19 (325–334). Odysseus also hears what she says to the suitors, and can observe that she is still loyal to her husband and remembers his parting instructions. As for talk of remarriage, Odysseus recognizes it for a cunning solicitation of gifts. Penelope claims that the hateful remarriage is approaching, but her disguised husband rejoices because he sees that she is not sincere and has other plans:

ὣς φάτο, γήθησεν δὲ πολύτλας δῖος Ὀδυσσεύς,
οὕνεκα τῶν μὲν δῶρα παρέλκετο, θέλγε δὲ θυμὸν
μειλιχίοισ' ἐπέεσσι, νόος δέ οἱ ἄλλα μενοίνα.

(*Odyssey* 18.281–283)

So she spoke, and godlike Odysseus rejoiced,
because she extracted gifts from them, and
charmed their minds
with her honeyed words, but in her mind she had
another intent.

At the beginning to Book 19 the suitors are gone, but the maids are still in the house, taunting Odysseus. He responds to their insults and Penelope overhears his words, upbraids the maids, and asks Eurynome to seat the stranger. As in books 17 and 18, there seems to be a conversational game being played in the room, not just a series of isolated exchanges between pairs of speakers. Odysseus addresses his words to the maid Melantho, but he is surely aware that Penelope is within earshot. At the end of his speech he warns Melantho that her overbold behavior might yet get her into trouble and that her mistress might become angry with her (*Odyssey* 19.83). As if prompted by Odysseus' words, Penelope at once threatens the offending servant (19.91–95). The beggar also warns Melantho that Odysseus may yet come back, that there is still hope (19.84), and this remark, like the previous one, is likely to be aimed at Penelope as much as at the maid. Finally, Odysseus says that Telemachus will no longer ignore the behavior of the women in his house, because he is no longer a child, something that is also manifestly true and well known to Penelope (19.85–88).

Both in Book 17, when Penelope makes her first attempt at conversation with the beggar, and also in Book 19, when the conversation is about to begin, we hear hopeful words about Odysseus' return and threatening words about destruction of the suitors and punishment of the maids. Plans for the murder of the suitors are indeed already afoot as Book 19 begins, with Odysseus and Telemachus removing weapons from the hall. The tone is thus set for the dialogue and reinforced: the same themes adhere to the planning of the interview in Book 17 and to its beginning two books later. Both Penelope and Odysseus come to their first conversation aware of each other's intelligence and complex motives, with the return of Odysseus, maturity of Telemachus, and destruction of the suitors on their minds and tongues. In a sense, a relationship is established between them even before the first words are exchanged. This relationship, like the dialogue itself, is unobserved by the suitors. The mutual awareness of the couple, the long delay of the actual dialogue, and Odysseus' request for privacy all increase the suspense and raise the audience's expectations of the dialogue. Even before husband and wife sit down to talk it seems unlikely that much of what will be said is going to be simple, straightforward, or lacking in ulterior motives.

The conversation, of course, does not disappoint. Penelope starts with a conventional introductory question about the beggar's name and origins, but her interlocutor does not respond to the question, gives no name, and says nothing of his polis and parents. Instead, he immediately moves beyond the ordinary and sets the tone for all that is to come. He compares Penelope to a perfect king:

> ὦ γύναι, οὐκ ἄν τίς σε βροτῶν ἐπ' ἀπείρονα γαῖαν
> νεικέοι· ἦ γάρ σευ κλέος οὐρανὸν εὐρὺν ἱκάνει,
> ὥς τέ τευ ἢ βασιλῆος ἀμύμονος, ὅς τε θεουδὴς
> ἀνδράσιν ἐν πολλοῖσιν καὶ ἰφθίμοισιν ἀνάσσων
> εὐδικίας ἀνέχῃσι, φέρῃσι δὲ γαῖα μέλαινα
> πυροὺς καὶ κριθάς, βρίθῃσι δὲ δένδρεα καρπῷ,
> τίκτῃ δ' ἔμπεδα μῆλα, θάλασσα δὲ παρέχῃ ἰχθῦς
> ἐξ εὐηγεσίης, ἀρετῶσι δὲ λάοι ὑπ' αὐτοῦ.
>
> (*Odyssey* 19.106–114)

Lady, none on the boundless earth would reproach you.
For indeed your fame reaches the broad sky,
just like the fame of some perfect king, who upholds justice,
god-fearing, as he rules over many and valiant men,
and the black earth bears wheat and barley, and trees are
    laden with fruit,
and sheep constantly bear young, the sea provides fish,
because of his good leadership, and the people under
    him prosper.

I will come back to this very complex utterance in another chapter to consider its peculiarities as a compliment to Penelope. For the moment, however, I set aside its implications for her and even for the development of the dialogue and focus on only one aspect of Odysseus' pronouncement, namely what it reveals about Odysseus himself.

This utterance has been identified by Watkins as an instance of "ruler's truth," a notion he defines as an "active intellectual force, verbally expressed, which ensures society's prosperity, abundance of food, fertility, and its protection from plague, calamity, and enemy attack."[1] On the basis of comparison between the Hindu act of truth and the Early Irish institution of ruler's truth, it is possible to reconstruct an Indo-European cultural notion of a vital force brought into being by the ruler's spoken word.[2] The power of this word derives from its truth, and this notion, as Watkins suggests, is expressed in Greek by the word δίκη, 'justice'. In a cognate passage from *Works and Days*, straight δίκη leads to peace and prosperity (225–235), whereas its opposite leads to devastation (235–247). In the same way, in the *Odyssey*, both the natural and social state of plenty depends on the king who can uphold good δίκη (εὐδικίας ἀνέχῃσι).[3]

The notion of the ruler's truth is at the core of the Audacht Morainn, the earliest known Irish example of the 'Instruction of Princes' (*speculum principum*) genre, and Martin suggests, on the basis of a detailed comparison between Greek and Irish evidence, that the same genre is the source of several cognate utterances in the *Odyssey* and Hesiodic poetry, among

---

[1] Watkins 1995:85.

[2] The comparison is first made by Dillon 1947. For a detailed discussion see Watkins 1979:182.

[3] It is interesting that in Hesiod ἀτάσθαλα appear as one of the opposite qualities to straight δίκη, just as in the *Odyssey* ἀτασθαλία is the quality of the suitors and Odysseus' companions that leads to their demise.

them Odysseus' description of the perfect king in Book 19.[4] It seems that the ruler's truth is not only an inherited cultural notion, but an inherited part of a king's education. As Martin puts it, "speaking well and truthfully is traditionally important advice in Irish Instruction of Princes."[5] He further argues that the very deployment of this genre characterizes the speaker as a king. Comparing what Odysseus says to Penelope and what he says to Euryalos in Book 8, where he describes an ideal speaker, Martin concludes that "Odysseus allows his interlocutor to know that he is king – provided the interlocutor recognizes the genre in which Odysseus is speaking."[6] In other words, Odysseus' very ability to perform in the genre of "ruler's truth" marks him as a king.

Odysseus' utterance, then, is essentially self-referential even though it is ostensibly about Penelope. He does not, to be sure, claim to be Odysseus, but in the context of Ithaca his very command of the relevant discourse identifies him as such: on Ithaca, there can be only one perfect king, Odysseus himself. Penelope may have had many visitors, and many of them may have made false claims, but this visitor is different because he reveals himself to be a true king not by claiming that he is one (that is the next step) but by speaking like one. Moreover, by describing the flourishing of the land under the perfect king's care, Odysseus verbally ushers in the recovery of Ithaca after the dark days of his absence. He begins his conversation with his wife by indirectly revealing himself, an action tantamount to a verbal enactment of his own return.[7]

When Penelope then repeats her question about her guest's identity, the dialogue moves onto a different level, and now Odysseus' response, which constitutes what is known as the Third Cretan Lie, is both specific and rich in detail. It has long been observed that the Cretan lies are highly polished rhetorical pieces, each one carefully aimed at its internal audience.[8] For example, the first lie (13.266–270), directed at Athena in the guise of a young shepherd, contains a veiled warning: Odysseus claims that he has killed a young man in an ambush, letting the shepherd know that he can defend himself.[9] The second lie (14.192–359) indirectly praises Eumaeus and makes Odysseus into a figure likely to win the swineherd's sympathy, a victim

[4] Martin 1984: 38, 46.
[5] Martin 1984: 36.
[6] Martin 1984: 46.
[7] See Martin 1984, esp. 44 and 47.
[8] See e.g. Haft 1984.
[9] Erbse 1972:154–155.

of abduction and enslavement like Eumaeus himself.[10] With these two lies Odysseus wins a favorable reaction from their respective addressees: Athena smiles with pleasure at his caution and cunning (13.287–288), while Eumaeus is full of sympathy for this guest, even if he does not believe all that the latter says (14.361–365).

The third and shortest of the Cretan lies, the one Odysseus addresses to his wife, is presumably equally well-aimed, but it elicits quite a different reaction from its audience, both unexpected and striking. Her guest describes his land, tells Penelope his genealogy and name, and says that he once offered hospitality to Odysseus who was blown to Crete by a storm on his way to Troy. No doubt one would expect Penelope to be moved by the tale, but the extent to which she is moved seems quite extraordinary:

> τῆς δ' ἄρ' ἀκουούσης ῥέε δάκρυα, τήκετο δὲ χρώς.
> ὡς δὲ χιὼν κατατήκετ' ἐν ἀκροπόλοισιν ὄρεσσιν,
> ἥν τ' εὖρος κατέτηξεν, ἐπὴν ζέφυρος καταχεύῃ,
> τηκομένης δ' ἄρα τῆς ποταμοὶ πλήθουσι ῥέοντες·
> ὡς τῆς τήκετο καλὰ παρήϊα δάκρυ χεούσης,
> κλαιούσης ἑὸν ἄνδρα, παρήμενον.

> (*Odyssey* 19.204–209)

> And as she listened her tears flowed and her face melted,
> just like the snow melts on the topmost mountains,
> when the East Wind melts it, after the West Wind has
>   poured it on,
> and the flowing rivers are in flood as it melts.
> In this way her fair cheeks melted as she poured tears,
> crying for her husband, who was present.

Although Penelope's weeping is frequently mentioned, nowhere else is her reaction described at such a length or compared to the melting of snow. In what follows, I will suggest that in a sense recognition has already happened here. Just as Odysseus will need to say much more to Penelope, but in a sense has already said it all by performing the ruler's truth, so Penelope by her tears makes evident the change that will happen and that is already happening in her life and in the world of Ithaca: the return of Odysseus. To be sure, she too will have much to say later, and in great detail, and a lot still to decide and

---

[10] On similarities between Eumaeus and the protagonist of the second lie see, e.g., Trahman 1952:37–39, Emlyn-Jones 1986:6–7. King (1999:75) argues that Odysseus uses this lie to "validate and commend Eumaeus' moral outlook."

to wait for. Nothing is made verbally explicit, yet the striking image of crying Penelope in a sense says it all: spring is coming to Ithaca after a long winter, the snow is melting, and change is in the air. This is not to say, of course, that the drama of Odysseus' return is over at this point or that Penelope's own struggles are at an end. Throughout the poem Penelope is praised, and sometimes blamed, for her immense self-control, her heart of iron, and she will continue to exercise this quality in her interactions with Odysseus even after the suitors are dead, all the way until the final recognition scene in Book 23. Yet already here, in the beginning, there is a sign that this stranger is not like the others questioned by Penelope and that something new is afoot. The verb τήκω, 'to dissolve, melt' occurs, in various forms, five times in as many lines in the description of Penelope's tears (19.204, 205, 206, 207, 208), and although there is perhaps nothing surprising about Penelope's emotion in reaction to memories of her husband alive and well on his way to Troy, this emphasis on dissolving in tears is remarkable.[11]

It may be hard to understand what it is exactly about the beggar's words that triggers such a reaction, but that is a different matter. The reaction itself suggests that there is more to the Third Cretan Lie than meets the eye, whether or not we can ever understand precisely what this is. Moreover, there are structural considerations that strengthen the suspicion that Penelope's crying on this occasion has special meaning.

There are two other similar breakdowns in the *Odyssey* that can shed some light on the broad outlines of the scene in Book 19: these are at 8.521–527 and 24.315–317. Before moving on to consider the details of Odysseus' tale itself, it is worthwhile to take a look at the broad structural elements of this scene in comparison with its simpler and clearer analogues.

To begin with the more remote parallel, Laertes gives way to grief when Odysseus, unrecognized, provides himself with a highly unusual and mysterious name (Eperitos, son of Apheidas, son of Polypemon, 24.305–306) and an equally mysterious place of origin (Alybas, 24.304–306).[12] There are only two occasions, apart from the quite different case of Outis in the cave of the Cyclops, when Odysseus invents a name for himself: his meeting with Laertes and his meeting with Penelope. The supposed Eperitos then mentions that he comes from a well-off family and that he had entertained Odysseus lavishly at his house, praises the latter as a guest, and recalls how he departed with good

---

[11] See Nagy 2009:305 and nn253–255 on the meaning and connotations of *tekesthai* in this scene and 2009:300–312 on its meaning in connection to the Orphic and Bacchic mysteries, in particular the theme of eternal flow.

[12] On these names see Heubeck 1992:395, ad loc., and Breed 1999:149–159.

omens (24.309–313). Laertes reacts with an intense outburst of grief that is not described as "melting," but is as extreme as Penelope's emotional reaction and erupts just as suddenly. The old man is 'covered by a cloud of grief' and pours dust over his head:

> ὣς φάτο, τὸν δ' ἄχεος νεφέλη ἐκάλυψε μέλαινα·
> ἀμφοτέρῃσι δὲ χερσὶν ἑλὼν κόνιν αἰθαλόεσσαν
> χεύατο κὰκ κεφαλῆς πολιῆς, ἁδινὰ στεναχίζων.
>
> (*Odyssey* 24.315–317)

So he spoke, and a black cloud of grief covered him;
with both hands he grasped the sooty dust
and poured it over his gray head, groaning incessantly.

The only exact parallel to these lines is *Iliad* 18.22–24 (*Iliad* 18.22–23 = *Odyssey* 24.315–316), where Achilles reacts to the news of Patroklos' death, which suggests that in the *Odyssey* Laertes is thinking of Odysseus' death.[13] The force of his grief is expressed by the idea of pouring of dust, just as Penelope pours tears in Book 19.

The two scenes thus share a number of elements: invented names, the noble origins of their supposed bearer, his guest-friendship with Odysseus, a mention of Odysseus' open-ended departure from some location (Crete, Alybas), and the reaction of extreme grief from the listeners, expressed through the diction of pouring and melting. Moreover, in both cases Odysseus feels pity looking at the suffering his words have caused, although he reacts differently in each scene. With Penelope, he has to keep back his tears by a superhuman effort (19.210–212), while with Laertes there is no call for such restraint: Odysseus is on the verge of crying, but instead he hugs his father and reveals directly who he is (24.318–322).

The revelation is followed by a test: Laertes asks for a clear sign, a proof of the stranger's identity, and Odysseus responds not only by demonstrating the scar, but by enumerating all the fruit trees that Laertes himself once gave to him (24.331–344). In response, Laertes is even more overpowered by emotion as he recognizes the signs:

> ὣς φάτο, τοῦ δ' αὐτοῦ λύτο γούνατα καὶ φίλον ἦτορ,
> σήματ' ἀναγνόντος, τά οἱ ἔμπεδα πέφραδ' Ὀδυσσεύς·
>
> (*Odyssey* 24.345–346)

---

[13] The formulaic verse ὣς φάτο, τὸν δ' ἄχεος νεφέλη ἐκάλυψε μέλαινα occurs also at 17.591 (but with a different continuation).

So he spoke, and his knees and heart went slack
as he recognized the sure signs that Odysseus showed him.

The effect that these signs have on Laertes is the same as a different set of signs has on Penelope in Book 23, where she subjects Odysseus to the famous test of the bed and the reunited couple finally fall into each other's arms:

ὡς φάτο, τῆς δ' αὐτοῦ λύτο γούνατα καὶ φίλον ἦτορ,
σήματ' ἀναγνούσῃ, τά οἱ ἔμπεδα πέφραδ' Ὀδυσσεύς·

(*Odyssey* 23.205–206)

So he spoke, and her knees and heart went slack
as she recognized the sure signs that Odysseus showed her.

The scene in Book 19, on the other hand, is both like and unlike these reunions. In Book 19, as in Book 24, Odysseus gives himself invented names and recalls entertaining "Odysseus" as a guest, and his story makes Penelope melt. Like Laertes, she asks for signs (but in this case ostensibly only to prove that her guests really did meet Odysseus) and like Laertes she grieves even more after receiving them:

ὡς φάτο, τῇ δ' ἔτι μᾶλλον ὑφ' ἵμερον ὦρσε γόοιο
σήματ' ἀναγνούσῃ, τά οἱ ἔμπεδα πέφραδ' Ὀδυσσεύς.

(*Odyssey* 19.249–250)

So he spoke, and roused her grief even more
as she recognized the sure signs which Odysseus showed her.

The occurrence of the same formula, which does not appear elsewhere in the *Odyssey*, unites the three episodes: only on these three occasions does a family member recognize Odysseus' signs as ἔμπεδα, 'firmly in place', a marked term in the poem.[14]

It appears, then, that some elements of the Laertes scene are paralleled in the Penelope scene in Book 19, while others are found in the scene in Book 23, as if the process of reunion that is condensed for Laertes is expanded and broken up into two parts for Penelope. Odysseus' dialogue with Laertes is much simpler than that with Penelope and much more direct, so that elements analogous to one scene with Laertes are dispersed over several scenes with Penelope. Nevertheless, the similar structure of all these episodes and the dictional echoes that unite them suggest that revelation is in the

---

[14] See Zeitlin 1995:125–127 on this term in the *Odyssey*.

air in Book 19 no less than in Books 23 and 24. In contrast to what happens with Laertes, there is no open disclosure of Odysseus' identity, but there is, I suggest, an indirect one. Like Laertes, Penelope tests her guest. But while in the Laertes scene a direct revelation is followed by a direct test, in Book 19 an indirect revelation is followed by an indirect test: Penelope asks the beggar to describe Odysseus' clothes as they were twenty years ago (19.215–219). The test is similar to the one that confirms Odysseus' identity in Laertes' eyes, a test of memory. For his father, Odysseus recalls the number and kinds of trees that Laertes himself once gave to him; for his wife, he recalls clothes and a pin that she herself once gave to him. On the surface, Penelope asks about the clothes only to check whether her guest really saw Odysseus twenty years ago, yet his reaction to her request suggests that there is a subtext to his claim. The "beggar" points out that it is hard to satisfy her demand after such a long time (19.221–223), then proceeds to describe the clothes in all their detail, eliciting a reaction from Penelope that is elsewhere associated only with the recognition of Odysseus.

Once he is tested by Laertes, Odysseus is openly acknowledged by his father. In Book 19 an equivalent stage is present too, although it takes a reduced form: Penelope announces that her guest has now put himself on an entirely different footing and has become both near and dear to her, an expression that is used of one's equals:

> νῦν μὲν δή μοι, ξεῖνε, πάρος περ ἐὼν ἐλεεινός,
> ἐν μεγάροισι ν ἐμοῖσι φίλος τ' ἔσῃ αἰδοῖός τε·
>
> (*Odyssey* 19.253–254)[15]

> Stranger, before I felt pity for you,
> but now in my house you are a respected friend.

In sum, the parallels between Odysseus' reunion with Laertes and the scene of the Third Cretan Lie suggest that not only the former but also the latter revolve around, or rather are structured by, the theme of Odysseus' self-revelation.[16]

The second meltdown comparable to that of Penelope is experienced by Odysseus himself, and this melting, designated by τήκω, plays a clear and crucial part in his self-revelation. Odysseus dissolves in tears at the end of Book 8, where he is compared to a woman lamenting for her husband:

---

[15] Cf. the same expression used by Nestor about Menelaos (*Iliad* 10.114), by Hera about herself in relation to Zeus (*Iliad* 14.210), by Kharis and Hephaestus about Thetis (*Iliad* 18.386, 425), Kalypso about Hermes (*Odyssey* 5.88), and by Odysseus about Idomeneus (*Odyssey* 19.191).
[16] See Breed 1999, esp. 147–159.

ταῦτ' ἄρ' ἀοιδὸς ἄειδε περικλυτός· αὐτὰρ Ὀδυσσεὺς
τήκετο, δάκρυ δ' ἔδευεν ὑπὸ βλεφάροισι παρειάς.
ὡς δὲ γυνὴ κλαίῃσι φίλον πόσιν ἀμφιπεσοῦσα,
ὅς τε ἑῆς πρόσθεν πόλιος λαῶν τε πέσῃσιν,
ἄστεϊ καὶ τεκέεσσιν ἀμύνων νηλεὲς ἦμαρ·
ἡ μὲν τὸν θνήσκοντα καὶ ἀσπαίροντα ἰδοῦσα
ἀμφ' αὐτῷ χυμένη λίγα κωκύει·

(Odyssey 8.521–527)

Thus sang the singer surpassing in glory. And Odysseus
melted, and tears from under his eyelids drenched his
    cheeks.
Just as a woman cries, falling and embracing her dear
    husband,
who fell defending his city and its people,
warding off the pitiless day from the city and children.
She sees him dying and gasping for breath
and she pours herself over him and cries in a piercing
    voice.

As with Penelope and Laertes, the diction of pouring is prominent, for not only is Odysseus said to shed tears and wet his cheeks (like Penelope: ὡς τῆς τήκετο καλὰ παρήϊα δάκρυ χεούσης, 'in this way her beautiful cheeks melted as she shed [χεούσης] streaming tears' 19.208), but the grieving woman to whom he is compared 'pours' herself in an embrace onto the body of her dying husband (χυμένη, 8.527).[17] There are no other such descriptions of melting in tears in the *Odyssey*. Odysseus' melting signals a turning point in his interactions with the Phaeacians: his tears prompt Alkinoos to ask the guest yet again who he is, and lead directly to Odysseus' announcement of his name and the telling of his story. Moreover, deliberate design on the part of Odysseus is involved in this self-revelation. In contrast with the first two songs of Demodokos, this one is requested by Odysseus, and if earlier he tries to hide his tears behind a cloak, no such attempt is mentioned when he listens to the third song.[18] Just as Penelope often cries, but never in the same way as when she listens to

---

[17] On the internalized lamentation of Odysseus in this scene, and on the distinction between *kleos* and *penthos/akhos* depending on a character's personal involvement in the song, see Nagy 1979:100–101.

[18] Cf. Ahl/Roisman 1996:85 for the observation that Odysseus' crying is here noticeably contrary to his usual "emotional restraint" and the idea that it is "carefully orchestrated" and designed "to precipitate his self-disclosure" (though Alkinoos is still the only one to notice the weeping).

Odysseus in Book 19, so Odysseus weeps on many occasions, but only here is his weeping described as melting and marked with an extended simile.[19]

It appears, then, that such "meltdowns" in the *Odyssey* signal key turning points in the process of Odysseus' self-revelation. This is not to say that we should ascribe to Penelope in Book 19 instant certainty about Odysseus' identity, or claim that she "recognizes" him. It is rather that the structure and diction of the scene suggest that the dialogue in Book 19, like the meeting with Laertes and the third song of Demodokos, has to do with Odysseus' self-revelation. Moreover, it is likely that the initial message is much more complex than simply "I am Odysseus," and has a negative side to it. With Laertes, Odysseus' story reflects his own grief and catalyzes his father's. Similarly, on Skheria the song about the Trojan horse and the sack of Troy prompts Odysseus' weeping, because the song both identifies Odysseus and brings him grief. What Odysseus says to Penelope has a similar effect: it both triggers grief and begins a process of self-revelation. I conclude that, quite apart from the content of the Third Cretan Lie, its context and the compositional structure into which it fits suggest that it should contain veiled claims to Odysseus' identity. Such evidence, external to the lie itself, is obviously insufficient to argue the point, and I will now proceed to the suggestion that there are indeed such veiled claims, based on the internal evidence of the lie itself. On the surface, the lie is a rather innocent utterance: Odysseus simply introduces himself as a Cretan named Aithon, a brother of Idomeneus, describes Crete, and tells the queen how he once entertained Odysseus at his house. And yet many details of the lie are rich in traditional meanings and implications that are directly functional in the *Odyssey*. In what follows I consider Odysseus' assumed name, his self-description as a younger brother of Idomeneus, and finally the effect of his references to Crete and Cretan landmarks.

[19] For an extended discussion of the diction of dissolving and pouring both in the simile and in the scene, see Nagy 2009:348–352. As Nagy shows, the diction of dissolving in this scene has far-reaching meanings and connotations having to do with lament, eroticism, and the fluidity of song.

CHAPTER TWO
THE NAME

THE NAME AITHON by which Odysseus introduces himself to Penelope is significant, just as his other assumed names in the *Odyssey* are. The word itself, αἴθων, is a nasal derivative from the root of αἴθομαι/αἴθω, 'to burn', and its essential meaning is 'burning' or 'fiery'. Although it is often conventionally translated as 'reddish brown', in Homer and archaic poetry the adjective is not a color term at all, but always means 'burning/blazing' and refers to the character or psychological state of those it describes.[1]

One of the many connotations of αἴθων is that of hunger and longing, since *aithon* can connote 'burning' with an urgent desire. This 'burning' can be physical, sexual, or social, that is, the adjective can designate burning for vengeance and restitution felt by a person somehow socially deprived, for example, an exile. By extension, the adjective is associated not only with deprivation and desire but with ways of acting to which these feelings lead. A person or animal who is αἴθων is likely to be relentless, cunning, aggressive, and stop at nothing. In extreme cases, *aithon* can even function as a proper adjective and Aithon as a proper name for a hybristic transgressor.[2] On the other hand, the name has a strong association with vengeance, and when vengeance is supported by a divine sanction, the fire implicit in *aithon* can become associated with the fiery power of Zeus himself as defender of the deprived. In fact, *aithon*

---

[1] For a more detailed discussion of the semantics of *aithon*, and arguments against its interpretation as a color term in Homer, see Levaniouk 2000a:26–36. Glossing *aithon* as a color term has had its impact on the interpretation of Aithon in *Odyssey* 19. See, for example, Russo 1992:86, LSJ, *DGE*. Cf. McKay 1959:12–13. The suggestion that Aithon in the *Odyssey* means 'foxy', 'cunning', is also usually based on taking *aithon* as a color term referring to fox's fur (see McKay 1959:9n2 with references). Although I believe, as will become clear, that one aspect of Aithon in the *Odyssey* is close to 'foxiness', and that the same semantic developments lead to the adjective's appearance as an epithet of foxes and to its appearance as a name of Odysseus, I do not think color is involved.

[2] An example is Aithon-Erysikhthon (Hesiod fr. 43a MW, cf. Callimachus *Hymn* 6, 66–67, where Callimachus alludes to Erysikhthon's name in Hesiod).

is used as an epithet of lightning.[3] Many of these connotations of *aithon* are relevant to the *Odyssey* and activated when Odysseus assumes his name in Book 19.

A typical example illustrating the semantics of *aithon* is its use as a simile in the *Iliad*, where Ajax is compared to a lion:

> ὡς δ' αἴθωνα λέοντα βοῶν ἀπὸ μεσσαύλοιο
> ἐσσεύαντο κύνες τε καὶ ἀνέρες ἀγροιῶται,
> οἵ τέ μιν οὐκ εἰῶσι βοῶν ἐκ πῖαρ ἑλέσθαι
> πάννυχοι ἐγρήσσοντες· ὁ δὲ κρειῶν ἐρατίζων
> ἰθύει, ἀλλ' οὔ τι πρήσσει· θαμέες γὰρ ἄκοντες
> ἀντίον ἀΐσσουσι θρασειάων ἀπὸ χειρῶν,
> καιόμεναί τε δεταί, τάς τε τρεῖ ἐσσυμένος περ·
> ἠῶθεν δ' ἀπονόσφιν ἔβη τετιηότι θυμῷ·

> (*Iliad* 11.548–555)

> As when dogs and rustic men drive away
> a ravenous [*aithon*] lion from their cows' enclosure,
> and do not allow him to tear the fat out of the cows,
> staying awake all night; and the lion, longing for meat,
> charges at them but gets nothing, for javelins spring
> from their strong arms and fly, thick and fast, at him,
> and blazing torches, and he shrinks from them for all
>   his eagerness,
> and at dawn he goes away, sore at heart.

The lion of this simile is *aithon* not because he has tawny fur, but because he is burning with a hunger strong enough to make him spend the entire night trying to break through to the food, in spite of all the spears and torches in his way. The animal is described as longing (ἐρατίζω) for meat, just as the verb αἴθομαι is often linked with love (ἔρως), specifically when the love is unconsummated, forbidden, or unattainable.[4]

A related connotation of αἴθων, something close to 'relentless', perhaps 'relentlessly resourceful', can be seen in Pindar, where αἴθων is used about a fox:

> τὸ γὰρ ἐμφυὲς οὔτ' αἴθων ἀλώπηξ
> οὔτ' ἐρίβρομοι λέοντες διαλλάξαιντο ἦθος.

> (Pindar, *Olympian* 11.19–21)

---

[3] E.g. Pindar *Olympian* 10.83. For more on *aithon* as applied to lightning, see below.
[4] E.g. Xenophon *Cyropedia* 5.1.16, *Anthologia Palatina* 12.83.2, Apollonius Rhodius 3.296.

> For neither the relentless [*aithon*] fox nor the loud-roaring lion
> could change their inborn temper.

Bundy has argued that the *gnome* refers to the poet, the *laudator*; foxes here symbolize the poets who are "mere technicians," while the lion is a poet who "disdains all device" and relies, with a "straightforward confidence" on his own inspiration.[5] The foxes have to resort to devices because they lack the inborn power of the lion and yet are so keen to get ahead that they are ready to try anything. This is how the *gnome* is interpreted in the A scholia: πανοῦργον ζῷον ἡ ἀλώπηξ· ὁ δὲ λέων δυναμικώτερος, 'the fox is an knavish animal, while the lion is stronger'. A similar sentiment is expressed in another Pindaric verse, spoken by the *laudator*: ὄπισθεν δὲ κεῖμαι θρασειᾶν ἀλωπέκων ξανθὸς λέων, 'I lie behind the venturous foxes, a tawny lion' (fr. 237), where the use of θρασύς sheds some light on the meaning of αἴθων in *Olympian* 11. The idea of persistence and daring (seen here in a negative light) is present in πανοῦργος, θρασύς, and also in αἴθων. There is a clear relationship between urgent desire and behavior, both bold and crafty, which is aimed at satisfying it.

The notion of burning hunger that is part of the semantics of *aithon* has a mythological manifestation in the character of Aithon-Erysichthon, so nicknamed, according to the Hesiodic *Catalogue of Women*, on account of his insatiable hunger:

> τὸν δ' Αἴθων' ἐκάλεσσαν ἐπ]ών[υ]μ[ο]ν εἵνεκα λιμοῦ
> αἴθωνος κρατεροῦ φῦλα] θνητῶν ἀνθρώπων.
>
> (Hesiod, *Catalogue* fr. 43a MW)[6]

> The tribes of mortal men called him by a nickname, Aithon,
> on account of his violent burning hunger.

In the *Catalogue*, Aithon has a crafty daughter, Mestra, who has magical abilities and provides for her hungry parent by being married off repeatedly and then returning home in animal shape. Mestra's name is derived from μήδομαι, 'to

---

[5] Bundy1962:30–32.

[6] 'Erysichthon' is restored in the fragment on the basis of 'son of Triopas' in line 3; Aithon occurs twice. Later sources give various versions of Erysichthon/Aithon's story, but his insatiable hunger is a constant. The sources are: Callimachus' *Hymn* 6, Lycophron 1393–1396 and Scholia, (2.384–385 Scheer = 43b MW), Suda s.v. αἴθων, Hellanicus in Athenaeus 416b (FGH 4 F 7), Antoninus Liberalis 17.5 (with an uncertain ascription to Nicander), Achaeus TrGF 20 F6–11 Snell (a satyr-play entitled *Aithon* which may be about Erysikhthon, but the fragments are insufficient to be certain) and Ovid *Metamorphoses* 8.738–878. For a detailed discussion of the sources, see McKay 1962:5–60 and Hopkinson 1984:18–31.

contrive' and signals her cunning and knowledge of "close counsels."[7] The myth of Erysichthon brings together the idea of burning hunger and the resourcefulness that satisfies it, a logical pairing. In this case the two features are distributed between the two members of this father and daughter team, but they can also be united and collectively evoked by *aithon*, as is the case with Pindaric foxes.

Both hunger and craftiness are also features of beggars and poets who have to ingratiate themselves with their audiences to get a meal.[8] When he calls himself Aithon, Odysseus assumes both the role of a beggar and of just such a poet. Just as Iros, the professional beggar of the *Odyssey*, has a 'raving' (μάργη, 18.2) belly, a stock characteristic of beggars in Homer and Hesiod,[9] so Odysseus, posing as a beggar (and as Aithon), suffers reproaches on account of his insatiable *gaster*:

> ἀλλ' ἐπεὶ οὖν δὴ ἔργα κάκ' ἔμμαθεν, οὐκ ἐθελήσει
> ἔργον ἀποίχεσθαι, ἀλλὰ πτώσσων κατὰ δῆμον
> βούλεται αἰτίζων βόσκειν ἣν γαστέρ' ἄναλτον.
>
> (*Odyssey* 17.226-228, cf. 18.362-364)

> But since he has learned worthless occupations he will
>   not agree
> to go to work, but wants to feed his insatiable belly by asking
>   for handouts,
> begging through the district.

At the same time, Odysseus, unlike Iros (who is not *aithon*), is also distinguished by his cunning. The affinity between the Hesiodic Mestra and Odysseus is obvious, and it is probably the force behind a development in Ovid, where Mestra is said to have married Odysseus' grandfather, Autolykos.[10] Short of new papyrus finds, it is probably impossible to establish whether Ovid invented this marriage or found it in Hesiod,[11] but Mestra is naturally associated with Autolykos through craftiness and a gift for transformations. In the extant fragments of the *Catalogue of Women* she interacts with another notorious trickster, Sisyphos, who, in his turn, is made a father of Odysseus in some post-Homeric

---

[7] Fr. 43a9 MW.

[8] *Odyssey* 14.124-127 and 11.363-369. See Svenbro 1976:50–59, Nagy 1979:261n4, 1985:77–80.

[9] On γαστήρ and themes associated with it, see Svenbro 1976.50–59; Arthur 1983.97–116, especially 102–4; Pucci 1987.173–180.

[10] Ovid *Metamorphoses* 8.738

[11] For an argument in favor of a lost Hellenistic model, see McKay 1962:44–47. For a reply to McKay, see Hollis 1970:128.

sources.[12] In the *Odyssey*, Odysseus seems to perform at once the role of Aithon and the role of Mestra: he may complain about his "accursed belly," but through his craftiness he always finds a way to survive.[13] When Odysseus assumes the role of a poet on Skheria he is both skillful and eager for reward.[14]

Like Homeric lions, but also like Pindaric foxes, Odysseus the beggar, posing as an exile, is a person deprived of all he had, a victim of a hunger, literal and metaphorical. He will prove himself deserving of the name, a character driven to undertake risks, resort to cunning, and stop at nothing.

Moreover, these connotations of Aithon fit not only Odysseus himself, but his Cretan persona (a royal offspring now deprived of his native land and status), and even the imaginary Odysseus in Thesprotia, whom Odysseus describes to Penelope: all of these characters have been separated from their respective households. The very social position of all these characters makes them eligible for becoming an Aithon.

These social connotations of Aithon can be placed, at least as far as the Homeric poems are concerned, within the framework of the institution of *xenia*. The relationship between the fundamental Homeric institutions of *oikos* and *xenia* has been much discussed, and I cite here Redfield's formulation: "Household self-sufficiency is modified by the positive reciprocities involved in relations with *xenoi* – and, at a deeper level, by marriage-exchange – and by the negative reciprocities of the vendetta."[15] The Homeric model of *xenia* involves a reciprocal exchange of hospitality and treasures (*keimelia*) between the representatives of two aristocratic households. Whenever a traveling aristocrat receives hospitality and gifts at a host's house, the expectation is that a member of the hosts' household should receive gifts and hospitality in return if he travels one day to the guest's land.

This aristocratic form of gift exchange is fundamentally different from other forms of gift-giving and receiving, such as the reception of gifts by the poet in return for his performance. Even if elevated to the point of being heroic or semi-divine, the poet can never have the same status as the host of his performance. Alkinoos will never receive gifts at Demodokos' house.

---

[12] fr. 43a MW, Sophocles *Philoctetes* 417 and Scholia.

[13] In Book 9, it is Odysseus' desire for *xenia* that compels him to wait for the arrival of Polyphemos, (an example of 'hunger', perhaps), but it is his cunning that allows him to escape (9.214–461). Cf. also Menelaos, who rescues himself and his starving crew (4.369) from Pharos with the help of a cunning plan devised by Eidothea (δόλον δ' ἐπεμήδετο, 4.437) and the wisdom of her equally cunning father Proteus (4.455).

[14] *Odyssey* 10.14–18, 11.363–369, 13.1–15, 14.124–132, 19.203. See Nagy 1985:77.

[15] Redfield 1983:231.

Having a household with a store of *keimelia* is therefore essential for participating in these aristocratic forms of exchange, while it is not necessary, for example, in order to be a poet.[16] A person who is deprived of his household through exile or other misfortune loses his ability to reciprocate, and has to become a perpetual "guest," someone who can be seen metaphorically as always "hungry."

Such social dislocation obviously applies to Odysseus until he regains his position on Ithaca, but it also applies in a different way to Aithon-Erysichthon in Hesiod and Callimachus. In Hesiod, Aithon violates the reciprocal agreement involved in marriage: instead of exchanging his daughter for a bride price (*hedna*), he takes the *hedna* but also keeps the daughter, which ultimately leads to conflict with the other household. In Callimachus, a very different Erysichthon eats through his family's possessions and is finally forced to abandon his previous social position and beg at the crossroads – the ultimate form of a non-reciprocal relationship.

The hungry exile burns for return and the restoration of his fortune, but not only this. He can have other goals, chief among them vengeance on those who are responsible for his deprivation or have occupied his former place. This is Odysseus' situation: return is unthinkable without his taking revenge upon the suitors. Aithon as a name in poetry also has associations that are particularly fitting to this situation, as can be seen from its appearance in an elegy of Theognis.

In deliberately enigmatic verses, of which I quote only the first two, Theognis calls himself Aithon:

> Αἴθων μὲν γένος εἰμί, πόλιν δ' εὐτείχεα Θήβην
> οἰκῶ, πατρῴας γῆς ἀπερυκόμενος.
>
> (Theognis 1209–1210)

> I am Aithon by birth, and I have my abode in the well-walled
>   city of Thebes,
> kept away by force from my native land.

Nagy suggests that the poet here alludes to his own burial in Thebes, since the verb οἰκῶ can be used in reference to a hero's abode after death, as it is in Sophocles' *Oedipus at Colonus* (27, 28, 92, 627, 637).[17] Within the same poem Theognis says

---

[16] The totality of the household wealth is expressed by the merism κειμήλιά τε πρόβασίν τε (*Odyssey* 2.75). For more on this formula, which is paralleled by English "goods and chattels" and Hittite *iyata damata*, see Watkins 1994. See also Watkins 1995:154.

[17] Nagy 1985:76–78.

that his city is next to the plain of Lethe, a reference to the underworld, which confirms this understanding of οἰκῶ (1215–1216). Elsewhere Theognis pictures himself as an exile, a person whose property has been taken by others (1197–2000) and who dies in exile (337–50).[18] Yet he also contemplates a return to his native city of Megara and revenge on those who have displaced him, even if it is after death (345–350). The name Aithon is thus as appropriate for Theognis as it is for Odysseus: both are destitute, separated from their native land, and both have a burning desire for return and vengeance on their enemies. Moreover, Nagy suggests further points of contact between Odysseus and Theognis, most of them having to do, directly or indirectly, with return and revenge.[19]

Theognis directly compares himself with Odysseus, who returns from the dead:

> Μή με κακῶν μίμνησκε· πέπονθά τοι οἷά τ' Ὀδυσσεύς,
> ὅστ' Ἀίδεω μέγα δῶμ' ἤλυθεν ἐξαναδύς,
> ὃς δὴ καὶ μνηστῆρας ἀνείλατο νηλέι θυμῶι,
> Πηνελόπης εὔφρων κουριδίης ἀλόχου,
> ἥ μιν δήθ' ὑπέμεινε φίλωι παρὰ παιδὶ μένουσα

(Theognis 1123–1127)

> Do not remind me of hardships. I have suffered the same
>   things as Odysseus,
> who came back after emerging from the great house of
>   Hades,
> and destroyed, with his pitiless will, glad in his heart,
> the suitors of Penelope, his wedded wife,
> who waited for him a long time remaining by her son.

Overcoming death is a theme present elsewhere in Theognis, and it is dependent, as in the *Odyssey*, on unflagging *noos* and cunning: no one can return once he enters Hades, except for Sisyphos, who did so by his wits:

> ἀλλ' ἄρα κἀκεῖθεν πάλιν ἤλυθε Σίσυφος ἥρως
> ἐς φάος ἠελίου σφῆισι πολυφροσύναις.

(Theognis 711–712)[20]

---

[18] See Nagy 1985:68–72.

[19] Nagy 1985:74–76.

[20] Sisyphos' return (like that of Odysseus) is directly connected to his *noos* (Theognis 305). See Frame 1978 on *nostos* as 'return' specifically from the dead, and on the etymological connection between *noos* and *nostos*, which is mirrored by the thematic connection. Theognis' own *noos* is equally crucial for his plans of return and retribution (350): see Nagy 1985:74–76.

But it turns out that Sisyphus returned even from there
to the light of the sun, using his great intelligence.

Both Sisyphos and Odysseus feature in the corpus of Theognis' poetry as heroic figures cognate with Theognis himself, figures of wisdom who return from the dead. But Odysseus is a fuller parallel to Theognis because of the themes of suffering and vengeance that he shares with the poet and that are not associated with Sisyphos. The initial point of comparison between Theognis and Odysseus in Theognis is their suffering (πέπονθά τοι οἶά τ' Ὀδυσσεύς, 1123), and the grievous necessity for Odysseus to descend into Hades before he can return. Odysseus' subsequent return is then connected with his pitiless vengeance upon the suitors.

When Theognis, for his part, contemplates vengeance, he pictures himself as a dog that crosses a wintry torrent wishing to drink his enemies' blood:

> αἶσα γὰρ οὕτως ἐστί. τίσις δ' οὐ φαίνεται ἡμῖν
> ἀνδρῶν, οἳ τἀμὰ χρήματ' ἔχουσι βίηι
> συλήσαντες· ἐγὼ δὲ κύων ἐπέρησα χαράδρην
> χειμάρρωι ποταμῶι πάντ' ἀποτεισάμενος·
> τῶν εἴη μέλαν αἶμα πιεῖν· ἐπί τ' ἐσθλὸς ὄροιτο
> δαίμων, ὃς κατ' ἐμὸν νοῦν τελέσειε τάδε.

(Theognis 345–350)[21]

This is how it is destined, but no retribution appears for me
against the men who robbed me by force and have
my possessions. But I am a dog and cross the ravine
with its wintry stream and will make them pay for all.
May I drink their black blood! And may a good spirit
        observe it,
and may it accomplish these things according to my intent.

Earlier in this fragment, Theognis longs to exact retribution from his offenders while he is still alive. Then, he says, he would 'appear to be a god among men' (339–340).

But since he does not see any retribution falling on those who seized his property, the poetic figure of Theognis contemplates death, and his wish for revenge transforms into the image of a dog crossing the stream,

---

[21] See Nagy 1985:68–72 for a justification of the emendation ἀποτεισάμενος in 348, as opposed to the transmitted ἀποσεισάμενος.

a prayer to drink the blood of his enemies, and the wish that a good *daimon* may oversee this post mortem revenge. As Murray has argued, the torrent in this case is likely to correspond to the river Styx, which is also ice-cold, and Theognis' infernal hound is thus comparable to the Erinyes, also imagined as deadly hounds coming from the underworld to drink the blood of their prey.[22] Although Odysseus is able to return from the underworld alive, while Theognis' return is only possible in the form of a ghostly dog, in both cases it is a return from the dead crowned with vengeance on the living. Burning for this return and vengeance seems to be captured in both cases by the name Aithon.

In the *Odyssey*, moreover, the themes of burning and revenge co-occur with a striking depiction of a dog. Immediately after the conversation between Odysseus-Aithon and Penelope, at the beginning of Book 20, Odysseus is so filled with indignation at the women who sleep with the suitors that he wants to kill them on the spot. Odysseus' emotional state is described by unique expression, κραδίη δέ οἱ ἔνδον ὑλάκτει, 'his heart barked inside him' (20.13)[23], which leads into a dog-simile:

> ὡς δὲ κύων ἀμαλῇσι περὶ σκυλάκεσσι βεβῶσα
> ἄνδρ᾽ ἀγνοιήσασ᾽ ὑλάει μέμονέν τε μάχεσθαι,
> ὥς ῥα τοῦ ἔνδον ὑλάκτει ἀγαιομένου κακὰ ἔργα.

> (*Odyssey* 20.14–16)

> Just as a dog stands over her tender cubs and,
>   not recognizing a man, barks and is crazed to fight,
> just so his heart barked inside of him as he looked in
>   indignation upon their wicked deeds.

It is clear from the simile that the violence of Odysseus' emotion is due to his defensiveness about his household: the dog in the simile is ready to fight for her pups. It is significant that this dog is female: in contrast, for example, to the hunting dog Argos, this one is the guardian of her "household" and "dependents." But the simile also reinforces the theme of vengeance, as has been shown by Franco in an extended study of the ancient Greek concept of the dog.[24] She argues that the dog's well-attested reputation as a mother is of a particular nature: it comes from the dog's fearlessness and even madness in defending and avenging her young.[25] This madness is marked in the *Odyssey*

---

[22] Murray 1965:279. Cf. *Choephori* 924, 1054. Drinking blood: *Choephori* 578, *Eumenides* 264–266.
[23] For a discussion of this expression and a discussion of the following simile, Rose 1979:215–230.
[24] Franco 2003:63–64, 207.
[25] Franco 2003:208–213.

by the use of the expression μέμονέν τε μάχεσθαι, 'is crazed to fight' (20.15). The association between the dog's motherly protectiveness and her raving rage can be seen most clearly in the figure of Hecuba, the Trojan queen, who is transformed into a dog. According to a tradition preserved by the scholia, Odysseus himself is involved in her story.[26] After sailing away from Troy, Odysseus and his men put in at a place called Maroneia, and plunder it. Hecuba, who is there, curses them, is killed by Odysseus' men and thrown into the sea, and the place where she is thus "buried" acquires the name 'Dog's grave,' Kynos Sema. This Kynos Sema was a known landmark on the Hellespont, mentioned by Thucydides and Strabo.[27] In Lycophron, Hecuba unleashes her curses on the Achaeans after the sacrifice of Polyxena and is stoned by them, and here again Odysseus is implicated more than others in her death: he is the first to cast a stone (*Alexandra* 330–334, 1174–1188). No transformation is mentioned directly, but Lycophron does say that in Hades Hecuba becomes the hound of Hekate (*Alexandra* 1174–1177).[28] In Euripides, the queen's fate of being turned into a dog and being immortalized in the Kynos Sema is foretold after her terrible vengeance on Polymestor (*Hecuba* 1265). Here again, Odysseus plays a central role in her fate since he is the one to take Polyxena away from her for sacrifice (339–432). Finally, in the *Trojan Women* Euripides brings together the two enemies, Odysseus and the Trojan queen, although in a different way: here she is allotted to Odysseus as a slave and is in despair (*Trojan Women* 227–292).

Odysseus consistently appears in a central role in the myths about Hecuba, and this connection is also likely to be part of the tradition. It is even possible that the dog in *Odyssey* 20 is an allusion to her, but whether this is so or not, Hecuba and her transformation story show what kind of a dog Odysseus is compared to. The simile operates by the logic of reversal, conspicuous elsewhere in the *Odyssey*. Just as at the court of Alkinoos Odysseus cries like a woman whose husband is killed and city sacked, whereas at Troy he was himself the killer and the sacker; so here he is compared to a furious mother-dog defending her young, whereas at Troy he is himself the destroyer of children (in the *Iliou Persis* he kills Astyanax)[29] and indeed the murderer of Hecuba, the vengeful mother-dog.

In Euripides' *Hecuba* there is an interesting detail: Polyxena tells her she will become a dog with fiery eyes, κύων γενήσῃ πύρσ' ἔχουσα δέργματα

---

[26] Hypothesis 10–15.

[27] Thucydides 8.104.5, 8.105.2, 8.106.4; Strabo 7.1.56, 13.1.28.

[28] Hecuba also turns into a dog in Nicander (*Scholia* on Euripides, *Hecuba* 3) and in Quintus of Smyrna (14.347–351).

[29] Proclus, *Chrestomathia* 268.

(1265). The dog's eyes are also full of fire in *PMG* 965, an anonymous fragment that may refer to the same transformation (χαροπὰν κύνα, 'bright-eyed dog,' *PMG* 965.1). Dogs in general were imagined as fiery and especially as fiery-eyed, and this quality is directly connected both to their function as guardians and to their proclivity towards *lussa*.[30] Hecuba is thus emblematic of the dog's fiery nature, as Franco suggests: "il case della cagna-madre no fosse che una manifestazione particolare, canonicamente emblematica, di questa lyssa canina, di questo eccesso di focosità sempre pronto a divampare."[31] The fire in the eyes of dog-Hecuba is akin to the burning for revenge experienced by the two Aithones, Odysseus and Theognis. The associations go deep, and although neither Hecuba's transformation into a dog nor Odysseus' involvement in her death is mentioned in Homer, these and similar themes are unlikely to be late. In fact, the Euripidean Hecuba is directly comparable to the Iliadic one. Segal observes that as the *Iliad* progresses, the escalation of violence and savagery gradually gives way to a more weary, reflective, and even conciliatory atmosphere in which broader horizons of human life and death can be contemplated. One person who takes little part in this development, however, is Hecuba. As Segal puts it, "For her, the bereaved mother, the hatred and savagery of the war are still alive. There can be no reconciliation, analogous to that between Priam and Achilles, between the killer and the mother who gave birth to the victim."[32] Just as Priam prepares to set off across the enemy lines in hopes of persuading Achilles to return Hektor's body, his wife reaches a horrible pinnacle of vengefulness in her desire to eat Achilles' liver raw:

> τῷ δ' ὥς ποθι Μοῖρα κραταιὴ
> γιγνομένῳ ἐπένησε λίνῳ, ὅτε μιν τέκον αὐτή,
> ἀργίποδας κύνας ἆσαι ἑῶν ἀπάνευθε τοκήων
> ἀνδρὶ πάρα κρατερῷ, τοῦ ἐγὼ μέσον ἧπαρ ἔχοιμι
> ἐσθέμεναι προσφῦσα· τότ' ἂν τιτὰ ἔργα γένοιτο
> παιδὸς ἐμοῦ . . .
>
> (*Iliad* 24.209–214)[33]

---

[30] Franco 2003:215: "Lyssa canina e fiamma che divampa, si diceva, son strettamente associati nell'immaginario greco. Ancor più precisamente, questa scintilla di follia latente che alberga nel cane si manifesta nel suo sguardo."

[31] Franco 2003:214–215.

[32] Segal 1971:69.

[33] For a detailed discussion of this passage see Segal 1971:61–62. Segal points out that when Hecuba calls Achilles 'raw-eating' (ὠμηστής) in 207 she is using an adjective not otherwise applied to humans, but only to fish (24.82) in the context of killing, and to dogs and birds scavenging on corpses (11.453–454, 22.67).

Somehow in this way strong Destiny
spun with his life-thread for him [Hektor] when he was born,
   when I myself bore him,
 to sate with his body the swiftfooted dogs, far away from his
      parents,
   at the hands of a strong man. I wish I could eat his liver,
   biting into the middle of it. Then I would pay him back for
      what he did
   to my son . . .

Hecuba's ghastly wish is an expression of vengeance (τότ᾽ ἂν τιτὰ ἔργα γένοιτο), a theme elsewhere connected to the figure of the dog, and dogs appear in her speech, feeding on the body of Hektor. This is a traditional cluster of themes, and Theognis' dream of drinking the blood of his enemies belongs to the same stock.

Both Theognis' ghastly hound and the dog-Hecuba have much in common with the Erinyes. In Euripides' *Hecuba*, Polymnestor compares Hecuba and the women who helped her to murderous hunting dogs, while he himself is the beast (1173), just as the Erinyes can be pictured as hunting dogs running down their prey (e.g. in Aeschylus, *Eumenides* 131–132 and 246–247). A little earlier, Polymnestor imagines the Furies ('maenads of Hades') dividing the bodies of his sons and the dogs feasting on them (1076–1077). The barking dog in the *Odyssey* is similar. Like Theognis and Hecuba, Odysseus is burning to avenge a transgression against his household; like Hecuba, the dog in the simile is defending her young; and like the Erinyes, Odysseus can even come back from the dead to reach his offenders.

In the *Odyssey*, the simile of the dog is accompanied by the diction of fire, and recasts in an unexpected way the themes embodied by Aithon and present throughout this part of the *Odyssey*. Restraining his violent emotions, Odysseus strikes his chest and addresses his own heart (τέτλαθι δή, κραδίη· καὶ κύντερον ἄλλο ποτ᾽ ἔτλης, 'endure, my heart; you have once endured an even greater outrage', 20.18), referring to the loss of his companions in the cave of the Cyclops. Yet his craving for revenge does not lessen, and now it is described as 'burning':

τῷ δὲ μάλ᾽ ἐν πείσῃ κραδίη μένε τετληυῖα
νωλεμέως· ἀτὰρ αὐτὸς ἑλίσσετο ἔνθα καὶ ἔνθα.
ὡς δ᾽ ὅτε γαστέρ᾽ ἀνὴρ πολέος πυρὸς αἰθομένοιο,
ἐμπλείην κνίσης τε καὶ αἵματος, ἔνθα καὶ ἔνθα
αἰόλλῃ, μάλα δ᾽ ὦκα λιλαίεται ὀπτηθῆναι,

ὣς ἄρ᾽ ὅ γ᾽ ἔνθα καὶ ἔνθα ἑλίσσετο μερμηρίζων
ὅππως δὴ μνηστῆρσιν ἀναιδέσι χεῖρας ἐφήσει

(*Odyssey* 20.23–29).

And his resilient heart obeyed
without letting up; but he himself tossed and turned
    this way and that.
Just as when a man turns a sausage full of fat and
    blood
this way and that over a high-blazing fire,
and wants it to be roasted very quickly,
in this way he turned back and forth, contriving
how he might lay hands on the shameless suitors.

Here there is once more a mention of the *gaster*, but now it is a sausage, not the belly. Nevertheless, it is surely still evocative of hunger, especially since the man roasting this sausage is impatient for it to cook quickly: Odysseus is on fire, burning with rage and impatient to get his revenge. Moreover, the use of κύντερον, 'more dog-like', about the gory meal of the Cyclops picks up the theme of the dog, and even the allusion to cannibalism resonates with the themes of vengeance.

To come back to Theognis, there is one more detail that unites his poetic persona with Odysseus. Both Aithon-Theognis and Aithon-Odysseus return from Hades to exact their vengeance, although Odysseus, of course, achieves this during his lifetime, making himself, from the point of view of Theognis, 'a god among men' (339), while Theognis can only prophesy his own return. Nevertheless, there is a striking possibility that both returns are (or will be) accomplished with the help of the same divine agent, Ino-Leukothea. In mysterious verses, Theognis claims that a 'sea corpse' is calling him home with a 'mouth that is alive':

Ἤδη γάρ με κέκληκε θαλάσσιος οἴκαδε νεκρός,
τεθνηκὼς ζωιῶι φθεγγόμενος στόματι.

(Theognis 1229–1230)

Already the corpse of the sea is summoning me back,
dead, but calling out with a mouth that is alive.

Nagy has argued that the 'corpse' in this version may be an allusion to the local traditions of Megara about the corpse of Ino being washed up on Megarian shores, suggesting that it is in fact Ino who is calling Theognis back.[34] After her fatal plunge off the Molourian rocks, Ino was believed to have emerged from the sea as the goddess Leukothea, but in Megara she also had a grave and a heroic precinct.[35] Ino and Leukothea are not easily separable, and while Leukothea was believed to aid sailors at sea, she is more than a marine goddess: her role of rescuing sailors is only one manifestation of her more fundamental role of assisting in transitions through death.[36] It is in this role that she appears in the *Odyssey* and rescues Odysseus from death at sea in the guise of a sea bird, *aithuia*, whose name is a feminine form of Aithon (*Odyssey* 5.337, 353).

What emerges from these parallels between Odysseus and Theognis is that their respective returns are cognate: both return from the dead with the assistance of Ino, both burn for revenge, both are pictured as or compared to a dog, and both bear the name Aithon. As Nagy suggests, the differences between the two returns may be conditioned by the distinction between relatively more local and more panhellenic levels of discourse.[37] In local Megarian cult, the focus is on Ino's death and burial, while on the panhellenic level it shifts to her deification as Leukothea. This difference is paralleled by Theognis and Odysseus. Megarian Theognis hopes to come back from the dead only as a vengeance on his enemies, while panhellenic Odysseus, like a god among men, literally comes back alive from the underworld.

For all his "lies" and disguises, Odysseus rarely invents a name for himself. When he talks to Penelope, his assumed name, Aithon, encapsulates in a very condensed form several themes that are essential for the hero: his fate of being a hungry wanderer, his displacement from the position typical of a king, his burning desire for return, his violent and implacable revenge, his passage through the underworld, and his return from the dead with its promise of rebirth. It would be an oversimplification to say that Odysseus selects a *nom parlant* for himself, because Aithon is more than a name: it is a type of a hero, a traditional figure. Odysseus is an Aithon, just as Erysikhthon and Theognis both are in their distinct ways.

---

[34] Nagy 1985:79.
[35] Pausanias 4.43.4, 1.42.7.
[36] Levaniouk 2000a:197–217.
[37] Nagy 1985:79–81.

CHAPTER THREE

ZEUS AND THE KING

ODYSSEUS APPEARS BEFORE PENELOPE as a long-suffering wanderer, and his rhetoric, including his assumed name, underscores his displacement from the aristocratic position in life that he once occupied. And yet Aithon's biography also serves to emphasize just how aristocratic, or, more precisely, how king-like that position actually was. The conceit of the *Odyssey* is that its hero is intrinsically a king, and recognizable as such. When he is reduced to having nothing, not even clothes, he could theoretically become any kind of a person – a beggar, a pirate, a wandering bard – but although he plays some of these roles, that is not what happens in the end. Instead, Odysseus shows himself to be a king already on Skheria, where he is offered the hand of a king's daughter. On Ithaca too, it is not a matter of simply regaining his position, but of proving this position to be truly his.

The qualities of a perfect king are also a preoccupation of Hesiod, and this is an important point of contact between the Hesiodic and the Odyssean traditions. Some of these core qualities are, I submit, evoked in the *Odyssey* by Aithon's descent.

In Hesiod, as in Homer, a true king is sanctioned by Zeus:

> ἐκ γάρ τοι Μουσέων καὶ ἑκηβόλου Ἀπόλλωνος
> ἄνδρες ἀοιδοὶ ἔασιν ἐπὶ χθόνα καὶ κιθαρισταί,
> ἐκ δὲ Διὸς βασιλῆες·
>
> (*Theogony* 94–96).

> For epic singers and cithara players on the earth
> come from Muses and far-shooting Apollo,
> and from Zeus come kings.

The kings appear here somewhat mysteriously along with the poets in the midst of praise for the Muses. But there is a connection, since one of the gifts of a true king is the true and well-spoken word, and related to it is another gift from Zeus, namely his *dike*, the ability to pronounce judgment.[1] In the *Theogony* a good king is both nourished by Zeus and favored by the Muses with the result that he can render 'straight judgment' and speak unfailingly:

> ὅντινα τιμήσουσι Διὸς κοῦραι μεγάλοιο
> γεινόμενόν τε ἴδωσι διοτρεφέων βασιλήων,
> τῷ μὲν ἐπὶ γλώσσῃ γλυκερὴν χείουσιν ἐέρσην,
> τοῦ δ' ἔπε' ἐκ στόματος ῥεῖ μείλιχα· οἱ δέ νυ λαοὶ
> πάντες ἐς αὐτὸν ὁρῶσι διακρίνοντα θέμιστας
> ἰθείῃσι δίκῃσιν· ὁ δ' ἀσφαλέως ἀγορεύων
> αἶψά τι καὶ μέγα νεῖκος ἐπισταμένως κατέπαυσε.

(*Theogony* 81–87)

> Whomever of the Zeus-nourished kings the daughters of
>   the great Zeus
> honor and look upon as he is born,
> for him they pour sweet dew on his tongue,
> and honey-sweet voice flows from his lips; and all the people
> look at him as he determines the established custom
> with his straight judgments. And he, speaking unfailingly,
> expertly and quickly stops a quarrel, even if it is a big one.

Both the proximity of Zeus and the power of *dike* are characteristics of the royal line of Idomeneus, Aithon's supposed brother. When Idomeneus boasts in the *Iliad*, he describes himself as the 'offspring of Zeus' and claims direct descent from the king of the gods:

> ὄφρα ἴδῃ οἷος Ζηνὸς γόνος ἐνθάδ' ἱκάνω,
> ὃς πρῶτον Μίνωα τέκε Κρήτῃ ἐπίουρον·
> Μίνως δ' αὖ τέκεθ' υἱὸν ἀμύμονα Δευκαλίωνα,
> Δευκαλίων δ' ἐμὲ τίκτε πολέσσ' ἀνδρεσσιν ἄνακτα.

(*Iliad* 13.449–452)

> So that you may see what kind of man I am as I come here,
>   a descendant of Zeus,
> who first begat Minos, the overseer of Crete.

---

[1] On the connection between poets and kings and the traditional diction associating kingship with the ability to speak well, see discussion and references above, pp27–28. Etymologically, δίκη is derived from the verbal root *deik, the root of Greek δείκνυμι and Latin *dicere* (Chantraine 1968 s.v. δίκη, δείκνυμι).

And Minos in his turn had a perfect son, Deukalion,
and Deukalion had me, a ruler over many men.

The special position of Minos seems to be marked here by an unusual and archaic title – *epiouros* of Crete.[2] In his talk with Penelope, Odysseus also claims a special relationship to Zeus for his supposed grandfather Minos and emphasizes it by a curious description of Minos as *oaristes* of the god.[3] Thus both in the *Iliad* and in the *Odyssey* Minos' connection to Zeus is singled out as his preeminent quality. It is in all likelihood as a result of this connection that Minos has a Zeus-granted gift of *dike*, shown by the role of judge over the dead that he assumes in the afterlife:

> ἔνθ' ἦ τοι Μίνωα ἴδον, Διὸς ἀγλαὸν υἱόν,
> χρύσεον σκῆπτρον ἔχοντα θεμιστεύοντα νέκυσσιν,
> ἥμενον· οἱ δέ μιν ἀμφὶ δίκας εἴροντο ἄνακτα,
> ἥμενοι ἑσταότες τε, κατ' εὐρυπυλὲς Ἄϊδος δῶ.

> (Odyssey 11.568–571)

> There I saw Minos, the splendid son of Zeus,
> sitting and holding a golden scepter, uttering judgments
> to the dead,
> and they consulted the lord about their cases,
> sitting and standing, all over the wide-gated house of Hades.

This role of an arbiter is precisely the role attributed by Hesiod to his ideal king (διακρίνοντα θέμιστας, *Theogony* 85).

It is worth emphasizing the loftiness of the lineage Aithon claims for himself, since it makes for such an astonishing statement in the mouth of a beggar. As we have seen, he begins his conversation with Penelope with a performance of the "ruler's truth," showing that he knows what a real king is and has mastered the discourse characteristic of such a king.[4] He then expands on this veiled demonstration of his identity by making a direct claim to belong not simply to a royal lineage, but to an exalted royal lineage with a

---

[2] It is interesting that the only other person to be called *epiouros* in Homer is Eumaeus, who is twice so named. When Athena tells Odysseus to visit him she describes the swineherd as follows: αὐτὸς δὲ πρώτιστα συβώτην εἰσαφικέσθαι, | ὅς τοι ὑῶν ἐπίουρος, ὁμῶς δέ τοι ἤπια οἶδε, | παῖδά τε σὸν φιλέει καὶ ἐχέφρονα Πηνελόπειαν (13.404–406). Lines 13.404–405 are the same as 15.38–39, where these instructions are given to Telemachus. Mycenaean has *opi . . . (h)oromenos* (PY AE 134), cf. ἐπὶ . . . ὄρονται (*Odyssey* 14.104). οὖρος Ἀχαιῶν is of the same origin (Janko1994:104 ad loc., Chantraine 1968 s.v. ὁράω).

[3] See below for further discussion of this word.

[4] See above, pp27–28.

special claim to Zeus's support. The genealogy is thus one step in a purposeful process of establishing himself as a "real" king during this dialogue, and of reminding Penelope what such a king is like. The theme of Zeus' sanction, moreover, resonates strongly in this part of the *Odyssey*, because it is after his return to Ithaca that Odysseus' own relation to Zeus becomes especially prominent. For example, beggar-Odysseus twice swears by Zeus that Odysseus will return soon (14.158 = 19.303), and on the morning of the bow contest prays for, and receives, an omen from Zeus, a thunderclap from the clear sky (20.105, 114).[5] Furthermore, Odysseus-the-beggar claims in his tales that Odysseus is in Dodona, consulting the oracle of Zeus (14.327–328 = 19.296–297).

The name Aithon fits this theme of Zeus' support and justice perfectly. As an adjective, *aithon* is applied to lightning, which is both the weapon Zeus uses to punish hybristic transgressors and a sign of victory, as thunder is for Odysseus. Such is the thunderbolt in Pindar's *Olympian* 10:

> καί νυν ἐπωνυμίαν χάριν
> νίκας ἀγερώχου κελαδησόμεθα βροντάν
> καὶ πυρπάλαμον βέλος
> ὀρσικτύπου Διός,
> ἐν ἅπαντι κράτει
> αἴθωνα κεραυνὸν ἀραρότα·

(*Olympian* 10.78–83)

> And now we shall sing the song of proud victory,
> celebrating thunder and lightning made of fire,
> weapon of thunder-rousing Zeus,
> a blazing thunder-bolt
> fitted to every supremacy.

Transgressors can be blazing in their turn, but nothing is a match for the fire of Zeus. An example illustrating these connections is the description of Kapaneus and his opponent, Polyphontes, in Aeschylus' *Seven against Thebes*. Kapaneus is a hybristic attacker, who cares nothing for Zeus and chooses fire as his weapon, in effect making himself out to be a human Zeus. Not only does Kapaneus have a torch-bearer and an inscription 'I will burn the city' on his shield, but he also claims that he will do so even against the will of Zeus, whose lightning he disparagingly compares to the warmth of noon (427–431). In response to a messenger's description of Kapaneus, Eteokles expresses his

---

[5] See Nagy 1999 on the omen and the apparently contradictory diction of 20.105 and 114.

hope that Zeus will strike the braggart with a lightning 'not at all similar to the midday warmth of the sun' (445–446). In the meanwhile, the opponent of Kapaneus, Polyphontes, is described as a man of 'burning purpose' (αἴθων . . . λῆμα, 448).[6] The appearance of the adjective *aithon* is hardly surprising in this context, full as it is of words relating to fire and lightning, but it has a connotation that goes deeper. Associations of *aithon* with Zeus, lightning, and the punishment of offenders all combine to make Polyphontes into a veritable human lighting bolt, a weapon of Zeus. In Euripides *Phoenissae*, Kapaneus is indeed eventually struck by lightning as he tries to scale the walls of Thebes (1181).

Such associations, made plain by Aeschylus, are present in a more compressed form in Homer, as may be seen in *Iliad* 15, where the battle has reached the Achaean ships and the Trojans, led by Hektor, are trying to set them on fire (15.702). In this episode Hektor enjoys the support of Zeus, and it is no accident that he is compared to a burning eagle (αἰετὸς αἴθων, 15.690) as he leads the attack and that the simile concludes with a vision of Zeus literally pushing Hektor ahead:

> . . . τὸν δὲ Ζεὺς ὦσεν ὄπισθε
> χειρὶ μάλα μεγάλῃ, ὤτρυνε δὲ λαὸν ἅμ' αὐτῷ.
>
> (*Iliad* 15.694–695)

And Zeus pushed him onward from behind
with his great hand, and roused his people along with him.

In the ensuing scene Hektor jumps on the ship of Protesilaos and demands fire (οἴσετε πῦρ, 15.718).

If the adjective *aithon* is a fitting epithet for lightning and thus evocative of the will of Zeus, so too is the very mention of Idomeneus, Aithon-Odysseus' supposed older brother. In the *Iliad*, Idomeneus is the only character to be actually compared to lightning, and moreover to lightning as brandished by Zeus:

> βῆ δ' ἴμεν ἀστεροπῇ ἐναλίγκιος, ἥν τε Κρονίων
> χειρὶ λαβὼν ἐτίναξεν ἀπ' αἰγλήεντος Ὀλύμπου
> δεικνὺς σῆμα βροτοῖσιν· ἀρίζηλοι δέ οἱ αὐγαί·
>
> (*Iliad* 13.242–244)

---

[6] Cf. the way Antigone curses Kapaneus in Euripides' *Phoenissae*: ἰώ, Νέμεσι καὶ Διὸς βαρύβρομοι βρονταὶ | κεραύνιόν τε φῶς αἰθαλόεν, σύ τοι | μεγαλαγορίαν ὑπεράνορα κοιμίζεις (182–184).

> And he moved on, looking like lightning when the son
>   of Cronos
> grasps and shakes it from shining Olympus,
> showing mortals a sign, and its rays are seen from afar.

The simile occurs during his *aristeia* in Book 13, and it is in the same scene that Idomeneus boasts of his descent from Zeus. In the same book, Idomeneus is compared to fire, a simile otherwise peculiar to Hektor: οἳ δ᾽ ὡς Ἰδομενῆα ἴδον φλογὶ εἴκελον ἀλκὴν (13.330), 'and when they saw Idomeneus, like a fire in his courage'. For Idomeneus, being Zeus' great grandson and being like lightning are two features that seem to go together.

To return to the *Odyssey*, Odysseus assumes the name Aithon as Idomeneus' brother, along with a Cretan descent from Zeus, and the special proximity to Zeus enjoyed by his ancestor Minos, a king *par excellence*. In this context, the name Aithon resonates with multiple connotations and sends multiple signals to Penelope. Not only is her guest "hungry" and burning for revenge, but, like Polyphontes in Aeschylus, he too is a human lightning bolt, a king sanctioned by Zeus who has the power and will of the god on his side.

CHAPTER FOUR
YOUNGER BROTHER

ONE OF THE UNEXPLAINED FEATURES of the Third Cretan Lie is Odysseus' self-characterization as Idomeneus' younger brother. By claiming to be a brother of Idomeneus he inserts himself into the Cretan royal family, but what is achieved by specifying that he is the younger one? Further, Odysseus adds that Idomeneus is not only older, but better.[1] Why this apparent self-denigration? It is especially puzzling given the tendency for single sons in Odysseus' family. As Telemachus explains, Akrisios has only one son, Laertes, who in turn has only one son, Odysseus, who also has only one son, Telemachus (15.117–120). There are, then, no younger brothers in the family: it is an ideal line of descent in which no wealth is dispersed among heirs.

The assumed persona of a younger brother is however just as fitting for Odysseus at the moment of the dialogue as the name Aithon, and conveys a related meaning: being a younger brother is another way of being hungry and deprived, and a particularly important one. In what follows I will suggest that posing as a younger brother sends a message about the fundamental nature of Odysseus as a hero and has specific meaning in its immediate context, in a larger context of the *Odyssey* as a whole, and even in a still broader context which includes the *Iliad*, and quite possibly Odysseus' hero cult.

First of all, what is entailed in being a younger brother? In the *Odyssey*, the question of siblings is, predictably enough, bound up with the question of inheritance. For example, one of the Ithacan elders, Aigyptios, is said to have four sons. Two of them apparently inherit his land (πατρώϊα ἔργα), while of the other two one goes to Troy with Odysseus and one woos Penelope:

---

[1] The same formula appears in the *Iliad* about Protesilaos, who is an elder and better brother of Podarkes: αὐτοκασίγνητος μεγαθύμου Πρωτεσιλάου | ὁπλότερος γενεῇ· ὁ δ' ἅμα πρότερος καὶ ἀρείων | ἥρως Πρωτεσίλαος ἀρήϊος (2.706–708). (ἅμα in 171 is an Aristarchean reading, while all the manuscripts have ἄρα).

καὶ γὰρ τοῦ φίλος υἱὸς ἅμ' ἀντιθέῳ Ὀδυσῆϊ
Ἴλιον εἰς εὔπωλον ἔβη κοίλησ' ἐνὶ νηυσίν,
Ἄντιφος αἰχμητής· τὸν δ' ἄγριος ἔκτανε Κύκλωψ
ἐν σπῆϊ γλαφυρῷ, πύματον δ' ὁπλίσσατο δόρπον.
τρεῖς δέ οἱ ἄλλοι ἔσαν, καὶ ὁ μὲν μνηστῆρσιν ὁμίλει,
Εὐρύνομος, δύο δ' αἰὲν ἔχον πατρώϊα ἔργα.

(*Odyssey* 2.17–22)

And his dear son, the spearman Antiphos,
went with godlike Odysseus in hollow ships to Troy,
> land of fine foals.
Brutal Cyclops killed him in his cavernous cave, and it was
> the last dinner he prepared.
There were three other sons, and one of them was among
> the suitors,
Eurynomos, and the two others kept and worked their
> paternal land.

Nothing can be said about the other three sons, but it seems that Eurynomos at least is young, since he is one of the suitors and they are repeatedly called 'youths'.[2] It is at least likely that the older sons inherit the land, but in any case it is clear that some of the brothers stay put and take over from their father, while others have to seek their fortune abroad.

A variation on the same theme occurs in the Second Cretan lie, where Odysseus represents himself as an illegitimate son of a wealthy Cretan named Kastor Hylakides (14.204). Odysseus says that although Kastor esteemed him as much as his other sons, who were numerous (200), the inheritance was not divided equally and he received very little (200–210). He then improves his fortunes by marrying a wealthy woman (211–213) and turning to war and plunder (216–234), all of which makes him powerful and respected (δεινός τ' αἰδοῖός τε, 14.234) among the Cretans. This particular Odyssean "ego" is a bastard, not a younger brother, but what unites both is the likelihood of not inheriting equally with the older or legitimate sons and thus having to rely on oneself. The Cretan bastard is versatile and alone pursues both strategies that are followed singly by the two sons of Aigyptios: setting out for plunder and marrying into wealth.

---

[2] νέοι: 13.425, 14.61, 17.494, 18.6, 20.361, 21.179, 184 and κοῦροι: 2.96, 16.248, 250, 17.174, 19.141, 24.131.

Odysseus assumes the role of a person somehow disadvantaged among his brothers both in the Second and in the Third Cretan Lies, and the repetition suggests that this is a meaningful pattern. Odysseus does indeed have something in common with such initially poor but adventurous characters, in spite of his position as the sole heir of Laertes. Odysseus does not live off his estate or even confine himself to war and plunder, but turns into a traveler, a potential suitor (of Nausikaa), a wandering bard, and a beggar: in short he has a career more suited to someone not provided with a comfortable inheritance. Moreover, he occupies a somewhat inferior position, as a king from Ithaca, vis-à-vis his peers with larger domains. Odysseus' circumstances are not as grand as those of other notable kings, and, like a typical younger brother, he compensates with personal qualities, first and foremost with cunning. The question of Odysseus' relatively small inheritance does surface in the *Odyssey*. When Telemachus visits Menelaos' palace he is astonished by its wealth, which to him seems divine, and suited for Zeus (4.74–75). Menelaos piously declines a comparison to Zeus, but does say that hardly any mortal could compete with him (4.77–80). Further, he later seems to imply (for Telemachus' benefit, no doubt) that he is powerful enough to relocate Odysseus from Ithaca with all his possessions and settle him at the border of his own realm. Apparently, only one town ruled by Menelaos would have to be emptied to take in Odysseus and all of his people, and this presumably would be an improvement in comparison with Ithaca, at least in Menelaos' eyes:

> καί κέ οἱ Ἄργεϊ νάσσα πόλιν καὶ δώματ' ἔτευξα,
> ἐξ Ἰθάκης ἀγαγὼν σὺν κτήμασι καὶ τέκεϊ ᾧ
> καὶ πᾶσιν λαοῖσι, μίαν πόλιν ἐξαλαπάξας,
> αἳ περιναιετάουσιν, ἀνάσσονται δ' ἐμοὶ αὐτῷ.
>
> (*Odyssey* 4.174–177)

> And I would have settled a city in Argos for him, and built
>   him a house,
> bringing him from Ithaca with his possessions and his son
> and all his people. I would have emptied one city
> of those that are in my territory and ruled by me.

The fanciful vision of relocation is presented as a sign of Menelaos' great friendship for Odysseus, but it is also a statement about his superior power. In fact, it strikingly parallels the insulting (but greater) offer that Agamemnon extends to Achilles in the *Iliad*, the offer of seven cities at the border of Agamemnon's own territory (*Iliad* 9.149–156). Telemachus seems to get the point, and when Menelaos later presents him with a gift of horses (probably again a hint that his domain is superior, 4.590) he refuses them on the grounds that Ithaca is not suitable for them, though it is excellent in other ways (αἰγίβοτος, καὶ μᾶλλον ἐπήρατος ἱπποβότοιο, 'good for pasturing goats, and even lovelier than places suitable for grazing horses' 4.606). Menelaos reacts to this with a smile and attributes Telemachus' polite but proud stance to his 'blood', suggesting that Odysseus too would have detected and resisted any implication that he might be inferior because his island is small and rocky:

> ὣς φάτο, μείδησεν δὲ βοὴν ἀγαθὸς Μενέλαος,
> χειρί τέ μιν κατέρεξεν ἔπος τ᾽ ἔφατ᾽ ἔκ τ᾽ ὀνόμαζεν·
> "αἵματός εἰς ἀγαθοῖο, φίλον τέκος, οἷ᾽ ἀγορεύεις·
> τοιγὰρ ἐγώ τοι ταῦτα μεταστήσω· δύναμαι γάρ.
>
> (*Odyssey* 4.609–612)

So he spoke, and Menelaos good at the battle cry
smiled and stroked him with his hand, and spoke and
    addressed him by name:
"You are of noble blood, dear child, the way you speak,
so I will change these things for you, since I can."

Defined as he is by his attachment to Ithaca, Odysseus does seem like a younger and less well-endowed "brother" in comparison to such Achaean kings as Menelaos. And, of course, as the *Odyssey* begins, he has lost everything, even what he had accumulated at Troy. If in the end he comes back with fabulous riches, more than he could have brought from the war,[3] and if he does acquire the kind of *kleos* that, at least as far as the *Odyssey* is concerned, Menelaos does not have, he does so after long adventures and trials of perseverance, cleverness and craft, and in this, as we will see, he again appears like a younger or illegitimate brother vis-à-vis Menelaos.

The same could be said about his position relative to Idomeneus, who is actually featured as his older brother in the Third Cretan Lie. According to the scholia on *Odyssey* 3.313, Zenodotos had in his edition variant verses in which Telemachus goes to Crete instead of Sparta. At *Odyssey* 1.93 Zenodotos read πέμψω δ᾽ ἐς Κρήτην καὶ ἐς Πύλον ἠμαθόεντα, 'I will send him to Crete and to sandy Pylos' (instead of ἐς Σπάρτην, 'to Sparta'), while at 1.285 he read κεῖθεν δ᾽ ἐς Κρήτην τε [δὲ Κρήτηνδε Buttmann] παρ᾽ Ἰδομενῆα ἄνακτα, 'and

---

[3] The gifts of the Phaeacians deposited on Ithaca are described as follows (13.137–138): πόλλ᾽, ὅσ᾽ ἂν οὐδέ ποτε Τροίης ἐξήρατ᾽ Ὀδυσσεύς, | εἴ περ ἀπήμων ἦλθε, λαχὼν ἀπὸ ληΐδος αἶσαν.

from there to Crete, to the lord Idomeneus', instead of κεῖθεν δὲ Σπάρτηνδε παρὰ ξανθὸν Μενέλαον, 'and from there to Sparta, to blond Menelaos'.[4] Crete and Sparta seem to be in some way interchangeable when it comes to Telemachus' journey. Presumably there was a corresponding variant narrative in which Telemachus went to Crete, and it may be asked whether it could have performed some of the functions of the Spartan episode within the macro-narrative of the poem. Was Idomeneus in this narrative in some way equivalent to Menelaos in our *Odyssey*? The answer, I think, is yes. Idomeneus too could easily have been presented as a fabulously grand and wealthy king who astonishes Telemachus and at the same time makes the young man proudly assert his own Ithacan identity. The effusive description of Crete in Book 19 would certainly fit with a Sparta-like role in a different *Odyssey*:

> Κρήτη τις γαῖ' ἔστι μέσῳ ἐνὶ οἴνοπι πόντῳ,
> καλὴ καὶ πίειρα, περίρρυτος· ἐν δ' ἄνθρωποι
> πολλοὶ ἀπειρέσιοι, καὶ ἐννήκοντα πόληες·
> ἄλλη δ' ἄλλων γλῶσσα μεμιγμένη· ἐν μὲν Ἀχαιοί,
> ἐν δ' Ἐτεόκρητες μεγαλήτορες, ἐν δὲ Κύδωνες
> Δωριέες τε τριχάϊκες δῖοί τε Πελασγοί·
> τῆσι δ' ἐνὶ Κνωσός, μεγάλη πόλις . . .

(*Odyssey* 19.172–178)

> There is a land called Crete, in the middle of the wine-like sea,
> beautiful and fertile, seagirt, and in it there are people,
> multiple, innumerable, and ninety cities,
> and many languages mixed one with another. There are
>   Achaeans there,
> and great-hearted Eteokretans, and Kydonians,
> and Dorians in three tribes and illustrious Pelasgians.
> And among the cities is Knossos, a great city . . .

This Crete is everything that Ithaca is not. In contrast to Odysseus' small and rocky territory, Crete is 'beautiful and fertile', filled with different and numerous peoples and dotted with ninety cities, including the grand Knossos.

---

[4] The scholia allege that Zenodotos invented this variant, but this seems unlikely (see West 1988:43 for a discussion of this question). West does not express a strong opinion on whether these variant verses are conjectures, but, as she admits, it is hard to imagine why such conjectures would arise and equally hard to see how they would become part of the written transmission of the poem (1988:43). Yet there must have been a reason for the existence of these variants, and the simplest reason is a corresponding narrative, a multiform of the *Odyssey* in which Telemachus does indeed go to Crete.

The size and wealth of Idomeneus' kingdom are similar to that of Menelaos, and even the proximity to Zeus is shared by both heroes. As we have seen, Idomeneus boasts a direct descent from the god, while Menelaos, though not a blood relation, is Zeus' son-in-law, and he knows that he will enjoy an afterlife reserved for the select few because of it (4.569).

In short, Idomeneus makes a good "older brother" for Odysseus: a king if there ever was one, close to Zeus, the only legitimate son, and a ruler of a vast and prosperous realm. And if his domain makes Idomeneus unlike Odysseus, so also does his return. According to Nestor's tale in *Odyssey* 3, Idomeneus returns safely from Troy, bringing all of his companions with him:

> πάντας δ' Ἰδομενεὺς Κρήτην εἰσήγαγ' ἑταίρους,
> οἳ φύγον ἐκ πολέμου, πόντος δέ οἱ οὔ τιν' ἀπηύρα.
>
> (*Odyssey* 3.191–192)

> And Idomeneus led all of his companions back to Crete,
> all those who had escaped from war, and the sea took none
> from him.

In the *Odyssey*, this mention of the companions acquires special significance, since it is just the opposite of what happens to Odysseus, as we are told in the prologue: ἀλλ' οὐδ' ὣς ἑτάρους ἐρρύσατο, ἱέμενός περ, 'But not even so could he rescue his companions, although he strove to do so' (1.6). Unlike Odysseus, Idomeneus keeps both his loot and his companions, and returns directly to his rightful position as a king, descendant of Minos.[5] In this sense he might indeed be called 'older and better', at least temporarily, even if in the end Odysseus does comes back more powerful and wealthier than before. While in the actual narrative of the *Odyssey* the structurally similar role is played by Menelaos, in

---

[5] See Frame 1978:81–115 on Nestor as 'returner' (the meaning of his name) and his role in the *Odyssey*. The information that Idomeneus arrives safely with all his men is relayed by Nestor, and the same Nestor suggests that Odysseus complicated his own return by making an initial mistake on departure from Troy. As Nestor explains, Odysseus and he always agreed while at Troy (3.126–129), but once the war was over, Zeus devised a grievous return for the Achaeans (3.130–132). The implication is that agreement between the two heroes ended, and indeed in what follows Nestor says that the Achaeans were divided in two groups, those who left earlier with Nestor himself and Menelaos, and those who remained at Troy for sacrifices with Agamemnon. Nestor makes it clear that Agamemnon's delay was a mistake (3.146–147). Odysseus at first sets off with the first group, but after reaching Tenedos turns around and goes back to Agamemnon (3.163–165), thus presumably also making a mistake. And while Nestor reaches home safely with all of his ships (3.165–183), Odysseus pays for this moment of blindness and his return becomes a very different matter from that point onwards.

the internal narrative that Odysseus constructs in his Third Cretan Lie, this role is played by Idomeneus.

There are, then, traits of Odysseus that make him suited for the role of a "younger brother," if only metaphorically. The question remains, however, why he should bring up this subject in his conversation with Penelope. To begin answering this question I suggest that the apparent inferiority of Odysseus in comparison with Menelaos and Idomeneus is only a symptom of his more fundamental character, and it is this character that is relevant in the dialogue. The character, I submit, has to do with Odysseus' special involvement with the young and with what, for lack of a better term, could be called the initiatory aspect of Odysseus' return.

It is, of course, a platitude to say that the *Odyssey* in general follows the typical pattern of a rite of passage: any story of return by definition involves a separation, a transitional period, and a return, and thus fits into van Gennep's famous tripartite scheme. However, what can be termed initiatory about Odysseus' return is not confined to this general structure, and involves details that do not necessarily flow from the structure itself. One of these less than obvious details is Odysseus' role as a younger brother, and, linked to it, the complicated question of his age in general. In what follows I will suggest an admittedly unprovable, but, I think, logical hypothesis that this particular detail has to do with Odysseus' role as a hero concerned with male maturation and one who emblematizes this process in epic. Such a role is, in turn, a crucial ingredient of Odysseus' return and reinstatement as a king and Penelope's husband.

To begin building up this hypothesis I will have to leave Odysseus for the moment and reconsider from another point of view the figure of the younger brother. The examples mentioned above, the sons of Aigyptios and the Cretan of the Second Lie, suggest that the younger brother is likely to be disadvantaged when it comes to inheritance. Now, I suggest that this disadvantaged position makes the younger brother an especially suitable protagonist for an initiation-related myth. In some sense, all young have to push against the older generation to make a way for themselves, and many youths, brothers or not, arrive in the world where many goods, social and economical, are already distributed among their elders. A younger brother is thus a particularly explicit and clear example of the condition of youth in general. Indeed, the best mythological model of a younger brother is to be found in a myth concerned precisely with the coming of a new generation, the *Homeric Hymn to Hermes*, an example that it will be useful to consider in more detail.

In the *Homeric Hymn to Hermes*, Hermes, Apollo's younger brother, starts out in his mother's cave having nothing and proceeds to use his wiles and tricks to win a status for himself among the Olympian gods. The stratagem he adopts to gain recognition is twofold: first, he invents the lyre, and second, he challenges Apollo by stealing some of the latter's cattle.[6] With the lyre, he will propitiate the elder god; with the stolen cattle, he will show that he has powers and resources, and is therefore worthy to be included into the community of adults. As Apollo looks at the condemning evidence of the two cowhides he draws just the conclusion that Hermes is aiming at: 'You don't need to grow up much more, Cyllenian one, son of Maia!' (*Homeric Hymn to Hermes* 407–8). Now that his abilities have been acknowledged, Hermes lets his elder brother know that his challenge is ultimately not hostile and that he does not want Apollo as an enemy, but as a sponsor and protector who will help him enter into his own proper position among the Olympian gods. The young god strikes up a song on his lyre, and Apollo is enchanted. Significantly, the song Hermes sings lists all the gods according to seniority (κατὰ πρέσβιν, 431) and tells how each of them has received his or her portion of the world:

> κραίνων ἀθανάτους τε θεοὺς καὶ γαῖαν ἐρεμνὴν
> ὡς τὰ πρῶτα γένοντο καὶ ὡς λάχε μοῖραν ἕκαστος.
>
> (*Homeric Hymn to Hermes* 427–28)

> He sang of the immortal gods and dark earth,
> how they first came to be and how each one received his share.

The song has to do with Hermes' fundamental concern in the *Hymn*: acquisition of a share for himself, now that he has arrived too late for the initial division.[7] Since Apollo has lost two cows he knows that his new brother is someone to reckon with; since he also marvels at his music and wants it for himself, he is inclined to make a deal with this new, and apparently resourceful, arrival to the world. Hermes willingly gives the lyre to Apollo, accepting for himself

---

[6] For a discussion of Hermes' strategy and parallels to it in modern Greece, see Johnston 2002, who also discusses cattle rustling as initiatory activity. Her interpretation is based on Herzfeld's anthropological insights into sheep stealing by youngsters on Crete (Herzfeld 1985).

[7] Johnston 2002:124 (citing Haft 1996:43 and Clay 1989:109, 138) points out how the content of each of Hermes' songs (54–61; 427–28) in the *Hymn* reflect his position and aspirations at the time he sings them, the first celebrating his mother and her home, the second, after his successful cattle raid, the cosmos and the gods and their privileges and honors, in which he hopes to share. Cf. also Shelmerdine 1986:52 on Hermes' lack of status among the Olympians, quoted below.

a lesser instrument, the syrinx, just as he agrees to a take a back seat to Apollo in divination: Apollo will have his glorious oracle in Delphi, while Hermes will be content with the lesser bee oracle, which Apollo himself used when he was younger. Under this condition, Apollo begins the process of creating a domain for his younger brother: he gives Hermes a 'shining whip' for shepherding of cattle (490–498) and later adds to it the 'wand of prosperity and wealth' (529). Hermes' invention and theft establish him in the world where he, the younger brother, gets nothing by default, but has to maneuver using both power and especially cunning in order to receive a share.

On the basis of her analysis of the myth of the *Hymn* in its particular manifestation, Johnston argues that it "expressed concerns that were most immediately relevant to young males, whom Hermes was expected to guide during their maturation."[8] She further suggests that a suitable context for performance of the *Homeric Hymn to Hermes* would have been the Hermaia, a festival that features athletic competitions for aristocratic boys and youths of different ages and that celebrated their maturation under the protection of Hermes. One of the features of the myth as it appears in the *Hymn* that makes it particularly suitable to such an occasion is the role of Apollo, Hermes' older brother. Apollo's prominence in itself is not surprising since he is the god most closely associated with the maturation of males, especially in its later stages, including the actual transition into the community of fully grown adults. His role in the *Hymn*, however, is so great as to require a more specific explanation. Johnston suggests that "the *Hymn* portrays the relationship between an older male and a younger male exactly as we would expect in a 'coming-of-age' tale: the older male will accept, support, and even train the younger male in skills that he himself has mastered, so long as the younger male acquiesces in his proper, subordinate role."[9] A younger male needs to balance the contradictory strategies of challenging and placating his elders in order to gain such a sponsor and ultimately to acquire, with his help, the "full honors" of an adult. In order to do so, the young male needs to be like Hermes – quick, strong, daring and cunning.

Apollo and Hermes represent two different stages of the maturation process: Hermes its difficult and treacherous beginnings, Apollo its shining culmination. In the *Hymn*, they are represented as a younger and older brother, but this is not the only possible model for such a relationship. In another maturation myth, that of Meleager, it seems that uncles, rather than an older brother, take on the role of "sponsors" in the coming of age process. A similar

[8] Johnston 2002:111.
[9] Johnston 2002:121.

relationship can also be conceptualized not in terms of relationship by blood, but in erotic terms, as in the famous *erastes-eromenos* pairs on Crete, described by Ephoros.[10] A younger brother, however, is a particularly good model of youth because by definition he needs to struggle for the full honor of adulthood in a world where the best positions are already occupied by his older brother or brothers, who are thus both his natural sponsors and his competitors. We will see that the subtle psychological game that is played out between Hermes and Apollo in the *Hymn* is to some extent paradigmatic of relationships between older and younger males, whether or not they are brothers.[11]

With Hermes in mind as a model, it is now time to return to the *Odyssey*. There is no need to reiterate in detail the similarities between Hermes and Odysseus, which are clearly manifested in their shared epithets. For example, πολύτροπος, 'of many turns', perhaps the most distinctive epithet of Odysseus and uniquely his in Homer, is used of Hermes in the *Hymn* (13, 439), and the god is also called ποικιλομήτης, 'of varied wiles' (155, 514) and πολύμητις, 'of many wiles' (319), both epithets used many times of Odysseus.[12] Not coincidentally, all these adjectives have to do with cunning, and the same connection is overtly expressed in the *Odyssey*, where Odysseus' maternal grandfather, Autolykos, who excels in perjury and theft, is said to enjoy the special favor of Hermes:

> μητρὸς ἑῆς πατέρ' ἐσθλόν, ὃς ἀνθρώπους ἐκέκαστο
> κλεπτοσύνῃ θ' ὅρκῳ τε· θεὸς δέ οἱ αὐτὸς ἔδωκεν
> Ἑρμείας· τῷ γὰρ κεχαρισμένα μηρία καῖεν
> ἀρνῶν ἠδ' ἐρίφων· ὁ δέ οἱ πρόφρων ἅμ' ὀπήδει.
>
> (*Odyssey* 19.395–398)

> the noble father of his mother, who surpassed men
> in theft and swearing of oaths; the god himself gave him
>> this gift,
> Hermes, for he burned for the god pleasing thighs[s]
> of lambs and kids. And the god readily favored him.

As has been observed, there are clear thematic parallels between the *Hymn* and the *Odyssey*. Odysseus' way home has to do with establishing and re-establishing his identity, with regaining his position as a hero, a king, and

---

[10] In Strabo 10.4.21. See following section for more on this.

[11] For an example, see the discussion of Antilokhos and Menelaos at the funeral games for Patroklos, below.

[12] For a fuller discussion of dictional and thematic parallels between the *Odyssey* and the *Homeric Hymn to Hermes*, see Shelmerdine 1986.

a husband: in short, with reclaiming his share in the world. Hermes, too, is preoccupied with establishing his identity. As Shelmerdine puts it: "He has no identity (except as Maia's son), no status in the Olympian world, and no 'heroic' (divine) sphere. Like Odysseus, he uses craft to win all three."[13] In both cases, the process is described as 'a long road' (δολιχὴν ὁδόν, *Odyssey* 4.393, 17.426; *Homeric Hymn to Hermes* 86).[14]

Odysseus' return involves regaining the position that he has already gained once in his youth, and thus echoes his youthful *rites de passage*, the steps that he had to take to become Odysseus in the first place. It is as if Odysseus' reconstitution of himself in the *Odyssey* involves not only re-birth, but also a re-growing up that culminates in re-marriage. At the conclusion of this long Hermes-like quest to "come of age" Odysseus achieves his goal at the festival of Apollo, Hermes' elder brother and "sponsor" in the *Hymn*. In the *Odyssey* this festival is distinctly associated with assemblies, which are attended by Telemachus and which are described at *Odyssey* 20.277 as a gathering of 'long-haired Achaeans'. These features of the festival certainly bring to mind the *apellai*, assemblies of the Dorians held at seasonally recurring festivals, from which the Doric form of the god's name, Apellon, may derive.[15] Burkert points out that the feast of the *apellai* at Delphi is the feast of the *epheboi*, young males who are coming of age. And, of course, Apollo himself is most often depicted as an ephebe, beardless and long-haired.[16] Given Apollo's primary concern with the transition of male youths to full adulthood, it is likely that the festival on Ithaca in the *Odyssey* is an occasion celebrating the maturation of a new generation, similar in this respect to the festival of the *apellai* in Delphi.[17]

The young man who triumphs most fully on this occasion is none other than Odysseus himself. The generation of Ithacan males coming to maturity follows the same strategies as the Cretan bastard, Odysseus' alter ego in the Second Lie: some of them, under the leadership of Odysseus, set out for Troy, no doubt hoping to improve their fortunes by war and plunder, while others, the suitors, hope to achieve the same end by marrying Penelope. The two sons of Aigyptios (2.15–22) who belong to these two groups respectively, Antiphos and Eurynomos, are typical representatives.[18] The adventurers and the suitors

---

[13] Shelmerdine 1986:52

[14] Shelmerdine 1986:52–53.

[15] Burkert 1975:10.

[16] Burkert 1975:11, 18–19.

[17] This need not, of course, be the only focus on the festival. On Apollo in this role see, e.g. Versnel 1993:313–334, Graf 1979:2–22.

[18] See Heitman 2005:15 for Aigyptios' family as representative of the interests of the Ithacans.

are brought together by numerous parallels and can be seen as in some way equivalent.[19] In the case of those who went to war, Odysseus is their leader, but also in a sense their competitor: they all face challenges and embark on adventures in the wilderness and Odysseus is the only one to survive. In the case of the suitors, Odysseus is not, of course, their leader literally speaking, but he is their model, because the suitors attempt to follow in his footsteps and accomplish what he accomplished – to marry Penelope. Here again, Odysseus competes against them, wins, and destroys them all. Moreover, quite apart from his success with Penelope, Odysseus succeeds in an equivalent task on Skheria: Alkinoos offers him Nausikaa's hand, and with it presumably his own wealth. Just as he outcompetes the youngsters of Ithaca, so too he outstrips the young men of Skheria, and the offer of Nausikaa's hand is the expected outcome of his victory. It is worth noting that this marriage, attractive as it may be, is also unequal: it would mean staying in Alkinoos' house as a son-in-law and owing everything to his wife's family.[20] Odysseus is offered an undoubtedly diminished position, fitting for a "younger brother" (or an illegitimate son) who has desirable personal qualities but does not have a household of his own. The marriage that benefits the Cretan bastard in the Second Lie is surely of the same kind, otherwise it probably would not be open to an illegitimate son. Odysseus' marriage to Penelope, on the other hand, is perfect and unblemished by such complications. Among those who went to war and competed for Penelope, Odysseus is the only one to return with wealth and to win a perfect marriage for himself, and thus the only one to accomplish fully that transition which the festival of Apollo celebrates.[21]

In keeping with this youthful role, a remarkable sliding of age-markers characterizes Odysseus: he is represented alternatively as an ageing married man and as a youngster. One of the clearest examples of such sliding is to be found in the Phaeacian episode. On the seashore Odysseus is rejuvenated by Athena and turned into a young and strong man with curls 'like a hyacinth

---

[19] Cf. Cook 1995:24–26 on parallels between Odysseus' crew, Aigisthos, and the suitors.

[20] For the lack of prestige and even humiliation attached to uxorilocal marriage, see Redfield 1975:15–16 and Donlan 1993:165–166 on Achilles' rejection of Agamemnon's offer of marriage to one of his daughters (*Iliad* 9.388–391).

[21] Cf. Nagy 1990a:122 for the notion of victory in competition as the survival of the victor and death of his competitors or opponents: "In some societies, the real death of one person is compensated proportionately: one other person 'dies' in a ritual contest, while the one or ones who competed with this other person 'live.' In other societies, however, including the Greek, the proportion is inverted: one person 'lives' by winning in a ritual contest, while the one or ones who competed with this person 'die' by losing."

flower' (6.229–235). This detail appears again on Ithaca, when Odysseus is described in the same way in a scene with Penelope:

> τὸν μὲν Ἀθηναίη θῆκεν, Διὸς ἐκγεγαυῖα,
> μείζονά τ' εἰσιδέειν καὶ πάσσονα, κὰδ δὲ κάρητος
> οὔλας ἧκε κόμας, ὑακινθίνῳ ἄνθει ὁμοίας.
> ὡς δ' ὅτε τις χρυσὸν περιχεύεται ἀργύρῳ ἀνὴρ
> ἴδρις, ὃν Ἥφαιστος δέδαεν καὶ Παλλὰς Ἀθήνη
> τέχνην παντοίην, χαρίεντα δὲ ἔργα τελείει,
> ὣς ἄρα τῷ κατέχευε χάριν κεφαλῇ τε καὶ ὤμοις.
>
> (*Odyssey* 6.229–235 = 23.156–162)[22]

> And Athena, born of Zeus, made him
> taller to look at and larger, and from his head
> she let down locks like the hyacinth.
> Just as someone overlays silver with gold,
> a knowledgeable man, whom Hephaestus and Pallas Athena
> have taught all kinds of craft, and he makes graceful things,
> just so did she pour grace over Odysseus' head and
>   shoulders.

An especially remarkable element in this passage is Odysseus' hair: the description suggests that it is long, as would befit a young man, indeed an ephebe. Further, his hair is like the hyacinth, a flower with strongly erotic associations; the comparison also brings to mind the hero Hyakinthos, a pre-adult male and Apollo's lover.[23] Described in this way, Odysseus seems not just beautified but restored to his ephebic appearance. A conflict between Odysseus and Nausikaa's potential suitors is then immediately imagined by the princess herself, who predicts that the Phaeacians might take Odysseus for her future husband (πόσις νύ οἱ ἔσσεται αὐτῇ, 6.177) and grumble that she dishonors local wooers (6.283–284). In this way, Odysseus is juxtaposed with an age-group younger than that of his natural peers, such as the kings who feast in the palace of Alkinoos. This juxtaposition continues when Odysseus participates

---

[22] Lines 6.229 and 23.156 are not however identical.

[23] For the erotic associations of the hyacinth, see e.g. Anacreon fr. 1.1.7, Anacreontea 31.1, Theocritus 11.26, Euripides *Iphigeneia in Aulis* 1299. Further references in Irwin 1990:214 n49, who specifically discusses *Odyssey* 6.231 and its meaning, pointing out in addition (215–218) the importance of the term *anthos* in the description, which itself has connotations of erotic youth (cf. ἄνθος ἥβης, *Iliad* 13.484).

in athletic competitions on Skheria, competing against men of the same younger generation. He challenges the age-mates of Alkinoos' son Laodamas, but not those of Alkinoos himself, in games introduced explicitly as a competition for the young:

> βὰν δ' ἴμεν εἰς ἀγορήν, ἅμα δ' ἔσπετο πουλὺς ὅμιλος,
> μυρίοι· ἂν δ' ἵσταντο νέοι πολλοί τε καὶ ἐσθλοί.
>
> *(Odyssey 8.109–110)*

> They went to the assembly and a great throng went along
>   with them,
> countless; and many excellent young men stood up.

Odysseus is invited to participate, and Laodamas mentions that he seems both strong and young enough: οὐδέ τι ἥβης δεύεται, 'he is not at all lacking in the vigor of youth' (8.137). Laodamas does, however, address Odysseus as one would an older man, ξεῖνε πάτηρ, 'father stranger', and Odysseus at first declines the invitation, calling it mockery and pointing to the troubles that now preoccupy him:

> Λαοδάμα, τί με ταῦτα κελεύετε κερτομέοντες;
> κήδεά μοι καὶ μᾶλλον ἐνὶ φρεσὶν ἤ περ ἄεθλοι.
>
> *(Odyssey 8.153–154)*

> Laodamas, why do you urge me to do these things,
>   mocking me?
> Sorrows are on my mind, not games.

Euryalos, however, immediately attributes Odysseus' decision not to his troubles or age, but to his lack of social status. Odysseus, he says, does not resemble a man skilled in athletic contest, but rather a merchant, the kind of man who sails around looking for profit (*Odyssey* 8.159–164). Under this provocation Odysseus does demonstrate his athletic abilities by throwing the discus farther than any Phaeacian, and then challenges them to match the throw. This challenge is issued specifically to the young: τοῦτον νῦν ἀφίκεσθε, νέοι, 'Now reach that, young men!' (8.202).

Odysseus' choice of the event, discus, may itself emphasize his superiority over the young in particular, including not only the Phaeacian youth, but also Penelope's suitors, against whom he will compete on Ithaca. Discus throwing is mentioned in the *Odyssey* as one of the suitors' pastimes:

μνηστῆρες δὲ πάροιθεν Ὀδυσσῆος μεγάροιο
δίσκοισιν τέρποντο καὶ αἰγανέῃσιν ἱέντες
ἐν τυκτῷ δαπέδῳ, ὅθι περ πάρος, ὕβριν ἔχοντες.

(Odyssey 4.626–628 = 17.168–170)

The suitors entertained themselves in front of
> Odysseus' house
with discus and throwing of goat-spears
on leveled ground, arrogant as before.

Discus throwing also occurs in connection with prime of youth (*hebe*) in the *Iliad*, where Antilokhos is separated from Menelaos in the chariot race by the length of a discus throw:

ὅσσα δὲ δίσκου οὖρα κατωμαδίοιο πέλονται,
ὅν τ' αἰζηὸς ἀφῆκεν ἀνὴρ πειρώμενος ἥβης.

(Iliad 23.431–432)

. . . as far as is the range of a discus, thrown from the
> shoulder,
that a lusty young man sends flying, probing the vigor
> of his youth.

In general, the confrontation of Antilokhos and Menelaos is at least in part a generational conflict, and it even bears similarities to the *Homeric Hymn to Hermes*. Like Hermes, Antilokhos challenges an older man, and does so by breaking the rules: he overtakes Menelaos in a narrow space by forcing him to hold back in order to avoid a crash. Like Hermes, he then retreats and by returning his unfairly gained prize shows deference to the very person he has challenged. Antilokhos tries to strike the same contradictory balance between challenging and placating the older generation that Hermes achieves in the *Hymn*. Like Apollo, Menelaos in the end shows favor to Antilokhos and allows him to keep the prize after all. Antilokhos, a very young man, is competing against an older, married man, and his youth is repeatedly brought up. Asked to swear an oath that he did not use trickery (*dolos*) against Menelaos, Antilokhos demurs and blames his youth for his rash behavior. Menelaos, he claims, is older and better, while he is young and simply behaves as such. Ostensibly, Antilokhos speaks of the folly of youth, but it is notable that the qualities he ascribes to youth are precisely the ambiguous qualities he shares both with Hermes and with Odysseus – a quick mind and cunning intelligence:

ἄνσχεο νῦν· πολλὸν γὰρ ἔγωγε νεώτερός εἰμι
σεῖο ἄναξ Μενέλαε, σὺ δὲ πρότερος καὶ ἀρείων.
οἶσθ᾽ οἷαι νέου ἀνδρὸς ὑπερβασίαι τελέθουσι·
κραιπνότερος μὲν γάρ τε νόος, λεπτὴ δέ τε μῆτις.

(*Iliad* 23.587–590)[24]

Stop now, for I am far younger than you,
lord Menelaos, while you are older and better.
You know of what sort are the transgressions of a young man:
for his mind is quicker, and his intelligence light.

Two features of this utterance are of importance for my argument. First, Antilokhos uses same formula about Menelaos as Aithon-Odysseus does about Idomeneus, his supposed older brother: πρότερος καὶ ἀρείων (*Iliad* 23.588, *Odyssey* 19.184). The relationship between Antilokhos and Menelaos in this episode thus parallels not only that between Apollo and Hermes in the *Homeric Hymn* but also that between Aithon and his older brother Idomeneus in the Third Cretan Lie. Secondly, in all these cases the younger man is also the cunning one. Quick mind and subtle intelligence, those quintessentially Odyssean features, turn out to be also generational: they are features typical of the young, and Odysseus emerges as their model. Antilokhos' behavior and rhetoric at the funeral games echo both the *Homeric Hymn to Hermes* and the *Odyssey*, suggesting that all three poems tap into a traditional nexus of themes having to do with youth and generational conflict. Moreover, an apparently arbitrary detail, the fact that Antilokhos is at one stage behind Menelaos by a discus throw, is not just a measure of distance, but part of the generational poetics that come to the fore in this scene. The same traditional tendency is active when Odysseus picks up a discus on Skheria.

All of these discus throws bring to mind the most famous myth involving this sport, that of Hyakinthos. Here too, Apollo appears as a sponsor for

---

[24] A similar expression is used by Diomedes at *Iliad* 10.226, where he explains that a second mind is useful in an ambush because a lone warrior may not think quickly, or well, enough: ἀλλά τέ οἱ βράσσων τε νόος, λεπὴ δέ τε μῆτις. Antilokhos uses κραιπνότερος 'quicker' where Diomedes has βράσσων 'slower' and, in contrast to Diomedes, seems to prevaricate: his words can be understood to mean that his decision was rushed and his intelligence slight, or they could mean that his mind was quick and his cunning subtle. Given Nestor's earlier advice that Antilokhos use "every kind of *metis*" (23.313–318) that latter meaning is certainly present in Antilokhos' words and the irony apparent. In his response, Menelaos also mentions Antilokhos' youth, but is understandably unwilling to grant his intellectual superiority. While Antilokhos says that his youthfully nimble mind took him too far, Menelaos says simply that his youth got the better of his mind: νῦν αὖτε νόον νίκησε νεοίη (*Iliad* 23.604).

a younger man, only this time the youth is not his brother, but his lover. A figure associated with the transition to maturity, Hyakinthos never makes this transition himself, but is killed by Apollo's discus, confirming the association between this game and achieving the flower of *hebe*.[25]

Odysseus' discus throw demonstrates not simply that he is better at the sport than the Phaeacians, but that he is best among the young. At the same time, the taunts to which Odysseus is subjected at the games emphasize his position as an outsider of questionable status, and this too is a variation on the same theme. Before he is fully accepted into the adult community, a young man is in a sense an outsider, and his status also remains to be determined. Different as these groups of people may be, there is something that the young share with foreigners and with illegitimate sons, such as the one that appears in the Second Cretan Lie: they all have yet to prove themselves to be worthy of becoming full members of their society, "kings" who can dine with Alkinoos.

At the conclusion of the Phaeacian games, Odysseus, now victorious, boasts of his warlike prowess in bow and spear and, in return, is treated by his hosts to a song and dance performance demonstrating the peaceful achievements of the Phaeacians. The themes associated with younger brother surface in this performance just as they do in Odysseus' own conduct on Skheria. The song of Ares and Aphrodite, performed by Demodokos on the occasion, remains one of the most difficult challenges to modern scholarship, and neither its meaning nor its relevance for Odysseus are fully understood, in spite of many arguments on the subject.[26] Here I can point out only one aspect of the song that is most relevant to the present discussion, namely that, like the athletic competitions that precede it, the song is concerned in part with generational differences. The main conflict is between a married older god, Hephaestus, and an unmarried younger one, Ares. Hephaestus is lame and therefore slow, while Ares is traditionally distinguished precisely by his speed, and this distinction between the two is emphasized in the song:

> οὐκ ἀρετᾷ κακὰ ἔργα· κιχάνει τοι βραδὺς ὠκύν,
> ὡς καὶ νῦν Ἥφαιστος ἐὼν βραδὺς εἷλεν Ἄρηα,
> ὠκύτατόν περ ἐόντα θεῶν, οἳ Ὄλυμπον ἔχουσι,
> χωλὸς ἐών, τέχνῃσι· τὸ καὶ μοιχάγρι' ὀφέλλει.
>
> (*Odyssey* 8.329–332)[27]

---

[25] The earliest attestation of this version of the myth is in Hesiod fr. 171.6–8.

[26] See, for example, Burkert 1960, Braswell 1982, Brown 1989, Olson 1989.

[27] One of the traditional epithets of Ares is θοός, 'swift' (e.g., *Iliad* 5.430, 8.215), derived from θέω, 'to run'. See Nagy 1979:327–328 on this epithet and related words.

Bad deeds bring no profit: a slow one overtakes a fast one,
just as now Hephaestus, while slow, captured Ares,
even though he is the fastest of the gods who dwell on Olympus
and Hephaestus is lame, but he did it by means of his craft.
And so now Ares owes him compensation for adultery.

Speed is a characteristic of Ares, and therefore of warriors, who are *therapontes*, 'ritual substitutes' of Ares, but this characteristic applies specifically to the young warriors.[28] As a quality of the young, speed has two sides to it, being essential not only in war but also in dance. An example of this equivalence can be seen in the *Iliad* when Meriones, one of the young Iliadic warriors known for his speed, (he is addressed by Idomeneus as πόδας ταχύ 'swift-footed' at *Iliad* 13.249), is mockingly called 'dancer' by Aineas:[29]

Μηριόνη τάχα κέν σε καὶ ὀρχηστήν περ ἐόντα
ἔγχος ἐμὸν κατέπαυσε διαμπερές, εἴ σ' ἔβαλόν περ.

(*Iliad* 16.617–618)

Meriones, even though you are a dancer,
my spear would have quickly stopped you forever, had I only
hit you.

Being a good dancer, in turn, is linked to being a good lover, as the example of Paris testifies.[30] Ares is swift in war, but is he also a good dancer? Nagy suggests that the Phaeacian dancers who perform along with Demodokos dance the parts of Ares and Hephaestus, and that in this performance Ares is a nimble dancer, while Hephaestus is a slow one. As Nagy puts it, "the Phaeacians' fleetfootedness in footracing and dancing matches the fleetfootedness associated with the god Ares himself, who is traditionally pictured as a nimble runner and dancer."[31] It seems likely that Ares' swiftness of foot is connected to his second traditional role, that of the quintessential lover and bridegroom. Evidence for such a role of Ares, apart from the song of Demodokos itself, is to be found in Sappho, where a bridegroom is described as 'equal to Ares', the same expression applied to warriors in the

[28] For more on this, see below on the distinction between Idomeneus, an older and slow warrior, and Meriones, a young and swift one. On warriors as *therapontes* of Ares see Nagy 1979:17.5–6.
[29] See below on the age of Meriones.
[30] Aphrodite compares Paris to a man returning from, or going to, a dance when she forces Helen to go to him: κάλλεΐ τε στίλβων καὶ εἵμασιν· οὐδέ κε φαίης | ἀνδρὶ μαχεσσάμενον τόν γ' ἐλθεῖν, ἀλλὰ χορὸν δὲ | ἔρχεσθ', ἠὲ χοροῖο νέον λήγοντα καθίζειν (*Iliad* 3.392–394).
[31] Nagy forthcoming: 215. On dance and Ares see also Muellner 1990:83–90.

Iliad.[32] Demodokos' depiction of Ares as a lover rather than a warrior is surely a response on the part of the Phaeacians to Odysseus' challenge. Odysseus makes no distinction between his athletic abilities and his military prowess: casting the discus, speed in running, and skill with the bow and spear are all listed together. In response, Alkinoos claims that Phaeacians are not good at warlike events. Though speed is indeed their distinctive quality, it is demonstrated not by racing, but by dancing, and accordingly their Ares appears in the song not as a warrior but as a lover.

In interpreting the song it is usually assumed that Odysseus should be compared to Hephaestus, because both are older, both are crafty, and both are defending their marriage bed. I have no doubt that this is indeed a valid parallel, but Odysseus plays multiple roles in the *Odyssey*, and if one of them is that of an older married man, another is that of a young man coming of age. If the Phaeacian bard celebrates Ares the lover, Odysseus is like both Ares the fighter and Ares the perfect bridegroom when he succeeds both on Skheria and on Ithaca. It is indicative of the thematics of the song that Apollo and Hermes also appear in it, and appear together, as older and younger brothers, in a way reminiscent of the *Homeric Hymn to Hermes*. As members of the younger generation, they seem to be impressed by Ares' achievement at least as much as by Hephaestus' cunning, and the words they exchange are those of a teasing older brother and his younger sibling, already hungry for erotic adventures:

> Ἑρμεία Διὸς υἱέ, διάκτορε, δῶτορ ἑάων,
> ἦ ῥά κεν ἐν δεσμοῖσ' ἐθέλοις κρατεροῖσι πιεσθεὶς
> εὕδειν ἐν λέκτροισι παρὰ χρυσῇ Ἀφροδίτῃ;"
> τὸν δ' ἠμείβετ' ἔπειτα διάκτορος Ἀργεϊφόντης·
> "αἲ γὰρ τοῦτο γένοιτο, ἄναξ ἑκατηβόλ' Ἄπολλον.
> δεσμοὶ μὲν τρὶς τόσσοι ἀπείρονες ἀμφὶς ἔχοιεν,
> ὑμεῖς δ' εἰσορόῳτε θεοὶ πᾶσαί τε θέαιναι,
> αὐτὰρ ἐγὼν εὕδοιμι παρὰ χρυσῇ Ἀφροδίτῃ.

> (*Odyssey* 8.335–342)

> "Hermes, son of Zeus, runner, giver of goods,
> would you want to lie in bed with golden Aphrodite,
> weighed down by strong bonds?"
> And runner slayer of Argos then responded to him:

---

[32] Sappho fr. 111.5 Voigt. For the formula in the *Iliad*, see *Iliad* 11.295, 13.802 (of Hektor); 11.604 (of Patroklos); 22.132 (of Achilles).

"If only this could happen, lord far-shooting Apollo!
May bonds three times as inextricable as these bind me,
and may all you gods look on and all the goddesses,
only let me lie with golden Aphrodite!"

Stages and aspects of male coming of age are reflected in the song of Ares and Aphrodite, and Odysseus, who listens to the song, is himself re-living this process. Granted, in the Phaeacian episode, Odysseus seems to disown his speed when he claims that he may not be able to compete in the footrace and blames the sea for this (8.230–233). He also seems to deny his youth when saying that he is no longer in possession of *hebe* (8.181). The situation is complicated, however. Even though exhausted by the sea, Odysseus does not completely distance himself from running, but only contemplates the possibility that someone may overcome him:

οἴοισιν δείδοικα ποσὶν μή τίς με παρέλθῃ Φαιήκων·

(*Odyssey* 8.230–231)

Only in the footrace do I fear that one of the Phaeacians
may overtake me.

In contrast to this caution is the confidence he displays when he challenges any Phaeacian except for Laodamas to compete with him in any event, including foot racing:

τῶν δ' ἄλλων ὅτινα κραδίη θυμός τε κελεύει,
δεῦρ' ἄγε πειρηθήτω, ἐπεί μ' ἐχολώσατε λίην,
ἢ πὺξ ἠὲ πάλῃ ἢ καὶ ποσίν, οὔ τι μεγαίρω,
πάντων Φαιήκων πλήν γ' αὐτοῦ Λαοδάμαντος.

(*Odyssey* 8.204–207)

Let one of the others, whomever his heart and spirit urges on,
come here and try me, since you have angered me very much,
in boxing or wrestling or in running, I have no objection,
anyone of the Phaeacians except for Laodamas himself.

It seems that Odysseus' progress towards Ithaca is represented both by an enactment of his "younger brother" role and by a gradual overcoming of it. Once he has defeated the suitors Odysseus will be able to stop playing a youngster. The final overcoming, however, will have to wait until Ithaca. In the meanwhile, the fluctuation in age, and with it, speed, remains a fundamental feature of Odysseus.

This feature is as relevant for the Iliadic Odysseus as for his Odyssean counterpart. There are several examples of Odysseus' age-fluctuation in the *Iliad*, but one of them is especially relevant for comparison with the Phaeacian games because it also occurs at an athletic competition, in the foot race at the funeral games for Patroklos. The fact that the sliding of Odysseus' age markers is present here too indicates that it is a traditional and deeply rooted element.[33]

Three competitors participate in the footrace: two of them, Ajax and Antilokhos, belong to the same generation. It is said specifically that Antilokhos is the fastest runner among the young: ὁ γὰρ αὖτε νέους ποσὶ πάντας ἐνίκα, 'For he used to overcome all the young ones in running' (*Iliad* 23.756). Throughout both the *Iliad* and the *Odyssey*, speed in running is consistently associated with youth,[34] and yet Odysseus wins the race, prompting Antilokhos to comment precisely on the question of age:

εἰδόσιν ὔμμ' ἐρέω πᾶσιν φίλοι, ὡς ἔτι καὶ νῦν
ἀθάνατοι τιμῶσι παλαιοτέρους ἀνθρώπους.
Αἴας μὲν γὰρ ἐμεῖ' ὀλίγον προγενέστερός ἐστιν,
οὗτος δὲ προτέρης γενεῆς προτέρων τ' ἀνθρώπων·
ὠμογέροντα δέ μίν φασ' ἔμμεναι· ἀργαλέον δὲ
ποσσὶν ἐριδήσασθαι Ἀχαιοῖς, εἰ μὴ Ἀχιλλεῖ.

(*Iliad* 23.787–792).

I am telling this to you, and all of you know it yourselves,
that the immortal ones still honor the elders.
For Ajax is a little older than I am,
but this one [Odysseus] is from a previous generation and
      previous people.

---

[33] It has been suggested that the competitors' performances in the foot race for Patroklos predict their *nostoi*, namely that Ajax Oileus falls during the race and subsequently dies during his *nostos*, while Odysseus wins both the race and his return with the help of Athena (Whitman 1958:264). On the same hypothesis, further details of the race may find correspondence in the quality, rather than the mere fact, of Odysseus' return.

[34] The epithet πόδας ταχύς and expressions such as ταχέες δὲ πόδες/ταχέεσσι πόδεσσι, for example, are applied to Paris (*Iliad* 6.514), Achilles (*Iliad* 13.348, 17.709, 18.354, 20.189, 21.564,), Meriones (*Iliad* 13.249), Aineas (*Iliad* 13.482), and Antilokhos (*Iliad* 18.2), all youthful characters. In his First Cretan Lie, Odysseus, talking to a youthful shepherd, who is actually Athena in disguise (ἀνδρὶ δέμας εἰκυῖα νέῳ, ἐπιβώτορι μήλων,| παναπάλῳ, *Odyssey* 13.222–223), claims to have killed a son of Idomeneus, a man one generation younger than himself and who is described as an excellent runner:
  φεύγω, ἐπεὶ φίλον υἷα κατέκτανον Ἰδομενῆος, | Ὀρσίλοχον πόδας ὠκύν, ὃς ἐν Κρήτῃ εὐρείῃ | ἄνδρας ἀλφηστὰς νίκα ταχέεσσι πόδεσσιν (13.259–261).

> They say he is in his unripe old age: it is hard for Achaeans
> to compete with him in speed, except for Achilles.

This victory is an anomaly. In the *Iliad*, Odysseus does not belong to the generation of unmarried young men, such as Antilokhos, but to a previous generation of married mature men. In age and status he is on his way to becoming a *geron*, even thought he is not yet old, as is indicated by Antilokhos' characterization of him as ὠμογέρων, literally 'an unripe old man', a Homeric hapax.[35] Moreover, it is interesting that in the *Iliad* Idomeneus, who becomes Odysseus' older brother in the Third Cretan Lie, is characterized in a similar way, namely as μεσαιπόλιος, 'half-grey' (13.361), another hapax. Idomeneus, then, is also on his way to becoming a *geron*. One of the crucial differences between them, however, is precisely swiftness of foot: Idomeneus is specifically described as slow because of his age. For example, he cannot strip off the armor of Oinomaos because he is no longer fast enough:

> οὐ γὰρ ἔτ' ἔμπεδα γυῖα ποδῶν ἦν ὁρμηθέντι,
> οὔτ' ἄρ' ἐπαΐξαι μεθ' ἑὸν βέλος οὔτ' ἀλέασθαι.
> τώ ῥα καὶ ἐν σταδίῃ μὲν ἀμύνετο νηλεὲς ἦμαρ,
> τρέσσαι δ' οὐκ ἔτι ῥίμφα πόδες φέρον ἐκ πολέμοιο.

> (*Iliad* 13.512–515)

> For in an onslaught his legs were no longer steady enough
> either to dart out after his own spear or to dodge that of
>   another man.
> And so in a standing fight he kept off the pitiless day,
> but his feet no longer carried him running quickly out of
>   fighting.

This feature is especially noticeable because at Idomeneus's side is his *therapon* and nephew, Meriones, who is a generation younger, and whom Idomeneus addresses with a mention of his speed in running: Μηριόνη, Μόλου υἱέ, πόδας ταχύ, φίλταθ' ἑταίρων, 'Meriones, son of Molos, swift-footed, most dear of my companions' (13.249).[36]

---

[35] The exact connotations of the epithet are unclear. As Falkner (1989:61n78) points out, the expression must be related to ἐν ὠμῷ γήραι at *Odyssey* 15.357, where Antikleia is said to place Laertes in 'raw' old age by her death. In this instance, 'raw' is usually taken to mean 'premature'.

[36] On Crete one way to define ephebic status seems to have been the ephebe's relationship to running. Ancient commentators explain the use of Cretan term *apodromos* to mean 'ephebe' since ephebes could not yet take part in this event: ἐν δὲ Κυρήνῃ τοὺς ἐφήβους τριακαδίους καλοῦσιν· ἐν δὲ Κρήτῃ ἀποδρόμους, διὰ τὸ μηδέπω τῶν κοινῶν δρόμων μετέχειν (*Aristophanes*

In contrast to Idomeneus, Odysseus is faster than the young and does not have a young companion at his side. It is as if Odysseus himself is both the ageing Idomeneus and the nimble Meriones. The fact that he is a fast runner and wins the footrace at the funeral games for Patroklos resonates with his *nostos*, when Odysseus will compete against the youths of the next generation. Instead of being like Idomeneus, Odysseus after the Trojan war at times comes closer to resembling Meriones, who is young, fast, and, in some versions of his genealogy, illegitimate.[37]

On Ithaca, the return of Odysseus signals at least a partial end to his life as a younger brother: opposed to his wanderings is a settled life amidst his family and property, an ideal repeatedly envisaged by the *Odyssey*. Telemachus, for example, wishes he could be the son of a man who is overtaken by old age on his estate:

> ὡς δὴ ἐγώ γ᾽ ὄφελον μάκαρός νύ τευ ἔμμεναι υἱὸς
> ἀνέρος, ὃν κτεάτεσσιν ἑοῖσ᾽ ἔπι γῆρας ἔτετμε.
>
> (*Odyssey* 1.217–218)

> And so I wish I could have been the son of some
>   fortunate man,
> whom old age has overtaken among his possessions.

Eurykleia attributes the same wish to Odysseus, recalling how he used to sacrifice to Zeus and pray to come to a 'sleek old age' and to bring up his son

---

Grammaticus, fr. 1.12). It is interesting that some commentators in a sense link the status of the ephebe with that of the old man when they reject the interpretation of apodromos as one no longer able to take part in the event: οὐ διὰ τὸ πεπαῦθαι τῶν δρόμων, καθ᾽ ὃ δὴ σημαινόμενον τῆς <ἀπο> προθέσεως ἄπιχθυς λέγεται ὁ μὴ ἐσθίων . . . ἀλλὰ δηλαδὴ ἀπόδρομοι ἐν Κρήτῃ, οἱ μήπω τῶν κοινῶν δρόμων μετέχοντες ἔφηβοι (Eustathius 2.630 on *Iliad* 8.518). Note Eustathius' comment on *Odyssey* 8.247, where he explains that Alkinoos takes Odysseus for an *apodromos*, a person who no longer takes part in the footraces (ὁ Ἀλκίνοος ἀπόδρομον τὸν Ὀδυσσέα ἐνόμισεν, ὡς ἤδη πεπαυμένον ἀπὸ τῶν δρόμων, Eustathius 1.292). There may have been real variation in the regional use of the term *apodromos*, but there is also a common core meaning to all instances: what unites the young with the old is that they are excluded from the competitions in running, which are thereby associated with full maturity and manhood. There is, of course, also an important difference between the young and the old: while the old are no longer as fast as they used to be, the ephebes, on the contrary, may be presumed to take part in races of their own and training for the grown-up races, where they will soon show their speed.

[37] Apollodorus 3.3.1, Diodorus Siculus 5.79. There is much more to be said about the similarities and points of contact between Odysseus and Meriones, and it has been suggested that Odysseus, in his Second Cretan Lie, makes himself out to be a Meriones-like figure (Clay 1983:88). For a detailed discussion of this question see Clay 1983:77–89 and Haft 1984. See also below, pp172–175.

(19.367–368). In his prophecy, Teiresias promises Odysseus that at the end of all his adventures a gentle death will come to him when he is 'worn out by sleek old age' (γήρᾳ ὕπο λιπαρῷ ἀρημένον, *Odyssey* 11.137). And although the same prophecy sends Odysseus away from Ithaca yet again, the vision of an old age at home is a positive prospect in the end, as Penelope acknowledges:

> εἰ μὲν δὴ γῆράς γε θεοὶ τελέουσιν ἄρειον,
> ἐλπωρή τοι ἔπειτα κακῶν ὑπάλυξιν ἔσεσθαι.
>
> (*Odyssey* 23.283–284)

> But if the gods accomplish a better old age,
> then there is hope for an escape from troubles.

The stability of Odysseus' promised old age is in contrast with the prime of his life, which he does not spend at home, and with the long road that brings him home in the end. To reiterate my earlier point: before Odysseus can become king again, he must once more go through the trials of youth, which culminates in his remarriage. In the process, Odysseus emerges as a hero of young men, a hero concerned with maturation and the achievement of full social standing, and there might well be a cultic dimension behind his epic persona. It is consistent with such a cultic role that in epic he is both a supremely successful "youngster" himself and also their destroyer. One might compare the role of Apollo, who is the patron god of males coming to maturity. In myth, he is himself a longhaired *ephebos*, but also, in the *Iliad*, an enemy and a destroyer of a youth most like him, Achilles.[38]

Initiatory or maturational activities are generational, recurring on a regular basis: each new generation has to go through these stages, and this process is part of the recurrent renewal of society. It is such a renewal that is afoot in Ithaca, set in motion by the return of Odysseus. This renewal occurs within the ritual framework of a seasonally recurring festival of Apollo, a festival which involves assemblies of young men and is likely to have had an initiatory component. In this context, Odysseus' re-becoming a king acquires a cultic flavor. Although in the *Odyssey* the return of Odysseus can obviously happen only once, the fact that it is a return, the fact that it re-enacts a transition into adulthood, and the fact that it happens within the context of a festival point to a ritual subtext, in which such return and renewal is a periodic occurrence. Viewed this way, some of the features that from the point of view of the Odyssean narrative may look like character-traits of Odysseus emerge

---

[38] Nagy 1979:62–63 and 142–144, with further references.

as generational. For example, Antilokhos in the *Iliad* attributes 'quick *noos*', a hallmark of Odysseus' personality, to the young in general (*Iliad* 23.589–90). These are qualities of Odysseus, but also of the "younger brothers," of those who need to make way for themselves in a world where older and well-established players are in control.

Within the *Odyssey*, the festival of Apollo is not only a celebration of a new generation but also more broadly a festival of renewal, perhaps something akin to a New Year festival: it is on this day, at new moon, that the dark period of inversion and dissolution on Ithaca comes to an end with the return of Odysseus. These two components, that of renewal, social and natural, and that of the entry of a new generation into the community, are in fact combined in actual festivals. For example, the Spartan Hyacinthia has been interpreted as a New Year festival, and is certainly a festival of renewal, but it is also concerned with maturation of males, a concern expressed in the corresponding myth, the death of Hyakinthos, a younger male, loved and "sponsored" by Apollo.[39] Similarly, it seems that festivals in honor of Zeus Kretaigenes on Crete celebrated both renewal in a larger sense and specifically the rise of new citizens.[40] Apollo's festival in the *Odyssey* seems akin to such historically attested festivals. On the one hand, Odysseus puts himself under Apollo's protection, thus occupying the position of a youth coming of age. At the same time, it is his return to Ithaca that ends a period of darkness and brings back prosperity and social stability, thus accomplishing renewal, both natural and social. In this association between Odysseus' return, the festival of Apollo, and renewal of life on Ithaca, there is, again, a glimpse of Odysseus as a cult hero. It may or may not be the case that some historical cults of Odysseus influenced the evolution of the *Odyssey*, but in any event he emerges as more than a king, a cult hero of the Odyssean Ithaca within the *Odyssey* itself. It is as if the panhellenic epic creates a virtual local community that is Ithaca, with its cult hero, Odysseus. As an epic hero, Odysseus returns only once, but as a cult hero he may be expected to "take part" in the festival of renewal on a seasonally recurring basis, and each time to be both the king/hero of Ithaca who can assure its flourishing and a patron and model for each new generation. Perhaps the strange redoubling of Odysseus' coming of age actually corresponds to this

---

[39] Hesiod fr. 171 MW, Apollodorus 3.10.3, Euripides *Helen* 1469–1474, Palaiphatos 46, Lucian *Dialogues of the Dead* 16, Ovid *Metamorphoses* 10.162–219, Pausanias 3.19.4. For a discussion of Spartan Hyakinthia, an annual festival of Apollo, as a rite of separation, the first step of the tri-partite rite of passage (separation, liminal period, integration) and also as a rite of passage aiming at marriage, see Pettersson 1992:9–41.

[40] West 1965, and see further below p104.

kind of ritual role, as does the fluctuation of his age and status between that of a mature and fabulously wealthy hero and that of an unmarried and "hungry" youngster.

When Odysseus introduces himself as the younger and lesser brother of Idomeneus, he sends a complicated message. The genealogy points to his place as a Zeus-nourished king, which Odysseus will in the end occupy, and which he claims as his own. At the same time, his role as a younger brother qualifies this message. This self-description reminds Penelope of the particular kind of heroism that is characteristic of her husband, and this reminder acquires special meaning on the eve of Apollo's festival. The Third Cretan Lie points to two related aspects of Odysseus: a husband and king, on the one hand, and a youngster coming to full adulthood on the other hand. This double identity seems to have cultic overtones: Odysseus' power to revive Ithaca is like that of a local hero, while his involvement with the rising generation is fitting for a hero concerned with male maturation. Within the *Odyssey*, this splitting of Odysseus' age is also paralleled by Penelope, who is depicted both as a married woman and as a girl on the verge of marriage. Perhaps the wavering in age for both Odysseus and Penelope has to do with the "cultic" mechanics of Odysseus' return and Ithaca's renewal, with all that is symbolized by the festival of Apollo.

CHAPTER FIVE

MINOS

ANOTHER SIGNIFICANT DETAIL OF THE THIRD CRETAN LIE is the famous and remarkably obscure description of Aithon's supposed ancestor, Minos, the king at Knossos:

> τῆσι δ' ἐνὶ Κνωσός, μεγάλη πόλις, ἔνθα τε Μίνως
> ἐννέωρος βασίλευε Διὸς μεγάλου ὀαριστής.

> *(Odyssey* 19.178–179)

> And among them there is Knossos, a great city,
> where Minos was king in nine-year periods and conversed
> with great Zeus.

It remains unclear what exactly is meant by ἐννέωρος βασίλευε, 'ruled in nine-year periods', and why Minos is designated by the highly unusual term ὀαριστής. Plato apparently took ἐννέωρος, 'nine-year-long', with ὀαριστής, 'conversation partner', rather than with βασίλευε, 'ruled', and explained that Minos went to talk with Zeus every ninth year, and brought back laws for the cities.[1] Nine-year cycles have been attested for Greek festivals and religious observances, the early *Pythian* games being one obvious example.[2] In the case of Minos' visits with Zeus, in Plato's version, this nine-year period seems to be implicitly connected with renewal of a social order through law. In later sources, Minos converses with Zeus in the Idaean cave, presumably the one

---

[1] *Minos* 319b (Minos is said to be 'educated' by Zeus) and *Laws* 624a (laws are set down according to Minos' conversations with Zeus). The same explanation is given in Strabo 10.4.8, 16.2.38.

[2] Russo 1992:85 (ad loc.) with references. Early Pythian games took place every eight years (ἐνναετηρίς, counted inclusively), see OCD s.v. "Pythian games" with references. According to Plutarch, Spartan kings were re-confirmed in their power every nine years (*Life of Agis* 11). According to Diodorus Siculus (4.61.3) and Plutarch (*Life of Theseus* 15.1), the Athenians had to send seven youths and seven maidens to the Minotaur every nine years. For more on connections between the Odyssean passage under discussion and the myth of Theseus' voyage to Crete with the youths, see below.

where the god was born.[3] This, again, suggests periodic renewal, since renewal in general is associated with the birth cave of Zeus. For example, according to a myth preserved in Antoninus Liberalis (19), on Crete there is a sacred cave in which Zeus is reported to be born and which is inhabited by the 'sacred bees', the nurses of the god. Every year a great fire is seen blazing out of the cave and it is said that this happens when Zeus' birth-blood 'boils out' (ἐκζέῃ). A yearly event in the cave seems to re-enact the birth of the god.

Just as the reference to nine years is suggestive but elusive in its meaning, so too is the term ὀαριστής applied to Minos. This is a rare word,[4] and precisely because of this its usage here deserves further consideration. In what follows I attempt to make some, albeit necessarily hypothetical, suggestions about the meaning and impact of this word in the mouth of Odysseus.

Words derived from the root of ὄαρ, 'wife', can carry a mildly erotic connotation, as is well known. For example, when Aphrodite gives Hera her waistband that contains all manner of allurements, including ὀαριστύς, a term conventionally translated as 'familiar converse':

> Ἦ, καὶ ἀπὸ στήθεσφιν ἐλύσατο κεστὸν ἱμάντα
> ποικίλον, ἔνθα δέ οἱ θελκτήρια πάντα τέτυκτο·
> ἔνθ' ἔνι μὲν φιλότης, ἐν δ' ἵμερος, ἐν δ' ὀαριστὺς
> πάρφασις, ἥ τ' ἔκλεψε νόον πύκα περ φρονεόντων.

> (Iliad 14.214–217)

> She spoke, and from under her breast she loosened the
>   embroidered strap,
> ornate, with all manner of charms in it:
> it contains affection, and desire, and seductive conversation,
> the kind that deceives the mind even of clever men.

The erotic connotation of *oaristus* is only one side of its meaning, however, and an optional one. It is certainly not present in every word derived from the same root, and even *oaristus* itself is not always primarily erotic. In the passage just cited, *oaristus* undoubtedly has to do with love, but it seems to be something more particular than simply an amorous conversation. Instead, it is a dangerous kind of discourse which leads to the loss of one's mind and therefore delivers one defenseless into the opponent's hands. Πάρφασις,

---

[3] Ephorus FGrH 70 F 14, Etymologicum Magnum 343.25 (s.v. ἐννέωροι), Eustathius 2.198.5–6 (on *Odyssey* 19.178), Strabo 10.4.8, 16.2.38.

[4] The Odyssean instance of *oaristes* is cited by Plato, *Minos* 319d, and Timo calls Pythagoras σεμνηγορίης ὀαριστήν in a hexametric distich (fr. 57 Diels).

the word with which *oaristus* is paired, usually designates a speech aimed at winning over the interlocutor and pressing him into a particular course of action.[5] *Parphasis*, and no doubt *oaristus* too, can be truthful or not, spoken in love or in hate, but in either case it is a question of one person prevailing over another. This suggests that the type of discourse contained in Aphrodite's waistband has to do with power and control, in other words, that it is agonistic as well as erotic.

Elsewhere the term ὀαριστύς seems to designate an openly agonistic equal exchange between a man and a woman. In a pseudo-Theocritean poem titled Ὀαριστύς a boy and a girl first tease and taunt each other and then make love in the bushes, parting with a promise of marriage from the boy (Theocritus 27.34–36). The girl insists that she is wooed by many and likes none, that she will escape Eros, that marriage brings grief, and that the shepherd boy with whom she talks is good enough only to kiss heifers. The boy responds that none can escape Eros and Aphrodite, that there is pleasure in marriage, and that the girl should not boast, because her youth will quickly pass. The following is a typical exchange:

> ΚΟ. καλόν σοι δαμάλας φιλέειν, οὐκ ἄζυγα κώραν.
> ΔΑ. μὴ καυχῶ· τάχα γάρ σε παρέρχεται ὡς ὄναρ ἥβη.
>
> (Theocritus 27.7–8)

> [Girl] You are fit to kiss heifers, not an unmarried girl.
> [Daphnis] Don't brag. Youth will quickly flee from you,
>   like a dream.

The whole poem consists of a dialogue equally divided between the two: one line from the boy, one line from the girl. In ancient Greece, most genres of speech and song are either male or female, but in this poem both speakers have equal parts. It is certainly an amorous conversation, but also an antagonistic one: the two are not yet lovers and jostle for a favorable position in their future relationship.

The same notion of even distribution between male and female may be present in the verb ὀαρίζω, from which the noun ὀαριστύς is derived. Thus

---

[5] LSJ glosses παραφήμι as 'advise', 'persuade', and also 'speak deceitfully', a range of meaning close to that of ὀαριστύς. Cunliff's (1963) gloss 'to induce to a course of action, persuade, prevail upon, win over' is more precise. The same meaning is evident in the noun παραίφασις/ πάρφασις, as it is used, for example, by Nestor at *Iliad* 11.793: ὡς ἐπέτελλ' ὃ γέρων, σὺ δὲ λήθεαι· ἀλλ' ἔτι καὶ νῦν | ταῦτ' εἴποις Ἀχιλῆϊ δαΐφρονι αἴ κε πίθηται. | τίς δ' οἶδ' εἴ κέν οἱ σὺν δαίμονι θυμὸν ὀρίναις | παρειπών; ἀγαθὴ δὲ παραίφασίς ἐστιν ἑταίρου (11.790–793).

the final conjugal conversation between Hektor and Andromakhe, in which each reacts to the fears and hopes of the other, is characterized by this verb (*Iliad* 6.516). When Hektor uses ὀαρίζω before his confrontation with Achilles, his very diction iconically expresses the idea of agonistic balance by twice repeating the expression παρθένος ἠΐθεός τε, 'a girl and a boy':

> οὐ μέν πως νῦν ἔστιν ἀπὸ δρυὸς οὐδ' ἀπὸ πέτρης
> τῷ ὀαριζέμεναι, ἅ τε παρθένος ἠΐθεός τε
> παρθένος ἠΐθεός τ' ὀαρίζετον ἀλλήλοιιν.
>
> (*Iliad* 22.126–128)

> Now there is no way to converse with him from a tree
>   or a rock,
> the way a girl and a lad,
> a girl and a lad talk together.

Lines 127–128 are an exercise in symmetry: not only is the expression παρθένος ἠΐθεός repeated, but it is put in a chiastic arrangement with two *oar*-words, ὀαριζέμεναι and ὀαρίζετον, and the whole construction is concluded with the dual ἀλλήλοιιν, 'to each other', which expresses the idea of mutuality not only semantically but iconically, being a doubling of *allos* and reflecting this origin in its repetitive phonetics. The idea of two equal opponents seems to be just as present in Hektor's syntax as it is evident in Pseudo-Theocritus' poem, and goes well with the setting of his musings: the confrontation between Achilles and Hektor is contrasted not simply with a love-chat, but, being an agonistic encounter, with an agonistic situation that is its extreme opposite. The logic behind Hektor's sudden foray into an apparent pastoral is also reflected in the formulaic system itself. The agonistic potential of the genre of *oaristus* is probably what accounts for its metaphorical use in the *Iliad* of hand-to-hand combat: πολέμου ὀαριστύς, 'amorous converse of war' (17.228), and προμάχων ὀαριστύν, 'amorous converse of front-rank fighters' (13.291). For Hektor and Achilles, however, the evocation of *oaristus* is especially meaningful because it is a premarital genre. Hektor's death in the *Iliad* is pictured as a negation of his marriage, so that it even becomes an occasion for a direct recollection of his wedding. When Andromakhe sees Hektor's dead body, she faints and loses her headband, which she received specifically on their wedding day:

> τῆλε δ' ἀπὸ κρατὸς βάλε δέσματα σιγαλόεντα,
> ἄμπυκα κεκρύφαλόν τε ἰδὲ πλεκτὴν ἀναδέσμην
> κρήδεμνόν θ', ὅ ῥά οἱ δῶκε χρυσῆ Ἀφροδίτη

ἤματι τῷ ὅτε μιν κορυθαίολος ἠγάγεθ' Ἕκτωρ
ἐκ δόμου Ἠετίωνος, ἐπεὶ πόρε μυρία ἕδνα.

(*Iliad* 22.468-472)

And far off from her head she cast the shining headdress,
the diadem and the cap and the plaited band,
and the head-band golden Aphrodite gave her
on that day when Hector of the shining helmet led her
    in marriage
from Eetion's house, after giving countless gifts.

As for Achilles, he is pictured as an ideal bridegroom in traditions outside of the *Iliad*, such as in Sappho (F 105b V),[6] and the *Iliad* itself envisages an impossible future in which Achilles will marry Briseis in Phthia (19.295–300). He is also a doomed bridegroom, destined never to become a husband. There are indications both in the *Iliad* itself and in what survives of the Epic Cycle that Achilles' identity as a perfect but doomed bridegroom was no less important than his identity as a perfect warrior, and moreover it has been argued that this identity as bridegroom is a matching counterpart to his identity as warrior.[7] If this is so, then the glimpse of *oaristus* that precedes the duel in *Iliad* 22 is as meaningful for Achilles as it is for Hektor, since it invites thoughts of marriage at the moment when Achilles is about to seal his fate to die an untimely death at war.

Further, Hektor's very utterance of the two words together, παρθένος ἠΐθεός τε, 'a girl and a lad', evokes another genre where the "girls" and the "boys" play equal parts, this time not a genre of speech, but rather the dance on the shield of Achilles, performed on a dancing ground like the one Daidalos once made for Ariadne in Knossos:

Ἐν δὲ χορὸν ποίκιλλε περικλυτὸς ἀμφιγυήεις,
τῷ ἴκελον οἷόν ποτ' ἐνὶ Κνωσῷ εὐρείῃ
Δαίδαλος ἤσκησεν καλλιπλοκάμῳ Ἀριάδνῃ.
ἔνθα μὲν ἠΐθεοι καὶ παρθένοι ἀλφεσίβοιαι
ὀρχεῦντ' ἀλλήλων ἐπὶ καρπῷ χεῖρας ἔχοντες.

(*Iliad* 18.590-594)

---

[6] See Nagy 2007b:21 for discussion.
[7] See Nagy 2007b:21 for a discussion of Achilles as 'equal to Ares' both as a warrior and as a bridegroom and Nagy 2005:80–81 on erotic aspects of Achilles, which are implicit but understated in the *Iliad*.

> And on it [the shield] the famed lame one fashioned a
>   dancing place,
> like the one that Daidalos once made for Ariadne in broad
>   Knossos,
> where lads and girls who attract bride-gifts of oxen
> dance holding each other by the wrists.

This dance is a parallel to an *oaristus*: most dances and choruses are either male or female, but here the girls and the boys are together, holding hands, and seem to play equal parts. This feature, along with the mention of Ariadne, brings to mind the famous *geranos* dance. According to Plutarch, when Theseus sailed back from Crete to Athens with the 'boys and girls' rescued from the Minotaur, they performed this dance on Delos, after Theseus dedicated an *aphrodision* he had received from Ariadne.[8] It is a mysterious story: Ariadne has already been abandoned at Naxos, and yet the dedication of the *aphrodision* suggests that the dance celebrates her love with Theseus. In an attempt to untangle the contradictions of the myth, Calame has suggested that an earlier setting for *geranos* was in fact not Delos, but Crete itself.[9] This would bring the *geranos* dance even closer to the dance on the shield, although Calame himself resists the identification of the two proposed by the scholia as worthless on the grounds that the *geranos* is danced without armor, while the dancers on the shield have daggers. Be that as it may, the two dances, even if they are not the same, are morphologically similar: both have something to do with Crete and Ariadne and both bring together boys and girls. In fact, a scholion on this passage even claims that Theseus' *geranos* was the first occasion on which males and females ever danced together:

> ἄμεινον δὲ ἐκεῖνο φάσκειν ὅτι πρώην διακεχωρισμένως χορευόντων
> ἀνδρῶν καὶ γυναικῶν πρῶτοι οἱ μετὰ Θησέως σωθέντες ἐκ τοῦ
> λαβυρίνθου ἠΐθεοι καὶ παρθένοι ἀναμὶξ ἐχόρευσαν.

> (Scholia (T) on *Iliad* 18.591)

> It is better to say that while previously men and women danced separately, Theseus and the lads and girls who were saved from the Labyrinth were the first to dance together.

---

[8] Plutarch, *Life of Theseus* 21.2.
[9] Calame 1996:118–120.

It is noteworthy that the scholiast uses exactly the same words for boys and girls, ἤϊθεοι καὶ παρθένοι, as Hektor does when he thinks of an *oaristus* before his confrontation with Achilles. Like the *geranos*, the dance on the shield of Achilles looks like an erotic and premarital genre. The emphasis is on the physical beauty and ornate attire of the dancers, the dancing floor belongs to Ariadne, the elders stand on the sides and admire the young, and the girls are described as ἀλφεσίβοιαι, 'attracting bride-gifts of oxen' (18.593), an epithet that applies to them only when they marry.[10]

By the same token, the *Oaristus* of Pseudo-Theocritus is a premarital discourse, and it seems likely that this circumstance is what accounts for the unusual equal distribution of male and female roles in both genres: as they meet and probe each other, boys and girls engage in the agonistic discourse of *oaristus*, and in a mixed dance, as a kind of mutual introduction. After marriage their relationship will presumably change and the balance will shift.

A similar coloring may be present in a related term *oaros*, which appears in a Hesiodic description of Aphrodite, in a context much like that of the Homeric *oaristus*:

> ταύτην δ' ἐξ ἀρχῆς τιμὴν ἔχει ἠδὲ λέλογχε
> μοῖραν ἐν ἀνθρώποισι καὶ ἀθανάτοισι θεοῖσι,
> παρθενίους τ' ὀάρους μειδήματά τ' ἐξαπάτας τε
> τέρψίν τε γλυκερὴν φιλότητά τε μειλιχίην τε.
>
> *(Theogony* 204–207)[11]

And from the beginning she received and has this honor,
her share among men and immortal gods:
girlish conversations and smiles and deceits,
and sweet pleasure and honey-sweet affection.

Like *oaristus*, *oaros* is associated with deceit, which suggests that it too is first and foremost a self-interested and manipulative way of speaking. Overtly erotic connotations, however, are optional in the case of *oaros*, and a more persistent connotation associates it more generally with the young and especially with coming to maturity. Pindar uses this term to refer to a song, and in three occurrences out of four in the victory odes it is a song performed

---

[10] Edwards 1991:229 ad loc., Lonsdale 1995. On the initiatory aspects of the *geranos* and its connection to Theseus' adventure on Crete see Condoléon-Bolanacchi 1989 and Delavaud-Roux 1992.

[11] Cf. ὄαροι νυμφᾶν in Callimachus *Hymn* 5.66.

by young men.[12] In *Pythian* 1, for example, Phalaris will never be welcomed, in contrast to a victor at the games, by the '*oaroi* of the boys':

οὐδέ νιν φόρμιγγες ὑπωρόφιαι κοινανίαν
μαλθακὰν παίδων ὀάροισι δέκονται

(Pythian 1.97–98).

And now no lyres resounding under the roof welcome him
in gentle companionship with songs [*oaroi*] of the boys.

Especially interesting is the use of *oaros* in *Pythian* 4, where it refers to a challenging speech Jason addresses to Pelias. The subject is the coming of the new generation. After a period of lawless rule by the usurper Pelias, Jason returns to take the place of his exiled father as rightful king. He addresses Pelias with an *oaros*:

πραῢν δ' Ἰάσων
μαλθακᾷ φωνᾷ ποτιστάζων ὄαρον
βάλλετο κρηπῖδα σοφῶν ἐπέων·

(Pythian 4.136–138)

And Jason,
letting fall gentle words [*oaros*] in a soft voice,
laid the foundation of wise speech.

Jason proceeds to say that he lays no claim to Pelias' wealth, but has come to take his position as king (139–156), his ancestral scepter (σκᾶπτον μόναρχον καὶ θρόνος, 'sole ruler's scepter and throne', 152–153). His demand is based on his descent, which he measures and finds equal to that of Pelias.

Like the *oaristus*, the *oaros* seems to have an agonistic side to it. The contents of the *oaroi* performed by youths in Pindar and maidens in Hesiod and Callimachus remain unknown, but it seems that like the *oaristus*, the *oaros* connotes both the joys and allurements of youth and the conflict-ridden process of confrontation as this youth comes to occupy its place in the world.

A confrontation between a young future king and an older king who is negatively viewed is itself likely to be a traditional theme, since Jason's confrontation with Pelias resembles on several counts the process that brings Theseus to the throne at Athens, as represented in Bacchylides 17. In both cases, there is a confrontation, an extreme and unfair trial successfully

[12] Pindar *Pythian* 1.98, 4.137, *Nemean* 3.11; in the fourth instance the *oaros* is in the poet's voice, *Nemean* 7.69.

undergone by the young man, and his eventual success in becoming a king. In Bacchylides 17, Theseus is on his journey to Crete with the boys and girls chosen for the Minotaur. While at sea he finds fault with Minos (who touches one of the girls) and challenges the older man. Like Jason, Theseus bases his claim on his regal pedigree, which is matched to that of Minos: the Cretan king is a son of Zeus, but Theseus is not inferior, since his father is Poseidon (Bacchylides 17.29–38). No words derived from the root *oar-* appear in Bacchylides' poem, but it is worth noting that it captures the same two aspects of coming of age that attach to such words, namely the erotic and the agonistic. Minos is aroused by the 'gifts of Aphrodite' (10) when he touches one of the Athenian maidens (11–12). The quarrel is prompted by this threatening touch and thus takes place in a sexually charged atmosphere, and yet it develops into a dispute over Theseus' worth and powers and results in a test and triumph of the younger man. The poem develops themes typically associated with youth, as indicated also by its transmitted title: Ἤίθεοι ἢ Θησεύς, 'The lads, or Theseus'.

It seems that terms derived from the *oar-* root designate genres of speech and song which are associated with the entry of a new generation into adult life. The themes of cyclical renewal and of a new generation's entry into maturity go hand in hand, just as in the *Odyssey* the return of Odysseus and renewal of life on Ithaca is accompanied by Telemachus' coming of age, while Odysseus himself takes on characteristics typical of a maturing adolescent. The same combination of themes may be implied in Minos' periodic conversations with Zeus. Part of this thematic nexus is signaled by the unusual word *oaristes* applied to Minos.

When in *Iliad* 22 Hektor imagines a boy and a girl having an *oaristus/ oaros*, the apparent subject is an old and formulaic one, 'the tree and the rock' (ἀπὸ δρυὸς οὐδ' ἀπὸ πέτρης, 22.126). The same formula surfaces in the *Odyssey*, and in the very conversation where Minos appears as *oaristes* of Zeus. When Penelope invites her guest to reveal his identity she says that he surely does not come 'from a tree or a rock':

οὐ γὰρ ἀπὸ δρυός ἐσσι παλαιφάτου οὐδ' ἀπὸ πέτρης.

(*Odyssey* 19.163)

For you are not from an old-renowned tree, nor from a rock.

In contrast to such primordial origins, perhaps the origins of the humankind itself, her guest must have a family and place of birth. But in response Odysseus claims for himself a genealogy which is impressively primordial.

Not only is he descended from Zeus in the third generation, but his grandfather is named Deukalion, a name that is connected to the very beginnings of the humankind. Nothing is known about this Deukalion, father of Minos, and there is no reason to think that he is the same as the hero of the flood myth, but the name, occurring as it does in close proximity to the tree and the rock, brings to mind the myth of the primordial couple, Deukalion and Pyrrha, who created people out of rocks by throwing these rocks behind them.[13]

It is in any case interesting that twice in Homer the undoubtedly old formula "the tree and the rock" co-occurs with the *oar*-words, *oaristes* and *oaristus*.[14] Jeanmaire speculated that the "tree and rock" conversation held by boys and girls and recalled by Hektor in Book 22 probably refers to "quelque mythe naif expliquant, par un couple primitif, l'origine de l'humanité."[15] Naive or not, the conversation about the tree and the rock may well have to do with the origins of the humankind, since both a renewal of order and an entry of a new generation into this order are a fitting occasion for a talk about such origins.[16] As a new cycle begins, the ultimate beginnings are revisited. If this is the case, then there may be an old mutual attraction between the tree and rock formula and the *oar*-words, an attraction that may explain their repeated proximity. This is not something that is made overt in the *Odyssey*. The tree and rock formula is spoken by Penelope, the *oaristes* is mentioned by Odysseus, and there is no immediate tangible link between these two elements as there is in Hektor's speech in the *Iliad*. Still, these are elements that belong together in a certain context and their occurrence can remind the audiences of such a context, thus setting the mood for the scene. On the surface of the narrative, skeptical Penelope is questioning a wandering beggar about his family, but just below the surface other themes begin to develop, triggered by key words: coming of age, renewal, the coming of the new king, and approaching marriage.

It is also worth noting that Crete has cropped up repeatedly in our discussion, both in contexts where *oar*-words are used and otherwise in connection with the relevant themes. The dance on the shield of Achilles is compared to

---

[13] Akousilaos 2F35, Pindar *Olympian* 9.42–46, Apollodorus 1.7.2.

[14] Apart from the two Homeric instances, a variation of the tree and the rock formula occurs in Hesiod *Theogony* 35 (see West 1966:268 ad loc. for a detailed discussion). On the formula, its Iranian cognate, and Indo-European origin see Watkins 1995:161–164.

[15] Jeanmaire 1939/1975:333.

[16] Eustathius (4.589, on *Iliad* 23.126–128) and the *Odyssey* Scholia (on 19.163) speculate that the phrase has to do either with the practice of exposing children, who were then said to be born from trees and rocks, or with the origins of humankind.

a Cretan dance performed on a dancing floor of Minos' daughter Ariadne. The *geranos* is performed on Delos but forms part of the story of Theseus' journey to Crete, his confrontation with Minos, and his love story with Ariadne. I have already mentioned above the possibility suggested by Calame that there were non-Athenian versions of the myth in which the *geranos* was actually performed on Crete. The Cretan journey and the same themes are also part of Bacchylides 17, where, as we have seen, Minos' descent from Zeus also comes into play. As in the *Odyssey*, this seems to be the ultimate qualification of a king. It seems that Crete and the family of Minos have a special connection with a nexus of various themes, premarital, erotic, and agonistic, all having to do with the rise of a new generation. If the preceding analysis has some validity, then in the Third Cretan Lie the word *oaristes* points to this nexus of themes. The bare mention of Minos may bring to mind the notions of king-ship and Zeus' protection, but Minos specifically as *oaristes* of the god triggers an additional set of associations. If the *oar*-words do indeed carry agonistic and youth-related connotations, then in what sense can Minos be *oaristes* of Zeus? It seems that he can be so described if those interactions, at nine year intervals, between the god and the king are imagined in some sense as Minos' re-becoming king, or perhaps even re-coming of age. The social renewal and reaffirmation that seems to be achieved goes hand and hand with the renewal and reaffirmation of the king himself. This Minos should be very much at home in the *Odyssey* precisely at the moment when his name appears – at the moment when the household of Odysseus, and Odysseus himself, are about to undergo just such a renewal.

CHAPTER SIX
CRETE AND THE POETICS OF RENEWAL

T HE SEMANTICS of *oaristes* are not the only hint at the notion of new beginnings that is present in the Third Cretan Lie. The theme of (re)birth, so prominent in the *Odyssey*, is brought to mind by the presence of Eileithyia in Odysseus' tale. After Idomeneus leaves for Troy, Aithon meets Odysseus in Crete when the latter is blown off course and lands near Amnisos, where there is a cave of Eileithyia:

> καὶ γὰρ τὸν Κρήτηνδε κατήγαγεν ἲς ἀνέμοιο
> ἱέμενον Τροίηνδε, παραπλάγξασα Μαλειῶν·
> στῆσε δ' ἐν Ἀμνισῷ, ὅθι τε σπέος Εἰλειθυίης,
> ἐν λιμέσιν χαλεποῖσι, μόγις δ' ὑπάλυξεν ἀέλλας.

> (*Odyssey* 19.186–189)

> And the force of winds brought him [Odysseus] to Crete,
> though he wished to go to Troy, and drove him off course
>   past Malea.
> He put in at Amnisos, where there is a cave of Eileithyia,
> in a difficult harbor, and he barely escaped the stormwinds.

This cave of Eileithyia is a known landmark and a site of continuous cultic activity (though not necessarily all associated with Eileithyia) from the Neolithic period onwards.[1] An offering of honey for Eileithyia (E-re-u-ti-ja)

---

[1] The cave was excavated by Marinatos (1929:94, 1930:91, cf. *BCH* 53.520n5, *Arch. Anz.* 1930.156), following a preliminary investigation and identification by Hatzidakis in 1885. On the cave and the cult see Faure 1964:82–90, Nilsson 1950:58, Rutkowski 1986:129–130, 138, 317, Hiller 1982:33–63, Burkert 1985:25–26. For a general overview of the cave, the finds, and the state of scholarship see Rutkowski and Nowicki 1996:21–24. It is unknown who was worshipped in the cave in the earlier periods, and indeed the finds consist entirely of pottery fragments that do not indicate any cultic activity clearly. In front of the cave there is a terrace with large stone blocks that might have served as altars (Rutkowski 1986:55). Most scholars who have studied the cave believe that it did have a cultic function. The cult of Eileithyia is likely to have begun

at Amnisos is recorded in a Knossos tablet.[2] Strabo (10.476) reports that there was also a temple of Eileithyia at Amnisos, and that the town was a port of Knossos during the times of Minos.[3] Pausanias mentions a Cretan tradition that Eileithyia, the goddess of childbirth, was herself born from Hera at Amnisos. He also says that it is from Crete and from Delos that Eileithyia came to Athens: there were three wooden figures of the goddess in Athens, two of them supposed to be Cretan (Phaedra's offerings), while the third and the oldest figure was said to have come from Delos (1.18.5).

The cave of Eileithyia at Amnisos is doubtless one of the nursery caves of Greece, caves associated with birth. Crete boasts some famous examples of such caves, including the cave where Zeus was supposed to be born,[4] and the cave of Eileithyia might have its own connection to Zeus. A nearby seashore sanctuary has been identified as belonging to Zeus Thenatas, so named after Thenai, where the newborn god is said to have lost his umbilical cord as he was being transported from Dikte to the Idaian cave.[5] Callimachus offers the

---

in the Mycenaean period and continued into the Geometric period; it then seems to decline and revives again in Hellenistic times. There are stalagmites in the cave that resemble a navel and female figures, and this opens the possibility that even if Eileithyia is a relative late-comer she continues the cult of a similar goddess (Chaniotis 1992:84). The Cretan form Eleuthuia can be understood as Greek, meaning 'she who comes'. This, if true, may indicate a relatively late flourishing of the cult in the Amnisos cave (Burkert 1985:26). On the etymology, see Dickinson 1994:285, Parker 1988:101–2. See also Chadwick-Baumbach 1963:188. Another possibility is that the word is pre-Greek (cf. the Cretan toponym Ἐλεύθερνα) and was assimilated to ἐλεύσομαι by popular etymology. See Wackernagel as cited by Nilsson 1955:1.313, Chantraine 1968 s.v. and Frisk s.v. In either case, an association between the verb and the goddess was felt by the native speakers, since Hesychius has a gloss ἐλεύθω· ἔρχομαι. Εἰλείθυια.

[2] (KN Gg 705 = Doc. no.206, Gérard-Rousseau 1968:101). On possible connections between Eleusis and Eileithyia, see Heubeck 1972.

[3] Eileithyia's association with Amnisos may also be evidenced by a title Ἀμνισία, glossed by Hesychius s.v. as ἡ Εἰλείθυια.

[4] In Hesiod's *Theogony* (477–480) Zeus is born on Crete, in a cave. There are several possible interpretations of the passage. Some assume that since Rhea first comes to Lyktos, the cave must also be somewhere in that area, the Psychro cave being the most popular candidate (see West 1966:297, on 477). It is also possible, however, that the cave in question is in fact the Idaean one, the place of Zeus' birth and/or upbringing in the majority of sources (e.g., Callimachus, *Hymn* 6.46–47, Apollonius Rhodius 2.1236–1237, 3.1134, Scholia on Apollonius Rhodius 3.134, Aratos, *Phaenomena* 32–36, Diodorus Siculus 5.70, Antoninus Liberalis 19). Apollodorus (1.1.6–7) says that Zeus was born in the 'cave of Dikte'. For an argument in favor of the presence of an infant figure in Eileithyia's cave at Amnisos and the possibility that it may be Zeus, see Faure 1964:87. For a general discussion of all the caves in question, see Faure 1964:81–131.

[5] Sporn 2002:133–134. It has been previously suggested that the sanctuary belonged to Artemis or Eileithyia herself, but an inscription found at the site (Sporn 2002:133 n901, SEG XXXIII 717–718, Chaniotis 1988:157) names Zeus Thenatas. The story of Zeus' umbilical cord is in Callimachus *Hymn* 1.42–44, Diodorus Siculus 5.70.4, Stephanus Byzantius s.v. Θεναί.

story as an aetiology explaining why the Kydonians call the plain of Thenai Ὀμφάλιον πέδον, 'Navel plain'.[6]

Another cave sacred to Eileithyia is attested at Olympia, where the cult was centered on the birth of a child and was administered by two priestesses, with males being banned from the site.[7] It is not clear who the child was in this case, but Pindar mentions a 'holy Idaian cave' at Olympia and this is in all likelihood the same as the cave of Eiliethyia, since it is mentioned in an invocation of Zeus as Soter, dwelling on the hill of Kronos. This is precisely where Pausanias locates the cave of Eileithyia, which was also sacred to Zeus Sosipolis.[8] It seems that the cave of Eileithyia at Olympia could be seen as analogous to the Idaian cave on Crete, even if it was not ultimately successful in establishing itself as an acknowledged place of Zeus' birth. What the Olympian cave does demonstrate is the close relationship between Eileithyia's cave and Zeus' birth-cave.

Within the *Odyssey*, the cave of Eileithyia is also reminiscent of the Ithacan cave of the Naiads, next to which Odysseus is left by the Phaeacians on his return. The Ithacan cave is located in a bay which serves as a harbor, has a source of water nearby, and is inhabited by nymphs (*Odyssey* 13.96–109). Similarly, Amnisos, both the site of Odysseus' landing and the reputed port of Minos, derives its name from a local river that was home to nymphs known as Amensiades or Amnesides.[9] The presence of a spring or river near a cave is significant, since life-giving (or even impregnating) water is often present in the sacred places of Eileithyia, such as at another Cretan cave of Inatos, and on Paros, and at Corinth.[10] Nonnus is probably not inventing anything new when he speaks of Ἀμνισοῖο λεχώιον ὕδωρ, 'the childbed water of Amnisos' (8.115), and παιδοκόμου δὲ πάτριον Ἀμνισοῖο ῥόον Κρηταῖον, 'ancestral Cretan steam of child-tending Amnisos' (13.250–251). Chaniotis speculates that the presence of several kourotrophic deities (Eileithyia, Artemis, the Nymphs) near the river Amnisos suggests that it played a role in weddings or initiations of the

---

[6] Callimachus *Hymn* 1.43–44. Kaczynska (2000) suggests that the plain is the small valley of the stream Ryakas, a tributary of Karteros, ancient Amnisos.

[7] Pausanias 6.20.2–4, 6.25.4. See Hampe 1951 on the function of the cave.

[8] Pindar, *Olympian* 5.17–18.

[9] Stephanus Byzantius s.v. Ἀμνισός.

[10] Stephanus Byzantius s.v. Εἴνατος· . . . τινὲς δὲ ὄρος καὶ ποταμός, ἐν ᾧ τιμᾶσθαι τὴν Εἰλείθυιαν Εἰνατίην. On Inatos see Faure 1964:90–94. On Paros the spring of Eileithyia was supposed to cause pregnancy: IG XII 5.185–208, and another such spring was located in the cave of Aphrodite Kolias on Hymettos (Faure 1964:85n5). For more on fertilizing powers of rivers and of Amnisos in particular, see Chaniotis 1992:87.

youth of Knossos, and points to other bathing places of young women, many of which seem to be connected with birth and fertility.[11]

It is tempting to imagine that the cave of the nymphs on Ithaca may have evoked similar associations. Apart from the presence of water and nymphs there is another detail that makes this cave similar to the birth caves, namely the fact that it is inhabited by bees (ἔνθα δ' ἔπειτα τιθαιβώσσουσι μέλισσαι, 'and there the bees deposit their honey[?]' 13.106).[12] In a myth cited above and reported by Antoninus Liberalis, Zeus is born on Crete in a sacred 'cave of the bees' and nurtured by their honey.[13] Similarly, Iamos, abandoned by his mother, is fed by bees in Pindar (*Olympian* 6.47), where Eileithyia is mentioned a few lines earlier (42) as assisting at his birth. It may or may not be an accident that Iamos then becomes a prophet at Olympia, coming to the 'hill of Kronos', where Eileithyia's cave was located (64–70). And again it may or may not be a coincidence that the offering recorded by the name of Eileithyia at Amnisos on a Knossos tablet is precisely that of honey, but it does seem that a set of ideas that belong to both poetry and cult binds together the Cretan cave of Eileithyia and the Ithacan cave of the nymphs.[14]

The reference to Eileithyia may be especially resonant in the context of the approaching festival of Apollo on Ithaca. The *Odyssey* leaves the nature of the festival vague, although its seasonal rhythm does suggest a return or birthday of the god, since that was imagined to take place in the spring. But however one imagines the festival, the fact remains that Eileithyia has strong ties with Apollo's mother Leto and with the god's birth. In the *Homeric Hymn to Apollo*, Leto gives birth as soon as Eileithyia steps on Delos:

εὖτ' ἐπὶ Δήλου ἔβαινε μογοστόκος Εἰλείθυια,
τὴν τότε δὴ τόκος εἷλε, μενοίνησεν δὲ τεκέσθαι.

---

[11] Chaniotis 1992:87.

[12] The meaning of the verb τιθαιβώσσουσι is unclear. Hesychius offers several glosses, including (s.v. τιθαιβώσσουσι) ἐναποτίθενται, ἀποθησαυρίζουσι τὴν τροφὴν αἱ μέλιτται, τὸν λεγόμενον μελίκηρον and τιθέασι. φυλάσσουσι; s.v.τιθαιβώσσειν: βόσκειν. ἐργάζεσθαι. τρέφειν, ἐθήβειν. θησαυρίζειν. ἀγαπᾶν. θορυβεῖν. τιθέναι τὴν βόσιν, τουτέστι τὴν τροφήν.

[13] With various permutations, bees are present in the myth of Zeus' nurture. Sometimes the god is brought up by nymphs, variously named Melissa ('bee') and Amalthea (Didymus via Lactantius, *Divinae Institutiones* 1.22), Amalthea and Kynosoura (Scholia on Euripides *Rhesus* 342), Adrasteia and Ida (Apollodorus 1.1.6), but invariably the daughters of Melisseus ('the bee one'). In Vergil *Georgics* 4.149–152, Iuppiter is fed by bees rather than nymphs. For fuller references, see Faure 1964:110–111.

[14] On the offerings of honey and other continuities between the Mycenaean testimonia and classical evidence for the cult of Eileithyia see Nagy 1969:128–129, where Nagy concludes that the classical/Mycenaean correlation in this case indicates "that the Homeric corpus here accurately transmitted the recollection of a Mycenaean cult-site in Crete."

ἀμφὶ δὲ φοίνικι βάλε πήχεε, γοῦνα δ' ἔρεισε
λειμῶνι μαλακῷ, μείδησε δὲ γαῖ' ὑπένερθεν·
ἐκ δ' ἔθορε πρὸ φόως δέ, θεαὶ δ' ὀλόλυξαν ἅπασαι.

(Homeric Hymn to Apollo 115–119)

And when the birth-pang bringing Eileithyia stepped
    onto Delos,
then labor seized her [Leto], and she desired to give birth.
She threw her arms around a palm tree, and planted
    her knees
on the soft meadow and the earth beneath her smiled,
and [the child] sprung forth into the light, and all the
    goddesses cried out.

Leto holds on to a palm tree, and a palm tree next to the altar of Apollo on Delos also appears in the *Odyssey*, where Odysseus compares Nausikaa to this young and slender tree:

οὐ γάρ πω τοιοῦτον ἴδον βροτὸν ὀφθαλμοῖσιν,
οὔτ' ἄνδρ' οὔτε γυναῖκα· σέβας μ' ἔχει εἰσορόωντα.
Δήλῳ δή ποτε τοῖον Ἀπόλλωνος παρὰ βωμῷ
φοίνικος νέον ἔρνος ἀνερχόμενον ἐνόησα.

(Odyssey 6.160–163)

For I have never seen such a mortal with my eyes,
neither a man nor a woman, and wonder takes hold of me
    as I look on.
Once on Delos I saw a young palm sapling like this shooting
    up by the altar of Apollo.

It has been observed that the poem's botany is imprecise here, as young palms are not slender but squat, and that this could not be the same palm that Leto used for support, since it would have aged and grown by the time of Odysseus' visit.[15] There is no reason, however, to adopt such a positivistic way of looking at the myth. The fact is that the mythology of Delos demands that it have a palm, and a Delian palm, young or old, can always be the tree under which Apollo was born. Like the indestructible olive tree at the Erechtheum, the Delian palm was still there and apparently a tourist attraction when Cicero visited the island (*De legibus* 1.1). Although Apollo never appears in the *Odyssey*

---

[15] Hainsworth 1988:305 (ad loc.).

in person, his presence is felt with Odysseus' return. It is following Apollo's calendar and with Apollo's weapon that Odysseus regains his home, and it can hardly be an accident that a radiant vision of Delos marks the beginning of this process on Skheria. It seems that the *Odyssey* is tapping into old religious and mythic associations that link Delos and its palm and altar of Apollo with return and renewal. Theseus' return from Crete, which I have had occasion to mention above, is also punctuated by a visit to Delos and a dance around the altar, and it too has to do with the end of a dark period and a new beginning, coinciding with the rise of a new generation. Moreover, similar imagery is associated with female coming of age. Sourvinou-Inwood has argued that in Attic iconography, especially of the fifth century, "altar and palm tree" is an established sign that points to "this important iconographical and semantic category: altar/ sanctuary/realm of Artemis in her persona as overseer of unmarried girls and of their preparation for marriage and transition to womanhood through marriage."[16] Altars and palms appear on vases in scenes of erotic pursuit and abduction which Sourvinou-Inwood interprets as pertaining to Artemis in her role as the protector of *parthenoi* as they transition into marriage and womanhood, a variation on a prenuptial theme "girls abducted from sanctuaries or choruses of Artemis."[17] Moreover, such scenes appear on vases otherwise associated with female maturation and marriage, such as *krateriskoi* from Artemis' sanctuaries at Brauron and Mounikhia and *alabastra*, which were used for storing perfumes and therefore associated with the world of women.

The themes of female coming of age apply directly to Nausikaa, who is for the first time thinking of marriage, whose meeting with Odysseus is a potential match, and who is famously compared to Artemis dancing with her companions.[18] Odysseus' reference to Delos is obviously deeply resonant in this context, but I suggest that it is resonant not for Nausikaa alone. The altar with the palm is polysemic and belongs both to Apollo and to Artemis, a connection verbalized by Callimachus, in whose *Hymn to Apollo* the god builds the altar out of the horns of the animals hunted by his sister (60–63). The Nausikaa episode is first and foremost prenuptial, but her forthcoming marriage and the renewal of life for Odysseus are closely joined. Odysseus does not become Nausikaa's bridegroom, but he is deemed suited for the role, and in that sense the meaning of the Delian palm applies to him as well.

---

[16] Sourvinou-Inwood 1991:99.

[17] Sourvinou-Inwood 1991:102–104.

[18] Sourvinou-Inwood (1991:127n33) mentions the Nausikaa episode as exhibiting the same associations (a girls about to be married, palm-tree, Artemis), and credits M. Lefkowitz with pointing this out.

Further, Odysseus' arrival on Skheria is assisted by Ino-Leukothea, who is associated with transition through death and has a kourotrophic function. It has even been suggested that Odysseus' landing is described in terms of physical birth.[19] Regardless of the validity of such interpretations the idea of rebirth is implicit, for example, in the simile at the end of Book 5, where Odysseus, concealed under a pile of leaves, is compared to a 'seed of fire' hidden under black soot.[20] Moreover, although Odysseus does not marry Nausikaa, he does attribute to her his revival: σὺ γάρ μ' ἐβιώσαο, κούρη, 'For you brought me back to life, maiden' (8.468). The reference to the Delian palm in Book 6 is therefore not only a compliment to Nausikaa, but an evocation of a whole cluster of ritual, mythic, and poetic associations that are relevant not only to the immediate context of their meeting on the seashore, but are also part of a much larger thematic scheme in the poem. It has long been observed that multiple thematic and dictional parallels link Nausikaa and Penelope together as well as the scenes that each woman shares with Odysseus.[21] Penelope has multiple roles, one of them being that of a nubile woman on the verge of marriage, just like Nausikaa. As Penelope enters this role, Artemis comes to the forefront in her life, and Penelope is both compared to Artemis (17.37 = 19.54) and prays to her (20.60–61). And just as on Skheria the mention of Artemis is linked to the mention of Apollo and his altar on Delos, so on Ithaca Penelope's prayer to Artemis coincides with the festival of Apollo. Eileithyia at Amnisos, for her part, might have shared her cultic space with Artemis.[22] The literary evidence is late, but there is no telling how far back it may go: Callimachus mentions

---

[19] Holtsmark 1966:206–210, Newton 1984:12–13. Newton further argues that Odysseus is presented as *deuteropotmos* and that his behavior when he first enters the palace of Alkinoos, including his apparently sudden appearance at Arete's feet, bears traces of a "rebirth ritual" (5–9).

[20] Russo 1993. On symbolism of rebirth in the Phaeacian episode in general see Segal 1962:20–25 and 1994:37–65.

[21] Lowenstam (1993:117) summarizes and expands on the parallels observed by Austin (1975:200–217) and Van Nortwick (1979): "Each woman speaks to the stranger alone, each rebukes a maid or attendants, each is immediately flattered by Odysseus, each offers a bath to the stranger, who refuses to be washed by a young maid, each recites a conventional homily about life, and each asserts that she is being importuned by her suitors to choose a husband." As Lowenstam points out (1993:117), the same formula is employed when Odysseus appears as a marriage prospect to Nausikaa and a husband to Penelope (6.229–235 = 23.156–162). Ingalls (2000) finds multiple initiatory elements in the Nausikaa episode and argues that the theme of initiation is also paralleled in the description of Penelope, who goes through several initiation-like steps in her preparation for remarriage with Odysseus.

[22] Archaeological evidence for Artemis at Amnisos is inconclusive. The nearby shore sanctuary, which had been thought to belong to Artemis, is now identified by an inscription as that of Zeus Thenatas: see note p95n5 above.

Artemis and Amnisos in one breath in *Iamb* 12, and the local nymphs, the Amnisides, appear as the goddess' companions in *Hymn* 3.[23] Artemis' presence at Amnisos would not be surprising, as she is both *lokhia*, a goddess of childbirth like Eileithyia herself, and, in Callimachus' *Hymn*, protector of harbors (λεμένεσσιν ἐπίσκοπος, 39 and λιμενοσκόπος, 259).[24] In Apollonius Rhodius (3.876–877) Artemis bathes in the waters of the Amnisos, waters that may bring fertility or be used for pre-wedding baths.[25] The nature of the goddess' ablutions here can be deduced from the name of another spring linked with her, Parthenios (3.876). The reference is made all the more telling by the fact that here Medea is being compared to Artemis as she drives out, surrounded by her companions, to a secret meeting with Jason, a scene that exhibits many parallels to the Nausikaa episode in *Odyssey* 6.[26]

Moreover, Eileithyia and Artemis are closely linked elsewhere: in Sparta, Eileithyia was worshipped in the *temenos* of Artemis Orthia and at Phaleron Artemis Lokhia and Eileithyia had a joint sanctuary.[27] It is no doubt their function as *kourotrophoi* that brings together Artemis, Eileithyia, and the local nymphs. Just as the reference to Delos in Book 6 is full of cultic echoes, so the reference to Eileithyia in Book 19 is no mere geographical detail, but carries with it a network of associations and resonates with its setting. Odysseus' actual return to Ithaca begins at the cave of the Nymphs, local divinities who, in their kourotrophic function, have the potential to watch over Odysseus' rebirth, coming of age, and remarriage. In his dialogue with Penelope Odysseus does not mention this cave, but he mentions another one that sends the same message even more clearly: the cave of Eileithyia on Crete, which supposedly gives Odysseus shelter from storm and thus ensures new life. In the context of the festival of Apollo, and with Penelope's marriage approaching, these details are especially poignant. Odysseus' household may seem to be in a desperate position, but Odysseus in disguise is already sounding the theme of rebirth.

Going a step further, one may ask whether Cretan lies as such, that is, the fact that they are Cretan, trigger a particular set of expectations. In other

---

[23] Callimachus *Iambus* 12 fr. 202.1 Pfeiffer, *Hymn* 3.15–17, 162–167.

[24] On the merging of Artemis and Eileithyia see Burkert 1985:151 and n26. Artemis is identified with Eileithyia, for example, in CIG 1596 (Chaeroneia, fourth century BCE) and a number of other inscriptions (see Farnell 1896.568) and is titled *lokhia* in CIG 3562, 1768 (λοχεία), Euripides *The Suppliants* 958, Plutarch *Quaestiones Convivales* 659a. She is also λυσίζωνος (Hesychius s.v., Scholia on Apollonius Rhodius 1.288) and σοωδίνα (CIG 1595). For women invoking Artemis in childbirth, see e.g. Euripides *Hippolytus* 165–169.

[25] See above, note p95n10.

[26] Apollonius Rhodius 3.828–1008.

[27] Chaniotis 1992:85 and n249 with references, SEG XXVIII 409, Pausanias 3.17.1, LSCG Suppl.17.

words, is the stranger's claim that he is Cretan itself a sign both to Penelope and the external audience of the lie? It is worth observing that parallel thematics of rebirth are present in another poem that features a Cretan lie, the *Homeric Hymn to Demeter*. Like Odysseus, Demeter appears in disguise and tells a tale in which she comes from Crete. The questions is: why Crete? Sometimes Crete is taken here to be simply an indication that Demeter is lying, since Cretan tales are also lies in the *Odyssey*.[28] Such an indirect way of hinting at the falsehood seems misplaced, however, since in each poem it is obvious in any case that the stories are not true. There is little doubt that Cretan tales go with disguise, and that a common tradition of "lies like the truth" unites the *Odyssey* and the *Hymn*, but this should not mean that references to Crete have no further significance.[29] Another explanation for Demeter's choice of Crete rests on historical grounds, namely that the mysteries or the cult of Demeter came to Eleusis from Crete and that the lie reflects this development.[30] But even if it could be shown that Demeter arrived from Crete, this would not explain the Cretan lie in the *Hymn*, since it would still be unclear why the *Hymn* should be interested in the Cretan connection. It seems more likely that there are poetic and mythological reasons for evoking Crete, independent of the goddess' actual origins. These poetic reasons are likely to be similar in the *Hymn* and in the *Odyssey*.

Like Odysseus, Demeter gives herself a name that points to her true nature and presages her epiphany: when the daughters of Keleus meet her by the well, she introduces herself as Δωσώ, the 'Giver' (*Homeric Hymn to Demeter* 122).[31] Moreover, just as with Odysseus' lies, Demeter's tale contains hints at her actual situation and concerns. For example, she says that she was forcibly abducted, just as Persephone is, and she rejects food, just as she rejects it in the macro-narrative of the *Hymn*.[32] It is as a Cretan woman that Demeter is then welcomed at Eleusis, and thus begins her return. Return and renewal

---

[28] Richardson 1974:188.

[29] The common tradition is noted by Foley 1994:42.

[30] Richardson 1974:188 with references, Adrados 1972:184. On possible Minoan origins of cult at Eleusis see, e.g. Nilsson 1950:558–572. Suter (2002:147) suggests that Demeter's Cretan lie is a remnant of a myth that described the arrival of Demeter, or of her worship, from Crete to Eleusis and Attica (whether such a myth corresponds to historical reality or not). She further compares Demeter's tale to the myths of Damis and Auxesia on Aegina, Hera on Samos, and Kore at Helios in Laconia, and inclines to the opinion that Demeter once was "the same kind of goddess from Crete" (221).

[31] See Richardson 1974:188 (ad loc.) on this emendation for the transmitted Δώς.

[32] Foley 1994:42. Foley also notes that Demeter herself is a victim of rape by Poseidon in one myth, and that in her lie she emphasizes the maternal links among females when she says that her name was given by her mother.

are, of course, central themes of the *Hymn* and they find their expression in the vision at the end of the poem of the previously barren plain of Rarion turning into fertile earth and sprouting vegetation.[33] Moreover, apart from natural transformation there are human institutions established by Demeter, and these include not only the Eleusinian mysteries, but the mock battle of the Eleusinian youths in honor of Demophoon:

> ὥρῃσιν δ' ἄρα τῷ γε περιπλομένων ἐνιαυτῶν
> παῖδες Ἐλευσινίων πόλεμον καὶ φύλοπιν αἰνὴν
> αἰὲν ἐν ἀλλήλοισι συνάξουσ' ἤματα πάντα.

> (*Homeric Hymn to Demeter* 265–267)

> But for him, in due seasons of revolving years,
> the sons of the Eleusinians will always join war
> and dreadful battle with one another, forever.

The mock battles in question are probably what is known from other sources as *balletus*, a ritual battle that involved stone throwing and was part of the Eleusinian games.[34] Since it is established to compensate for the fate of baby Demophoon, who fails to grow up, the battle probably has to do with the growing of a new generation, especially since the combatants are παῖδες, 'youths'.[35] There are other examples of mock battles as the activity of the rising generation, the most famous perhaps being the battles of Spartan youths at Platanistas.[36]

Both natural and human renewal are present, then, in the *Hymn*, even if these themes are submerged in a sea of others, the *Hymn* being a very complex poem that fuses multiple myths. Demeter's Cretan lie may not be overtly linked to the themes of renewal in its content, but it is linked to them in the framework of *Hymn* as a whole: it is her first self-introduction to mortals and a

---

[33] *Homeric Hymn to Demeter* 471–473.

[34] Richardson 1974:208–209, Càssola 1975 ad loc.

[35] Demophoon does not die in the *Hymn*, but is described as if he were near death (253, 289). In other versions he is burned in Demeter's fire (Apollodoros 1.5.1, Orphic fr. 49 Kern. Games were often founded to compensate for the death of child-heroes (e.g. Melikertes at the Isthmia, Opheltes at the Nemea), and Demophoon also may be presumed to die young. On Demophoon in the *Hymn*, see Felson-Rubin and Deal 1994, Foley 1994.44–45, 48–50, 52–53. For a detailed discussion of the *balletus*, see Richardson 1974.246–248 (on lines 265–267) and Càssola 1975; on ritual battles of young men see, e.g., Jeanmaire 1939:396–397.

[36] Pausanias 3.14.8–10, 11.2. For these battles as an initiatory rite see Burkert 1985:263. Among other examples are contests for Androgeos or Eurygues, son of Minos, killed by the Athenians (Hesychius s.v. ἐπ' Εὐρυγύῃ ἀγών, Hesiod fr. 146 West). For more on Androgeos see Calame 1996:79–81.

first step towards her return. When Demeter says that she comes from Crete, she gives the audience of the *Hymn* a sign not just that she is telling a lie, but that this tale is a beginning of her self-revelation, that it should be scrutinized for signs, that an epiphany is coming, and that this epiphany will be associated with the ultimate return of the goddess and renewal of her functions. The Third Cretan Lie in the *Odyssey* plays a similar role: it is a crucial step in Odysseus' heroic "epiphany," and it hints at the rebirth, both natural and cultural, that is associated with his return.

These are hypothetical suggestions, but if ever a place were to connote return, rebirth, and epiphany, Crete is an excellent candidate for that role, since there is hardly a place in ancient Greek culture where the principle of rebirth and renewal, both natural and social, is more strongly expressed. The cult of Eileithyia is prominent in Crete not only at Amnisos but also, for example, at Lato.[37] The union of Demeter and Iasion, mentioned both in the *Odyssey* and in the *Theogony*, is also localized on Crete and takes place in a thrice-ploughed field (νειῷ ἔνι τριπόλῳ), thus doubtless having to do with fertility (*Odyssey* 5.125–127, *Theogony* 969–971) and seasonal renewal of nature. It is also on Crete that Bacchylides localizes the abduction of Kore (fr. 47 SM), an event firmly connected with the same periodic renewal.

It seems that myths and rites of coming of age also had a special importance on Crete. The famous *erastes-eromenos* pairs are described by Ephorus, as we have seen in the previous section: an older man "abducts" a younger one, (the abduction was arranged with the relatives of the boy and was accompanied by a mock pursuit), takes him to the country to hunt and to feast, and at the end makes presents symbolizing a boy's entry into manhood: a warrior's robe, an ox, and a wine cup. Being chosen for such an abduction distinguishes the boy among his peers, so that afterwards he is called *kleinos* and allowed to wear special clothes.[38] Cretan myths of coming of age seem to cling especially to the family of Minos. For example, a myth about Minos' son Glaukos, who dies while playing and is then revived by a seer, has been analyzed as reflecting the stages and processes of a boy's maturation.[39] As has been mentioned above, Minos and Crete play a crucial role in Athenian myth, providing the stage for Theseus' attempt to prove himself as a hero, save the Athenian youths, and become the king of Athens. Further, Crete is home to the Kouretes, a mythic group of young warriors who protect the divine child

---

[37] Willetts 1962:169.

[38] Ephorus FGrH 70 F 149 = Strabo 10.4.21.

[39] See Muellner 1998. The myth involves several familiar elements, such as bees and honey, and the cave.

after his birth and perform war dances.[40] An epigraphic example illustrating the connection between natural renewal, the new generation of citizens, and Cretan Zeus survives in the *Palaikastro Hymn to the Greatest Kouros*, which must have been performed by young males, probably at a festival celebrating the epiphany of Zeus Kretaigenes (the hymn was discovered in the sanctuary of Zeus Diktaios at Palaikastro).[41] In the hymn, the devotees ask the god to 'leap into' flocks and fields, ships, cities and customary law (Themis).[42] Significantly, the 'greatest *kouros*' is also invoked to leap into the new (and young) citizens: ν[έος πο]λείτας, 34. Here, as in the *Odyssey*, the renewal of nature and society goes hand and hand with the maturation of a new generation. Nilsson speculated that the hymn was probably sung at a spring festival that celebrated the "graduation" of youths from the *agela*, which, according to Willetts, "coincided with a time of general birth and rebirth, a time to celebrate the city's birthday and the continuity of life and its functions."[43] A more recent analysis of the hymn focuses on its Hellenistic historical context (the inscription is dated to the second or third century CE and will have been a replacement of an earlier original, perhaps of the fourth or third century BCE).[44] But whatever its political and territorial aims, the hymn still taps into very old themes, and still assimilates the real youth, who are pictured performing it (strophe 1) to the mythic Kouretes.[45] If indeed the seasonal setting for the hymn was spring, then that too is paralleled in the *Odyssey*, where spring begins to be mentioned and the weather seems to turn just as Odysseus arrives in his house.[46]

In 1962, Willetts wrote confidently that "the mention of the cave of Eileithyia at Amnisos, in the *Odyssey*, indicates that the Homeric tradition derives from the Minoan Age."[47] Since then, the security of such conclusions has eroded. It has become clear that archaeological continuity at a cult place can coexist with massive changes in culture and ideology, and that projection from the historical period of Crete back to the Minoan era is a treacherous undertaking.[48] The very fact of the continuity of cult at Amnisos opens the possibility that the mention of it could have entered the Odyssean tradi-

---

[40] Burkert 1985:261–262 with references.
[41] IG III 2.2, Guarducci 1974, Murray 1908–1909, West 1965. For text with commentary see Furley and Bremmer 2001:2.1–20, and a more general discussion in 1.68–75.
[42] IG III 2.2, strophes 5–6.
[43] Nilsson 1950:549 and n56, Willetts 1962:214.
[44] Perlman 1995.
[45] See Burkert 1985:262.
[46] See below on spring and the *Odyssey*.
[47] Willetts 1962:169.
[48] See, e.g., Marinatos 1993.8–12.

tion at almost any time. Indeed, such mentions do not even have to derive directly from Crete, since once the island acquired a certain "personality" in poetry this personality could have been evoked by any poet and in any poem, whatever his own origins and whatever the origins of the poem. Conversely, there is also nothing to preclude a direct connection between the *Odyssey* and Crete. My point here, however, is not about the origins but about the artistry of the *Odyssey*, an artistry that depends on a long performative tradition. Elements in the conversation between Odysseus and Penelope may not go back to early traditions of Crete, but they do evoke Cretan themes and associations, including those having to do with renewal of life and the rise of a new generation.

That said, Odysseus does seem to have ties to the two Cretan heroes Idomeneus and Meriones that reach beyond Homeric poetry. One striking piece of evidence is a red-figure Attic *stamnos* from about 480 BCE that depicts the escape of Odysseus and his companions from the cave of the Cyclops.[49] The Cyclops holds the stone that he uses to close the entrance to the cave, and next to him, hanging under a ram's belly with a sword in hand, is none other than Idomeneus (inscribed ΙΔΑΜΕΝΕΥΣ). Odysseus, also identified by an inscription (ΟΔΥΣΥΣ) is behind Idomeneus, under another ram. Apparently, then, there existed narratives in which Odysseus and Idomeneus traveled and had adventures together: it was not inconceivable for someone in fifth-century Attica to put Idomeneus in the Cyclops' cave. There is also evidence of Meriones traveling with Odysseus after Troy, and though this evidence is late, it is noteworthy because here the notions of renewal may be part of the connection. Plutarch (*Life of Marcellus* 20) reports that in Sicily, in a city called Enguium, there was a temple of goddesses known as The Mothers. Cretans reportedly founded the town and built the temple, dedicating spears and helmets in it, including a bronze helmet with the name of Meriones and another one with the name of Odysseus. The legend, then, brought Odysseus and Meriones together to the temple of The Mothers, goddesses rather reminiscent of Eileithyia and concerned with birth. Diodorus certainly sees these divinities as Cretan transplants (with what justification is a different matter) and remarks that they were worshipped in an unusual manner, as in Crete, and that numerous dedications decorated their temple.[50] Like Eileithyia, these divinities seem to be concerned with the protection of baby Zeus, since, according

---

[49] Beazley 5343, attributed to the Siren Painter. Now in the Shelby White and Leon Levy Collection, New York.
[50] Diodorus Siculus 4.79.

to Diodorus, they hide the newborn god from his father, Kronos.[51] Is it possible that the name of the town, Enguium in Latin, Engyon in Greek, may itself be connected to the cult, which was its main claim to fame? Diodorus describes the town's location as a 'stronghold' (χωρίον ὀχυρὸν) and in Classical Greek the name Engyon should mean something like 'safe, secure'.[52] It is derived from the root γυ- (of γύη, γυῖα, γύαλον etc.), the basic meaning of which is 'curve', 'hollow'. In particular, the term γύαλον can apply to caves and subterranean caverns, and as Ferrari has shown, its meaning comes close to the English 'vault' in the sense that it is a cavern where something can be hidden and kept safe.[53] The notion of a protective hollow space comes close to describing the cave of Eileithyia on Crete, and also the same cave in Odysseus' Cretan Lie, with its harbor where he finds refuge. Diodorus claims that the town got its name from a local stream, but even that may be part of the similarity between the Mothers and Eileithyia, whose cave was in proximity to the nourishing Amnisos. It seems possible that the mythical Cretans arrived in Sicily along with their mythic themes, and that Odysseus shares in these themes, just as he does in the *Odyssey*.

To sum up, several details of Odysseus' Third Cretan Lie – Deukalion, Minos the *oaristes* of Zeus, the cave of Eileithyia – resonate with the theme of renewal. The message contains signs addressed to the audience and to Penelope, signs relevant to Odysseus' present rather than his past. Whether or not Penelope understands these signs is a separate question, which I set aside for later chapters. For the moment I would like simply to revisit Penelope's tearful reaction to Odysseus' story, a reaction which seems so outwardly dark and desperate, yet itself contain a premonition of renewal. These tears flow in response to the signs, hints, and premonitions that Odysseus slips into his story, and it is both paradoxical and fitting that they should be an outburst of grief, yet also a favorable sign. In response to Odysseus' tale Penelope melts the way snow melts in the mountains: ὡς δὲ χιὼν κατατήκετ' ἐν ἀκροπόλοισιν ὄρεσσιν, 'as the snow dissolves on the topmost mountains' (19.205). The melting of the snow is a sign of spring, and spring in the *Odyssey* is correlated with Odysseus' return, as has been long observed.[54] As the poem nears its climax, Athena appears as a swallow (22.240), the suitors are compared to cattle attacked by flies in the spring (ὥρῃ ἐν εἰαρινῇ, 22.301), and Penelope compares herself to a nightingale who sings at the beginning of spring (ἔαρος

---

[51] ibid.
[52] Diodorus Siculus 4.79.5
[53] Ferrari 2002:184–186.
[54] See Austin 1975, chapter 5, and Borthwick 1988.

νέον ἱσταμένοιο, 19.519). The change of season is implied in the mysterious but twice repeated prophecy that Odysseus will return at the waning of one moon and the beginning of another (14.162, 19.307), and another mysterious astronomical reference seems to be contained in Eumaeus' description of his native land, located 'where the turns of the sun are' (15.404). Last, but not least, the arrival of spring is signaled by the festival of Apollo that coincides with the bow contest, since Apolline festivals do not usually take part in winter, and several cities celebrated the god's epiphany in spring and early summer.[55] Penelope's tears, then, are not an isolated detail but one of the scattered but persistent signs of spring that accompany Odysseus' return, and thus her tears themselves are a sign of a turn in the world and the return of Odysseus.

The surreptitious hints at return, rebirth, and renewal both in Odysseus' story and Penelope's reaction to it not only resonate thematically with each other, but also heighten the drama of the moment, creating the tense atmosphere of expectation and uncertainty. The signs are tantalizing, but there are trials still ahead. Moreover, certain elements in Odysseus' story complicate the picture and increase the tension by bringing to mind the open-endedness of Odysseus' travels, which has given so much trouble to Penelope and Telemachus. In contrast to the bay of Phorkys on Ithaca, which is sheltered from the wind (αἵ [sc. ἀκταί] τ' ἀνέμων σκεπόωσι δυσαήων μέγα κῦμα, 'they [the promontories] offer shelter from the big waves driven by the stormy winds', 13.99), the anchorage next to the cave of Eileithyia is less secluded, and just barely allows Odysseus to escape the storm: μόγις δ' ὑπάλυξεν ἀέλλας (19.189). It is not Crete, but Ithaca that is the setting of rebirth and renewal in the *Odyssey*. On Crete, Odysseus receives only a temporary respite as he waits out twelve days of a particularly strong northern wind:

> εἴλει γὰρ βορέης ἄνεμος μέγας οὐδ' ἐπὶ γαίη
> εἴα ἵστασθαι, χαλεπὸς δέ τις ὦρορε δαίμων.
>
> (*Odyssey* 19.200–201)

> For the great northern wind kept them [Achaeans from
> sailing],
> and a man could not even stand on earth. Some harsh
> divinity roused it.

---

[55] Farnell 1907:258. In Delphi the birthday of Apollo was celebrated on the seventh of Busios, the first month of spring (Plutarch, *Greek Questions* 292).

The cave of Eileithyia points to birth and life but does not offer decisive salvation within the framework of the Cretan tale, which ends in a pointedly open-ended way, with Odysseus and his companions embarking to continue their journey:

τῇ τρεισκαιδεκάτῃ δ' ἄνεμος πέσε, τοὶ δ' ἀνάγοντο.

(*Odyssey* 19.202)

But on the thirteenth day the wind fell, and they set forth.

CHAPTER SEVEN

THE CLOAK

AFTER THE CONCLUSION OF ODYSSEUS' CRETAN TALE, once her tears stop flowing, Penelope returns to the task at hand, the testing of her interlocutor. This transition from emotion to practicality, from premonitions of the poem's denouement to Penelope's suspicions about her guest's veracity is a good illustration of the narrative tension peculiar to this part of the *Odyssey*. At the same time, the questioning by no means negates the impression created by Penelope's tears, and in a sense only strengthens it. The questions Penelope asks seem too difficult to be addressed to a stranger, however intelligent and trustworthy. She demands that her guest tell her what clothes Odysseus wore when he came to Crete, twenty years ago, and that he describe his companions (*Odyssey* 19.215–219). Harsh suggested long ago that Odysseus has already aroused Penelope's curiosity by initially withholding his name and then skillfully bringing the conversation back to Odysseus. By following this up with a minute recollection of Odysseus' clothing while commenting that it is difficult to remember such details, Odysseus, in Harsh's words, "designedly suggested his identity but warned Penelope by his reserve and by his disclaimers, especially by a slyly humorous one that Odysseus may have been dressed differently when he left Ithaca, that he does not desire open recognition at the crucial point."[1]

Harsh does not, however, see the same level of design behind Penelope's words, and that is the only way in which I would emend his admirable reading of the scene. At this (or any) point, Penelope hardly needs to be told that open recognition is undesirable, and her questions seem to be designed precisely to give her guest the opportunity of proving to her that he is Odysseus. Unlike a stranger, the real Odysseus should remember not simply his clothes but also those items that were particularly closely tied to his identity, and it is precisely such things that Odysseus mentions, including a red double cloak of wool,

[1] Harsh 1950:11.

a shining and soft *khiton*, and a memorable golden pin with a dog hunting a fawn (19.225–234). These possessions serve, of course, to identify Odysseus, and Penelope duly recognizes them, cries even more than before, and remarks that she herself gave these clothes to her husband and that the stranger is now *philos* and *aidoios* to her (19.253–257).

Much can be said about the way clothes function as part of Odysseus' lies, his disguise and his revelation in the *Odyssey*. As Block nicely puts it, "the return of Odysseus is not a simple revelation, but a process through which deception identifies the hero by concealing him, as clothing identifies a man by covering him."[2] I will not dwell here on clothing as a disguise. Instead, I will comment briefly on the way mentions of the clothes function rhetorically in the dialogue with Penelope and related episodes, and then focus on the way in which the mention of the cloak and the pin continue to modulate the themes of Odysseus' previous utterance, the Third Cretan Lie.

The first item the beggar mentions in response to Penelope is the cloak:

> χλαῖναν πορφυρέην οὔλην ἔχε δῖος Ὀδυσσεύς,
> διπλῆν· ἐν δ᾽ ἄρα οἱ περόνη χρυσοῖο τέτυκτο.
>
> (*Odyssey* 19.225–226)

Odysseus had a woolen purple cloak,
a two-fold one, and in it was a pin of gold.

To begin with the obvious, the cloak and the *khiton* together are apparently a sign of status and a gift that a guest might expect from his host. These two items of clothing, which form a complete costume, are repeatedly given, received, requested and desired, presumably because their presence and absence distinguishes a man who is a member of a social group from an outcast, a beggar, a person in trouble. The character who comes closest to making this function of clothes explicit is Odysseus himself, when, in the *Iliad*, he threatens to humiliate Thersites by stripping him:

> μηδ᾽ ἔτι Τηλεμάχοιο πατὴρ κεκλημένος εἴην,
> εἰ μὴ ἐγώ σε λαβὼν ἀπὸ μὲν φίλα εἵματα δύσω,
> χλαῖνάν τ᾽ ἠδὲ χιτῶνα, τά τ᾽ αἰδῶ ἀμφικαλύπτει.
>
> (*Iliad* 2.260–262)

---

[2] Block 1985:11.

> May I no longer be called the father of Telemachus
> if I do not seize you and strip off your clothes,
> the cloak and the *khiton*, which cover your private parts.

Once he arrives on Ithaca and assumes the appearance of a beggar, Odysseus seems to begin a quest for cloak and *khiton*. He tells Eumaeus how he was previously entertained by Pheidon in Thesprotia and received these items of clothing (though they were later stolen), hinting that this is the way to treat a guest. Eumaeus, being a gracious host but nobody's fool, holds off and does not offer the clothes. When the time comes for the beggar to meet Penelope, the loyal swineherd clearly worries that his guest may tell false tales about Odysseus in order to win her over and finally acquire the clothes he desires. Meanwhile, Odysseus does obtain from Eumaeus the loan of a cloak for one night by means of his famous and problematic tale about going into an ambush with Odysseus at Troy, almost freezing to death, and then being saved by Odysseus who says that reinforcements are needed and thus causes another member of the group to fling his cloak aside and run for help. The speaker then sleeps comfortably through the rest of the night in that discarded cloak.[3] At least one message of the tale is obvious – Eumaeus' guest is as cold now as he was then, and he would like a cloak. Eumaeus makes a point of saying that he has no extra cloaks, but does let his guest borrow one for the night, adding that Telemachus will give him a cloak and a *khiton* when he comes back (14.516). When the latter arrives in the hut he lives up to this promise and offers the clothing to Odysseus. Penelope, too, offers clothes, on two occasions. First she asks Eumaeus to invite the beggar in so she can question him about Odysseus and promises that she will give him a cloak and a *khiton* if he speaks the truth. And secondly, she pacifies the suitors before the bow contest by saying that should the beggar string the bow his reward will not be her hand in marriage but rather clothing, a spear, a sword, and shoes. Variants of the same one-line formula are used on most of these occasions:

---

[3] *Odyssey* 14.462–506. For analysis of Odysseus' cloak tale see Block 1985:6 (who believes the tale to be modeled on the Doloneia) and Newton 1998:143–56, who discusses the way the story alludes both to other parts of *Odyssey* 14 and to the *Iliad*, and analyzes its rhetorical effects as an *ainos* for Eumaeus. See also Brennan 1987:1–3, for whom the fact that it is Aetolian Thoas who is duped by Odysseus is significant, since he believes that this is a joke at the expense of what he sees as a rival Aetolian epic tradition. Though I find it reductive to say that this tale is based on the Doloneia, there are certainly similarities between these two ambush narratives. For more on this question, see below, pp130–131.

αὐτός τοι χλαῖνάν τε χιτῶνά τε εἵματα δώσει.

(Eumaeus, *Odyssey* 14.516)

He will give you clothes, a cloak and a *khiton*.

ἔσσω μιν χλαῖνάν τε χιτῶνά τε, εἵματα καλά.

(Telemachus, *Odyssey* 16.79; Penelope, 17.550)

I will dress him in good clothes, a cloak and a *khiton*.

Beggar-Odysseus seems to be looking for a cloak and a *khiton*, but in reality he is not. In the hut of Eumaeus he utters a promise that Odysseus will come back soon, and he specifically proclaims that he will only receive his gift of a cloak and *khiton* if this promise comes true:

ἀλλ' ἄγε νῦν ῥήτρην ποιησόμεθ'· αὐτὰρ ὄπισθεν
μάρτυροι ἀμφοτέροισι θεοί, τοὶ Ὄλυμπον ἔχουσιν.
εἰ μέν κεν νοστήσῃ ἄναξ τεὸς ἐς τόδε δῶμα,
ἔσσας με χλαῖνάν τε χιτῶνά τε εἵματα πέμψαι
Δουλίχιόνδ' ἰέναι, ὅθι μοι φίλον ἔπλετο θυμῷ·
εἰ δέ κε μὴ ἔλθῃσιν ἄναξ τεὸς ὡς ἀγορεύω,
δμῶας ἐπισσεύας βαλέειν μεγάλης κατὰ πέτρης,
ὄφρα καὶ ἄλλος πτωχὸς ἀλεύεται ἠπεροπεύειν.

(*Odyssey* 14.393–400)

But let us now make a pact, and in the future
let the gods who hold Olympus be witnesses for both of us.
If your master returns to this house,
you shall give me clothes, a cloak and a *khiton*, and send
    me off
to Doulikhion, where I want to go.
But if your master does not come as I say,
order your servants to throw me off a high cliff,
so that the next beggar will think twice before taking
    advantage of you.

Eumaeus refuses the pact, but the gift becomes impossible: Odysseus the beggar can never accept clothes from his own household because once the condition for his acceptance is met he will no longer be a beggar and clothes will no longer be a gift. In this way Odysseus both requests clothing and declines it. In fact he never receives his cloak and *khiton* as a beggar: it is only after the suitors are dead and his identity proclaimed that he changes his clothes.[4]

Because Odysseus' request for clothes is a pretense, in effect itself a disguise, it can be seen as an element of the different strategies he employs in talking to Penelope, Telemachus, and Eumaeus. There are some telling differences in the ways the clothes are mentioned in these three cases, and they fit into the larger framework of each episode. Examining the way Odysseus talks about clothes to Eumaeus and to Telemachus can shed light on the way he talks about this to Penelope in Book 19. Eumaeus is uncertain of his guest's identity as he entertains Odysseus in his hut and remains so until Odysseus actually reveals himself and demonstrates his identifying scar.[5] Telemachus learns that the stranger is his father almost immediately, right there in the swineherd's dwelling, and, unlike others, requires little proof to accept this fact. Odysseus' emphatic assertion and Athena's magic seem to suffice. Penelope, in my opinion, suspects that the beggar is Odysseus right away, but does not reveal her suspicions directly, so that there is no recognition scene between husband and wife. In accordance with these three different situations, the question of Odysseus's clothes is handled very differently.

Eumaeus persists in thinking that the stranger needs a cloak and *khiton*, or at least in acting as if he does. In Book 17, when Penelope asks to see the stranger and promises to reward him with clothing if he speaks the truth, Eumaeus relates her words to Odysseus and then adds his own remark about the urgency of the beggar's need for clothes:

> εἰ δέ κέ σε γνώῃ νημερτέα πάντ' ἐνέποντα,
> ἕσσει σε χλαῖνάν τε χιτῶνά τε, τῶν σὺ μάλιστα
> χρηΐζεις· σῖτον δὲ καὶ αἰτίζων κατὰ δῆμον
> γαστέρα βοσκήσεις· δώσει δέ τοι ὅς κ' ἐθέλῃσι.

> (*Odyssey* 17.556–559)

> And if she finds that all you tell is true,
> she will give you clothes, a cloak and a *khiton*,

---

[4] See also below pp115-116.

[5] Though Eumaeus may have his suspicions. Roisman (1990) and Ahl and Roisman (1996:167–181) offer a detailed discussion of Eumaeus' first encounter with Odysseus and suggest that the swineherd entertains suspicions regarding the beggar's identity, or at least regarding his status, since he treats him as an important person.

which you need very much. As for food, you can feed your belly
begging through the district. And whoever wants to will give
to you.

Eumaeus' remark seems to be indirect advice to the stranger about how
to proceed: now is a good time to speak the truth since it would be in the
stranger's own interests. Eumaeus takes good care of his guest from the first
moment the latter arrives at the hut, and here he paints a practical picture of
how the beggar-Odysseus could manage to survive on Ithaca, starting with the
most urgent need of acquiring serviceable clothes.

With Telemachus, the question of clothes disappears through Athena's
divine powers. The goddess touches Odysseus with her staff and changes not
only his appearance but, first of all, his clothes. Instead of his rags Odysseus
now wears a well-washed *khiton* and not a *khlaina*, but a *pharos*, a different type
of cloak or mantle:

φᾶρος μέν οἱ πρῶτον ἐϋπλυνὲς ἠδὲ χιτῶνα
θῆκ' ἀμφὶ στήθεσφι, δέμας δ' ὤφελλε καὶ ἥβην.

(*Odyssey* 16.173–174)

First she put a well-washed mantle and a *khiton*
around his chest, and increased his stature and youth.

After that, the question of Telemachus' providing the beggar with clothes
naturally disappears, since Telemachus now knows that the rags are a disguise
and he hopes soon to help his father in regaining all of his possessions, not just
a cloak.

With Penelope, too, the question of cloak and *khiton* is dropped in its
simple form, even though her guest passes her tests of truthfulness. Penelope
does mention the possible gift of clothing again in Book 21, but there she is
speaking not to the disguised Odysseus but to the suitors, and thus has to
sustain their illusion that the beggar is only a beggar and not to be feared
(*Odyssey* 21.331–342). In Book 19, by contrast, both Penelope's offer and
Odysseus' reaction become more complex. When beggar-Odysseus swears
an oath that Odysseus will come back 'within this very *lukabas*', Penelope
responds with a promise of gifts if he is right, but immediately adds that she
does not have such hopes (*Odyssey* 19.309–316). In the meanwhile, however, she
offers her guest a wash, a warm bed, a bath in the morning, and Telemachus'
company at dinner the next day. This offer seems to involve not only being
clean and rubbed with oil but also being well-dressed, since Penelope says:

πῶς γὰρ ἐμεῦ σύ, ξεῖνε, δαήσεαι, εἴ τι γυναικῶν
ἀλλάων περίειμι νόον καὶ ἐπίφρονα μῆτιν,
εἴ κεν ἀϋσταλέος, κακὰ εἱμένος ἐν μεγάροισι
δαινύῃ;

(Odyssey 19.323–326)

For how will you learn, stranger, whether I in any way surpass
the rest of women in awareness and shrewd intelligence,
if you feast in our halls unwashed and wearing bad clothes?

I interpret this offer as part of Penelope's testing strategy, based primarily on her later reaction to Odysseus' reply. A suggestion that this question is not to be taken literally is also perhaps contained in Penelope's reference to *metis*, a quintessentially Odyssean quality that usually involves scheming and clever contrivance.[6] In this case, if Penelope's question is taken at face value, it is not clear what the reference to *metis* is doing here: there is nothing surpassingly cunning about offering one's guest a bath and a bed. In any case, Odysseus refuses everything – the bed, the bath, and the clothes, saying that cloaks and blankets have been hateful to him ever since he left his land behind, and that his nights are sleepless, not comfortable (*Odyssey* 19.336–347). This reply wins emphatic approval from Penelope, who never offers either clothes or bedding again to her guest and who claims that none of the other strangers that have come to her house have been so *pepnumenos*. A difficult word that has received much scholarly attention, *pepnumenos* eludes simple translation, ('wise', 'prudent', 'intelligent', 'shrewd', 'honest', 'daring', and 'artless' have all been suggested), but is consistently connected with positively evaluated speech.[7]

---

[6] *Metis* might be translated as 'artifice' or 'stratagem', as suggested by Nagy 1979:45–49. For an expanded and informative discussion of the meaning of *metis* in Homer see Detienne and Vernant 1978:11–26.

[7] See Heitman 2005:54–55 for a brief survey of suggested translations, including his own, 'artless'. This translation, however, does not fit certain instances: Nestor, for example, can hardly be called 'artless', yet Athena calls him *pepnumenos* at *Odyssey* 3.20, right after mentioning, at 3.18, that he is likely to hide some *metis* in his mind. When Athena says that Nestor will not tell a lie because he is so *pepnumenos*, she is not saying that Nestor is artless or straightforward, but rather that he will understand that at this point it would be inappropriate to lie to Telemachus. I am grateful to Robin Greene (unpublished work) for clarifying this point. Moreover, 'artless' adds a negative tinge to the adjective, which is always positive in Homer. Finally, this translation completely divorces the participle from its verb πέπνυμαι, which has nothing to do with being artless. The verb, in Homer at least, quite clearly has to do with mental vigor and intelligence, perhaps especially with moral intelligence (*Odyssey* 10.495 is an especially clear example; the verb is applied to Odysseus and seems to have a moral aspect to it at *Odyssey* 23.210). The use of

Here it is clearly complimentary and Penelope repeats it again, saying that all the stranger says is *pepnumena* and that he says it *euphradeos*, 'sensibly':

ξεῖνε φίλ'· οὐ γάρ πώ τις ἀνὴρ πεπνυμένος ὧδε
ξείνων τηλεδαπῶν φιλίων ἐμὸν ἵκετο δῶμα,
ὡς σὺ μάλ' εὐφραδέως πεπνυμένα πάντ' ἀγορεύεις.

(Odyssey 19.350–352)

Dear stranger – for never has such an intelligent man
come to my house from among the strangers who live
    far away,
and none has been dearer, so sensible and wise is
    everything you say.

The complexities of this reply, as with the whole Eurykleia episode which follows, are not my subject here, but there are two aspects of Penelope's utterance that are important to mention. First of all, she makes a distinction between this stranger and all others that have come to her in the past. According to Eumaeus, many have come to Penelope with tales of Odysseus, and all have lied, and Eumaeus is clearly suspicious that his guest will do the same. In a sense, he of course does so, and yet for Penelope this beggar is entirely unlike all others who have come to her. Secondly, at this point in the dialogue it already becomes hard to comprehend what is being said on the assumption that Penelope has no suspicion about the guest's identity. It is not clear, for example, why it should be so wise (or astute, or sagacious, or honest, or proper) of Odysseus to refuse a bath and a bed, if he is in fact a wanderer in need of all these things and one who has, moreover, honestly deserved them. On the other hand, if he is, or could be, Odysseus, it is in his interest both to keep his disguise intact and to avoid making himself in any sense at home in his house until the house is won back. By offering him the creature comforts of home, Penelope can test the seriousness of his intentions and the value of his claims regarding Odysseus' forthcoming return. If he accepts the clothes then perhaps that is what he wanted all along. If he does not accept them, then he has other goals and the probability increases that he is in fact Odysseus and that he is determined to get it all back. In his reply, the stranger stresses

---

pepnumenos in the *Odyssey* as it applies to Telemachus is analyzed by Roisman (1994) and Heath (2001). For a full survey and a balanced analysis of meaning see Cuypers in *Lexikon des früh-griechischen Epos* s.v. One of the difficulties with the word is that it seems to combine a cognitive evaluation (intelligent, reasonable, able to correctly interpret social situations etc.) with a moral one (gentlemanly, proper, wise).

that his refusal of comforts has to do with being away from his native Crete, implying that only after returning home will he enjoy what Penelope offers. When Penelope says that Odysseus' response is *pepnumenos*, she thus indicates that his response is both discreet and based on a correct evaluation of what is appropriate in his situation. For Odysseus, in contrast to any other stranger, this is not the time to accept gifts or be seen in good clothes, and in fact that time is postponed for longer than might be expected. Even in Book 23, when the suitors are already dead, Odysseus still initially faces Penelope in his rags, now bespattered with the suitor's blood, in spite of the fact that Eurykleia has offered him a change of clothing at the end of Book 22 (22.487). Only after the couple sit for a while facing each other in silence, and Telemachus reproaches his mother for being too hard, and Penelope mentions the signs that she and Odysseus both know, and Odysseus gives instructions about a fake feast to be put on by his household, only then does Odysseus finally have a bath and put on new clothes. And, interestingly, what he dons then is not the *khlaina* that was offered to him by Eurykleia, but a *pharos* (*Odyssey* 23.155).

Odysseus seems to have a complicated relationship with cloaks. Just as his reunion with Penelope is a much more subtle process than his acceptance by Telemachus or recognition by Eumaeus or even his return to Laertes, so the motif of clothing receives a more intricate and elaborate treatment in Penelope's case. All the more important, then, to understand, what signals Odysseus is sending by describing the *khlaina* and a *khiton* he used to have on Ithaca, a long-lost costume that he seems to seek, but any substitution of which he refuses to accept as a beggar.

First of all, does it make any difference whether the cloak Odysseus recalls is a *khlaina* as apposed to *pharos*? The two garments have some overlapping uses, and can be worn on similar occasions. For example, when he cries at Alkinoos' feast, Odysseus hides behind a *pharos* (8.84), but when Telemachus cries at Menelaos' dinner, he covers his eyes with a *khlaina* (4.115, 4.154). The overlap, however, is smaller than the difference between the two. The *pharos* is in essence simply a large piece of cloth (the size of which is its canonical feature, encapsulated in the formula *mega pharos*: *Iliad* 2.43, 8.221, *Odyssey* 5.230, 8.84, 10.543, 15.61), and in Homer it is often made of a luxurious fabric. It can be worn both by men and by women (for example, by Calypso at *Odyssey* 5.230) and it is also used to clothe the dead (Hektor is wrapped in one at 24.588, and Penelope pretends to weave one for Laertes). The *khlaina* is smaller, usually made of wool, sometimes double and worn only by males. It too can be luxurious, but it is first and foremost a practical cloak. In Homer, the *pharos* tends to be worn on occasions of leisure, festivity, or great importance, and it is never connected with great physical effort. It may be an indication of status that Agamemon is the only character in the *Iliad* to wear the *pharos* in an assembly (*Iliad* 2.43) and even in battle, though he is shouting encouragement to his troops rather than fighting (*Iliad* 8.221). Otherwise, the *pharos* seems to be connected with female company: for example, Telemachus dons a *pharos* after he is bathed by Nestor's daughter Polykaste (*Odyssey* 3.467). This tendency holds for *pharea* worn by Odysseus: it is a *pharos*, not a *khlaina*, that Odysseus receives from Nausikaa (*Odyssey* 6.214) in a scene permeated with the signs of romance and, more specifically, of wedding.[8] He continues to wear this purple *pharos* at the feast of Alkinoos, and it is with this that he covers his head while crying. He also wears it when he appears to Nausikaa after his bath, made younger and more handsome by Athena (*Odyssey* 6.227–237). An almost identical transformation of Odysseus occurs one more time in the poem, when Odysseus appears to Penelope on the verge of their final reunion, again wearing a *pharos*:

> αὐτὰρ Ὀδυσσῆα μεγαλήτορα ᾧ ἐνὶ οἴκῳ
> Εὐρυνόμη ταμίη λοῦσεν καὶ χρῖσεν ἐλαίῳ,
> ἀμφὶ δέ μιν φᾶρος καλὸν βάλεν ἠδὲ χιτῶνα·
> αὐτὰρ κὰκ κεφαλῆς χεῦεν πολὺ κάλλος Ἀθήνη
> μείζονά τ' εἰσιδέειν καὶ πάσσονα· κὰδ δὲ κάρητος
> οὔλας ἧκε κόμας, ὑακινθίνῳ ἄνθει ὁμοίας.
>
> (*Odyssey* 23.153–158)

> And the housekeeper Eurynome bathed the great-hearted
>   Odysseus
> in his own house, and anointed him with oil,
> and dressed him in a beautiful mantle and a *khiton*.
> And Athena shed great beauty over his head and made him
> taller and stronger to look at. She made thick locks
> tumble down his head, like the hyacinth flower.

The *khlaina*, on the other hand, is worn in situations when what is needed is not beauty but warmth (though it may, of course, provide both). Odysseus in Eumaeus' hut needs a *khlaina* to keep warm, and *khlainai* are precisely what are worn by Eumaeus himself and his men, people who work rather than sit at banquets. While the *khlaina* clearly encumbers running, since on several occasions Homeric characters fling off their *khlainai* to run (Thoas at *Odyssey*

---

[8] More on this below, pp271, 279, 322.

14.499–500, Odysseus himself at *Iliad* 2.183–184), it is still worn by men in action, those going into ambush, those taking part in an emergency night council, those traveling. On Calypso's island, for example, Odysseus puts on a *khlaina* when he sets out to cut trees for his raft (*Odyssey* 5.229).

But of course, the *khlaina* is not all about practicality. Precisely because it is a male garment associated with the active life, it seems especially suited for reflecting the wearer's achievement, and there is some evidence in Homer that it does precisely that. It may be significant that on Skheria Odysseus continues to wear the *pharos* that Nausikaa gave him both at the feast and then at the games, where he intends to remain only a spectator. After the games, however, and after he proves his abilities by winning in discus-throwing without even taking off the *pharos*, he receives a new set of clothing, and this time it includes a *khlaina* (*Odyssey* 8.455), as if Odysseus' demonstration of his athletic abilities has entitled him to one.

But the most elaborate *khlaina* in Homer is worn in the *Iliad* by the eldest of the heroes, Nestor:

> ἀμφὶ δ' ἄρα χλαῖναν περονήσατο φοινικόεσσαν
> διπλῆν ἐκταδίην, οὔλη δ' ἐπενήνοθε λάχνη.

> (*Iliad* 10.133–134)

> And he pinned about his shoulders a dark-red cloak,
> two-fold and flowing, with a thick pile of wool.

It is noteworthy that nobody else in Homer has a similar *khlaina*, except for Odysseus on the way to Troy, in his own description. Only Nestor and Odysseus have cloaks that are both purple and wooly, though Telemachus also wears a purple cloak and many characters have wooly ones. In addition, both Nestor's and Odysseus' cloaks are double and they are the only characters in Homer who are mentioned as having pins for their *khlainai*.

The parallel, I think, is significant, because there are so many other ways in which Nestor and Odysseus are connected to each other, and because Nestor plays such an important role in the *Odyssey*. To point out the obvious, both Nestor and Odysseus are heroes famed for their intelligence rather than their physical power (though both boast of that too), both are equally known for their eloquence, and they are, according to Nestor himself, always of one mind in council during the Trojan war (*Odyssey* 3.126–129). Both heroes are also central figures of the *nostos* traditions, though here their fates are very different. Nestor himself tells the story (already mentioned above) of their disagreement and parting at Tenedos, which results in two divergent fates:

Nestor returns home safely and quickly, Odysseus returns late, in trouble, and without his men.[9] Odysseus fails to do what Nestor succeeds in doing, namely returning and bringing back his crew, and through this failure he temporarily loses his very status as Odysseus, a king, a wealthy person, leader of men and 'sacker of Troy'. Nestor never undergoes such a reversal, certainly not on his way back from Troy. When Odysseus describes his cloak and pin to Penelope, he seems to represent his pre-Trojan self as a younger Nestor, his cloak and pin symbolizing his status and function as an accomplished hero. Like the details of the Third Cretan Lie, this description not only reminds Penelope of what Odysseus used to be, but also of what he failed to be, or to remain, especially when it is delivered by the suspected Odysseus himself, dressed not in that purple cloak but in beggar's rags. Odysseus' previous words contain premonitions of his return, but also hint at his particular role and fate as a hero, a role that involves losses and returns, being a king but also being a "younger brother."[10] In a similar way, the description of his splendid cloak, spoken by an ill-dressed beggar, points both to Odysseus' achievement and the peculiar nature of that achievement. Odysseus' refusal to accept bed, bath, and clothing also acquires an added meaning in this context. Like his assumed Cretan self, who has rejected comforts ever since he left Crete behind, Odysseus will accept nothing less than the restoration of his former status, marked by the purple cloak and golden pin in which he left for Troy. Not just any cloak will do.

Further, the description of Odysseus' cloak and pin echoes the Third Cretan Lie in the broader sense of having to do with the overall ritual and mythic scheme that operates in the *Odyssey*, namely the idea of coming of age and becoming a king, associated with periodic social and natural renewal. One of the ways of marking a young man's transition into manhood is by new clothing, most commonly a cloak. On Crete, when an *eromenos* returns to town having spent time in the wilderness with his elder abductor, he received presents which suggest that he is now a man and a warrior, including a warrior's

---

[9] *Odyssey* 3.126–183. Nestor does not say that he quarreled with Odysseus, but I am persuaded by Frame's (2009:175–193) detailed discussion of the scene that this is implied. According to Nestor's narrative, Odysseus first sails from Troy to Tenedos along with Nestor, while Agamemnon stays on at Troy. In Frame's analysis (2009.182), this represents a division between those who will return safely and those who will not, and Odysseus initially joins the former. Then Nestor and Odysseus apparently quarrel at Tenedos and Odysseus returns to Agamemnon. Frame shows that the quarrel and Odysseus' subsequent separation from Nestor ensures for him a long and difficult return instead of the quick and safe return that Nestor provides for those who stay with him. Further, the divergence of the two heroes at this point correlates to their different types of intelligence (Frame 2009.192–193).

[10] On Odysseus as a younger brother of Idomeneus in the Third Cretan Lie see Chapter Four.

outfit: στολὴν πολεμικὴν καὶ βοῦν καὶ ποτήριον, 'attire for war, an ox and a drinking cup' (Ephorus, FGrH 70 F 149.110 = Strabo 10.4.21). In the city of Pellene in Achaea, the winners in the athletic competitions at the Hermaia received warm cloaks as prizes.[11] This particular Hermaia attracted competitors from beyond its local area already in the first half of the fifth century, and receives several mentions in Pindar.[12] The city was famed for these cloaks, but this can hardly be the only reason they were awarded at the games, and it is probably not a coincidence that competitions of pre-adult males are a distinctive feature of Hermaia all over Greece.[13]

There is also a mythological competition for a cloak, and yet another splendid mythological cloak on a hero's shoulders in the myth of Jason and the voyage of Argo. The parallels between the *Argonautica* and the *Odyssey* are not exact, yet their accumulation is striking, especially considering the general similarities and points of contact of these two traditional tales. The latter is a well-established fact and needs no additional explanation, except to say that perhaps the parallels and contacts go beyond what has long been appreciated. Quite apart from such obvious elements as the Clashing Rocks and Skylla and Kharybdis, which the two traditions simply have in common, there are less obvious echoes.[14] For example, Odysseus is strangely good at carpentry. Not only does he built his own house with its famous bed, but he also builds a raft for himself, and the construction is described in detail in the *Odyssey* (5.234–261). This is a distinctive feature: we hear nothing of Achilles, Agamemnon, Menelaos, or even the clever Nestor, wielding a chisel. This feature, however, is apparently shared by Jason in Apollonius' *Argonautica*, since he is instructed by

---

[11] Pindar *Olympian* 7.86, 9.97–98 with scholia and *Nemean* 10.44, Photius *Lexicon* s.v. Πελληνικαὶ χλαῖναι, Hesychius s.v. Πελληνικαὶ χλαῖναι, Suda s.v. Πελληνικαὶ χλαῖναι (which names the games Heraia, rather than Hermaia, probably by mistake), Strabo 8.7.5, Pollux *Onomasticon* 7.67, Scholia to Aristophanes *Birds* 1421.

[12] Pindar *Olympian* 9.98 with scholia; *Olympian* 13.109, *Nemean* 10.44 mention Pellenian games and these may well be the Hermaia, though the scholia identify them as Theoxenia in honor of Apollo. The relationship between the two is unclear, and the information provided by scholia inconsistent: a scholion to *Olympian* 9.98 mentions both games as if they were independent, but another scholion to *Olympian* 7.86 claims that these were the same games. Johnston hypothesizes that the Theoxenia may have been added to the existing Hermaia at some point under Delphic influence, since elsewhere festivals called Theoxenia were usually held in honor of the Dioskouroi (or Herakles), whereas Delphi held a well-known Theoxenia in honor of Apollo (Johnston 2002:117).

[13] Plato (*Lysias* 206d) and Aeschines (1.10) mention only παῖδες and νεανίσκοι as competitors at the Athenian Hermaia, and there is plentiful (though mostly Hellenistic) epigraphical evidence for Hermaia as games for youngsters. See Johnston 2002:116 for a discussion with references.

[14] See Meuli 1921 for a discussion of the *Odyssey*'s relation to an oral *Argonautica*.

Athena in carpentry, even if he does not build the ship himself (1.724).[15] When Odysseus sets out to build his raft, his attire includes a cloak (*khlaina*), and though nothing appears to be remarkable about this particular cloak, the very fact that it is mentioned may point to a traditional association. In Apollonius' *Argonautica* Jason's instruction in ship-building is mentioned in connection with nothing less than his famous and most elaborately described cloak, which Jason receives from Athena:

> Αὐτὰρ ὅγ' ἀμφ' ὤμοισι, θεᾶς Ἰτωνίδος ἔργον,
> δίπλακα πορφυρέην περονήσατο, τήν οἱ ὄπασσε
> Παλλάς, ὅτε πρῶτον δρυόχους ἐπεβάλλετο νηός
> Ἀργοῦς, καὶ κανόνεσσι δάε ζυγὰ μετρήσασθαι.

(*Argonautica* 1.721–724)

> But around his shoulders he pinned the work of the Itonian goddess,
> a two-fold purple cloak, which Pallas had given him
> when he first put in place the shores for building the ship,
> Argo, and learned to measure the thwarts with a rule.

What follows is an extended ecphrasis of the cloak, but the initial description is very reminiscent of the *Odyssey*: both cloaks are double and purple, and both are fastened with a pin (*perone*). Needless to say, it is quite possible that Apollonius' description of Jason's cloak is influenced by the *Odyssey*, but that hardly reduces it in significance. If Apollonius decided to echo the description it may have been precisely because he was sensitive to the similarities in poetic and mythological function of both.

In the *Argonautica*, Jason makes an impression on the women of Lemnos, as Apollonius describes in an elaborate simile:

> Βῆ δ' ἴμεναι προτὶ ἄστυ, φαεινῷ ἀστέρι ἶσος,
> ὅν ῥά τε νηγατέῃσιν ἐεργόμεναι καλύβῃσιν
> νύμφαι θηήσαντο δόμων ὕπερ ἀντέλλοντα,
> καί σφισι κυανέοιο δι' αἰθέρος ὄμματα θέλγει
> καλὸν ἐρευθόμενος, γάνυται δέ τε ἠιθέοιο
> παρθένος ἱμείρουσα μετ' ἀλλοδαποῖσιν ἐόντος

---

[15] See Murray 2005, especially 92–99 on the question of who actually builds the ship in Apollonius' *Argonautica* and its ramifications.

ἀνδράσιν, ᾧ κέν μιν μνηστὴν κομέωσι τοκῆες -
τῷ ἴκελος προπόλοιο κατὰ στίβον ἤιεν ἥρως·

(Argonautica 1.774–781)

And he went towards the fortress, like a shining star,
which maidens, confined in their newly-built bowers,
look at as it rises above the houses.
And through the dark-blue air it enchants their eyes
with its beautiful red gleam and a maiden brightens up,
a maiden pining for a youth, who is far away among
    strangers,
and for whom her parents keep her as a promised bride.
Like such a star the hero went, following in the tracks of
    his attendant.

The simile looks ahead to the improvised nuptial arrangements between the Argonauts and the Lemnian women, which will lead to the repopulation of the island, but it also taps into the mythological layers both crucial to the *Arognautica* and especially potent in this Lemnian episode. The use of the term *eitheos* to denote the young man who is absent, and perhaps even the fact that he is away, all suggest the period of transition into full maturity, a period when young men in myth typically undergo trials, and which often conclude with marriage. It is noteworthy that Jason's entry into Hypsipyle's city in his splendid cloak triggers this particular set of associations.

Cloaks, in any case, play an important role in the Lemnian myth long before Apollonius. Pindar mentions what seems to be a well-established myth that the Argonauts held games on Lemnos and that cloaks served as prizes in competition:

ἔν τ' Ὠκεανοῦ πελάγεσσι μίγεν πόντῳ τ' ἐρυθρῷ
Λαμνιᾶν τ' ἔθνει γυναικῶν ἀνδροφόνων·
ἔνθα καὶ γυίων ἀέθλοις ἐπεδείξαντο κρίσιν ἐσθᾶτος ἀμφίς,
καὶ συνεύνασθεν.

(Pythian 4.251–254)

They reached the expanses of Okeanos and the Red Sea
and the man-slaying race of Lemnian women.
There they displayed the trial of their limbs in contests for
    the prize of a cloak,
and slept with the women.

A sexual encounter with the women follows closely upon the acquisition of cloaks, and a new generation is produced. The unions between the Argonauts and the women represent a fresh start for Lemnos, but in myth this fresh start is also a revitalizing of the old, a restoration rather than a completely novel beginning. The most visible sign of this is the continuation of the royal line. Indeed, while all the other men are killed, the king of the island, Thoas, is saved by his daughter, and it is the same daughter, Hypsipyle, who gives birth to the next king, thus accomplishing her role of linking the generations of males, exactly as if nothing ghastly and abnormal has happened on the island. Euneos, the son of Jason and Hypsipyle, and his grandfather Thoas are both mentioned in the *Iliad*, where Euneos is the current ruler of Lemnos (*Iliad* 23.747).

Burkert writes of the cloaks that Argonauts receive on Lemnos that "[t] he attire is linked with marriage or, rather, a disorganized mass celebration of the nuptials, ending *e contrario* the period of hate between the sexes and the lack of men."[16] In some sense, this assessment seems self-evident, since the competition for which the cloaks are awarded is followed so closely by the "nuptials." But the same assessment, I think, applies to Odysseus' cloak in Book 19: its description is designed to remind Penelope not just of Odysseus, but specifically of their marriage. In contrast to the *pharos*, which may be a proper garment for the wedding itself, or at least is associated with love-making,[17] the double purple cloaks worn by both Odysseus and Jason seem to be connected with marriage in a less direct way, as the visible signs of male achievement, the precursor and precondition of marriage in the mythic sequence of events. As he enters the city of Hypsipyle in his cloak Jason is ogled by women presumably because he looks like such splendid marriage prospect. Odysseus is actually married already when he sets out on his Trojan adventure, yet in the *Odyssey* too there is a mention of women staring at Odysseus:

---

[16] Burkert 1983:192.

[17] As mentioned above, we find Odysseus wearing a *pharos* in both wedding-tinged scenes in the *Odyssey*, one involving Nausikaa and the other in Book 23, when Odysseus faces Penelope. In the *Argonautica* too, while Jason first appears to Hypsipyle wearing his double cloak, the robe that is later specifically associated with their love is a different one, a *pharos*, which is said to be a memento of much love-making (3.1204–1206). There are also female garments that are explicitly associated with weddings both in the *Odyssey* and in *Argonautica*, and in both poems these pass through the hands of the males. In the *Odyssey*, Helen gives Telemachus a *peplos* for his bride (15.123–129). In the *Argonautica*, Dionysus gives a *peplos* to his son Thoas, who in turn gives it to his daughter Hypsipyle, and she to Jason (4.421–428).

ἦ μὲν πολλαί γ' αὐτὸν ἐθηήσαντο γυναῖκες.

(*Odyssey* 19.235)

And many women gazed at him in admiration.

Sitting in front of her as a ragged old beggar, Odysseus seems to remind Penelope of a subject that is her own preoccupation too, namely what an excellent match she once made in marrying Odysseus. It is a painful subject, because the promise of that splendid marriage has been replaced by twenty years of waiting, material losses, and recent dangers to Telemachus. This promise is now threatened with complete extinction by another marriage, and yet it is no doubt in part this very promise that makes Penelope despise the prospect of marrying one of the suitors, none of whom is a match for Odysseus. Penelope herself alludes to the perfection of her and Odysseus' start in life and the grievous reversals that followed when she says that the gods were jealous of them and begrudged them the enjoyment of their youth:

θεοὶ δ' ὤπαζον ὀϊζύν,
οἳ νῶϊν ἀγάσαντο παρ' ἀλλήλοισι μένοντε
ἥβης ταρπῆναι καὶ γήραος οὐδὸν ἱκέσθαι.

(*Odyssey* 23.210–212)

The gods gave us pain,
they begrudged us enjoyment of our youth,
our staying together
and coming to the threshold of old age together.

We never see Odysseus talking about these things to Penelope, and indeed such a conversation is hard to imagine. Once they acknowledge each other openly, the resilient couple exchange words about the trials still to come. But by describing himself in his pre-Trojan attire Odysseus does communicate to Penelope his own awareness of the contrast between the promise of that time and the miseries of the present. By doing so he prepares the ground for his forthcoming indirect claims that the promise still holds, that he is still Odysseus.

All of this suggests additional possible connotations for Odysseus' cloak in Book 19. In the context in which it is mentioned, following the Third Cretan Lie, the cloak brings to mind the peculiar fate of Odysseus: to be, in a sense, the great adolescent, to re-compete for his wife and re-earn his cloak, or at any rate to prove that he is still the man who did so as a youth. In this sense, the change of clothes Odysseus talks about and undergoes on Ithaca follows the same pattern as that of Jason on Lemnos. In Pindar, the competitions for a cloak are followed by sex and procreation. Pindar mentions no particular clothing at that later stage, but if this were Homer the item of choice would have been a *pharos*. In Apollonius Rhodius there is no contest, but there is a splendid cloak in which Jason arrives and which is then replaced by a *pharos* symbolic of his love encounter with Hypsipyle. In either case, a manly competitive event is associated with a *khlaina* and comes first, while erotic intercourse with women is associated with the *pharos* and comes second. The same sequence is observed on Ithaca. First, there is the mention of Odysseus' *khlaina*. He does not appear to Penelope wearing it, as he might have done twenty years prior, and as Jason appears to Hypsipyle, but its description serves a parallel function: both to remind her of that earlier appearance and in a sense to re-enact it verbally. Later, after the bow contest and what he himself ironically and cruelly calls an *aethlos* (*Odyssey* 22.25), namely the murder of the suitors, Odysseus wears a *pharos*, in a wedding-tinged scene. The *khlaina* appears only in words, but in its proper place.

There may in fact be specifically ritual undertones to the appearance of this *khlaina*. It is impossible to demonstrate this with any certainty, and we lack the cultural background to sense these ritual connotations with the clarity that may have been easy for ancient audiences, but we can at least be aware of their presence, and even guess something of their general nature. As has been mentioned above, in Pellene *khlainai* were prizes at the Hermaia, the games in honor of Hermes, but the games, in turn, are repeatedly associated by our sources with Theoxenia, the festival of Apollo.[18] Johnston surmises that the two festivals may have been combined, and if this is correct, then these cloaks were won and worn at a festival of Apollo. In any case, the setting for the mention of Odysseus' *khlaina* in the *Odyssey* is the approaching festival of Apollo, a festival which will be the crowning point of Telemachus' passage to maturity, which will involve a contest, and which will separate, with the cruelty and exaggeration typical of myth, those who will now be honored men worthy of heading a household (Odysseus and Telemachus) from those who will die before marriage (the suitors).[19]

The *khlaina* may be actually a part of the festival, one of its ritual props. Just as Odysseus' cloak is similar to Jason's in terms of the morphology of myth, so its setting, widely understood, is, in terms of its ritual echoes, uncan-

---

[18] See note 11 above.

[19] See Nagy 1990:122 for a discussion of the notions of struggling for one's life, symbolic death (for those who lose), and survival (for the winner) in actual ritual contest in Ancient Greece, building on the findings of Meuli (1968) and Sansone (1988).

nily reminiscent of the mythical Lemnos visited by the Argonauts. Burkert discusses in detail the parallels between the myth of the Lemnian women and the Argonauts, and a yearly ritual on Lemnos, one of the clearest examples of a ritual period of reversal, dissolution, and devastation followed by a renewal of life.[20] Philostratus of Lemnos reports that every year fire would be extinguished on the island for nine days and during this time funerary sacrifices would be performed and secret subterranean deities would be called upon. The new, pure fire would then be brought from Delos and distributed for all necessities of life, especially the crafts of Hephaestus, and then it would be said that a new life began on the island.[21] Burkert suggests that one of these nine fireless days is also mentioned by Myrsilus of Lesbos, who says that for one day every year the women of Lemnos would stay away from men and even somehow drive men away by their smell, surely the ritual equivalent of the terrible stench inflicted by Hera on the Lemnian women in myth.[22] Burkert hypothesizes that there was also a departure of the king, corresponding to the departure, in myth, of Thoas, the king of the island and the only male to escape death.[23] Somehow, though it is hard to say exactly how, Dionysus seems to have been involved, perhaps playing a role in the return of the fire. Burkert points to the popular motif of the drunken Hephaestus being brought back to Olympus by Dionysus. Thoas is Dionysus' son and has a distinctly Dionysiac name ('the fast one').[24] The coins of the city of Hephaistia, where the festival took place, show a ram, suggesting that a ram sacrifice was part of the festival, felt caps of the Cabiri, and grapes and vines.[25] The felt caps of the Cabiri establish a connection with nearby Samothrace and their cult and

---

[20] Burkert 1983:190–195.

[21] Philostratos *Heroikos* 740 Kayser.

[22] FGrH 477 F1 = Scholia to Apollonius Rhodius 1.615. Burkert 1983:193. Athenian women at Skira achieve the same effect by chewing on garlic: Philochorus FGrH 328 F 89.

[23] Euripides *Hypsipyle* fr. 64.111, *Anthologia Palatina* 3.10, Apollonius Rhodius 1.620–626, Theolytos FGrH 478 F 3, Xenagoras FGrH 240 F 31, Scholia to Apollonius Rhodius 1.623, scholia to Pindar *Olympian* 4, scholion 31b.4 Drachmann. Euneos, son of Jason and Hypsipyle mentioned in the *Iliad* 23.747, was also the founder of the line of Euneidai, priests of Dionysus Melpomenos at Athens (Toepffer 1889:181–206).

[24] Maenads (in poetry, at least) are prone to rushing and run already in Homer. For example, Andromache rushes out like a maenad (διέσσυτο μαινάδι ἴση, *Iliad* 22.461) when she hears the sounds of upheaval and suspects that Hektor has come to harm. The adjective θοός and the verb θοάζω are frequently applied to maenads or appear in Dionysiac contexts. For example, both words are attested in Euripides *Bacchae* about maenads and the women of Thebes: θοάζω Βρομίωι πόνον ἡδὺν (65), ἐν δὲ δασκίοις ὄρεσι θοάζειν (219), ἴτε θοαὶ Λύσσας κύνες (977). Cf. also the occurrences in Euripides' *Trojan Women*: μαινὰς θοάζει (307), μαινὰς θοάζουσ' (349), and the name of the maenads associated with Parnassus: Thyiades.

[25] Head 1967:262–263, Cook 1940, vol.III. 232–235.

mysteries there, but there were also cults of the Cabiri on Lemnos itself and a shrine to them near the city of Hephaistia.[26] In one myth, the Cabiri are children or grandchildren of Hephaestus who fled from Lemnos in horror at the women's grisly act.[27] Burkert writes: "From the standpoint of the cult and the pre-Greek perspective, the Argo is the ship of the Cabiri bringing new fire and new life," adding that the Dioskouroi, who accompany Jason, were often identified with the Cabiri.[28] Even Jason's name may point to a connection with the Cabiri or at any rate to Samothrace, since it is hardly different from Iasion, a character who is, in various sources, the husband of Demeter, brother of Dardanus, husband of Cybele, and father of Plutus, and who played a role in the Samothracian mysteries.[29]

The Lemnian city of Hephaistia dedicated its festival of dissolution and renewal to Hephaestus, its patron deity, not to Apollo, and it took place in August, not in winter or early spring as Odysseus' return does. In the *Odyssey* there is no hostility between the sexes (rather, the opposite is the problem in Odysseus' household) and fire does not disappear from Ithaca. In short, there is no question of drawing direct parallels between the *Odyssey* and the Lemnian rites. Moreover, the connections between the myth of the Argonauts and these rites are themselves problematic, though tantalizing. A ship is involved in both cases, and it brings new life to the island. Beyond that core event the analogies and connections are harder to tease out: was the day of bad-smelling women really a part of Hephaistia's festival, one of the nine fireless days? Do the images on Hephaistia's coins necessarily have to do with the city's main festival? What was the role of the Cabiri on the island and how far back does it go? These are all unanswered questions, compounded by the fact that the evidence we have ranges from the myth of the Argonauts, too ancient for us to see its roots, to the observations of a philosopher during the Second Sophistic.

The quality and quantity of the evidence makes any attempt to look at the *Odyssey* through the Lemnian lens more of a mental exercise than an argument. And yet it is striking how much of Burkert's reconstruction is paralleled, piecemeal, in the *Odyssey* and beyond it in visual depictions of Odysseus. On vases Odysseus is surprisingly often depicted wearing a *pilos*, the pointed felt cap worn by Hephaestus and the Cabiri and entirely uncharacteristic of the

---

[26] Excavation reports in *ASAA* 1939/40.223–224, 1941/43.75–105, 1952/54.317–40. See Burkert 1983:194 for further references.

[27] Photius, *Lexicon* s.v. Κάβειροι.

[28] Burkert 1983:195.

[29] *Odyssey* 5.125–128, Hesiod *Theogony* 969–974, *Catalogue of Women* fr. 185.6 MW, Hellanicus FGrH 4 F 23, Diodorus Siculus 5.48–49.

other epic heroes. In Boeotia, scenes involving Odysseus appear repeatedly on the distinctively grotesque vases from the Cabirion, and although nothing concrete is known about the connection between Odysseus and the Cabiri, there must have been one.[30]

On Lemnos, King Thoas is the son of Dionysus, and the same god, who is rarely on stage in Homer, may be lurking behind the scenes in the *Odyssey*. Suitors are repeatedly depicted as drinking, and when the first of them, Antinoos, is struck down by Odysseus' arrow the drinking cup falls out of his hand (22.17). The suitors also suffer from terror and mental distraction, and although it is Athena, not Dionysus, who afflicts them, the description of their fright has a distinctly Dionysiac flavor, including even the *oistros*, the gadfly, which often appears in connection with Dionysus and is so common a metaphor for frenzy that the word itself acquired the meaning 'madness':[31]

> δὴ τότ' Ἀθηναίη φθισίμβροτον αἰγίδ' ἀνέσχεν
> ὑψόθεν ἐξ ὀροφῆς· τῶν δὲ φρένες ἐπτοίηθεν.
> οἱ δ' ἐφέβοντο κατὰ μέγαρον βόες ὣς ἀγελαῖαι·
> τὰς μέν τ' αἰόλος οἶστρος ἐφορμηθεὶς ἐδόνησεν
> ὥρῃ ἐν εἰαρινῇ, ὅτε τ' ἤματα μακρὰ πέλονται·

(*Odyssey* 23.297–301)

And then from high above on the roof Athena held up
  her aegis
that destroys mortals. Then their minds grew distraught,
and they stampeded all over the hall, like cows in a herd
when a darting horse-fly attacks them and sends them spinning,
in the season of spring, when the days are long.

[30] The most famous vase is a black-figure *skyphos* from the fourth or late fifth century BCE (Oxford, Ashmolean Museum G249) which shows on one side Odysseus and Circe at her loom; on the other side Odysseus (inscribed Olyteus) is shown on an improvised raft holding a trident and being blown along by Boreas (inscribed Borias): Wolters and Bruns 1940:109. There are several other Cabirion vases with Odysseus, including, for example, another *skyphos* from the fourth century with Odysseus and Circe and Odysseus' companions turned into swine (Nauplion, Archaeological Museum 144) and yet another *skyphos* with Odysseus, Circe, a loom, and vines (University of Mississippi P116, Wolters and Bruns 1940:100). The initial publication of ceramics from the Cabirion is Wolters and Bruns 1940, augmented by Braun and Haevernick 1981. Braun (Braun and Haevernick 1981:26–29) suggests that these caricature images may represent scenes from Middle Comedy, and is followed in this assessment by Webster and Green (1978:39). Schachter (1986:99) notes, in support of this idea, that the *cavea* at the site was enlarged during the same period when most of the Cabirion-ware vases were produced. See Schachter 1986:99–100 on theatrical performances at the Cabirion during the *panegyris*.
[31] Levaniouk 2007:190–191.

Thracian wine also plays an all-important role in the cave of the Cyclops (*Odyssey* 9.198, 345–374). Is it an accident that the name Thoas also appears in the *Odyssey*? The Aetolian Thoas, who in Odysseus' lying tale runs off and leaves behind his cloak, is not so remarkable a character in the *Iliad* as to justify his inclusion in the ambush along with big-shots like Odysseus and Menelaos. It has been suggested that his appearance in the *Odyssey* is completely ad hoc, has no traditional background, and is simply invited by his name, which means 'swift'. Alternatively, it may be rhetorically advantageous for Odysseus to describe an Aetolian being deceived, since Eumaeus reports being taken in by an 'Aetolian man' (*Odyssey* 14.379). But the Aetolian Thoas is also a grandson of Oineus, whose name is derived from the word for 'wine', suggesting that in this case too, as clearly in the case of the Lemnian Thoas, this swiftness is specifically of Dionysiac nature. What went into the choice of Thoas will remain a mystery, but it is at least possible that the name was felt to have connotations appropriate to the moment. Casting off one's cloak and running seems to be a pattern, since it is repeated in the *Iliad*, where the person doing it is none other than Odysseus himself. This may seem (or be) too slight a connection to justify any talk of traditional collocation, but it equally well may be just such a collocation, its outlines faint only because we are lacking so much of the relevant lore. To make things even more complicated, Odysseus runs in order to stop the Achaeans from leaving and to call them back to order, and the person whom he has to chastise most personally is another Aetolian, Thersites, whom Odysseus beats and threatens with taking away his cloak and *khiton* (*Iliad* 2.261–262). Was there actually something specifically Aetolian about casting off one's cloak and running? The circle of associations closes with the interaction of Odysseus and Thoas beyond Homer: just as Odysseus hits Thersites in the *Iliad*, so Thoas thoroughly thrashes Odysseus in the Cycle, in order to make him unrecognizable.[32] A version of the same story is present in the *Odyssey*: Odysseus dresses up as a beggar and enters Troy where he is recognized by Helen alone (4.244–258). The assistance of Thoas is not mentioned, perhaps because being bruised, even voluntarily, does not enhance Odysseus' nobility. Beyond the

---

[32] Scholia to Lycophron 780. The scholiast first reports a story in which Odysseus persuades Thoas to strike him with violent blows (πληγαῖς βιαίαις) in order to make him unrecognizable. This seems to echo the account of the episode in *Odyssey* 4, where Odysseus disfigures himself with 'unseemly blows' (πληγῇσιν ἀεικελίῃσι, *Odyssey* 4.244). Then the scholiast comments specifically on what is reported in the *Little Iliad*. Presumably the part about Odysseus' request is also from the *Little Iliad*, but that is not clear from the scholia. What is definitely ascribed to the author of the *Little Iliad* is that Thoas wounded Odysseus (ὁ τὴν μικρὰν Ἰλιάδα γράψας φησὶ τρωθῆναι τὸν Ὀδυσσέα ὑπὸ Θόαντος, ὅτε εἰς Τροίαν ἀνήρχοντο), and possibly scarred him with sticks (the text is corrupt here).

Odyssey, however, Odysseus has a definite tendency toward the comedic and grotesque, and it is possible that in other poems he cut quite a different figure from his Odyssean self. In any case, his associations with the Aetolians may have some reality behind them, since Odysseus also has a cultic connection to the region. Aristotle mentions that there was an oracle of Odysseus among the Eurytanes in Aetolia.[33]

In the Lemnian myth a herald named Aithalides negotiates between the women and the Argonauts, and Odysseus too seems to have peculiarly strong ties with heralds. He describes for Penelope the herald Eurybates, who followed him from Ithaca to Troy, and adds that he was close to Odysseus (*Odyssey* 19.244–248). This Eurybates appears in the *Iliad* as well, in Book 2, precisely when Odysseus, in a hurry to stop the Achaeans from fleeing, flings away his cloak and runs. Eurybates picks up the cloak (*Iliad* 2.183–184). As with Thoas, one may wonder whether the fact that Eurybates appears in connection with a cloak in both poems is a coincidence or a result of the association of ideas whose meaning is no longer transparent. It seems more prudent and realistic to assume that there is something here we are missing than to accept such an intricate network of coincidences.

In Apollonius Rhodius, Aithalides is a Thessalian, but his only moment in the limelight comes on Lemnos, when he approaches Hypsipyle on behalf of the Argonauts. It is on this occasion that Apollonius tells of Aithalides's unusual fate: as a gift from his father Hermes, the herald has an unfailing memory, which he will keep even in the Underworld, and in addition to this, his soul will alternate between being in Hades and being among the living. The same information regarding Aithalides was known to Pherecydes.[34] Burkert sees a connection between the name Aithalides and the fact that

---

[33] Scholia to Lycophron 799: (Aristotle fr. 508 Rose) Ἀριστοτέλης φησὶν ἐν Ἰθακησίων πολιτείᾳ Εὐρυτᾶνας ἔθνος εἶναι τῆς Αἰτωλίας ὀνομασθὲν ἀπὸ Εὐρύτονος (Εὐρύτου Tzetz. ad Lyc. p. 790 Müller), παρ' οἷς εἶναι μαντεῖον Ὀδυσσέως.

[34] Apollonius Rhodius 1.641–651, Pherecydes FGrH 3 F 109 = Scholia to Apollonius Rhodius 1.641. Unfortunately, neither Pherecydes nor Apollonius comment further on this strange fate, reminiscent of the Dioskouroi (who are also among the Argonauts). Aithalides has one more distinction: Pythagoras claimed that the herald was his own pre-Trojan incarnation (followed by Euphorbus, Hermotimos, Pyrrhos, and finally Pythagoras), presumably in connection with Hermes' gift which supposedly allowed the soul of Aithalides to remember all of its past lives and intermittent sojourns among the dead as it continued to migrate into new bodies (Diogenes Laertius, *Vitae Philosophorum* 8.4–5.). The form of the name, Aithalides, is puzzling: it looks like a patronymic or a clan or guild-name (of the Eupatridai, Homeridai type), but, being the son of Hermes, Aithalides does not have an ancestry that would explain the name. Stephanus Grammaticus (46.21) reports that the deme Aithalidai was part of the Leontis phyle in Athens, and that its name derived from Aithalides.

Lemnos was called Aithale ('the sooty one'). Both names are derived from *aithale*, 'soot, ashes', and seem fitting for the island of Hephaestus, especially since Stephanus of Byzantium connects the name Aithale with metallurgy.[35] The festival of Hephaistia has to do with fire, and the root *aith-* fits into this context. This is, of course, also the root of Odysseus' assumed name, Aithon, and of the bird-name *aithuia*, in whose guise Ino-Leukothea assists Odysseus in his return to the living by saving him from death at sea (*Odyssey* 5.337). What makes these connections seem noteworthy is partly the fact that all these words are relatively rare and partly the fact that both personal names, Aithalides and Aithon, are associated with return from the dead. Ino-Leukothea certainly shares this association. This suggests that the root *aith-* was associated with the notion of survival and return from the dead. Or, to put it in another way, it is possible that when fire and burning were associated with this notion, ritually and otherwise, they tended to be denoted by the root *aith-*. Odysseus' salvation with Ino's help is certainly metaphorically expressed in the *Odyssey* through the image of fire. When Odysseus finally reaches the shores of Skheria, he finds some dense bushes and makes a shelter for himself under their branches. As he falls asleep there under a pile of dry leaves, Odysseus is compared to a firebrand concealed by ashes:

ὡς δ' ὅτε τις δαλὸν σποδιῇ ἐνέκρυψε μελαίνῃ
ἀγροῦ ἐπ' ἐσχατιῆς, ᾧ μὴ πάρα γείτονες ἄλλοι,
σπέρμα πυρὸς σῴζων, ἵνα μή ποθεν ἄλλοθεν αὔοι,
ὣς Ὀδυσεὺς φύλλοισι καλύψατο.

(*Odyssey* 5.488–491)

As when someone conceals a firebrand under the black ashes,
far away in the country, where there are no neighbors,
saving the seed of the fire so that he will never have to
    rekindle it from elsewhere.
That is how Odysseus concealed himself under the leaves.

In another instance of a striking echo, the language used in Book 5 to describe Odysseus' makeshift refuge is repeated almost exactly in Book 19, when Odysseus as Aithon is already on Ithaca. There, the thicket conceals not Odysseus himself, but the boar, who leaps out of his lair with fire in his

---

[35] Stephanus Byzantius 46.10, Polybius 34.11.4. There were other places of the same name: Stephanus reports an 'Etruscan island' (νῆσος Τυρσηνῶν, 46.5) called Aithale because iron was produced there (he also connects the Lemnian byname with metallurgy).

eyes to inflict the identity-laden thigh wound on Odysseus and be killed by him (*Odyssey* 19.439–454).

Odysseus' helper Ino has a strong connection with Dionysus, (she is the god's nurse in myth), and might have connections to Samothrace, just as Lemnos is connected to it through the Cabiri.[36] At any rate, the connection between the Ino episode in the *Odyssey* and mysteries on Samothrace was perceived by one of the scholiasts. Odysseus receives a veil from Ino and has to tie it around his torso to swim safely to shore. This veil was compared in antiquity to the ribbon tied around the torso of initiates at Samothrace, whose initiation, it was believed, protected them from drowning. In the *Odyssey* and beyond, Ino is a figure who has to do with transcending death, as she herself does: born a mortal, she leaps to her death into the sea and is transformed into Leukothea, the white goddess. Progression from mortal to divine, the experience of death, and the transcending of it are all features typical of mystery cult, and in that sense Ino might well have affinities with the mysteries of the Cabiri. In any case, the co-occurrence of the *aith-* words, fire and returns from the dead both in the *Odyssey* and in the Lemnian myth is striking.

According to Pindar, the race in armor at the Argonaut games on Lemnos is won by Erginos, whose hair is gray as if with age (*Olympian* 4.19–26). According to the scholia, Erginos is first mocked by the women for competing with the young, but then demonstrates his actual age in the contests.[37] Burkert sees here a hint at Hephaestus' victory in his own city, since the name Erginos, 'Worker', seems appropriate for the god.[38] This is another point of contact within the *Odyssey*, the notion of an older man winning in competition with the young, or perhaps of a man seeming old but in fact being young. Odysseus wins both against the Phaeacian youths and against the suitors. The games on Skheria, moreover, are followed by the song of Ares and Aphrodite, where

---

[36] Apollodorus 3.4, 3.28, Pausanias 1.44.8, 2.1.3, Zenobius Cent. 4.38, Tzetzes Scholia to Lycophron 107, 229–231, Scholia to *Iliad* 8.86, Scholia to *Odyssey* 5.334, Scholia to Euripides *Medea* 1284–1289, Hyginus *Fabulae* 2.4, Ovid *Fasti* 6.481–498, Servius on *Aeneid* 5.241. Ino's frantic flight from her maddened husband, Athamas, and her final jump into the sea are also Dionysiac, and paralleled by the god himself in the *Iliad* (6.135–136). Jeanmaire saw in Ino a prototypical maenad (1951:208–210); see also Henrichs 1978:137–143. On Ino's flight see further Burkert 1983:178, and on chase as part of Dionysiac ritual see Burkert 1983:178. See also above, n24, on Dionysiac rushing. Curiously enough, Ino also seems to have a negative connection to the Aetolians, since the latter were excluded, along with slaves, from the precinct at Chaeronea. Plutarch gives an *aition* for this custom: Ino went mad out of jealousy, because she suspected Athamas of having an affair with a slave girl, who was an Aetolian by the name of Antiphera (Plutarch *Greek Questions* 267D).

[37] Scholia to Pindar, *Olympian* 4, scholion 32c.

[38] Burkert 1983:195.

Hephaestus appears in person and triumphs over a younger and mightier god.[39] This has long been seen as a reflection on Odysseus, though the parallel is not exact (Odysseus does not do on Ithaca what Hephaestus does in the song).[40] Still, the very appearance of Hephaestus, and the fact that in the song the apparently weak and older craftsman is, if not more, then certainly no less capable than the young and powerful Ares, is indeed reminiscent of Lemnian notions about the god, as reconstructed by Burkert. Moreover, Odysseus' repeatedly mentioned skill at carpentry also allies him with both Erginos and Hephaestus, both artisans. In a scene that has already been mentioned above, Odysseus wins a race at the funeral games of Patroklos, and Antilokhos, a youth, comments on the unusual fact that an older man, his hair half-gray, is faster than the young. In Pindar's *Olympian* 4, Erginos also triumphs in speed, and claims that his gray hair is no indication of age:

οὗτος ἐγὼ ταχυτᾶτι·
χεῖρες δὲ καὶ ἦτορ ἴσον. φύονται δὲ καὶ νέοις
ἐν ἀνδράσιν πολιαί
θαμάκι παρὰ τὸν ἁλικίας ἐοικότα χρόνον.

(Olympian 4.24–26)

> Such am I in speed.
> My hands and heart are equally good. Even
>   on young men
> gray hair often grows
> before the fitting time of their age.

Here, Erginos only gets a crown, but there is little doubt that in other versions of the story he must have received a cloak too, since these are the same games on Lemnos which elsewhere, including in Pindar, are said to have cloaks for prizes.[41]

---

[39] See above, pp72-74.

[40] On the relevance and resonance of the Song of Ares and Aphrodite, see, e.g, Braswell 1982, Alden 1997.

[41] Erginos has a speaking name which is reminiscent of another mythological carpenter, Polytekhnos, whose name, in turn, is reminiscent of Odysseus' characteristic epithets, *polymetis* and *polytropos*. Polytekhnos, moreover, is reminiscent of Odysseus in other ways. He is married to Aedon, and the couple is extremely well-matched and happy until they become too complacent and boast that their marriage is better than that of Zeus and Hera (Antoninus Liberalis 11, Boeus fr. 1229.8 Powell 1229.8 Powell). Needless to say, the gods destroy the marriage. As I will argue below, Penelope also has a name derived from a bird-name, and shares certain features with Aedon. Moreover, as has already been mentioned, she also thinks that the jealousy of the gods is the source of her and her husband's trouble. In different ways, Odysseus has points of

The mental exercise of teasing out similar elements in a Lemnian myth and festival complex and in Odysseus' return does reveal unexpected points of contact. Elements such as the prominence of the root *aith-* or the superior speed of a white-haired hero are especially valuable because they are not obviously motivated by their immediate contexts. There is no clear reason why Ino should appear as an *aithuia* and not some other bird, or why Odysseus should win the footrace in the *Iliad*. These are points of contact, though not necessarily of direct contact. There is no reason to think that the *Odyssey* was influenced by Lemnian myth or ritual, or vice versa. It is more likely that what the comparison reveals are elements of a cultural vocabulary that was used at different times, in different ways, and in different places to communicate related ideas. The Lemnian festival and the *Odyssey* can be seen as two different utterances that both make use of this traditional vocabulary, and there must have been other such utterances that are lost to us.

Tracing the connotations of Odysseus' cloak has lead to a wide range of associations congruent with themes and notions already present in the Third Cretan Lie. The cloak adds another element to these themes and plays its own role in the conversation. Like everything else Odysseus says to Penelope, his description of the cloak is not just a recollection, nor even just a sign for his wife, though it is all these things. In the setting of Apollo's festival and in the context of so many other ritual hints, signals, and echoes, the cloak-speech acquires special weight and potency. It also, like everything else Odysseus says, becomes a speech act in the sense that by saying it Odysseus takes part in Apollo's festival and enacts, within its ritual framework, his own return. In addition to its immediate function of making Penelope recognize Odysseus' clothes and confirming the beggar's identity, the cloak is part of a deeper communication between Odysseus and his internal and external audiences, because it is a part of an intricate, variable, but resilient and probably very ancient complex of ideas.

---

contract with two carpenters, Polytekhnos and Erginos, suggesting that his own carpentry skills have deep mythological roots.

CHAPTER EIGHT

THE PIN

A S REMARKABLE AS THE CLOAK ITSELF IS the golden pin Odysseus uses to fasten it, another object Penelope herself gave to Odysseus on departure:

χλαῖναν πορφυρέην οὔλην ἔχε δῖος Ὀδυσσεύς,
διπλῆν· ἐν δ' ἄρα οἱ περόνη χρυσοῖο τέτυκτο
αὐλοῖσιν διδύμοισι· πάροιθε δὲ δαίδαλον ἦεν·
ἐν προτέροισι πόδεσσι κύων ἔχε ποικίλον ἑλλόν,
ἀσπαίροντα λάων· τὸ δὲ θαυμάζεσκον ἅπαντες,
ὡς οἱ χρύσεοι ἐόντες ὁ μὲν λάε νεβρὸν ἀπάγχων,
αὐτὰρ ὁ ἐκφυγέειν μεμαὼς ἤσπαιρε πόδεσσι.

(*Odyssey* 19.225–232)

Odysseus wore a woolen purple cloak,
a two-fold one, and in it was a pin of gold,
with double grooves, and on the front was
    a marvelous design:
a dog held a dappled fawn in its front paws,
grasping it as it struggled. And everyone admired it,
how, though they were golden, the dog grasped the fawn,
    strangling it,
while the fawn thrashed with its feet, trying to escape.[1]

Like the cloak, the pin has an obvious role within the dialogue – it is a sign (*semata*, 19.250) for Penelope. As we feel wonder at the intricate object and the thrilling hunting scene it depicts we may also wonder, along with Penelope, at her guest's very ability to describe it in such detail. The implication of this ecphrastic feat is surely not that the Cretan stranger has a photographic memory, but that he is none other than the former wearer of the pin. Beyond

---

[1] See below on the translation of λάω.

this, however, the description of the pin sends a more complex message to its audiences, both external and internal. Like much else in this densely packed conversation, the pin fits into the mythic and ritual framework of the approaching festival, evoking yet another related nexus of ideas, and interacting with multiple elements both in the *Odyssey* itself and beyond.

The pin itself appears to combine several realistic features into an imaginary object and several brooches have been proposed as close parallels. The general consensus is that this type of a pin requires techniques belonging to the late eighth or seventh century, though attempts have been made to compare it with archaeological finds of all periods, from Minoan gems to Etruscan brooches.[2] The bigger problem, however, has to do not with the type of object, but with the language used to describe it. It has to be acknowledged that there is at least one lexical difficulty that has not been solved, namely the meaning of the verb λάω. Lexica list 'grip' as one of its meanings, but this is only a guess based on our passage alone. Worse still, the other meanings of the verb, 'to see' and 'to cry', are also badly attested, so that the status of λάω as a full-fledged verb is altogether doubtful.[3] In the sense 'to cry', the verb may be a poetic back-formation from λεληκώς (in reality from λάσκω), while the sense 'to see' may result from a reinterpretation of the expression ὀξὺ λάων (from 'loudly crying' to 'sharply seeing'). This expression is used about an eagle in the *Homeric Hymn to Hermes* (360) in a context where sight is important, and this and other such instances could form the basis of a reinterpretation. On the other hand, Hesychius does attest a λάω meaning to see, and the possibility should be considered that it is simply another such verb, though one with unclear etymology.

In either case, the meaning of λάω in *Odyssey* 19 remains problematic. Russo suggests that 'to see' fits the context better since "it is more difficult to imagine a visual depiction of a dog's bark than of his fierce look."[4] Such considerations cannot be decisive, but there is another difficulty with the meaning 'to bark', namely that it would result in syntactical awkwardness in line 229,

---

[2] Nilsson 1933:123–125, Lorimer 1950:511–515, Roes 1951:216–222, Russo 1992:88 ad loc.

[3] Leumann (1950:233–6) observes the similarity between the two poetic expressions, ὀξὺ λάων and ὀξὺ λεληκώς and explains λάω in the sense 'to cry' as an artificial poetic back-formation from the participle form λεληκώς. The verb λάω 'to cry' is also suspiciously similar to another verb, attested as a gloss in Hesychius, namely λαίω, meaning 'to bark', a meaning which would perhaps better suit the Odyssean dog. In contrast to λάω, λαίω has a good etymology: it is cognate with Vedic *rajati*, Lithuanian *lóti* and Slavic *lajati*, all meaning 'to bark', and appears in Avestan, probably meaning 'to shout', in the compound *gathro.raiiant* (Yt.13.105). Perhaps the existence of λαίω encouraged the poetic formation of metrically different λάω.

[4] Russo 1992:89 ad loc.

where the participle λάων appears to be transitive. The meaning 'to see', for its part, does not complicate the syntax, but seems strangely anticlimactic, although it is possible to imagine a dog staring at the convulsions of its prey. Still, it is easy to see why some modern commentators insist on taking λάω as 'to grasp', even though there is no evidence for such a meaning beyond our passage.[5] It is also easy to see why this verb caused scholarly disagreement already in antiquity.[6] The problem still awaits a satisfactory solution.[7]

In addition to the unexplained verb, the pin ecphrasis involves a Homeric hapax, ἐλλός, in line 228. In this case, the meaning and the etymology are clear enough (the word is derived from ἔλαφος and must be synonymous with νεβρός),[8] but the rarity of the word is impressive. Apart from this instance, the word appears primarily in lexica, etymological works, and once in a mythographical work by Antoninus Liberalis (28.3). The pin is thus a prime example of the unusual and difficult diction that characterizes this part of the poem.

But if the background and precise impact of this unusual diction is hard to discern, something can nevertheless be said about its resonance in the *Odyssey*. First and foremost, an analogy suggests itself between Odysseus and the dog, the suitors and the fawn.[9] In a repeated simile, the suitors are compared to suckling fawns in a lion's lair, which seems to reflect the situation in the *Odyssey*:

> ὡς δ' ὁπότ' ἐν ξυλόχῳ ἔλαφος κρατεροῖο λέοντος
> νεβροὺς κοιμήσασα νεηγενέας γαλαθηνοὺς
> κνημοὺς ἐξερέῃσι καὶ ἄγκεα ποιήεντα
> βοσκομένη, ὁ δ' ἔπειτα ἐὴν εἰσήλυθεν εὐνήν,
> ἀμφοτέροισι δὲ τοῖσιν ἀεικέα πότμον ἐφῆκεν.
>
> (*Odyssey* 4.334–338 = 17.126–130)

> As when a doe puts her fawns, newly born and still suckling,
> to sleep in a lion's lair

---

[5] Rutherford 1992:170.

[6] Both the scholia and Eustathius record diverging opinions of Aristarchus and Crates on this matter: Aristarchus understood λάων as ἀντὶ τοῦ ἀπολαύων, while others, among them Crates, took it as ἀντὶ τοῦ βλέπων (Scholia on the *Odyssey* 19.229.1, Eustathius 2.200 on *Odyssey* 19.229). Hesychius s.v. λάων appears to clarify Aristarchus's gloss ἀπολαυστικῶς ἔχων as ἐσθίων and adds a further twist to the matter by mentioning yet another interpretation: some take the verb to mean 'to lap, lick with the tongue' (οἱ δὲ λάπτων τῇ γλώττῃ).

[7] Perhaps λάω, 'to bark', could refer here to the dog's open mouth, with which it is strangling the fawn, thus 'grasping with its teeth'.

[8] Chantraine 1968 s.v. ἔλαφος.

[9] Rutherford 1992:170 ad loc.

and goes to search though the hills and grassy glens,
grazing. And then the lion comes back to his sleeping place
and brings ugly destruction to both of them.

The biologically improbable fact that the doe beds her young in a lion's den is a distinctive feature of these Odyssean similes, and it reflects specifically the fact that the suitors are in Odysseus' house (Menelaos, who utters the simile in Book 4, makes this explicit). This seems, however, to be a variation on a traditional theme, since there is also a simile in the *Iliad* with a lion coming upon a doe's hiding place and destroying the fawns:

ὡς δὲ λέων ἐλάφοιο ταχείης νήπια τέκνα
ῥηϊδίως συνέαξε λαβὼν κρατεροῖσιν ὀδοῦσιν
ἐλθὼν εἰς εὐνήν, ἀπαλόν τέ σφ' ἦτορ ἀπηύρα·

(*Iliad* 11.113–115)

Just as a lion easily crushes the innocent young of a swift doe,
when he comes upon their lair, taking them in his powerful
        teeth
and ripping out their soft hearts.

In the *Iliad*, the deer is the quintessential hunted animal, ever fearful and swift, and prey to people with their dogs as much as to lions. When Achilles is chasing Hektor around the walls of Troy he is compared to a determined dog running down a fawn (*Iliad* 22.188–192). In the *Odyssey*, Odysseus has a special connection to hunting dogs and in Book 19 he will emerge as a hunter, accompanied by dogs, in the recollections of his youthful boar hunt on Mount Parnassus:

οἱ δ' ἐς βῆσσαν ἵκανον ἐπακτῆρες· πρὸ δ' ἄρ' αὐτῶν
ἴχνι' ἐρευνῶντες κύνες ἤϊσαν, αὐτὰρ ὄπισθεν
υἱέες Αὐτολύκου· μετὰ τοῖσι δὲ δῖος Ὀδυσσεὺς
ἤϊεν ἄγχι κυνῶν, κραδάων δολιχόσκιον ἔγχος.

(*Odyssey* 19.435–438)

The hunters came into the wood and the dogs ran ahead
        past them,
searching out the tracks, while behind were the sons
        of Autolykos.
And among them went godlike Odysseus,
close behind the dogs, brandishing his long spear.

It is noteworthy that on two occasions in the *Odyssey*, one of them on the day of Apollo's festival, Telemachus also appears with a spear and in the company of dogs, as if to indicate that he too is a hunter and therefore a man, not a child:

> Τηλέμαχος δ' ἄρ' ἔπειτα διὲκ μεγάροιο βεβήκει
> ἔγχος ἔχων· ἄμα τῷ γε κύνες πόδας ἀργοὶ ἔποντο
>
> (*Odyssey* 17.61–62)[10]

> And then Telemachus went through the house,
> holding his spear. And the swift-footed dogs went along
>   with him.

Moreover, the opposition between the hunting dogs and the other kinds of dogs is active and operative in this part of the *Odyssey*, and it is articulated by Odysseus himself at the very moment when he enters his household for the first time in twenty years. The scene in question is the only instant and complete recognition of Odysseus on Ithaca – by his dog Argos. Looking at his old hunting companion lying on a pile of dung, Odysseus asks about his speed and in so doing makes a distinction between fast hunting dogs and the decorative dogs who fidget under their masters' feet at dinner:

> καλὸς μὲν δέμας ἐστίν, ἀτὰρ τόδε γ' οὐ σάφα οἶδα,
> ἢ δὴ καὶ ταχὺς ἔσκε θέειν ἐπὶ εἴδεϊ τῷδε,
> ἦ αὔτως οἷοί τε τραπεζῆες κύνες ἀνδρῶν
> γίνοντ', ἀγλαΐης δ' ἕνεκεν κομέουσιν ἄνακτες.
>
> (*Odyssey* 17.307–310)

> His body is excellent, but it is not clear to me
> whether in addition to his appearance he is also swift
>   at running,
> or whether he is just one of those table dogs men have,
> whose masters keep them for the sake of their beauty.

In his reply, Eumaeus stresses Argos' former hunting qualities, especially his ability to run fast (*Odyssey* 17.312–317). The expression κύνες ἀργοί, 'swift dogs' (used in connection with Telemachus, once with a modification), has

---

[10] Cf. *Odyssey* 2.10–11: βῆ ῥ' ἴμεν εἰς ἀγορήν, παλάμῃ δ' ἔχε χάλκεον ἔγχος, | οὐκ οἶος, ἄμα τῷ γε δύω κύνες ἀργοὶ ἔποντο.

roots of Indo-European antiquity, and the word used for 'fast' in this formula is also the source of the name Ἄργος, by the minimal means of accent shift.[11]

When Odysseus enters his house, the first being to see him and be seen by him is a quintessential hunting dog. Argos is also the dog of Odysseus' youth and the fact that he dies at the very moment of his master's return seems to mark the end of the hunter-Odysseus as he used to be on Ithaca before his departure and the beginning of the new, returned, hero.[12] Of the youths currently in Odysseus' house only Telemachus appears equipped as a hunter, while the suitors are mostly distinguished by their attachment to Odysseus' table, so that an analogy is drawn between Odysseus, Telemachus, and the hunting dogs, on the one hand, and the suitors and the table dogs on the other.

The speed of hunting dogs goes hand in hand with the nimble feet of their hunting companions, the young men. In the *Iliad*, it is the youngest of the Achaeans, Antilokhos, who is compared to a hunting dog, and the point of comparison is again his speed. Menelaos asks Antilokhos whether he could run out and hit one of the Trojans, since he is the youngest and fastest of all the Achaeans:

> Ἀντίλοχ' οὔ τις σεῖο νεώτερος ἄλλος Ἀχαιῶν,
> οὔτε ποσὶν θάσσων οὔτ' ἄλκιμος ὡς σὺ μάχεσθαι.
>
> (*Iliad* 15.569–570)

> Antilokhos, there is no one younger than you among
>   the Achaeans,
> nor anyone quicker on his feet, nor as brave as you
>   at fighting.

Antilokhos then rushes (ἔθορε, 15.573) out of the front ranks, kills a Trojan with a spear throw, and runs up to despoil him, like a hunting dog. The dog in the simile chases a fawn:

> Ἀντίλοχος δ' ἐπόρουσε κύων ὥς, ὅς τ' ἐπὶ νεβρῷ
> βλημένῳ ἀΐξῃ, τόν τ' ἐξ εὐνῆφι θορόντα
> θηρητὴρ ἐτύχησε βαλών, ὑπέλυσε δὲ γυῖα
>
> (*Iliad* 15.579–581)

---

[11] Schultze 1933:124 compared Vedic r̥jíśvan- ἀργίποδας κύνας (*Iliad* 24.211), κύνας ἀργούς (*Iliad* 1.50), κύνες πόδας ἀργοί (*Iliad* 18.578). For further comments, see Watkins 1995:172.

[12] At Kalydon, there was a κυνὸς σῆμα, supposedly the grave of Atalanta's dog Aura, who was killed by the boar: Pollux 5.45. Here too, perhaps, the death and burial of the dog mark the end of the hunt.

> Antilokhos rushed at him, as a dog leaps upon
>> a wounded fawn,
> whom a hunter has struck as he darted from his lair,
> and has loosened the limbs under him.

The animals of this Iliadic simile are the same as those on Odysseus' pin, confirming the intuition of the scholia that the pin points both to Odysseus' youth and to his 'education' as a hunter: οὕτω γὰρ οἱ εὐγενεῖς τῶν νέων ἐπαιδεύοντο, 'for this is how the noble young men used to be educated'.[13]

The hunting scene on the pin seems to be a vivid reminder of what Odysseus used to be before leaving for Troy. But if the young Odysseus was a hunter, what about the beggar who is now sitting before Penelope? The remarkable thing is that as he describes the dog and the fawn on his old pin, Odysseus is himself dressed in a deerskin, since such is the begging costume created for him by Athena:

> ἀμφὶ δέ μιν ῥάκος ἄλλο κακὸν βάλεν ἠδὲ χιτῶνα,
> ῥωγαλέα ῥυπόωντα, κακῷ μεμορυγμένα καπνῷ·
> ἀμφὶ δέ μιν μέγα δέρμα ταχείης ἕσσ' ἐλάφοιο,
> ψιλόν· δῶκε δέ οἱ σκῆπτρον καὶ ἀεικέα πήρην.
>
> *(Odyssey* 13.434–437)

> And she threw around him a horrible tattered cloth
>> and a torn
> squalid *khiton*, sullied with foul smoke,
> and she clothed him in the large, smooth-worn skin
>> of a swift deer.
> And she gave him a staff, and an ugly sack.

Not only are Odysseus' tattered rags in sharp contrast with the splendid cloak and *khiton* he recalls, but the deerskin seems to make him the very opposite of his former hunting self. The detail of the deerskin is curious because nobody else in Homer wears such a garment, and even outside of Homer it is extremely unusual for a male: only the bacchants regularly wear the spotted hide of the fawn, *nebris*. Putting on an animal hide is often a symbolic act equating, fully or partially, the human and the animal. Thus Paris wears a leopard skin and Menelaos a lion skin when they confront each other, and

---

[13] Scholia to the *Odyssey* 2.10. For a discussion of hunting as a pre-military training for young men, see Barringer 2001:10–69. See Isler-Kerényi 2001:135 on Dionysus as patron of young men engaged in hunting.

the characteristics of the two animals mirror those of the two heroes.[14] Even more clearly, Dolon wears a wolf's skin in the Doloneia episode, uniquely in Homer, and he is depicted in this attire on vases, sometimes also standing on all fours and plainly playing the wolf.[15] The hide transforms its wearer, literally or metaphorically, into the animal, and the boundaries between literal and metaphorical can be very fluid.

Another example of a male in a deerskin is Aktaion, who, according to Stesichorus, is clothed in one by Artemis:

Στησίχορος δὲ ὁ Ἱμεραῖος ἔγραψεν ἐλάφου περιβαλεῖν δέρμα
Ἀκταίωνι τὴν θεόν, παρασκευάζουσάν οἱ τὸν ἐκ τῶν κυνῶν
θάνατον, ἵνα δὴ μὴ γυναῖκα Σεμέλην λάβοι.

(Pausanias 9.2.3 = Stesichorus PMG 236)

> Stesichorus of Himera wrote that the goddess threw a skin of a deer
> around Aktaion, preparing for him death by his hounds, in order
> that he might not take Semele as wife.

As Nagy argues, this is a way of describing the transformation of Aktaion into a stag.[16] The iconography of Aktaion is such that he is most often depicted not as a deer, but as his human self attacked by the dogs.[17] On some of these depictions he wears a deerskin, sometimes has horns, and on one vase he is depicted in a complete deer costume including a deer-head hat.[18] Rather than

---

[14] Naiden 1999.

[15] Dolon on all fours: Attic *lekythos* ca.480–470 BCE in Paris (Louvre CA 1802, LIMC Dolon 2), a terracotta plaque from Curti, near Capua, probably third century BCE (Munich, Antikenslg., LIMC Dolon 3). Dolon wearing wolf pelt with the animal's head covering his head, Herakles-style: Attic red figure cup, ca. 490–480 BCE (St. Petersburg, Hermitage 1542, LIMC Dolon 13). On identification between heroes and animals in similes and on the analogy between the simile and the mask, see Schnapp-Gourbeillon 1981. On Dolon as wolf, see Gernet 1981:125–140.

[16] Nagy 1990:263–265.

[17] Bowra 1961:99–100, 125–26, Richter 1950 fig. 411.

[18] The depictions of Aktaion's metamorphosis begin to appear on vases around the middle of the fifth century, while the earlier depictions represent him as wholly human. Examples of vases with Aktaion clothed in deerskin include an amphora attributed to the Eucharides Painter (Hamburg, Museum für Kunst und Gewerbe 1966.3, ca. 490–480 BCE), and a *pelike* from Vulci by the Geras painter (Musée du Louvre G224, c.480 BCE). Aktaion appears in full-body deer costume on fragments of a volute crater attributed to the Pan Painter (Athens, National Museum, Acropolis 760). On the Hamburg *pelike* a doe's head appears above Aktaion's own. It has been suggested that this represents a theater costume and that the depiction as a whole is inspired by theatrical performances (Hoffman 1967:17). Aktaion appears with a pair of horns on an Attic red-figure krater by the Lykaon Painter (Boston, Museum of Fine Arts 00.346, ca. 440 BCE).

proving that Artemis in Stesichorus merely dressed Aktaion in a deerskin instead of transforming him, such depictions seem to me to prove precisely the opposite, namely that wearing a deer skin is a way of expressing the notion of transformation. In the *Odyssey* too, a goddess, Athena, puts the deerskin around the hero's body, though a different verb is used for the action (ἕννυμι rather than περιβάλλω, 13.436). Odysseus is not transformed into a deer, of course, but I suspect that Odysseus' deerskin is still related to Aktaion's and has some of the same meanings.[19]

The central fact of Aktaion's myth in all its various versions is the young man's dreadful death: transformed into a stag, he is torn apart by his own hounds.[20] The reasons for this unalterable event are, in contrast, variable. In the early sources, the earliest being the Hesiodic *Catalogue of Women*, Aktaion desires marriage with Semele. Stesichorus' treatment of the myth follows the same outline: Artemis transforms Aktaion into a deer and causes his gruesome death in order to prevent his marriage to Semele.[21] In both cases Aktaion's transgression seems to have nothing to do directly with Artemis, and it is not clear whether she herself is angered (for whatever reason) by Aktaion's marriage plans, or whether she fulfills the will of Zeus. Nothing is said about Semele's own willingness or not, nor indeed is it clear why Aktaion's desire for Semele should be so terribly punished: is it because Semele belongs to Zeus, or simply because it would be incestuous to marry an aunt? In any case, there is an intriguing parallel to this mysterious plot in the story of Orion as presented by Calypso in *Odyssey* 5:

> ὡς μὲν ὅτ' Ὠρίων' ἕλετο ῥοδοδάκτυλος Ἠώς,
> τόφρα οἱ ἠγάασθε θεοὶ ῥεῖα ζώοντες,
> ἕως μιν ἐν Ὀρτυγίῃ χρυσόθρονος Ἄρτεμις ἁγνὴ
> οἷσ' ἀγανοῖσι βέλεσσιν ἐποιχομένη κατέπεφνεν.

> (*Odyssey* 5.121–124)

> Just as when rosy-fingered Dawn picked Orion,
> you, the easy-living gods, begrudged her this,

---

[19] Frontisi-Ducroux (1997:442–443) observes the similarity between this passage in the *Odyssey* and Stesichorus' language and suggests that the latter deliberately echoes Homer, and that the action of Artemis, like the action of Athena in the *Odyssey*, is deliberately ambiguous: both a metamorphosis and a disguise.

[20] For an analysis of the myth and a detailed discussion of its pictorial representations see Barringer 2001:128–138.

[21] *The Catalogue of Women*: P.Mich. inv. 1447 verso, published by Renner 1978:281–287 and P.Oxy. 2509 (there is disagreement as to whether the latter papyrus belongs to the *Catalogue*: see Heath 1992:8 and 20n13 with references); Stesichorus PMG 236.

until pure, golden-throned Artemis came
and killed him on Ortygia with her gentle arrows.

Here another human, a youthful hunter like Aktaion, becomes the sexual partner of a goddess, (in this case apparently willingly), and is killed by Artemis. Again, there is no explanation as to why Artemis should object to a union between Orion and Eos. Perhaps there is a clue, however, in the fact that both Orion and Aktaion are hunters. One possibility is that Artemis is acting as a patron deity of the hunters, whose sexual behavior is subject to restriction, (an extreme example is Hippolytus in Euripides' play, also a hunter, but the one who shuns Aphrodite and devotes himself fully to Artemis).[22] What is unacceptable to Artemis in Orion's and Aktaion's behavior may be whom they want to marry, or it may be the fact that they want to marry at all. The version of the myth in which Aktaion's transgression consists in chancing upon Artemis bathing is first attested in Callimachus' *Hymn* 5, and is made famous by Ovid.[23] Apollodorus mentions it as the prevalent version, though he also knows the one with Semele.[24] In Euripides' *Bacchae* there is yet another reason for this divine anger: Aktaion boasts that he is a better hunter than Artemis. In all three cases, Aktaion seems to fail to observe the correct etiquette of a hunter, whether by importing sexuality into the hunting sphere or by being arrogant towards the goddess of the hunt.

Apollodorus also reports a version of the myth by Akousilaos, the most interesting feature of which is not the motivation for the murder, but its aftermath: Aktaion's fifty hounds, having devoured their master in a fit of madness, become distraught and look for him. The search brings them to the cave of Chiron, who makes an image of Aktaion and in this way calms the dogs.[25] This apparently human behavior of the dogs may be attested already in Hesiod, depending on the attribution of P.Oxy. 2509, and it is probable that a catalogue of their names, attested in later sources, also goes back to Hesiodic poetry.[26] The lamentation of the dogs for Aktaion is described in curiously human

---

[22] Euripides *Hippolytus* 10–19, 58–113, Burkert 1983:60–61. See Barringer 2001:128–174 on hunting and transgression, invariably involving sexuality (apart from Aktaion, the examples include Kallisto and Meleager).

[23] Callimachus *Hymn* 5.107–118, Ovid *Metamorphoses* 3.128–252.

[24] Apollodorus 3.4.4.

[25] Apollodorus 3.4.4. The grief of the dogs for Aktaion is also mentioned in P.Oxy. 2509, which is probably part of the Hesiodic *Catalogue of Women* (assigned by Lobel 1964, followed by Casanova 1969 and Gallavotti 1969; arguments in support in Janko 1984, rejected by West 1985:88. Translation and a brief discussion of the myth in Heath 1992:7–9).

[26] Apollodorus 3.4.4, Aeschines fr. 423 Mette, Ovid *Metamorphoses* 3.206–224, Hyginus *Fabulae* 181.

terms, and Burkert sees in this a reflection of a ritual that corresponds, in some sense, to the myth: "These animals are performing a human ritual of the sort we find attested again and again: the 'search' for a torn-up victim ending in a symbolic restoration. Aktaion's death is a sacrificial ritual of the hunt, consecrated by the Mistress of the Beasts and performed in the form that had been standard since Palaeolithic times."[27] The dogs, in this case, emerge as a masked secret society, just as Aktaion is transformed into a deer by wearing a deerskin.

The cornerstone of Aktaion's myth is reversal, the transformation of hunter into the hunted. If indeed it is linked, however vaguely, to an ancient ritual as envisaged by Burkert, then the ritual would presumably involve the familiar movement from dissolution to restoration, and Aktaion's drama would fit squarely into the dissolution part. In the *Odyssey* too, the deerskin appears during the dark period of inversion on Ithaca, and it is surrounded by multiple references to the hunt. The logic of reversal seems to be behind Athena's choice of attire for her protégé. Before he can triumph, Odysseus has to sink even deeper than before; before he can regain Penelope's coveted bed he will not accept any bed at all, but sleep on the floor; before he regains his youth and sprouts hyacinth-like hair by Athena's magic he has to lose his hair completely and shrivel into an old man; before he can kill the suitors he has to take their verbal and even physical abuse. By the same token he seems to temporarily masquerade as a deer before he can regain his place as a hunter.

Odysseus' deer hide invites thoughts of Aktaion, and it is hard not to connect it to the beginning of the next episode, because the first thing that happens to Odysseus in his new attire is an attack by dogs:

> ἐξαπίνης δ' Ὀδυσῆα ἴδον κύνες ὑλακόμωροι.
> οἱ μὲν κεκλήγοντες ἐπέδραμον· αὐτὰρ Ὀδυσσεὺς
> ἕζετο κερδοσύνῃ, σκῆπτρον δέ οἱ ἔκπεσε χειρός.
> ἔνθα κεν ᾧ πὰρ σταθμῷ ἀεικέλιον πάθεν ἄλγος·
> ἀλλὰ συβώτης ὦκα ποσὶ κραιπνοῖσι μετασπὼν
> ἔσσυτ' ἀνὰ πρόθυρον, σκῦτος δέ οἱ ἔκπεσε χειρός.
> τοὺς μὲν ὁμοκλήσας σεῦεν κύνας ἄλλυδις ἄλλον
> πυκνῇσιν λιθάδεσσιν, ὁ δὲ προσέειπεν ἄνακτα·
> "ὦ γέρον, ἦ ὀλίγου σε κύνες διεδηλήσαντο
> ἐξαπίνης, καί κέν μοι ἐλεγχείην κατέχευας.

(*Odyssey* 14.29–38)

---

[27] Burkert 1983:112–113.

Suddenly the barking dogs noticed Odysseus,
and ran at him baying. And Odysseus
cleverly sat down, and his staff fell out of his hand.
There, by his own farm house, he might have suffered
    an unseemly pain,
but the swineherd rushed through the gate,
quickly coming to Odysseus on his swift feet, and a piece of
    oxhide [he was holding] fell out of his hand.
He shouted at the dogs and scattered them in every direction
with a shower of stones, and then he addressed his master:
"Old man, a little more and the dogs would have torn you to
    pieces right there,
and you would have poured reproach over me."

These are the dogs that guard Eumaeus' property, not hunters, and Odysseus is in no immediate danger of losing his life. In comparison with Aktaion's dismemberment, and indeed in comparison with Odysseus' own grand adventures of the past, the whole scene seems almost comic: here is Odysseus, the king of Ithaca, coming home after many adventures, about to be badly mauled by some farm dogs. Humor, however, is by no means incompatible with mythic and ritual undercurrents, and Odysseus, dressed in a deerskin, and crouching helplessly as the dogs attack him strikes a curiously Aktaion-like pose. The episode, at any rate, does not seem likely to be simply decorative, since it is the very first thing that happens to Odysseus after he parts from Athena and ventures inland on his island. Moreover, Eumaeus' dogs receive a lot of attention: we are told, for example, that there are four of them and that Eumaeus brought them up himself. They even deserve a heroic-sounding epithet, ὑλακόμωροι, which occurs in Homer only here and again at *Odyssey* 16.4, when the same dogs greet Telemachus very differently from the way they greeted Odysseus, with tails wagging.[28] For whatever reason, these dogs seem important. Their behavior with Odysseus forms a sharp contrast to that of Argos, who recognizes and greets his old master. The scene with Argos, like the earlier one near Eumaeus' hut, may involve playing with the themes of Aktaion's myth, since Argos' ability to recognize Odysseus even in deerskin is in sharp contrast to the failure of Aktaion's dogs to do the same. It is interesting, in this regard, that the dogs' inability to

---

[28] The meaning of the second part of the compound is unclear. It occurs also in ἰόμωρος, ἐγχεσίμωρος and probably goes back to *mêros, as in Germanic and Slavic names such as Volk-mar, Vladi-meru (Risch 1974:213).

recognize Aktaion is commented upon in several sources, which attribute it not just to the fact of his transformation, but also to the madness (*lussa*) sent by Artemis, as if the deerskin itself were not sufficient. Pausanias opines that the dogs killed Aktaion in madness and without recognizing him (μανέντες δὲ καὶ οὐ διαγινώσκοντες, 9.2.4), under the influence of the 'disease *lussa*'. Apollodorus also blames *lussa* and says that the dogs commit their ghastly mistake in ignorance, κατὰ ἄγνοιαν (3.31).[29]

The crouching Odysseus who is saved from the dogs by Eumaeus makes an emphatic contrast not only to the young boar-hunting Odysseus but also to the stag-hunting Odysseus of his own storytelling (*Odyssey* 10.156–184). Odysseus kills a stag on Circe's island and it has even been suggested that the *Odyssey* alludes to Aktaion's myth in *that* scene, both because any beast on Circe's island could potentially be a metamorphosed human and because the stag is so unusually large that it is called a 'monster' (*pelor*, *Odyssey* 10.168).[30] I doubt that a human should be imagined under the skin of that stag, but it is indeed relevant to the Aktaion allusion in Books 13 and 14, yet in a different way. The size of the stag is an emblem of Odysseus' hunting prowess and his ability to survive and sustain his men in the wilds. In contrast to that role, Odysseus on Ithaca himself becomes a deer, and not an impressive one at all. Moreover, just as Odysseus' boar hunt on Mount Parnassus has an initiatory flavor to it, so does the killing of the stag on Circe's island. In the latter case this impression is created not by the killing itself, but by the emphasis placed on the animal's size and weight and the fact that Odysseus carries it to his companions, including the description of how Odysseus binds the stag, exactly how he lifts it up, and finally how he deposits it in front of the ship (*Odyssey* 10.164–172). These details, which have no immediate motivation in the *Odyssey*, are in fact strongly reminiscent of a well-attested motif (and perhaps practice) of lifting animals in connection with transition to adulthood. During the festival of Proerosia, for example, the Athenian ephebes lifted bulls on their shoulders before sacrifice.[31] This finds a mythic parallel in Theseus: according to Pausanias, upon his return from Crete the Athenian hero threw some oxen high in the air and thereby proved to bystanders that he was a man.[32] Crete

---

[29] Frontisi-Ducroux 1997 cites these sources and discusses in detail the role of vision and (non) recognition in Aktaion's myth as well the myth's other various inversions and oppositions.

[30] See Roessel 1989 for the suggestion that this episode is an allusion to Aktaion's myth.

[31] Lebessi 1985:84, 125, Pelekidis 1962:224 ff., Durand and Schnapp 1989:59 fig.83, Marinatos 2003:133.

[32] Pausanias 1.19.1. This is discussed as an initiatory scene by Graf 1979 and Waldner 2000:190. One typically "initiatory" detail of the scene is the fact that Theseus, because of his dress and hairstyle, is teased by the bystanders for being a 'girl'. There are obvious initiatory elements in

provides early archaeological evidence for similar practices or at least similar ideas. Multiple bronze plaques depicting beardless youths lifting animals on their shoulders were found at the sanctuary of Kato Syme, which originated in the Bronze Age and flourished in the early Archaic period, and where Hermes, it has been argued, was worshipped as a mediator in the transition of males from adolescence to adulthood.[33] On one of these plaques a beardless youth carrying a goat on his shoulders faces an older bearded male who carries a bow. Lebessi suggested that this scene depicts a homosexual lover and beloved, pointing out that homosexuality as part of male upbringing is attested on Crete by later authors. Following Lebessi, Marinatos points out that the older male touches the elbow of the younger one as if in approval, and suggests that he is the younger male's tutor. It seems that the beardless youth here demonstrates his prowess by carrying the goat, while the older male approves. The bow indicates that he is a hunter.[34] On another plaque a youth carries a goat on his shoulders, supporting it with one hand while holding his bow in the other, making it clear that, unlike Theseus, he is lifting not a domesticated animal but prey from the hunt.[35] On most of the Kato Syme plaques the carried animal is tied up, but it can be carried in different ways. Sometimes the animal is relatively small and carried over the shoulders supported with one hand, but on at least one plaque a man is depicted in the process of trying to stand up with a large bound animal that obscures his entire head (as the smaller ones do not) and rests both on his shoulders and neck. The man is leaning on a spear.[36] This seems to be what is described in the *Odyssey*. Odysseus uses pliant twigs to bind up his deer and carries it on his neck, leaning on a spear. He specifically mentions that the stag has to be carried in this way because it is too large to be transported 'on the shoulder holding with one hand':

> τῷ δ' ἐγὼ ἐμβαίνων δόρυ χάλκεον ἐξ ὠτειλῆς
> εἰρυσάμην· τὸ μὲν αὖθι κατακλίνας ἐπὶ γαίη
> εἴασ'· αὐτὰρ ἐγὼ σπασάμην ῥῶπάς τε λύγους τε,
> πεῖσμα δ' ὅσον τ' ὄργυιαν ἐϋστρεφὲς ἀμφοτέρωθεν
> πλεξάμενος συνέδησα πόδας δεινοῖο πελώρου,

Theseus' Cretan voyage as a whole.

[33] Marinatos 2003:131–137 with references. Marinatos follows the assessment of the excavator, A. Lebessi, synthesized in Lebessi 1981, 1985, 2000. For illustrations of the plaque see Lebessi 1985 pl. 46 no. Γ8, pl. 40 no. Γ7, pl.41 no. Γ5, rendered as figures 7.2, 7.3, and 7.4 in Marinatos 2003.

[34] Lebessi 1985 pl.41, no. Γ5, Marinatos 2003 figure 7.4. The plaques of Kato Syme represent hunting, wresting and carrying of animals, alive and dead: see Marinatos 2003.132–137 with references.

[35] Lebessi 1985 pl.46, no.Γ8, Marinatos 2003 figure 7.2.

[36] Lebessi 1985 pl.40, no.Γ7, Marinatos 2003 figure 7.3.

βῆν δὲ καταλλοφάδια φέρων ἐπὶ νῆα μέλαιναν,
ἔγχει ἐρειδόμενος, ἐπεὶ οὔ πως ἦεν ἐπ' ὤμου
χειρὶ φέρειν ἑτέρῃ· μάλα γὰρ μέγα θηρίον ἦεν.

(Odyssey 10.164–171)

And stepping on him I drew my bronze spear out of his
    wound,
and left him right there, laying him down on the ground.
And in the meanwhile I broke off twigs and pliant
    branches and,
having plaited a rope, well-twisted from both ends, about
    a fathom in length,
I bound the legs of this great monster,
and went towards the black ship, carrying it on my neck
and leaning upon a spear, for it was impossible to carry
    him on my shoulder
holding him with one hand – it was a very large beast.

It seems that on Circe's island Odysseus performs a feat typical of a successful young male and especially a hunter, namely killing and then lifting a large herbivore such as a deer or a goat. In this, as in so many other aspects, he seems to be going through the trials of a youth on his way to becoming a man. On the same island he also, of course, confronts dangerous female sexuality and withstands it, with Hermes' help.[37] Aktaion stumbles on the same path, whether through an error in timing or in choice of a woman.

Returning to Aktaion, there are no direct indications of his extra-literary life, but some general sense of direction can be gathered from a consideration of the myth alongside those about Aktaion's cousins. All three daughters of Cadmus have sons, and their myths seem to be in some sense parallel. Aktaion is transformed into a deer and torn apart by his dogs. His cousin Pentheus is torn apart by the maenads, including his mother, who think they are hunting a wild beast. Their cousin Learchus is killed by his own father, and

---

[37] Cf. the *Homeric Hymn to Aphrodite*, where the goddess, in a wilderness setting, seduces a young hunter, Anchises. See Marinatos 2003:142–144 for an interpretation of the *Hymn* and a discussion of a plaque from Kato Syme that shows a female figure provocatively parting her skirts and revealing her genitalia. Following Lebessi, Marinatos argues that these plaques "reflect a male clientele at Kato Syme" and are "a declaration of the act of heterosexual initiation." Note further that such an initiation does not equal marriage: see Marinatos 2003:145–146. On Aphrodite Skotia as connected to male maturation on Crete see Willets 1962:285–286, Leitao 1995, Waldner 2000:201–229.

this death is also pictured as a hunt: according to Apollodorus, Athamas hunts him down 'like a deer', (καὶ Ἀθάμας μὲν τὸν πρεσβύτερον παῖδα Λέαρχον ὡς ἔλαφον θηρεύσας ἀπέκτεινεν, 'and Athamas killed his older son, Learchus, after hunting him down like a deer' Apollodorus 3.4.3). In all cases, there is a chase and a terribly perverted hunt. There are references to *sparagmos* and to hunting deer, and they are combined in Aktaion's case: Pentheus is torn apart, Learchus is killed like a deer, Aktaion is torn apart as a deer. Euripides' dramatization of Pentheus' myth in the *Bacchae* is full of references to the hunt, including a mention of Aktaion as a negative example for Pentheus (337–342). As Heath remarks, the cousins "are both portrayed here as hybristic hunters – one literal, one metaphorical – who eventually meet nearly identical sparagmatic fates as hunters-turned-hunted."[38] The analogy between Pentheus and Aktaion is remarkably sustained in the *Bacchae*, and it would be out of place to discuss it here in all its multiple aspects.[39] Suffice it to say that Pentheus is pictured as a hunter, (he tracks and chases both Dionysus and the women who have escaped to the mountains), that he dies dressed in a traditional maenadic costume that includes 'the dappled skin of a fawn' (835), and that Agave calls her fellow female hunters 'my running dogs' as she incites them to the hunt (731).[40] In both cases the chasers are overtaken by madness and do not recognize their prey: the dogs do not suspect the deer is their master, and the maenads do not realize that their prey is human. This is also true for the third cousin, Learchus, since his father Athamas is struck with madness when he kills his son (μανείς, 'maddened', Apollodorus 1.9.2; ἀγανακτήσασα δὲ Ἥρα μανίαν αὐτοῖς ἐνέβαλε, 'Hera, being vexed, put madness into them', Apollodorus 3.4.3). In all these cases, moreover, the horror is magnified by the fact that the murderers and the murdered are in a nurturing relationship. Aktaion is killed by his own dogs, as every source remarks, and Cadmus in Euripides' *Bacchae* emphasizes that Aktaion raised the dogs himself:

> ὁρᾷς τὸν Ἀκταίωνος ἄθλιον μόρον,
> ὃν ὠμόσιτοι σκύλακες ἃς ἐθρέψατο
> διεσπάσαντο, κρείσσον' ἐν κυναγίαις
> Ἀρτέμιδος εἶναι κομπάσαντ' ἐν ὀργάσιν.

> (*Bacchae* 337–340)

---

[38] Heath 1992:11.
[39] For a fuller discussion see Heath 1992:10–18, to whom this account is indebted.
[40] Heath 1992:10–18.

You see the miserable fate of Aktaion,
whom the raw-eating dogs tore to pieces, the dogs
   he reared himself,
because he boasted in the mountain meadows
to be better than Artemis at hunting.

Learchus and Pentheus are killed by their parents and Pentheus at least is also lamented by the murderers, just as Aktaion is sought and bewailed by his dogs. I wonder if an echo of this last element, the notion of proximity between the victims and the hunters, is not present in the *Odyssey*, where we are told that Eumaeus raised the dogs himself:

πὰρ δὲ κύνες θήρεσσιν ἐοικότες αἰὲν ἴαυον
τέσσαρες, οὓς ἔθρεψε συβώτης, ὄρχαμος ἀνδρῶν.

                       (*Odyssey* 14.21–22)

And by them [the swine] always lay four dogs
that were like wild beasts, whom the swineherd himself,
   a leader of men, reared.

There is no direct parallel here, but there is a somewhat chilling confluence of similar elements: Odysseus, unrecognizable in his deerskin, is threatened by the dogs raised by his most loyal servant.[41] Eumaeus remarks on how narrowly he escaped the disgrace of having his dogs harm a guest, adding that he has enough grief already in missing Odysseus (*Odyssey* 14.37–44). Little does he realize what an outrage he has indeed avoided.

Burkert connects the myth of Athamas and Learchus with a festival of dissolution, perhaps specifically the Agrania, which was especially prominent in Boeotia, the home turf of all three grandsons of Cadmus, but if the elements of a cultic action are indeed contained in the myths of Learchus, Pentheus, and Aktaion, their outlines are dim and hardly distinguishable.[42] Still, there are elements that unite all these myths, such as the notion of reversal and dissolution in its application to the hunt, the Dionysiac element of madness, and the presence of deer. All of these elements are also present in the *Odyssey*, and

---

[41] Eumaeus' exceptional position as a person particularly close to Odysseus is indicated by the story of his upbringing together with Odysseus' sister (15.362–370), his own mention of Antikleia's feelings for him (φίλει δέ με κηρόθι μᾶλλον, 15.369), and by the fact that Odysseus, once on Ithaca, goes first of all to the swineherd's hut. Eumaeus also has the distinction of being the only person in the *Odyssey* to be addressed through apostrophe (e.g. 14.55, 165).

[42] Burkert 1983:178–179.

in their proper place, in the final period of darkness that precedes Odysseus' return.

To come back to Odysseus' golden pin, another layer can be added to its already impressive significance. The pin plays against the deerskin that Odysseus now wears to reveal the depth of the reversal and devastation that has taken place, to suggest a temporary transformation of the hunter into the hunted. At the same time, the recollection of the cloak and pin in the mouth of the squalid beggar is a veiled promise to Penelope, a prediction of the revival and restoration to come. This double contrast between the splendid past, the murky and anxiety-ridden present, and the uncertain but tempting promises of the future creates a much more potent message than a simple confirmation that Penelope's guest has indeed entertained Odysseus. In contrast to Aktaion, Odysseus does not in fact turn into a hunted animal, but by wearing a deerskin he does create this potentiality, as if it has to be activated before it can be laid to rest. This way of evoking a myth while avoiding it is a pattern in the *Odyssey*: in the same way, Penelope mentions Aedon, the murderous mother of her own son, while doing all she can to avoid the same fate. In a sense, these ghastly stories, whether hinted at or explicitly mentioned, function in the *Odyssey* as a myth might function in the context of an actual festival. The murder and dismemberment that are present in myth were not, of course, part of any Greek festival, including those dramatizing dissolution and reversal. Rather, references are made to myths, and masks and play-acting may also be involved. In the same way, the festival of Apollo in the *Odyssey* seems to function as a context in which certain myths are told, implied, and even enacted. The difference is that the action of the *Odyssey* itself shares many features with the evoked myths: Odysseus really does face the possibility of being killed and Penelope really does face the possibility of causing her son's death. Still, even as its characters live their own myth, the *Odyssey* activates many other relevant myths in the context of Apollo's festival.

CHAPTER NINE

EURYBATES

THE FINAL TOKEN Odysseus-Aithon gives to Penelope is the description of his herald Eurybates:

καὶ μέν οἱ κῆρυξ ὀλίγον προγενέστερος αὐτοῦ
εἵπετο· καὶ τόν τοι μυθήσομαι, οἷος ἔην περ·
γυρὸς ἐν ὤμοισιν, μελανόχροος, οὐλοκάρηνος,
Εὐρυβάτης δ' ὄνομ' ἔσκε· τίεν δέ μιν ἔξοχον ἄλλων
ὧν ἑτάρων Ὀδυσεύς, ὅτι οἱ φρεσὶν ἄρτια ᾔδη.

(*Odyssey* 19.244–248)

And a herald, a little older than himself,
came along with him. I will tell you about him, what sort
     of a person he was.
He was round-shouldered, dark-skinned, with wooly hair,
and his name was Eurybates. Odysseus valued him above
his other companions, because they thought alike.

Like everything else in this conversation, the mention of Eurybates has its share of complications and unsolved puzzles. All three adjectives describing the herald are Homeric hapaxes, which means we are ill-positioned to evaluate their effect. Overall, Eurybates has struck commentators as physically unattractive, though possibly concealing an "inner excellence" behind his "un-heroic" façade.[1] This impression seems to be primarily created by the herald's rounded shoulders, a characteristic which is also present, in grotesque form, in Thersites:

φολκὸς ἔην, χωλὸς δ' ἕτερον πόδα· τὼ δέ οἱ ὤμω
κυρτὼ ἐπὶ στῆθος συνοχωκότε· αὐτὰρ ὕπερθε
φοξὸς ἔην κεφαλήν, ψεδνὴ δ' ἐπενήνοθε λάχνη.

(*Iliad* 2.217–219)

---

[1] Russo 1992:90 ad loc.

He was bandy-legged and lame in one foot. His shoulders
    were arched,
coming together over his chest. And above,
his head was deformed, with sparse hair.

It is doubtful that this comparison is justified. The adjective used of Thersites'
shoulders is *kurtos*, and it regularly describes humped backs such as that of a
camel, a bull rearing for attack, and, above all, of hunchbacks.[2] Since Thersites'
shoulders come together over his chest and go together with a limp and sparse
hair, there can be little doubt that he is far removed from any conventional
notions of beauty or fitness. In contrast, *guros* is not conventionally used to
describe humps and has no associations with deformity. Eurybates' shoulders
are curved or rounded, but it is not even clear whether this is good or bad, or
either. His other features, dark skin and wooly hair, are equally hard to place.
Some have thought that this combination suggests an African type, but this
seems unlikely.[3] As Irwin has shown, *melas* is often used to describe the tanned
skin of males who spend much time in the sun, and there is no reason to think
that it means anything different here.[4] In fact, though there is no exact match
elsewhere for Eurybates' physical characteristics, the person whom he comes
closest to resembling is in fact Odysseus, and Odysseus at his best. When
Athena restores Odysseus' youth, once for Nausikaa and once for Penelope, the
hero acquires dense hair described in terms reminiscent of that of Eurybates
(οὔλας ἧκε κόμας, 'let down wooly hair' *Odyssey* 6.231 = 23.153), and when
Odysseus regains his normal appearance to reunite with Telemachus, he
becomes dark-skinned (ἂψ δὲ μελαγχροιὴς γένετο, 'he became dark-skinned
again' 16.175). Since Odysseus in these scenes is certainly meant to be
handsome, young, and strong, it seems doubtful whether Eurybates is indeed
such an unattractive, Thersites-like character as he is sometimes thought to
be. Indeed, in view of the similarities in skin and hair between Eurybates and
Odysseus, it seems noteworthy that in the Teikhoskopia when Priam looks at
the Achaeans from the wall of Troy and describes Agamemnon, Odysseus, and
Ajax, he mentions Odysseus' wide shoulders:

> μείων μὲν κεφαλῇ Ἀγαμέμνονος Ἀτρεΐδαο,
> εὐρύτερος δ' ὤμοισιν ἰδὲ στέρνοισιν ἰδέσθαι.

(Iliad 3.194–195)

---

[2] See LSJ s.v.
[3] See Snowden 1970:101–102, 122, 181, Russo 1992:90 ad loc.
[4] Irwin 1974:112–116, 129–135.

> Shorter by a head than Agamemnon son of Atreus,
> but in appearance broader in shoulders and chest.

Eurybates is presumably less heroic-looking than Odysseus, but they do resemble each other. On balance, I wonder whether γυρὸς ἐν ὤμοισι in *Odyssey* 19 does not mean something like 'with bulging shoulders', a feature that is not necessarily handsome, but indicative of physical aptitude. If so, Eurybates may be reminiscent of the short and bow-legged warrior praised in Archilochus fr. 114.[5] In any case, Eurybates' physical similarity to Odysseus is matched by their apparent trust and mental accord, which leads Odysseus to value the herald above his other companions. The mental qualities of Eurybates are described as ἄρτια ᾔδη (19.248), 'he thought things in accordance with him'.[6] The only other time this expression is used in Homer it applies to Diomedes' trusty companion, Deipylos. On that occasion too, Diomedes is said to value Deipylos above the rest of his age group (*Iliad* 5.325–326). Eurybates, then, seems to be a kind of Odysseus-double, both because of their shared physical characteristics and because of their intellectual cohesion.

In this connection it is tempting to speculate on the possible implications of the name Eurybates. The name should mean something like 'wide-ranging' or 'wide-striding', (from εὐρύ and βαίνω), and may be a generic name for a herald, since Agamemnon's herald in the *Iliad* is also so named (*Iliad* 2.320). Agamemnon's second herald, Talthybios, certainly has a life beyond Homer, since he had a hero precinct (ἱρόν) in Sparta, where the Talthybiadai were a family (or possibly a guild) of heralds.[7] The name Eurybates, however, has a different set of associations outside of Homer. According to Aristotle, Eurybatos or Eurybates of Aegina was a particularly successful thief who escaped from captivity under the pretence of demonstrating to his drunken guards how he used to get into houses (he scrambles over the wall using goads and sponges).[8] Another Eurybatos mentioned in literature is a native of Ephesos, but he shares with his Aegenitan namesake an inclination to cheat: when Croesus sends him to Delphi with a supply of gold in order to negotiate with the Greeks, he instead defects to Cyrus (and presumably keeps the

---

[5] The two are compared by Russo 1992:90 and 1974:139–52.

[6] As rendered by LSJ s.v. ἄρτιος A.1, with reference to *Iliad* 5.326 and *Odyssey* 19.248.

[7] Herodotus 7.134.

[8] Aristotle fr. 84 Rose. The same story is retold in various sources, e.g. Suda s.v. Εὐρύβατος, Eustathius on *Odyssey* 19.247, Aristaenetus *Epistulae* 1.20.

gold).[9] This second Eurybatos is presented as a historical character, but this may be a deceptive appearance. Eustathius mentions that there are even more Eurybatoi, and that they are all πανοῦργοι, which certainly does not inspire any confidence in their historicity, but does suggest that the name, at least in its second-declension form, had strong and clear associations with trickery and deception. In fact, the name Eurybatos apparently became proverbial for a knave relatively early on. Already Aristophanes calls Zeus 'Eurybatos' on account of the god's multiple affairs and shapeshifting aimed at eluding Hera's wifely anger.[10] A learned poet such as Euphorion apparently knew many various Eurybatoi.[11] One of the more interesting, and certainly mythological, bearers of the name is one of the two brothers collectively called the Kerkopes, famous as robbers and liars. This is important because the stories about them are likely to be quite early, since they are widely represented in visual arts from the early sixth century onwards.[12] The early representations mostly show Herakles carrying the two Kerkopes on a pole over his shoulder: the captured thieves are hanging upside-down, one from each end of the pole. The representation seems to refer to a story that is fully attested only in much later sources, to the effect that the Kerkopes are warned to watch out for a Melampygos, ('black-bottomed one'), attempt to steal Herakles' armor, are captured, and then make jokes, as they are hanging upside-down on the pole, about Herakles' hairy bottom, which they only now recognize as their warning sign. Amused by the teasing of the Kerkopes, Herakles laughs and lets them go.[13] Herodotus is aware of the Kerkopes and appears to locate them near Thermopylae, where he mentions 'the rock of the Melampygos and the haunts

---

[9] Ephorus FGrH 70 F 58a, Diodorus Siculus 9.31.3, Michael Apostolius Paroemiographer, *Collectio paroemiarum* 8.11.2 = Aristotle fr. 84, Suda s.v. Εὐρύβατος, Constantinus Porphyrogenitus *De virtutibus et vitiis* 57.

[10] Aristophanes fr. 184 (*Daidalos* 1).

[11] Euphorion fr. 83, Ἠδ' ὅσσα προτέροισιν ἀείδεται Εὐρυβάτοισιν. The fragment is hard to interpret since we lack any further context.

[12] Visual representations of the Kerkopes far antedate literary mentions. The early examples include a (probably) Middle Corinthian cup from Perachora (Athens, National Museum, Perachora 2542, LIMC Kerkopes 1, Perachora II, 262–263, no. 2542, pl.106, 110, Amyx 1988:565), two Corinthian *pinakes*, probably also of the early sixth century (Berlin Ch F766, F767, LIMC Kerkopes 10), a shield-band from Olympia, ca. 575–550 BCE (B 975, LIMC Kerkopes 14), and metopes from Foce del Sele (about 550 BCE, Paestum, Museo Nazionale, LIMC Kerkopes 11) and Temple C at Selinous (about 540–530 BCE, Palermo, Mus. Reg. 3920, LIMC Kerkopes 12).

[13] Suda s.v. Kerkopes, Pseudo-Nonnus, *Scholia mythologica* 4.39.6. Apollodorus mentions that the Kerkopes were captured by Herakles but gives little detail (2.6.3). He locates them in Ephesos. Diodorus Siculus also locates them in Asia Minor and says that Herakles killed some of them and brought others to Omphale (4.31.7).

of the Kerkopes'.[14] Diotimus locates their activity in the same part of Greece, namely in Boeotia:

> Κέρκωπές τοι πολλὰ κατὰ τριόδους πατέοντες
> Βοιωτῶν σίνοντο· γένος δ' ἔσαν Οἰχαλιῆες,
> Ὦλός τ' Εὐρύβατός τε, δύω βαρυδαίμονες ἄνδρες.
>
> (Ἡρακλέους Ἆθλα = *Supplementum Hellenisticum*, fr. 394)

> The Kerkopes used to maraud constantly, trampling through
>   the crossroads
> of the Boeotians. In origin they were from Oikhalia,
> Olos and Eurybatos, two luckless men.

Later sources, however, picture them near Ephesos, and say that it was there that Herakles captured them (Apollodorus 2.6.3, Diodorus 4.31.7). There is no mention of the 'black-bottomed one' in those accounts that place the Kerkopes in Asia Minor. Since some of the Ephesian population derived from Boeotia and Thessaly it is quite possible that they brought the story of Kerkopes and Herakles with them and transferred it to their environment. In any case, the story is attested in Asia Minor, mainland Greece, and Italy, in the latter two regions as early as the sixth century. Harpocration even mentions poetry about the Kerkopes ascribed to Homer:

> ἐν τοῖς εἰς Ὅμηρον ἀναφερομένοις Κέρκωψιν δηλοῦται ὡς
> ἐξαπατητῆρές τε ἦσαν καὶ ψεῦσται οἱ Κέρκωπες.
>
> (Harpocration s.v. Κέρκωψ)

> In the *Kerkopes*, attributed to Homer, it is said that the Kerkopes
> were deceivers and cheats.

Given this wide and early distribution it is not surprising to find several versions of the myth, including the names of the rascally brothers. Aeschines, for example, gives the names Andoulos and Atlantos, while the Suda gives Passalos ('peg') and Akmon ('anvil') – both sexual puns – among others.[15]

Still, there are features of the Kerkopes which seem to go well with the name Eurybates. In anonymous verses cited by Pausanias (the Atticist), the Kerkopes are said to do precisely what is indicated by their name, wander and cover large distances:

---

[14] Herodotus 7.216.
[15] Harpocration s.v. Κέρκωψ (citing Aeschines), Suda s.v. Κέρκωπες.

ψεύστας, ἠπεροπῆας, ἀμήχανά τ' ἔργ' ἐάσαντας,
ἐξαπατητῆρας· πολλὴν δ' ἐπὶ γαῖαν ἰόντες
ἀνθρώπους ἀπάτασκον, ἀλώμενοι ἤματα πάντα.

(Pausanias s.v. Κέρκωπες)

. . . liars, cheats, deceivers, enablers of irremediable
   deeds.
Traveling over a large territory,
   they used to deceive people, roaming all the time.

Similarly, Diotimus presents them as wandering robbers (κατὰ τριόδους
πατέοντες, 'trampling over the crossroads' fr. 393).

It is obvious that Kerkopes have certain features that align them with
Odysseus. Although the *Odyssey*, of course, presents an elevated picture of
its hero, he, like the Kerkopes, has a definite comic potential, not entirely
ignored even in Homer. Like Odysseus, they are famous for telling lies, wander
in search of gain, and use their wits to escape from captivity. In this, both
Odysseus and the Kerkopes are also similar to the Aeginetan Eurybates, who
escapes from prison. The Kerkopes are especially reminiscent of Odysseus'
grandfather Autolykos, famous for theft and perjury, and Eustathius mentions
both Sisyphus and Autolykos as rivals of the Kerkopes in deceit.[16] Although the
name of Odysseus' herald is Eurybates rather than Eurybatos, the difference
in declension would probably not erase the relevant connotations. The Suda,
at any rate, glosses Eurybatos as *poneros* and proceeds to list possible sources
of this meaning, including the Aeginetan thief, the Ephesian traitor, and, with
reference to Douris, the companion of Odysseus.

It is impossible to say when the association between the name Eurybatos
or Eurybates and the notion of villainy and deceit arises, but it is quite possible
that it forms early enough to be active in the *Odyssey*. Granted, we hear nothing
of any particular lawlessness on the part of Odysseus' herald or indeed of that
of Agamemnon, who has the same name. Both appear in the *Iliad* strictly as
heralds and seem to perform their function without incident. Moreover,
heralds, like wanderers, have to walk a lot, so that the name Eurybates fits a
herald as well as it does a traveling thief. Yet if the name Eurybates was associ-
ated with villainy at an early date, then a companion who is particularly close
to Odysseus could hardly bear that name without evoking that association.
Eurybates is a man after Odysseus' own heart more than anyone else of his
companions, and such a man is unlikely to be an honest simpleton.

---

[16] Eustathius 2.202 (on *Odyssey* 19.247).

There can be no certainty in such matters, but it seems possible that by describing Eurybates, a character physically resembling Odysseus himself and close to him in mentality, Aithon-Odysseus reminds Penelope of the transgressive qualities of her husband, whose long absence from home does, after all, involve plunder, lies, arrogant looting, and tricky escapes from captivity. This is what Odysseus is like when he sets out for Troy. Even the name of Odysseus can be taken to indicate not only the suffering the hero endures, but also the harm he causes others, through the Homeric folk-etymology, which derives it from ὀδύσσομαι, 'to be angry with, hate'. Autolykos gives the infant Odysseus a name designed to recollect the anger his own thefts and deceits inspire in his victims:

> πολλοῖσιν γὰρ ἐγώ γε ὀδυσσάμενος τόδ' ἱκάνω,
> ἀνδράσιν ἠδὲ γυναιξὶν ἀνὰ χθόνα βωτιάνειραν.
>
> (*Odyssey* 19.407–408)[17]

> For I come here hated by many
> all over the man-feeding earth, both men and women.

Perhaps some similar notions contribute to Diotimus' choice of adjective to describe the Kerkopes, βαρυδαίμονες, a word that usually means 'of ill luck' rather than 'bringing ill luck to others', as might be expected of robbers. Like the cloak and the pin, the description of the herald seems to say much about Odysseus and the nature of his absence and return, suggesting both the reasons he might be somewhere in unknown trouble and the likelihood that he will extricate himself.

Finally, if the mention of Eurybates indeed carries some of the connotations suggested above, then the next question is how such connotations would fit in with the general tone of Odysseus' Third Cretan Lie and also with

---

[17] The question whether Odysseus' name should be taken in active or passive sense (hater or hated, bringing pain or feeling pain) is an old one (the scholion V at 19.407 glosses *odyssamenos* both as μισηθείς and as βλάψας). Stanford (1952:209–213) argues for a coexistence of the active and the passive sense. Rank believes that both "the hater" and "the hated" are possible meanings of Odysseus' name, but that the first predominates (1951:51–65). More recently, scholars have favored the notion of balance between the active and passive meanings, Odysseus as both "victim and victimizer" (Clay 1983:64) and explored the resulting ironies. For a discussion of this question see Clay 1983:54–64, Peradotto 1990. In his two-way relationship with suffering, as in many other aspects, Odysseus is similar to Herakles. Nagy (1990:13–14) comments on dictional similarities between the *Homeric Hymn to Herakles* (5–6) and the proem of the *Odyssey* (1.1–4). In the *Hymn*, Herakles is said both to commit and to suffer many reckless deeds (*atasthala*). Arguably, the same can be said about Odysseus, though the *Odyssey* foregrounds the suffering of Odysseus and the recklessness of his crew and the suitors.

the setting of Apollo's festival. Is Eurybates a character particularly suitable to evoke the figure of absent Odysseus and therefore the stage in Odysseus' life that is marked by wandering and transgression and that comes to its end and culmination with Apollo's festival? On the verge of reclaiming his place as a king, on the eve of the festival, Odysseus in the period leading up to this moment of crisis hints at what he has been and is. On Ithaca he is first and foremost a king, and yet he also has been, and is, a hungry and vengeful wanderer, a younger brother struggling for his place in the world, and a youthful hunter. Perhaps a clever wandering looter and acquisitive transgressor should be added to the list. That all Odysseus' looting, both at Troy and in Cyclops' cave, does nothing to enrich him, while his lasting acquisitions are gained peacefully as gifts from the Phaeacians, is a different matter. The point remains that Odysseus is certainly not averse to looting on his travels, though perhaps there is a difference here between his youthful and his older self.

It would be too simplistic to suggest that Odysseus follows the paradigmatic path through adolescence to maturity as outlined by Vidal-Naquet in his influential work on the black hunter.[18] The actual situation in the *Odyssey* is much more complex, since Odysseus' actual growing up and becoming Odysseus is telescoped into his re-becoming Odysseus, and since there seems to be a cyclical element in Odysseus' departures and returns (he is, after all, forced to leave Ithaca again after the end of the *Odyssey*), an element that does not fit into the linear progression from childhood to adulthood, though it does fit well with the idea of dissolution and restoration. Yet the *Odyssey* certainly taps into the mythological themes that Vidal-Naquet connects to the figure of the black hunter, and taps into them very deeply. The activities and ideas associated with Greek adolescence include hunting, use of deception and stealth, use of the bow, abnormal sexuality, and lack of participation in political life, i.e. separation from the social group. Most of these features apply to Odysseus during his period of wandering, except for the bow, which on Ithaca stands for the opposite of what it does in Vidal-Naquet's scheme: legitimate kingship and full manhood, rather than the liminality of adolescence. The trickery and knavery that might be associated with Eurybates may not carry any specifically initiatory meaning, since these qualities are permanent features of Odysseus. At the same time, Odysseus himself is liable to become an initiatory kind of a figure, and perhaps these qualities are part of what is involved. A recent critique of the black hunter model demonstrates how unconvincing it can be when applied to a particular work of poetry, and Vidal-Naquet's own

---

[18] Vidal-Naquet 1983:106–156.

attempt to analyze Neoptolemus in Sophocles' *Philoctetes* as a typical initiand is certainly open to objections.[19] Yet the problems may be caused not by defects of the model but by attempts to use it reductively, as the primary (or only) vehicle for interpreting the play. In the course of criticizing Vidal-Naquet's arguments regarding Neoptolemus, one scholar observes that another character in the same play seems to be a better example of the black hunter. That character is Odysseus, who, in the play, "obeys authority unquestioningly, pursues a quarry in the wilderness that he intends to master through deception, and seeks military victory through the use of the non-hoplite bow" and, outside of the play, "is characterized by a recurrent rejection of marriage along with nearly unrestricted sexual activity," all of which makes him "the most perfect example of the black hunter in Greek mythology."[20] The scholar who so describes Odysseus sees this as the downfall of the black hunter model, since it seems arbitrary and nearly nonsensical for another character instead of the supposed initiand Neoptolemus to exhibit these qualities, and since, not being an adolescent, Odysseus does not seem to be a fitting candidate for them. This may indeed be so within Sophocles' play, and it may well be true that the initiation model is not helpful for the play's interpretation. In general, however, Odysseus is a very fitting candidate indeed for a role such as the black hunter not because he is literally an adolescent, but because it is his specific quality as a hero to forever go through an adolescence-like process. For this, Eurybates seems to be a suitable companion.

As I have argued above, the name Eurybates is a fitting one not only for a herald but also for an all-penetrating rogue, and there may indeed be a link between these two occupations. So far, I have been treating the two options as distinct, but they may not be so. The two functions, being a herald and being a thief, may seem unrelated, but they are in fact united in the figure of Hermes, a god who is both a messenger and a rogue and who, in both functions, has to do with the crossing of boundaries. This is perhaps not so surprising, since any go-between is liable to be unreliable and has a ready-made opportunity for skullduggery. I have already had a chance to comment on the similarities between the epithets of Hermes in the *Homeric Hymn*, which has to do with the god's growing up, and Odysseus' epithets in Homer, as well as on the more general similarities between the journeys of Odysseus and Hermes. To this overarching similarity can be added the special relationship with Hermes enjoyed by Odysseus' thievish grandfather Autolykos and the latter's actual

---

[19] Dodd 2003. For another recent critique of Vidal-Naquet see Polinskaya 2003.
[20] Dodd 2003:74.

descent from Hermes in non-Homeric sources.[21] Further, Hermes helps Odysseus in his wanderings when the hero has to confront one dangerous female (Circe) and escape from another one (Calypso). This role too is suitable for Hermes as the patron of young males, since Hermes sometimes appears as a lover of Aphrodite, and it has been suggested that in such depictions the two gods function as patrons of sexuality rather than marriage and oversee the young men's premarital introduction to sex.[22] It is in this role that Hermes appears in the *Odyssey* when he helps Odysseus to withstand Circe's charms and share her bed. Moreover, Hermes is also a fast runner and later a patron of gymnasia and athletic competitions, especially those of adolescents, and I have argued that this quality is shared by Odysseus.[23] It is at the Hermaia at Pellene that young males earned their cloaks. There are, to sum up, multiple elements that have to do with male maturation and are typical both of Hermes and of Odysseus. In these circumstances, the hero's special proximity to a herald named Eurybates contributes to his Hermes-like aspect. Finally, I come back to the peculiar fact that Eurybates appears both in the *Odyssey* and in the *Iliad* in connection with Odysseus' cloak. The scene in *Iliad* 2 where Odysseus casts off his cloak and Eurybates picks it up has already been mentioned. Various scholars have found that this scene resonates with the *Odyssey*, in particular in Book 14, where Odysseus tells Eumaeus his 'blameless *ainos*' about a cloak.[24] The co-occurrence of Eurybates and the cloak suggest that a dialogic relationship exists also between that scene in *Iliad* 2 and *Odyssey* 19. In the *Odyssey*, Odysseus recalls his old cloak and attempts to gain a new one. In the *Iliad*, in contrast, he flings the cloak away as he runs. In *Odyssey* 14, he tells Eumaeus a lying tale about how he went into ambush without a cloak and acquired one with Odysseus' help. In this version of the Iliadic ambush, Odysseus himself has a cloak and helps the speaker acquire one. This story has a point of contact with the Doloneia, the only extended ambush-narrative in the *Iliad*, and, curiously, here it is Odysseus, like the pseudo-Cretan of *Odyssey* 14, who sets out with a shield, but without a cloak (*Iliad* 10.149). Observing this correspondence, Muellner poses the question: "Is epic too unsophisticated for a cross-reference here in the *Odyssey* to another version of this tale in which Odysseus himself needed a χλαῖνα?"[25] After surveying the evidence, Clay inclines toward

---

[21] Pherecydes FGrH 3 F 120 (FHG 1.63b).
[22] Marinatos 2003:145–148.
[23] Hermes' epithet ἐριούνιος (folk-etymologized in antiquity as 'beneficial') is derived from the root of οὖνος, 'running course', and means 'good runner'.
[24] See pp111, 131, above.
[25] Muellner 1976:96n43.

the possibility of "such subtle cross-referencing."[26] A further question might be whether or not going into an ambush without a cloak is in fact a repeated and therefore recognizable element of such tales, in which case it too could have connotations and meanings which may or may not be recoverable by us. As it is, the *Iliad*, for Odysseus, seems to be for losing or not having his cloak, while the *Odyssey* is for wearing and regaining it. Anyone, of course, can throw away a cloak and run, and running presupposes getting rid of the cloak for the simple reason that it impedes movement. Yet we do not see Nestor or Idomeneus running and undressing, and the action, while natural, seems to be particularly suited to swift-footed youths. References to people dashing off without their clothes in later literature, including a supposedly real-life example in Lysias 3, involve mostly adolescents (*meirakion* in Lysias 3.12 and 3.35, *neaniskos* in Gospel of Mark 14.51–52). On Skheria, by contrast, Odysseus does not run, and retains his cloak even while participating in athletic competitions. On Ithaca, where he is a king, he used to wear a cloak matched only by Nestor's (double, purple, and with a pin). It seems, in short, that Odysseus undergoes a development from the Ithacan king to the pseudo-adolescent figure of the *Iliad*, and then in a long and torturous way back to being the king on Ithaca. In a subtle way, Odysseus' mention of Eurybates in connection with the cloak seems to allude to this trajectory. Even the fact that Eurybates is identified as 'the Ithacan one' in *Iliad* 2 contributes to this impression: it is as if Odysseus' cloak (the one given by Penelope, perhaps) properly belongs in an Ithacan context, and so is picked up by the Ithacan herald.[27] In *Odyssey* 19, having played his Hermes-like role and traveled along his 'long road', Odysseus is about to get his cloak back and fully establish himself as man and a king at a festival of Apollo.

Just as Penelope's melting in tears at the beginning of her dialogue with Odysseus is both an immediate reaction to what Odysseus has said and a token of larger developments in the poem (whether or not it is so interpreted by Penelope herself and Odysseus), so the signs Aithon-Odysseus gives his wife are rich with layers of meaning. Ostensibly, the description of the clothes and the herald serves to prove that the Cretan stranger did indeed meet Odysseus long ago. Implicitly, but still close to the surface, the same signs suggest that

---

[26] Clay 1983:87.

[27] It could be argued that Eurybates is here identified as the Ithacan one in order to distinguish him from Agamemnon's herald with the same name, but this, while plausible, does not preclude other considerations and effects. Moreover, in *Iliad* 9 Eurybates the herald is mentioned without any further comment, so that it is actually not clear whose herald he is and nothing is done to resolve the ambiguity there (*Iliad* 9.170).

the stranger actually is Odysseus. Beyond this immediate purpose, the signs carry a wealth of connotations and hint at Odysseus' past, his identity as a hero, and the nature of his return. These allusions, some strong and clear, some remote and faint, activate a broad associative network and contribute to the highly charged atmosphere on the eve of Apollo's festival. The festival is both an end to the period of dissolution and an occasion marking the growing up of a new generation, and both these events can be thought of using the traditional vocabulary of themes, (such as hunt, cloak, dogs), and characters, (such as Hermes, Ino, Aktaion), evoked in the *Odyssey*. Odysseus' signs for Penelope are fitted not only to the knowledge shared by the couple, but also to the poetic environment in which they are given: they both serve to (re)create the occasion of the festival within the poem and derive some of their meaning from this fictional occasion. The scope and meaning of each association may be variable, and no doubt much is irretrievable for us, but it seems likely that the combined effect of Odysseus' allusions would have been felt by the poem's audiences, at least to the extent that it contributed to the recognizable atmosphere of the festival's eve and to the rich and densely traditional texture of Odyssean poetry.

CHAPTER TEN

ODYSSEUS AND THE BOAR

HE DIALOGUE BETWEEN PENELOPE AND ODYSSEUS is broken into two parts by Odysseus' footbath and the recollection of his boar hunt on Mount Parnassus. The change of scene is dramatic: here we see Odysseus just reaching maturity (*hebe*), unmarried, and performing a hunting feat in the company of his relatives. Eurykleia's recognition of Odysseus by his scar prompts the digression, but the explanation of how Odysseus received this mark is only a small part of its significance. The poetic effect of the boar hunt has to do not only with Eurykleia, but with Penelope, since it marks a change in her conversation with Odysseus. This change is prepared by what comes before it, and the hunt fits in with the thematic agenda of its narrative surroundings, first and foremost Book 19 itself. I will confine my remarks here to those aspects of the hunt that are relevant, directly or indirectly, to its role as an intermission in the conversation between husband and wife, beginning with the less obvious resonances and concluding with more direct relevance of the boar hunt for Odysseus and Penelope as a couple.

Just as Odysseus' description of his hunting pin stands in sharp contrast to the deerskin he is wearing for the moment, so the flashback to Mount Parnassus reverses a very different association with the pig that Odysseus appears to acquire once back on Ithaca. The goatherd Melanthios meets Odysseus in beggar's disguise on his way to town with Eumaeus and refers to him by an abusive word, μολοβρός. The meaning of this term, although not entirely clear, has something to do with pigs:

> πῆ δὴ τόνδε μολοβρὸν ἄγεις, ἀμέγαρτε συβῶτα,
> πτωχὸν ἀνιηρόν, δαιτῶν ἀπολυμαντῆρα;
>
> (*Odyssey* 17.219–220)

> Where are you leading this *molobros*, you wretched
>   swineherd,
> this tiresome beggar, a spoiler of feasts?

Aelian notes that the young of wild boar are called μολόβρια and that Hipponax refers to the boar as μολοβρίτης.[1] Ancient (and folk) etymologies derive *molobros* from μολοῦντα πρὸς τὴν βρῶσιν, walking towards food[2] and the etymology fits with Odysseus' assumed persona of a hungry beggar, who complains of his ever-demanding belly and is accused of gluttony. On the other hand, a different explanation for the term has been proposed by Coughanowr on the basis of modern Greek evidence, which suggests that *molobros* should mean something like 'hairless' or 'with uneven coat'.[3] According to Coughanowr, μαλάβρα in the dialect of Epirus refers to a kind of disease like ringworm that leads to hair loss, which would also fit Odysseus, who is, of course, made bald by Athena as part of this disguise (*Odyssey* 13.431). Whatever its meaning, the evidence of Aelian and Hipponax makes it clear that for an ancient audience the term would call to mind pigs, especially in the *Odyssey*, where, as Stanford points out, calling Odysseus a pig as he is being led by Eumaeus the swineherd makes for a good joke.[4] Moreover, if Coughanowr is on the right track, there may be a further joke when Melanthios predicts that Odysseus will 'rub his shoulders' on many doorposts: ὃς πολλῆς φλιῆσι παραστὰς θλίψεται ὤμους (17.221). Pigs have a habit of rubbing against trees, (perhaps to get rid of pests, thus making their coats uneven?), and this fact is noted by Aristotle, who thinks that boars do so to toughen the skin.[5] Odysseus is called a pig and his begging is described in corresponding terms.

Further, the porcine terminology continues to cling to Odysseus as he confronts Iros in Book 18, for here too Odysseus is again insulted by the mysterious term *molobros* and then immediately compared to a swine:

> τὸν δὲ χολωσάμενος προσεφώνεεν Ἶρος ἀλήτης·
> "ὢ πόποι, ὡς ὁ μολοβρὸς ἐπιτροχάδην ἀγορεύει,
> γρηῒ καμινοῖ ἶσος· ὃν ἂν κακὰ μητισαίμην

---

[1] *De natura animalium* 7.47, Hipponax fr. 77.

[2] Scholia on the *Odyssey* 17.219, Eustathius 2.141.2 (on *Odyssey* 17.219). Cf. Chantraine 1952:203–205 (on the meaning 'glutton'). LSJ offers 'greedy fellow', while Cunliffe (1977 s.v.) restricts himself to "a term of abuse or depreciation of unknown meaning."

[3] Coughanowr 1979.

[4] Stanford 1965:287 ad loc.

[5] Jacobson 1999. *Historia Animalium* 6.18, 571b. Toughening of the skin in preparation for battle with other boars: καὶ πρὸς ἀλλήλους δὲ ποιοῦνται μάχας θαυμαστάς, θωρακίζοντες ἑαυτοὺς καὶ ποιοῦντες τὸ δέρμα ὡς παχύτατον ἐκ παρασκευῆς, πρὸς τὰ δένδρα τρίβοντες καὶ τῷ πηλῷ μολύνοντες πολλάκις καὶ ξηραίνοντες ἑαυτούς. Jacobson notes that "Lucilius evidently used this fact for vituperative purposes," *scaberat ut porcus contritis arbore costis*, 333 M = 331 K.

κόπτων ἀμφοτέρῃσι, χαμαὶ δέ κε πάντας ὀδόντας
γναθμῶν ἐξελάσαιμι συὸς ὣς ληϊβοτείρης.

(*Odyssey* 18.25–29)

Angry at him, Iros the vagabond said:
"Look at that, how glibly this *molobros* talks,
like an old furnace-woman. I would devise some bad plans
for him,
hitting him with both hands, and I would knock all the teeth
from his jaws onto the ground, as if he were a pig that is
devouring the crops."

It is curious that the pig in this comparison loses its teeth, and the scholia offer little clarification. In Eustathius' opinion, the verses in question may refer to a Cypriot law that allowed a person whose crops are damaged by another's pig to knock its teeth out.[6] A reference to a particular Cypriot law is unlikely, to say the least, but perhaps Iros' threat could reflect some similar, and more widely known, practice of detoothing pigs in defense of crops. What seems tolerably clear is only that Odysseus is being teased and threatened by this uncomplimentary comparison. Teeth, of course, are the primary characteristic of the boar, the words for tooth and tusk being the same in Greek, just as the words for the wild boar and domestic swine are too. The boar's white tusks, which the animal menacingly sharpens, are a constant presence in similes, and a toothless pig seems to be the very opposite of its fiery wild counterpart. Odysseus conceals his muscles under squalid rags, and his symbolic identity with the fierce boar is hidden, it seems, under the mask of a toothless and perhaps patchy-coated pig. Of course, when he girds himself for a fight with Iros, Odysseus begins to look not so miserable after all, and the suitors comment on his strong body (*Odyssey* 18.71–74). Iros is first terrified and then badly beaten, and the suitors get a glimpse of what is behind the mask, but do not recognize what they see.

If Iros and Melanthios use pig language to dishonor Odysseus, Eumaeus uses pigs themselves to do just the opposite. The importance in the poem of the swineherd and his swine is a subject too large to be discussed here fully and does not relate directly to the conversation in Book 19, but the very fact that Eumaeus is Odysseus' most important ally, that Odysseus goes first of all to his cabin and there, next to the pig sties, and meets with his son, does

[6] Eustathius 2.165 on *Odyssey* 18.29.

support the idea that the hero has a special relationship to the animal. One detail of Odysseus' stay with Eumaeus seems worth mentioning in connection with Book 19. As they feast at Odysseus' house, the suitors consume its wealth, and in particular they diminish the number of male pigs, with Eumaeus always sending the best of them:

> πεντήκοντα σύες χαμαιευνάδες ἐρχατόωντο,
> θήλειαι τοκάδες· τοὶ δ' ἄρσενες ἐκτὸς ἴαυον,
> πολλὸν παυρότεροι· τοὺς γὰρ μινύθεσκον ἔδοντες
> ἀντίθεοι μνηστῆρες, ἐπεὶ προΐαλλε συβώτης
> αἰεὶ ζατρεφέων σιάλων τὸν ἄριστον ἀπάντων.

> (*Odyssey* 14.15–19)

> Fifty swine who sleep on the ground were confined [in each
>   enclosure],
> the breeding females, while the males slept outside,
> many fewer in number. For the godlike suitors diminished
>   their number
> by eating them, since the swineherd always sent them
> the best of all the well-fed pigs.

When Odysseus arrives at the swineherd's hut he is naturally treated to more modest fare, namely piglets (*khoirea*), and Eumaeus remarks that this is what the servants eat, while the grown and fattened male pigs are for the suitors (18.80–81). Eumaeus then goes on to explain to his guest how the suitors carelessly devour Odysseus' flocks and seem to feel safe doing so, (he presumes they have information 'from the god' about Odysseus' death), and concludes by mentioning that every day he selects the best of the pigs for them:

> αὐτὰρ ἐγὼ σῦς τάσδε φυλάσσω τε ῥύομαί τε
> καί σφι συῶν τὸν ἄριστον ἐῢ κρίνας ἀποπέμπω.

> (*Odyssey* 14.107–108)

> But I guard and watch over these pigs,
> and carefully choose the best of the pigs and send it off
>   to them.

The suitors also get to eat the best of goats (14.105–106) but in the setting of Eumaeus' hut the emphasis is on the pigs, and in both cases the impression is created that the suitor's choice of victims for their daily sacrifice has to do with more than gastronomical considerations. The male animals are more expendable that the female ones if the flocks are to be sustained, but quite apart from such practical considerations, there is obvious symbolism in the suitors' choice of always sacrificing the best of Odysseus' male animals. The suitors, it seems, want to be what they eat, the strongest males around. Their daring choice of victims implies that they are no worse than Odysseus, since they can take the male flower of his flocks with impunity.

Eumaeus and his guest talk over their meal, and Odysseus tells his Second Cretan Lie. It has been suggested that in telling this fictional biography he is in fact hinting to Eumaeus at his real identity.[7] He also claims that Odysseus is currently in Thesprotia and that his return is imminent. Eumaeus deplores this claim, refuses to believe it, and thereby casts doubt on his guest's entire story, and yet his attitude to the beggar undergoes a noticeable change. Whereas before the beggar-Odysseus was told to be content with a servant's meal, now Eumaeus orders the best of pigs to be sacrificed for him. All of a sudden the swineherd has had enough of giving up the fruit of his labors to the suitors and he will share an honorific meal with his guest. The suitors do not even know yet that a new person has appeared on the island, but he has already taken their place as the one who gets to eat 'the best of pigs'. The pig is described in some detail, (he is very fat and five years old) , and so is the sacrifice, (Eumaeus does everything in a ritually correct way). As he casts into the fire the hairs from the pig's head, Eumaeus prays to all the gods for Odysseus' return (14.422–424).[8]

It is an open question whether or not Eumaeus' sacrifice indicates that he has suspicions about his guest's identity. But regardless of what Eumaeus is supposed to think, the very fact that Odysseus is treated to the best of pigs is significant in itself. This sacrifice is a step in the hero's return, and it is surely notable that he not only partakes in it, but also receives the honorific portion, the back. The language used to describe this presages Odysseus' reestablishment on Ithaca, since he is here called *anax*, and the way he is treated is described with the verb γεραίρω, also used in the *Iliad* when Ajax receives an honorific portion (also the back) at the feast of kings in Agamemnon's tent (*Iliad* 7.321):

> νώτοισιν δ' Ὀδυσῆα διηνεκέεσσι γέραιρεν
> ἀργιόδοντος ὑός, κύδαινε δὲ θυμὸν ἄνακτος.
>
> (*Odyssey* 14.437–438)

[7] Roisman 1990:222–233.
[8] On the ritual details of Eumaeus' sacrifice see Kadletz 1984 and Petropoulou 1987.

But he honored Odysseus by giving him the long chine
of the white-toothed pig, and gratified the heart of
his master.

There seems to be a touch of irony in the way Odysseus both praises Eumaeus for the honor and notes the discrepancy between his assumed persona and the treatment he receives:

αἴθ' οὕτως, Εὔμαιε, φίλος Διὶ πατρὶ γένοιο
ὡς ἐμοί, ὅττι με τοῖον ἐόντ' ἀγαθοῖσι γεραίρεις.

(*Odyssey* 14.440–441)

Eumaeus, may you be as dear to father Zeus
as you are to me, since you honor me, such as I am,
with good things.

Is there a bit of teasing in this remark? Eumaeus professes to disbelieve his guest, but his actions belie his words. He may not yet be convinced that his guest is Odysseus, but he certainly no longer seems to believe that he is a simple beggar. Does Odysseus here let Eumaeus know that the discrepancy does not escape his notice? Eumaeus' response is also far from simple, and can be taken in several ways:

ἔσθιε, δαιμόνιε ξείνων, καὶ τέρπεο τοῖσδε,
οἷα πάρεστι· θεὸς δὲ τὸ μὲν δώσει, τὸ δ' ἐάσει,
ὅττι κεν ᾧ θυμῷ ἐθέλῃ· δύναται γὰρ ἅπαντα.

(*Odyssey* 14.443–445)

Eat, remarkable stranger, and enjoy the things
that are here. God will grant one thing, and let another
thing fall through,
whatever he wants in his heart: for he can do anything.

By urging him to enjoy what there is, Eumaeus seems to let his guest know that further probing into the reasons for the honor is unwelcome. When he adds that gods can give and take as they wish, he seems both to suggest that nothing is secure, and that much is possible. In any case, the conclusion, namely that everything is doable for the gods, is certainly the kind of commonplace that reverberates with suggestiveness in this setting, for surely one of its implications is that the gods could even bring back Odysseus. In Eumaeus' hut, Odysseus progresses from eating piglets like servants to receiving the honorific portion at the sacrifice of the best of pigs, a progress that represents a step in his gradual return, a move away from the nameless beggar and towards the king that Eumaeus so fondly remembers.

And if there is a wild animal with which that king is generally associated, it is certainly the boar and not, for example, the lion or the leopard. This association is present not only in the *Odyssey* but also in the *Iliad*, and fits Odysseus in part because the boar's aggressive behavior, as it is represented in Homer, is a good match for Odysseus' particular type of violence. In the *Iliad*, Odysseus' association with the boar is marked, most strikingly, by the fact that he is the only character in the poem to wear the boar tusk helmet:

> Μηριόνης δ' Ὀδυσῆϊ δίδου βιὸν ἠδὲ φαρέτρην
> καὶ ξίφος, ἀμφὶ δέ οἱ κυνέην κεφαλῆφιν ἔθηκε
> ῥινοῦ ποιητήν· πολέσιν δ' ἔντοσθεν ἱμᾶσιν
> ἐντέτατο στερεῶς· ἔκτοσθε δὲ λευκοὶ ὀδόντες
> ἀργιόδοντος ὑὸς θαμέες ἔχον ἔνθα καὶ ἔνθα
> εὖ καὶ ἐπισταμένως· μέσσῃ δ' ἐνὶ πῖλος ἀρήρει
> τήν ῥά ποτ' ἐξ Ἐλεῶνος Ἀμύντορος Ὀρμενίδαο
> ἐξέλετ' Αὐτόλυκος πυκινὸν δόμον ἀντιτορήσας,
> Σκάνδειαν δ' ἄρα δῶκε Κυθηρίῳ Ἀμφιδάμαντι·
> Ἀμφιδάμας δὲ Μόλῳ δῶκε ξεινήϊον εἶναι,
> αὐτὰρ ὃ Μηριόνῃ δῶκεν ᾧ παιδὶ φορῆναι·
> δὴ τότ' Ὀδυσσῆος πύκασεν κάρη ἀμφιτεθεῖσα.

(*Iliad* 10.260–271)

> And Meriones gave Odysseus his bow and quiver,
> and a sword, and put on his head a helmet
> made out of leather. On the inside it was firmly strung
> with leather thongs; on the outside white tusks
> of a shining-tusked boar were closely set this way
>   and that,
> well and skillfully. And in the middle a felt cap was fitted
>   into it.
> This helmet Autolykos once stole out of Eleon, from Amyntor,
>   son of Ormenos,
> penetrating into his close-built house,
> and gave it to Amphidamas of Cythera to take to Skandeia.
> And Amphidamas gave it to Molos as a guestgift,
> and he in turn gave it to Meriones, his son, to wear.
> But then it was put on the head of Odysseus and protected it.

Although the helmet belongs to Meriones, he never actually wears it. Odysseus, on the other hand, is linked to the helmet doubly, not only because he wears it into ambush, but also because the helmet comes to Meriones through Odysseus' own grandfather, Autolykos, who acquires it by theft. This "coincidence" was noted and commented upon by a scholiast, who found it pleasant that the helmet came back by such a complex route to Autolykos' grandson.[9] It is curious that Odysseus' connection with the boar repeatedly intersects with his maternal grandfather, both in the *Iliad* and in the *Odyssey*. In neither case does Autolykos himself hunt, and it has been argued that the helmet in the *Iliad* even symbolizes Odysseus' "Autolycan heritage," his darker side, and his proclivity towards guile, in short his excellent suitability for a secret nocturnal mission such as he performs in the Doloneia. This may well be true, but I think there is more to the helmet. As was mentioned above, costumes have a special significance in the Doloneia, and are described both in great detail and in rare language. Diomedes' costume, for example, includes a very strange helmet, the subject of a memorable alliterative phrase, ἄφαλόν τε καὶ ἄλλοφον, 'without horn or crest' (10.258). The helmet is said to be called καταῖτυξ (10.258), a Homeric *hapax* of unclear meaning that stumped the scholiasts. From the way it is explained in the *Iliad* (10.257–259) it is clear that *kataitux* was not a widely known word, and needed glossing. All of this suggests that the *Iliad* here touches upon subjects of some antiquity, and this impression is strengthened by the appearance of the boar tusk helmet, certainly a bronze-age object.[10] This helmet also receives a very detailed description, so that it draws a lot of attention to itself. Moreover, the costumes of the Doloneia have some of the properties of masks, as has long been recognized.[11] If Dolon's wolf skin hints at playing the wolf, and if Diomedes' lion skin similarly links the hero to the animal, then Odysseus is here identified with the boar. This is striking enough, since Odysseus does not always cut such a brave figure in the *Iliad*, while the boar is depicted as the most ferocious of the wild beasts. In fact, it has been suggested that, in contrast to Dolon and Diomedes' outfits, Odysseus' is to be interpreted as a disguise, in the sense that Odysseus is precisely not a boar and

---

[9] Scholia bT on *Iliad* 10.271.

[10] Hainsworth 1993:179–180 ad loc., with references. The significance of dress in the Doloneia was noted by Reinhardt (1961:247). For a discussion of costumes in the Doloenia and especially of Odysseus' boar-tusk helmet see Clay 1983:76–89, on Dolon's wolf-costume see Gernet 1981:125–139.

[11] Reinhardt 1961:247, Clay 1983:76–77. See also above, p143.

that a fox or a wolf might be a better match for him.[12] The helmet, according to this argument, belies and dissembles Odysseus' true character. I think that, on the contrary, the boar tusk helmet is indeed emblematic of Odysseus in the way the lion's hide is emblematic of Diomedes, and the wolf pelt of Dolon. Odysseus may not always behave with the greatest nobility in the *Iliad*, but he does have boar-like qualities, including the animal's uncompromising aggression, a subject to which I will come back shortly. The fact that Autolykos is associated with the boar hunt in the *Odyssey* and with the boar tusk helmet in the Doloneia suggests that being boar-like is not incompatible with having Autolycan qualities, and that the two aspects of Odysseus' personality might indeed be connected. In fact, one of the distinctive qualities of the boar which is illustrated in *Odyssey* 19 is its habit of hiding in a lair and then bursting out of it, right upon the hunters, a quality well suited for a master of ambush such as Odysseus. There is even a lexical link between the word of the boar's lair used in Book 19 (λόχμη, 19.441) and the word for ambush, λόχος, both derived from the root of λέχεται, 'to lie down'.[13]

Odysseus is also compared to the boar in an extended simile, and the comparison between it and other such similes reveal more of the hero's boar-like qualities. The Achaeans retreat in fear (φόβος ἔλλαβε πάντας, *Iliad* 11.402) and leave Odysseus alone among the Trojans. For a second Odysseus hesitates, contemplating the shameful option to flee (φέβομαι) and the chilling option to stay and perish now that Zeus has scattered (ἐφόβησε) all the Achaeans. He decides to stand firm, and it is at this moment that he is compared to a boar coming out of a thicket and being met by a throng of dogs and men:

> ὡς δ' ὅτε κάπριον ἀμφὶ κύνες θαλεροί τ' αἰζηοὶ
> σεύωνται, ὃ δέ τ' εἶσι βαθείης ἐκ ξυλόχοιο
> θήγων λευκὸν ὀδόντα μετὰ γναμπτῇσι γένυσσιν,
> ἀμφὶ δέ τ' ἀΐσσονται, ὑπαὶ δέ τε κόμπος ὀδόντων
> γίγνεται, οἳ δὲ μένουσιν ἄφαρ δεινόν περ ἐόντα,
> ὥς ῥα τότ' ἀμφ' Ὀδυσῆα Διῒ φίλον ἐσσεύοντο
> Τρῶες·

(*Iliad* 11.411–420)

---

[12] Clay 1983:77.

[13] The verb is attested only in Hesychius: λέχεται· κοιμᾶται and λελοχυῖα· λεχὼ γενομένη. The aorist form ἔλεκτο may also belong to the same verb. The root *legh is attested in Hittite, Germanic, Celtic, and Slavic, and has multiple derivatives in Greek, including various words for bed such as λέκτρον and λέχος. See Chantraine 1968–1980 s.v. λέχεται for a full discussion. See further on the similarities between the boar's lair in *Odyssey* 19 and Odysseus' bed of leaves in *Odyssey* 5 (εὐνήν, 482; λέκτο, 487). Russo (1992 on 19.439–443) comments on this dictional link.

As when dogs and lusty young men
rush around a boar, who comes out of a deep thicket
whetting the white tusks in his curved jaws,
and they dart around him, and the gnashing of his teeth
    is audible,
but they stand firm and await him, though he is terrible,
so at that time Trojans rushed around Odysseus dear to Zeus.

It is interesting that the only other hero to receive a boar simile of this type in the *Iliad* is Idomeneus, Odysseus' Cretan older brother in *Odyssey* 19. As an aside, it seems noteworthy that Crete crops up so consistently in the proximity of the boar. In the *Odyssey* the boar hunt follows after Odysseus' Third Cretan Lie and interrupts his conversation as a Cretan prince with Penelope. In the Doloneia, Odysseus receives his boar tusk helmet from a Cretan, Meriones. And the other of the two Cretan leaders, Meriones' uncle Idomeneus, is the only warrior in the *Iliad* to be featured in a boar simile matching that of Odysseus. It has been suggested that Odysseus and Meriones are similar in many ways, and they are certainly connected beyond Homer, as are Odysseus and Idomeneus.[14] It is perhaps not a coincidence, but a reflection of deeper and older connections, that Odysseus receives his helmet from Meriones and that he and Idomeneus are linked though their boar-similes. In Book 13, Idomeneus is also facing an intimidating foe, and the possibility of flight is raised immediately before the boar simile:

ἀλλ' οὐκ Ἰδομενῆα φόβος λάβε τηλύγετον ὥς,
ἀλλ' ἔμεν' ὡς ὅτε τις σῦς οὔρεσιν ἀλκὶ πεποιθώς,
ὅς τε μένει κολοσυρτὸν ἐπερχόμενον πολὺν ἀνδρῶν
χώρῳ ἐν οἰοπόλῳ, φρίσσει δέ τε νῶτον ὕπερθεν·
ὀφθαλμὼ δ' ἄρα οἱ πυρὶ λάμπετον· αὐτὰρ ὀδόντας
θήγει, ἀλέξασθαι μεμαὼς κύνας ἠδὲ καὶ ἄνδρας·
ὣς μένεν Ἰδομενεὺς δουρικλυτός, οὐδ' ὑπεχώρει.

                        (*Iliad* 13.470–476)

Fear did not grasp Idomeneus like an overgrown child,
but he stood firm, like some boar in the mountains, sure in
    his own valor,

[14] On the similarities and connections between Meriones and Odysseus see Clay 1983:84–89 and Haft 1984. One particularly striking example involves both heroes and also concerns helmets. Plutarch (*Life of Marcellus* 20) reports that helmets with the names of Meriones and Odysseus were consecrated at a temple to goddesses known as the Mothers in the Sicilian town Enguium (see also above, p105).

who stands up to a large gang of men advancing upon him,
in a deserted place, and bristles his back.
And his eyes blaze with fire, and he whets
his tusks, keen to fight off dogs and men.
So Idomeneus famed for his spear held his ground,
    and did not give way.

Like Odysseus, Idomeneus is pictured as a lonely beast facing a band of men and dogs, though the two similes are not identical. Odysseus is in fact only a secondary subject of the simile in which the Trojans are compared to dogs and men attacking a boar, and this placement of emphasis seems to predict the course of the following fight: Odysseus is eventually wounded and forced to begin retreating before the superior numbers of the Trojans. In contrast, Idomeneus at first faces the enemy on his own, but then calls for reinforcements and emerges unscathed from the encounter. In his boar simile, accordingly, there is more focus on the boar and less on the men who confront him. Still, the two similes show multiple similarities, which seem significant especially in view of their rarity.[15] The closest parallel elsewhere comes from the Hesiodic *Shield*, where Herakles is compared to a boar as he confronts Kyknos:

οἷος δ' ἐν βήσσῃς ὄρεος χαλεπὸς προϊδέσθαι
κάπρος χαυλιόδων φρονέει [δὲ] θυμῷ μαχέσασθαι
ἀνδράσι θηρευτῆς, θήγει δέ τε λευκὸν ὀδόντα
δοχμωθείς, ἀφρὸς δὲ περὶ στόμα μαστιχόωντι
λείβεται, ὄσσε δέ οἱ πυρὶ λαμπετόωντι ἔικτον,
ὀρθὰς δ' ἐν λοφιῇ φρίσσει τρίχας ἀμφί τε δειρήν·
τῷ ἴκελος Διὸς υἱὸς ἀφ' ἱππείου θόρε δίφρου.

                              (*Shield* 384–390)

Just as in mountain woods, difficult to detect,
a large-tusked boar plots in his heart to fight
against hunters and whets his white tusks,
turning sideways, and foam flows about his mouth
as he gnashes his teeth, and his eyes are like blazing fire,
and he lifts his bristling hair along his spine and neck,
looking like this creature the son of Zeus jumped off his
    horse-drawn chariot.

---

[15] Idomeneus' connection to the boar is not limited to this simile. At *Iliad* 4.253 he is called συῒ εἴκελος ἀλκήν, ('like a boar in might'), an expression that appears only three times in Homer (the other two are about Hektor at *Iliad* 11.293 and about Ajax at *Iliad* 17.281).

In all of these cases a single boar faces multiple enemies and is not intimidated by them. In the *Iliad*, the battle circumstances which prompt these similes are themselves similar: both Idomeneus and Odysseus are alone, both overcome fear, and both try to hold out while calling for reinforcement (αὖε δ' ἑταίρους, 'shouted for companions', Odysseus at *Iliad* 11.461, Idomeneus at *Iliad* 13. 477). There are, besides, several elements that are shared by all or most of these similes and also by the description of the boar hunt in Book 19 of the *Odyssey*. The boars in *Odyssey* 11, *Iliad* 13, and the *Shield* all sharpen their white tusks, and this is described in diction that illustrates both the formulaic qualities of this element and the flexibility of the formulaic system: *Shield* has θήγει δέ τε λευκὸν ὀδόντα, 'and he whets his white tusk' (386), *Iliad* 13 has αὐτὰρ ὀδόντας | θήγει, 'but he whets his tusks' (474-75), while *Iliad* 11 has θήγων λευκὸν ὀδόντα, 'whetting his white tusk' (413). Just as white tusks are traditional so is the bristling of the boar's back: ὀρθὰς δ' ἐν λοφιῇ φρίσσει τρίχας ἀμφί τε δειρήν, 'he makes the hair on his spine and neck bristle' (*Shield* 389), φρίσσει δέ τε νῶτον ὕπερθεν, 'and he bristled his back above' (*Iliad* 13.473), φρίξας εὖ λοφιήν, 'bristling his spine strongly' (*Odyssey* 19.446). Similarly, fire flashing in the beast's eyes is a recurrent feature: ὄσσε δέ οἱ πυρὶ λαμπετόωντι ἔικτον, 'his eyes were like blazing fire' (*Shield* 388), ὀφθαλμὼ δ' ἄρα οἱ πυρὶ λάμπετον, 'his eyes blazed with fire' (*Iliad* 13.474), πῦρ δ' ὀφθαλμοῖσι δεδορκώς, 'looking with fire in his eyes' (*Odyssey* 19.446). The boar in *Iliad* 11 comes out of a thicket (βαθείης ἐκ ξυλόχοιο, 412) and so does the boar in *Odyssey* 19 (ὁ δ' ἀντίος ἐκ ξυλόχοιο, 445), the two expressions being metrically-equivalent sequences. A similar idea is expressed in the *Shield*, where the boar is called 'hard to see in advance', (χαλεπὸς προϊδέσθαι, 384). In all these cases, the animal's power, apart from its spirit and physical strength, lies in the fact that it appears suddenly out of concealment.

The cumulative picture of the boar that emerges from these similes is that of a beast who appears suddenly out of a hidden lair and who fights alone, even in a desperate position, against a large numbers of foes. Such an animal is a particularly fitting double for Odysseus. The ability to lie in hiding and then emerge suddenly is precisely the trait he utilizes in the Doloneia, when he notices Dolon from afar and hides together with Diomedes away from the road in order to jump out when Dolon is close. When Odysseus confronts the suitors in the *Odyssey*, he reveals himself suddenly as he emerges out of his rags to face, almost single-handedly, enemies who are individually lesser than him but are dangerous in greater numbers, just like the Iliadic boars surrounded by men and dogs. Nor should these enemies expect any mercy from a boar-like opponent. Whatever the zoological facts, it is an ancient belief expressed in the *Iliad* that no animal is as violent, relentless, and untameable as a wild boar.[16] In the same way, Odysseus is merciless to Dolon and equally merciless to the suitors.

As Odysseus converses with Penelope he prepares the ground for bursting out of his disguise and confronting the suitors. The first part of the conversation contains veiled claims regarding his identity as Odysseus. In the second part, Penelope will propose the bow contest, thus providing Odysseus with the next step that he will take in order to substantiate these claims. The contest also provides an occasion and means for casting off his disguise and attacking his rivals. His boar-like qualities will shine in the process and the boar hunt that divides the dialogue in Book 19 is a suggestive background against which to view the second part of the conversation.

It is a much-observed fact that when large game is killed there often appears a relationship of equivalence between the hunter and the hunted, the hero and the beast. It has been argued that in Ancient Greece (and Europe in general) the boar in particular tended to enter into this relationship, being the prevalent large quarry, the nearest equivalent to men among predators, and more violent than any other animal.[17] In the *Odyssey* the equivalence between the boar and Odysseus is marked by the deployment of formulaic diction: the description of Odysseus' first shelter in overgrown bushes on Skheria is almost identical to that of the boar's shelter in Book 19. Before he is disturbed by the footsteps of humans and dogs, the boar is invisible, hidden in a lair so impenetrable that neither wind nor sun can reach him:

> ἔνθα δ' ἄρ' ἐν λόχμῃ πυκινῇ κατέκειτο μέγας σῦς·
> τὴν μὲν ἄρ' οὔτ' ἀνέμων διάη μένος ὑγρὸν ἀέντων,
> οὔτε μιν ἠέλιος φαέθων ἀκτῖσιν ἔβαλλεν,
> οὔτ' ὄμβρος περάασκε διαμπερές· ὣς ἄρα πυκνὴ
> ἦεν, ἀτὰρ φύλλων ἐνέην χύσις ἤλιθα πολλή.

(*Odyssey* 19.439–443)

---

[16] E.g. *Iliad* 17.20–22: οὔτ' οὖν παρδάλιος τόσσον μένος οὔτε λέοντος | οὔτε συὸς κάπρου ὀλοόφρονος, οὔ τε μέγιστος | θυμὸς ἐνὶ στήθεσσι περὶ σθένεϊ βλεμεαίνει. Eustathius comments on these lines (4.4): οὐ μάτην ἐπὶ συὸς ἔφη τὸ "οὗ θυμὸς μέγιστος", ἀλλ' ὅτι ἀφυλάκτως ἔχει ὁ σῦς πρὸς τὸ παθεῖν διὰ τὸ ἄγαν θράσος. θρασὺ μὲν γὰρ καὶ ἡ πάρδαλις, ὁ λέων δὲ καὶ ἀνδρεῖον. ἄμφω δὲ φυλάξονται ποτε παθεῖν μᾶλλον ἤπερ ὁ σῦς θυμῷ πολλῷ ῥέων. Ἔτι πάρδαλις μέν, φασί, καὶ λέων ἡμεροῦνται, σῦς δὲ ἄγριος ἀεὶ ἄγριος.

[17] Meuli 1946:248–252, Burkert 1983:12–22, esp. 20–21 with references, Davies 2001, referring to Hatto 1980:xiii and 230.

There a great boar lay in its closely-knit lair.
The power of wet-blowing winds could not blow through it,
nor the shining sun strike it with its rays,
nor yet did the rain penetrate it, so solid it was,
and there was a great pile of fallen leaves on it.

On Skheria, Odysseus similarly lies under a cover of bushes and leaves so dense that he is completely protected from the elements, and he too is awakened by a sound (of Nausikaa and her friends playing ball). The boar emerges suddenly, close by Odysseus, while on Skheria Odysseus has to walk a bit to reach the maidens, but he still startles and terrifies them. The closest verbal echo is in the description of the shelter itself:

> δοιοὺς δ' ἄρ' ὑπήλυθε θάμνους
> ἐξ ὁμόθεν πεφυῶτας· ὁ μὲν φυλίης, ὁ δ' ἐλαίης.
> τοὺς μὲν ἄρ' οὔτ' ἀνέμων διάη μένος ὑγρὸν ἀέντων,
> οὔτε ποτ' ἠέλιος φαέθων ἀκτῖσιν ἔβαλλεν,
> οὔτ' ὄμβρος περάασκε διαμπερές· ὣς ἄρα πυκνοὶ
> ἀλλήλοισιν ἔφυν ἐπαμοιβαδίς· οὓς ὑπ' Ὀδυσσεὺς
> δύσετ'. ἄφαρ δ' εὐνὴν ἐπαμήσατο χερσὶ φίλησιν
> εὐρεῖαν· φύλλων γὰρ ἔην χύσις ἤλιθα πολλή.

> (*Odyssey* 5.476–483)[18]

> He crept underneath two bushes
> that grew from the same spot, one of *phylie* and one
>   of olive.
> The power of wet-blowing winds could not blow through
>   them,
> nor the shining sun strike them with its rays,
> nor yet did the rain penetrate them, so close together
>   did they grow,
> intertwining one with the other. Odysseus entered
> under them and with his hands heaped up a wide
> bed for himself, for there was a great pile of fallen leaves
>   there.

---

[18] Russo 1993 discusses in detail the verbal parallels and their significance, arguing for a momentary merging of identity between Odysseus and the boar. My discussion of this thematic echo is indebted to him, though I believe the merging he suggests is more than momentary.

This echo, it has been argued, creates a "temporary merging" of Odysseus and the boar, so that the beast becomes in a sense Odysseus' double.[19] The impression of the boar and Odysseus as equals is strengthened by the image of their reciprocal attack: Odysseus raises his spear, but the boar is quicker in striking with his tusk, only to be brought down by the wounded Odysseus. This equivalence between the hunter and the beast is an especially fitting element in this hunt, because it is also a rite of passage for the youthful Odysseus. As one scholar puts it: "Odysseus has met his 'animal other,' killed him, and taken on the animal power of the boar as a constituent element of his new manhood."[20]

It is a scholarly commonplace that Odysseus' hunt on Parnassus has initiatory undertones (though it is not an initiation, of course).[21] Odysseus comes to Parnassus in fulfillment of Autolykos' request that he should come once he reaches *hebe*, a request which Autolykos utters as he first sees baby Odysseus and gives him his name:

τῷ δ' Ὀδυσεὺς ὄνομ' ἔστω ἐπώνυμον. αὐτὰρ ἐγώ γε,
ὁππότ' ἂν ἡβήσας μητρώϊον ἐς μέγα δῶμα
ἔλθῃ Παρνησόνδ', ὅθι πού μοι κτήματ' ἔασι,
τῶν οἱ ἐγὼ δώσω καί μιν χαίροντ' ἀποπέμψω.

(*Odyssey* 19.406–409)

Let "Odysseus" be his given name. And whenever
he reaches the pinnacle of youth and comes into his mother's
    great paternal house,
and to Parnassus, where I have my possessions,
from these I will give him a gift and send him back rejoicing.

The trip to Parnassus to meet his grandfather and name-giver, be received into maternal family, and carry away the promised gifts is therefore closely bound up with Odysseus' identity.[22] The fact that Odysseus hunts with his mother's brothers is significant, because in many societies, including those of Ancient Greece and other Indo-European cultures, the mother's father and her brothers have a special connection to their sister's or daughter's sons, and play

---

[19] Russo 1993:57.

[20] Russo 1993:58.

[21] See, e.g. Detienne 1973:303 (on boar hunt as a male initiatory rite), Schnapp-Gourbeillon 1981:138–139, Felson-Rubin and Sale 1983 and 1984.

[22] For the name of Odysseus and its connection to the hero's identity, see above p.160. Some representative studies on the question are Sulzberger 1926, Stanford 1952, Dimock 1956, Russo 1985:248–250, Clay 1983:59–65, Peradotto 1990.

a large role in their education. The role of mother's brothers as educators and helpers is attested both in myth, (Daidalos and Talos, Achilles and Menesthios, Adrastos and Hippomedon, Priam and Eurypylos, Creon and Amphitryon, etc.), and in historical record: Pindar mentions boys competing alongside their maternal uncles, and several of his *laudandi* follow in the footsteps of their maternal uncles by winning in the same events.[23] In his study of the importance of the maternal uncle and grandfather in Greece, Bremmer concludes his analysis of multiple examples of this phenomenon by suggesting that, "MoBr [mother's brother] had an active role in his SiSo [sister's son] education" and that "for the young nephew the MoBr functions as the model par excellence for imitation."[24] He further notes that when maternal uncles hunted with their nephews, their supervision of the hunt "most likely had an initiatory significance, as probably also in other cases where a SiSo accompanied this MoBr into war."[25] The most famous example of such a hunt in the company of maternal uncles is also the most famous boar hunt of Greek myth, the hunt for the Calydonian boar. Like Odysseus, Meleager is accompanied not just by uncles, but specifically by his mother's brothers, and this detail is central to the myth and present from its earliest attestation. A conflict with these uncles and the (accidental or deliberate) killing of some of them is the turning point of the myth and the reason for Meleager's own death. It has been suggested that while Odysseus' hunt represents a successful passage from boyhood to manhood, Meleager's represents a failed one, though not all versions of the latter myth fit this interpretation with equal ease.[26] Nevertheless, while it may be simplistic to see the Calydonian hunt as nothing but a failed initiation, it certainly has features of a rite of passage. Boar-hunts in general seem to play a special role in male upbringing, and Pausanias (3.14.10) even describes ritualized boar-fights staged by Spartan ephebes, with each boar representing a group of youths. On fifth-century vases the Calydonian hunters are beardless youths dressed only in the chlamys, a typical way of depicting ephebes. As Barringer remarks, "Contemporary views may have understood the youthful hunters in the Calydonian boar hunt depictions as ephebes or pre-adults

---

[23] Pindar *Pythian* 8.35–38, *Nemean* 5.41, *Isthmian* 6.57, *Nemean* 9.79–81, *Isthmian* 3.24. Bremmer 1983a:179 discusses these examples and lists further ones.

[24] Bremmer 1983b:180.

[25] Bremmer 1983b:178.

[26] Felson-Rubin and Sale 1983, critiqued by Most 1983, response in Felson-Rubin and Sale 1984. For a comprehensive discussion of the Meleager myth see Honea 1991. For a discussion of the Calydonian hunt, including its initiatory aspects and the possible nature of Meleager's transgression, see Barringer 2001:147–161.

engaged in a hunt that exalts them to manhood."[27] Certainly Odysseus' hunt on Parnassus does just that: it exalts him to manhood.

A recollection of this moment seems especially potent at the end of Odysseus' first conversation with Penelope, the conversation in which he evokes many themes associated with coming of age and with his youthful identity as a hunter. The recollection of the boar hunt takes these themes one step further, since hunting deer may be both typical and expected of a young hunter, but killing a boar represents an entirely different level of manhood. The particular importance for the establishment of manhood of this life-threatening hunt is evidenced by the story told by Athenaeus, (with reference to Hegesandros), that in Macedonia it was not customary for a male to recline at dinner until he had speared a boar without the use of nets. As a result of this rule, a Macedonian named Kassandros, though a brave man and a good hunter, had to eat sitting up next to his father, because he was not lucky enough to have accomplished this feat.[28] In Herodotus' story, Croesus' son Atys cannot bear to be prohibited from taking part in a boar hunt, because he believes that such abstention would render him both an inferior citizen and an inferior man in the eyes of others:

Ὦ πάτερ, τὰ κάλλιστα πρότερόν κοτε καὶ γενναιότατα ἡμῖν ἦν ἔς τε πολέμους καὶ ἐς ἄγρας φοιτῶντας εὐδοκιμέειν. Νῦν δὲ ἀμφοτέρων με τούτων ἀποκληίσας ἔχεις, οὔτε τινὰ δειλίην μοι παριδὼν οὔτε ἀθυμίην. Νῦν τε τέοισί με χρὴ ὄμμασι ἔς τε ἀγορὴν καὶ ἐξ ἀγορῆς φοιτῶντα φαίνεσθαι; κοῖος μέν τις τοῖσι πολιήτῃσι δόξω εἶναι, κοῖος δέ τις τῇ νεογάμῳ γυναικί; κοίῳ δὲ ἐκείνη δόξει ἀνδρὶ συνοικέειν;

(Herodotus 1.37)

Father, in times past it was the best and most noble thing for us to win a good reputation through warfare and hunting. But now you keep me from both these things, even though you are aware of no cowardice or faintness of heart on my part. Now what kind of appearance should I present as I go to and from the market? What kind of man will I seem to the citizens, or to my newly wedded wife? With what kind of husband will she think she lives?

---

[27] Barringer 2001:154. Barringer provides a detailed discussion of the iconography. A clear example with hunters wearing only the chlamys is an Attic red-figure *dinos* by the Agrigento Painter, c. 459 BCE (Athens, National Museum 1489), Barringer 154.
[28] Athenaeus 1.31.

Atys concludes his list of concerns with his anxiety about the opinion of his young wife. This seems to be a particular worry of his, since he saves it for the end and then repeats it twice. In so doing he touches upon yet another connotation of the boar hunt, its connection not only to manhood but more specifically to sexual virility. This connotation is not always active and visible, but it is both noticeable and naturally connected to the hunt's manhood-affirming power.

Hatto observes that in a mythic boar hunt the boar is identified with the hero, and that, at the same time, the boar becomes a "symbol of overmastering virility," not only because of its exceptional ferocity, but also "in view of the boar's masterful way of mounting his sow."[29] Moreover, as Davies observes, "because of the physical construction of his body, the boar's most frequent mode of wounding his human pursuers was in the groin with this tusk."[30] Davies appeals to Burkert's ideas about sexual excitement at the climax of the hunt to suggest that death by a boar's tusk is akin to emasculation. Some such ideas may be behind the variation in the myth of Attis, who emasculates himself in some versions, but is killed by the boar in the Lydian version.[31] Adonis too is killed by a boar, and the description of his boar-inflicted wound in Bion's *Epitaph* has clear sexual connotations:

> κεῖται καλὸς Ἄδωνις ἐν ὤρεσι μηρὸν ὀδόντι,
> λευκῷ λευκὸν ὀδόντι τυπείς, καὶ Κύπριν ἀνιῇ
> λεπτὸν ἀποψύχων· τὸ δέ οἱ μέλαν εἴβεται αἷμα
> χιονέας κατὰ σαρκός, ὑπ᾽ ὀφρύσι δ᾽ ὄμματα ναρκῇ,
> καὶ τὸ ῥόδον φεύγει τῶ χείλεος· ἀμφὶ δὲ τήνω
> θνᾴσκει καὶ τὸ φίλημα, τὸ μήποτε Κύπρις ἀποίσει.

> (Bion *Epitaph* 8–13)

> Beautiful Adonis lies in the mountains, wounded in his thigh
>   by a boar's tusk,
>   in his white thigh by a white tusk, and he brings pain to
>   Cypris,
>   softly ceasing to breathe. And his black blood drips
>   over his snow-white skin, and beneath his brows his eyes
>   grow dim

---

[29] Hatto 1980:303 and 225.

[30] Davies 2001:5.

[31] Pausanias 7.17.8, 10–12 (both versions). Other sources of the myth include Ovid *Fasti* 4.221–222, Diodorus Siculus 3.58.

and the rose color flees from his lips, and about him
dies also his kiss, which Cypris will never have.

Other examples include the murder of Tlepolemus during a boar hunt in
Apuleius' *Metamorphoses*. Tlepolemus' killer, Thrasylus, proceeds to propose to
his victims' widow, which suggests that sexual rivalry is the motive. Thrasylus
throws Tlepolemus' body in the boar's way to be mangled as if the boar really
did kill him, and then spears his dead opponent on the right thigh to imitate
a typical boar-tusk wound.[32] In the context of rivalry over a woman, both the
boar hunt in general and the location of the wound in particular are suggestive.
Ovid seems to be playing with similar themes in his description of Ancaeus'
death in the Calydonian boar hunt. Atalanta wounds the boar with an arrow,
and the male hunters are ashamed that a woman was the first to draw blood.
Shouting that male weapons are superior to the female ones, Ancaeus lifts his
axe and at this moment the boar stabs him with both tusks in the groin.[33]

Odysseus, of course, is wounded by the boar 'above the knee', in other
words, in the thigh. The boar dies, while Odysseus establishes his manhood
and has a mark on his thigh as a trace of the danger that he confronted. The
location of Odysseus' scar is emphasized in the *Odyssey*, especially at the
moment when he receives the wound, with the words 'above the knee' in an
effective enjambment:

> ὁ δέ μιν φθάμενος ἔλασεν σῦς
> γουνὸς ὕπερ, πολλὸν δὲ διήφυσε σαρκὸς ὀδόντι.
>
> (*Odyssey* 19.449–450)

But first [before he could strike] the boar struck him
above the knee, and gashed much of his flesh with his tusk.

Odysseus' thighs, moreover, receive some attention in the part of the poem
leading up the boar hunt. As he girds himself for the fight with Iros, a preview
of what is in store for the suitors, Odysseus bares his body and reveals muscles
unexpected in an aged beggar. First on the list are his thighs:

> αὐτὰρ Ὀδυσσεὺς
> ζώσατο μὲν ῥάκεσιν περὶ μήδεα, φαῖνε δὲ μηροὺς
> καλούς τε μεγάλους τε, φάνεν δέ οἱ εὐρέες ὦμοι.
>
> (*Odyssey* 18.66–68)

---

[32] Apuleius *Metamorphoses* 8.1–15.
[33] Ovid *Metamorphoses* 8.392–400.

But Odysseus
girded himself with rags around his genitals and showed his
thighs,
splendid and great, and his wide shoulders became visible.

Further, just a few verses later, the suitors comment precisely on the strength of his thighs:

ἦ τάχα Ἶρος Ἄϊρος ἐπίσπαστον κακὸν ἕξει,
οἵην ἐκ ῥακέων ὁ γέρων ἐπιγουνίδα φαίνει.

(*Odyssey* 18.73–74)

"Soon our Iros Non-Iros will have trouble of his own making,
to judge by the thigh muscle the old man reveals from under
his rags."

The overarching context both for this comment and for the boar hunt is Odysseus' opposition to a crowd of young men who are both visibly lusting after his wife and enjoying sex with his maids. Similar concerns can be detected even in the battle between the two beggars. Threatening Iros with all manner of retribution if he loses, Antinoos concludes with a threat that they will send him to king Ekhetos, who will cut off his sexual organs and feed them to the dogs (*Odyssey* 18.87). With Iros being symbolically a representative of the suitors in this fight with Odysseus, Antinoos is understandably annoyed at the beggar's evident fear and the strong possibility of his loss. The implications of Iros' disgrace bode ill for his own self. Conversely, the threat to his manhood, which Odysseus once had to face on Parnassus, is present again. In his confrontation with the suitors, Odysseus' manliness is being tested, and a flashback to the boar hunt is one of the ways in which it is reaffirmed.

There are intriguing items of comparative evidence for the connection between the boar hunt and access to women. In the Irish and Scottish folk tale of Diarmuidd and Grainne, Diarmuidd, a maternal nephew of king Fionn, both steals his uncle's wife Grainne and kills the boar his uncle was hunting.[34] Moreover, it is remarkable that here again a maternal uncle and his sister's son appear together in connection with the boar hunt. Like Meleager, Diarmuidd undermines the typically warm and supportive relationship between mother's brother and sister's son, and does so in connection with a boar hunt. And like Meleager, Diarmuidd is not allowed to get away with his transgression: he walks barefoot on the back of the boar and is pierced by one of the animal's

---

[34] Ni Shéaghdha 1967.

poisonous bristles.[35] In his consideration of the pedigree of Shakespeare's boar in *Venus and Adonis*, Hatto concludes that it can be traced back to the twelfth century, and that "it is in these boars of the High Middle Ages that the animal stands out essentially as a symbol of overbearing masculinity in love and war, with unmistakable and long-standing associations with nobility."[36] A particularly clear example is the *Tristan and Isold* of Godfried von Strassburg. Here, Tristan is associated with the boar, which is an emblem on his shield. High Steward Marjodo, who at this time shares a bed with Tristan, dreams one night that a boar bursts into the bed-chamber of King Mark, Tristan's maternal uncle, and befouls the sheets. When he awakes from the dream, Marjodo discovers that Tristan is gone, follows him to Isold's chamber, and overhears the lovers.[37] Here again the boar is associated with Tristan's sexual incursion into his uncle's territory. In an eleventh-century Persian romance, *Wis and Ramin*, King Moabad is robbed of his wife Wis by his younger brother Ramin. He is waiting for Ramin in an ambush when a boar runs out of the forest and sets his army to flight. Moabad confronts the beast and is torn by its tusk from navel to the heart.[38] The loss of a woman and defeat in confrontation with boar go hand in hand.

I do not suggest that there is a straightforward connection between these medieval boars and the one Odysseus kills on Parnassus, but taken together with the ancient examples where the boar is associated with sexual dominance, they suggest that this is a wide-spread idea, no doubt aided and sustained by actual observation of the animal, and this increases the likelihood that some such association is active in the *Odyssey*.

A woman and *eros* also complicate the plot of the Calydonian boar hunt. In some versions of the tale, the disastrous outcome of the hunt is precipitated by Meleager's love for the Amazon-like female hunter, Atalanta. Although he kills the boar, Meleager presents Atalanta with its hide, since she was the first to strike the boar with an arrow. It is this gift of the hide that leads to

---

[35] Ni Shéaghdha 1967, K.H Schmidt in *Enzyklopädie des Märchens* s.v. Diarmuid (3.604).

[36] Hatto 1946:355.

[37] Gottfried von Strassburg, *Tristan und Isold*, Hrsg. F. Ranke 1930, 13512–13596.

[38] Hatto 1980a.xi. *Wis and Ramin* was composed ca. 1050 by the Persian poet Gorgani (also rendered as Gurgani, Jurjani) and is thought to be based on a still-earlier popular tale. Persian text and translation in Ali and Lees 1864–5. English translation by Morrison 1962, French by Massé 1959.

the quarrel between Meleager and his uncles.[39] It has been suggested that this version of Meleager's myth dramatizes the failed rite of passage as a result of premature and excessive indulgence in love, though this is a debated point. Some versions of the myth do not have Atalanta, yet Meleager kills his uncles nevertheless, and even when Atalanta is present, both on vases and in literary accounts, there is often no mention of Meleager's love for her. Many scholars trace the erotic involvement between Meleager and Atalanta to Euripides' *Meleager* (c. 416 BCE), though Atalanta appears as one of the Calydonian hunters on vases much earlier.[40] She seems to be a suitably "initiatory" figure: a female hunter, who is sometimes depicted on vases as a warrior and often wears the Scythian garb of an "outsider." The antiquity of Atalanta's part in Meleager's myth remains a matter of dispute, but it does in any case illustrate the potentialities of the myth, the ultimate suitability of erotic involvement with a woman as a subject to be raised in the context of a boar hunt.

Moreover, it has been observed that depictions of the Calydonian hunt appear on vases associated with women, namely on an *exaleiptron* (c. 570–560) and on five *dinoi*, a type of vase associated with wedding, because it was apparently a typical wedding gift.[41] In addition, the depiction of the Calydonian hunt appears on the François Vase, which both depicted a wedding, that of Peleus and Thetis, and might have served as a wedding gift.

The same subject is raised indirectly in Bacchylides 5, where Meleager dies "leaving behind shining youth," (ἀγλαὰν ἥβαν προλείπων, 154), and unmarried. That he would have made a perfect bridegroom can be inferred from the question addressed to his poor shade by Herakles, namely whether he has a sister similar to himself, whether there is a bride comparable to the bridegroom who was not to be:

---

[39] *Iliad* 9.529–99, Hesiod fr. 25.12–13 MW, Stesichorus *Suotherai* (PMG 221), Pausanias 10.31.4 (referring to Phrynichus *Pleuroniai*), Bacchylides 5.71–154, Aeschylus *Choephori* 603–12, Sophocles *Meleager* (Radt 1977, fr. 401–406), scholia to Aristophanes *Frogs* 1238, Euripides *Meleager* (Nauck 1964, fr. 515–539), Apollodorus 1.8.1–2, Accius fr. 428–450, Diodorus Siculus 4.34.2–5, Ovid *Metamorphoses* 8.270–525. Arrigoni 1977:9–47 provides a full discussion of literary sources, Barringer 2001:147–161 discusses visual as well as literary evidence. It is widely thought that the Homeric version of the myth may not be the earliest, but rather presupposes a pre-Homeric version more similar to those attested later. For a discussion of this question see Hainsworth 1993:131–132 ad loc., Bremmer 1998, Kakridis 1987:11, 18–41, Felson-Rubin and Sale 1983 and 1984.

[40] E.g., Page 1937:179, Most 1983:204–205, Séchan 1967:423–426, Woodford (LIMC, s.v. "Meleagros"). The opposite opinion is expressed by Felson-Rubin and Sale 1984:215–215 (in response to Most 1983) and Arrigoni 1977:21.

[41] Barringer 2001:159–160.

Ἥρά τις ἐν μεγάροις Οἰ-
νῆος ἀρηϊφίλου
ἔστιν ἀδμήτα θυγάτρων,
σοὶ φυὰν ἀλιγκία;
Τάν κεν λιπαρὰν <ἐ>θέλων θείμαν ἄκοι-
τιν.

(Bacchylides 5.164–169)

Is there in the halls of Oineus,
dear to Ares,
an unwed daughter,
similar to you in appearance?
Her I would gladly make my radiant wife.

The idea of marriage is thus introduced into the poem, and not only the marriage of Herakles and Deianeira, but of the marriage that should have been Meleager's lot. The last words spoken by Meleager, and the last devoted to his myth in the ode, once again seem to cut both ways, with Meleager himself brought to mind by the description of his sister, as yet ignorant of Aphrodite:

Λίπον χλωραύχενα
ἐν δώμασι Δαϊάνει-
ραν, νῆϊν ἔτι χρυσέας
Κύπριδος θελξιμβρότου.

(Bacchylides 5.172–175)

I left tender-necked
Dianeira at home,
as yet inexperienced of golden
Aphrodite, enchanter of mortals.

Returning to the *Odyssey*, when the boar hunt intrudes between the two halves of the dialogue in Book 19, it resonates with the themes of that dialogue and its context, and moreover it fits into its proper place in the sequence of these themes. Prior to the hunt interlude, Odysseus presents himself as Idomeneus' (and therefore in some sense his own) "younger brother," someone who has to regain everything already gained in his youth. The hunt picks up the theme of coming-of-age, but has to do most directly with the affirmation of Odysseus' manhood. Odysseus has begun the process of winning back his wife and destroying those who challenge his manhood, and the boar hunt is a fitting flashback to appear at this point. It has been observed that the digression prompted by Eurykleia's discovery of the scar replays a complete sequence of events that made Odysseus into Odysseus in the first place. As Russo puts it:

> We have been told of Odysseus' birth, naming, and entry into manhood. All that is lacking now to complete the heroic identity is the reacquisition of his wife and his royal power of the Ithacans. The remainder of the interview makes significant moves towards these goals.[42]

I agree with this, but think that the process of reacquisition of his wife and kingdom has already began in the first part of the interview. Within the digression, the boar hunt completes Odysseus' transition to adulthood and points to the next step, which is marriage. Within the dialogue, the boar hunt recaps and re-affirms the themes that have been in the background of the dialogue so far, themes having to do with growing up. Because manhood, virility, and access to women are associated with hunting the boar, the hunt also points to the resumption of marriage between Penelope and Odysseus. And just as within the hunting digression marriage is the logical next step, it is also thus outside the digression, within the dialogue. In effect, Odysseus has made a claim that he is ready to regain his wife, and the flashback to the boar hunt re-affirms this claim. When Penelope resumes the conversation, she moves at once to the question of her marriage, so that the hunt not only continues the themes of the first conversation, but ushers in those of the second. Penelope may have her doubts or fears, but the flashback to the boar hunt predicts that Odysseus will re-assert his manhood with the unmitigated violence of his animal double.

[42] Russo 1992:7.

PART II

PENELOPE

INTRODUCTION TO PART II

I T IS NO SURPRISE that the tales Odysseus tells Penelope in Book 19, including first and foremost his final Cretan lie, emerge as fully-fledged poetic performances, just as the long narrative of his wanderings with which he enchants the Phaeacians is a poetic performance on a grand scale.[1] Odysseus' propensity to turn into an *aoidos* and even merge with the poetic voice of the *Odyssey* has been much commented upon and I will not restate these well-accepted arguments.[2] To be sure, Odysseus' creation of false identities on Ithaca has been seen as a different kind of poetic art than his extended narrative at the court of Alkinoos. In the words of Segal,

> If the hero/bard honored at the Phaeacian feasts is the vehicle of
> a divinely authored truth among men, the beggar/bard is a figure
> for the adaptability of the poetic art, its multiplicity and variety
> and therewith its capacity for reaching men and women of different
> types and classes with tales of endlessly varied moods and registers.[3]

If the first type of performance, at least in its large-scale form, seems to be a male prerogative, the second type, exemplified by Odysseus' Cretan lies, is open to Penelope as well, and the differences between the two types should not be overstated. Odysseus' Cretan lies may indeed exemplify a different side of his poetic art than the extended tales of his wandering during which an audience is apt to forget to whom they are listening, to Odysseus or to Homer. But even so, the long narrative for the Phaeacians is not quite "divinely authored," (Alkinoos hints that its poetic form is of more importance than its factual accuracy), and it is certainly adapted to please its

---

[1] On Homeric speeches as performative events that can be analyzed as genres, see Marin: 1989.1–42.

[2] For an extended discussion see Segal 1994:113–183, Ford 1992:90–130, and Nagy forthcoming: Chapter Four.

[3] Segal 1994:158. See also Peradotto 1990:169–170 on the distinction between the "discourse of representation" and the "discourse of production," and Clayton's discussion of the Cretan lies in the light of this distinction and as an example of Penelopean poetics (Clayton 2004:53–82).

audience and indeed to benefit from that audience. Conversely, the Cretan lies, which may appear, in the words of Clayton, to "showcase the process of poetic improvisation in a combination of free-form invention with skillful interweaving of elements that appear in more than one version,"[4] in other words, to be more about fitting the occasion and less about conforming to the truth, may on closer analysis reveal little that is invented in the usual sense of the word and instead represent a way of performing that is as traditional as that of the lengthier narratives. The difference between these performances seems to be less the question of tradition vs. improvisation than a question of more public vs. more private settings. Penelope, therefore, though she does not tell long tales at a feast, can nevertheless assume the role of an *aoidos* in her own right. This too has been long recognized. As Felson puts it, speaking of Penelope's scenes in Books 17–23, "the scenes ... reveal Penelope improvising, like a performing poet, as a weaver of her life-history. She also uses poetic devices – simile, paronomasia, mythic exemplum – to make her points. In a sense, the interview of Book 19 is Penelope's *aristeia* as a bardic figure."[5] I could not agree more, and in what follows I take this assessment of Penelope as my starting point in attempting to analyze her performances during the dialogue and, in particular, her use of mythological allusion within them.

[4] Clayton 2004:61.
[5] Felson 1994:25.

CHAPTER ELEVEN
THE CONVERSATION

I FOCUS INITIALLY ON THE SECOND PART of the dialogue, after Odysseus' footbath. At this point, the conversation between Penelope and Odysseus changes in tone and substance: Penelope now takes the center stage, the beggar primarily expresses his agreement, and the fictional Odysseus in Thesprotia drops out of view. The focus shifts back to Penelope's position and options, and now there is talk of her next step. Tears are never far from the surface, but they no longer well up to interrupt the conversation, and large emotion-laden speech-frames disappear with them. The interpretation of this part of the dialogue is strongly affected by the question of recognition, and therefore particularly problematic. It is here that Penelope announces her decision to hold the bow contest, a decision that can be understood in different and even opposite ways depending on one's answer to the recognition question. What Penelope says to Odysseus before the announcement is equally hard to decode, and here the meaning of each utterance depends not only on its internal qualities but also on its role in the unfolding conversation.

Before turning to the concluding part of the dialogue, therefore, it may be useful to take stock of how things stand before the conversation is interrupted by Odysseus' foot-bath. The great difference between the way Penelope and Odysseus talk before and after that interruption is, in my opinion, best explained on the assumption that recognition takes place in the first part. In response to Odysseus' description of his own long-gone clothes Penelope cries and recollects how she herself folded the cloak and khiton and put in a pin. She says that the beggar is now no longer a stranger to her, but someone dear and respected:

> νῦν μὲν δή μοι, ξεῖνε, πάρος περ ἐὼν ἐλεεινός,
> ἐν μεγάροισιν ἐμοῖσι φίλος τ' ἔσῃ αἰδοῖός τε.

> (*Odyssey* 19.223–224)

Stranger, before I felt pity for you, but now
you are for me, in my house, a dear and respected friend.

Later, she addresses him as ξεῖνε φίλ', 'dear stranger' (19.350), and a hint at recognition may be present in her words. Athanassakis suggests, on the basis of comparative evidence from Modern Greek, that the phrase ξεῖνε φίλε used here by Penelope may mean more than 'dear guest'.[1] In Modern Greek songs, a person long absent from home, or dead, is said to be away in a 'foreign place', (ξενιτειά), and sometimes the absent person himself is talked of as a *xenos*, as in the following lines, addressed "to an absent husband or to the dead in the underworld," two overlapping situations that are intertwined in the *Odyssey*:[2]

τί νὰ σοῦ στείλω ξένε μου, τί νὰ σοῦ προβοδήσω;
νὰ στείλω μῆλο σέπεται, κυδῶνι μαραγκιάζει.

What shall I send you, my stranger, what can I bring to you?
An apple will rot, and a quince will wither.[3]

Athanassakis concludes that possibly "given the semantic compass of ξεῖνος, ξεῖνε φίλε means also 'my stranger', a collocation which definitely shows her [Penelope] alert to the possibility that this stranger may be the one for whom she has been pining away."[4] Be that as it may, the expression doubtless indicates that Penelope quickly identifies the beggar as someone close to herself. He is no longer an unknown wanderer, protected, to be sure, by Zeus *xenios*, but not expected to receive anything beyond the minimal hospitality granted to all. Instead, he now resembles an old and treasured friend. In Homeric diction, the collocation of *xenos* and *philos* always seems to refer to those especially valuable among friends, and is frequently connected with gifts. For example, Diomedes calls himself ξεῖνος φίλος, 'dear stranger', to Glaukos when he realizes that they have ties of hospitality inherited from their fathers and manifested in gifts (*Iliad* 6.224). The bow Odysseus leaves at home is referred to as a memory of a dear friend (μνῆμα ξείνοιο φίλοιο, *Odyssey* 21.40). This could quite possibly be Odysseus' first alliance, made with Iphitos during his youthful trip to the Peloponnese (*Odyssey* 21.13–16), and there is no need to comment on the significance of the gift, Odysseus' bow. In the *Odyssey* the combination of *xenos* and *philos* is used surprisingly

---

[1] Athanassakis 1994:127–131.
[2] Athanassakis 1994:130.
[3] Saunier 1983:103,108 (10A and15A respectively), cited by Athanassakis 1994:130.
[4] Athanassakis 1994:131.

sparingly (considering the centrality of hospitality in the poem) and always weightily. Telemachus addresses Athena disguised as Mentes as ξεῖνε φίλ', 'dear stranger/guest', not yet knowing who his guest is but imagining, and perhaps hoping, that he might be one of his father's friends (*Odyssey* 1.175–177). The guest does not disappoint, and soon Telemachus is grateful to the pseudo-Mentes for speaking to him as a father would and wants to reciprocate with a precious gift that would remain in Mentes' family as a long-lasting and valuable possession, a κειμήλιον (*Odyssey* 1.308–313). Telemachus surely does not treat all his guests in this way, but on this occasion he is specific about wanting the stranger among his friends, and the gift is supposed be such as to solidify and memorialize the relationship.

> τιμῆεν, μάλα καλόν, ὅ τοι κειμήλιον ἔσται
> ἐξ ἐμεῦ, οἷα φίλοι ξεῖνοι ξείνοισι διδοῦσι.
>
> (Odyssey 1.312–313)

> "An honorable [gift], very beautiful, which will be
>   a treasure for you
> from me, such as dear strangers/guest-friends give
>   to each other."

As for the combination of *xenos*, *philos*, and *aidoios*, it is used in the *Odyssey* only twice, in the passage under discussion where Penelope so describes her beggar-guest, and just a little earlier in the same conversation, where the beggar himself so describes Idomeneus in relationship to Odysseus:

> αὐτίκα δ' Ἰδομενῆα μετάλλα ἄστυδ' ἀνελθών·
> ξεῖνον γάρ οἱ ἔφασκε φίλον τ' ἔμεν αἰδοῖόν τε.
>
> (Odyssey 19.190–191)

> And immediately he came to the citadel and asked for
>   Idomeneus,
> for he said that Idomeneus was a dear and respected guest-
>   friend to him.

When Penelope calls the beggar ξεῖνε and says that he is *philos* and *aidoios* in her house, her words resonate with Odysseus' Cretan story, as if confirming its validity. Just as Idomeneus was a dear friend to Odysseus, so now the beggar, Idomeneus' supposed younger brother, becomes a dear friend to Penelope, as if he has established his credentials as a person belonging to the world of Odysseus' closest guest-friendships. He achieves this, of course, not by giving

Penelope any proof that he actually belongs to Idomeneus' household, but by recalling Odysseus' own clothes with precision. The beggar's Cretan story is a vehicle for his riddling claim to be Odysseus, and perhaps by playing along with this story Penelope hints that she understands who its subject really is. When she then uses ξεῖνε φίλ' (*Odyssey* 19.350) at the conclusion of the conversation, it is to remark on the beggar's intelligence and to say that no other guest has ever been nearer and dearer to her, a remarkable statement to be uttered at a first meeting, and another hint that this guest is not, in truth, a stranger:

> "ξεῖνε φίλ'· οὐ γάρ πώ τις ἀνὴρ πεπνυμένος ὧδε
> ξείνων τηλεδαπῶν φιλίων ἐμὸν ἵκετο δῶμα,
> ὡς σὺ μάλ' εὐφραδέως πεπνυμένα πάντ' ἀγορεύεις.
>
> (*Odyssey* 19.350–352)[5]

> Dear stranger – for never has such an intelligent man come
>   to my house, from among the strangers who live far
>   away,
> and none has been dearer, so sensible and wise is everything
>   you say.

Needless to say, Penelope also denies the possibility of ever seeing Odysseus again and blames the Trojan war and grievous fate for the loss:

> ... τὸν δ' οὐχ ὑποδέξομαι αὖτις
> οἴκαδε νοστήσαντα φίλην ἐς πατρίδα γαῖαν.
> τῷ ῥα κακῇ αἴσῃ κοίλης ἐπὶ νηὸς Ὀδυσσεὺς
> ᾤχετ' ἐποψόμενος Κακοΐλιον οὐκ ὀνομαστήν.
>
> (*Odyssey* 19.257–260)

> I will not welcome him home again
> upon his return to his dear native land.
> And so with bad fate did Odysseus leave in his hollow ship
> to look at Accursed-Troy, a city not to be named.

It is possible to see Penelope's words as an indication of her sincere despair and complete absence of any suspicion regarding her guest. In this case, her words do not advance the conversation, but simply reflect her emotion. On the other hand, the way Penelope talks about the absent Odysseus shifts depending

---

[5] On the meaning of *pepnumenos*, see Cuypers 2001 and above p115-116.

on the demands of the situation. Here Penelope says that Odysseus will not come back and seems to imagine him as dead, and yet just a hundred lines further she says that Odysseus must now look as aged as her guest, apparently imagining her husband alive and wandering somewhere far away from Ithaca (19.358–360). In each case, Penelope's words cannot be understood simply as statements about herself, because they are part of a dialogue. It is possible to see her words at 19.257–260 as a prompt for Odysseus to go further with his claims. In this case, her words do advance the conversation: by offering her *philia* to the stranger, yet asserting that Odysseus will not come back, Penelope lets him know that she is sensitive to his suggestions but her doubts are not yet dispelled. She also brings him to the question at hand, namely the return of Odysseus.

And this is precisely the subject to which Odysseus turns next. Nothing more is said about Crete or Aithon's own past misfortunes, no further comment made on his own transition from riches to rags.[6] Instead, the beggar announces that he has news of Odysseus' return and will reveal this unfailingly:

> ἀλλὰ γόου μὲν παῦσαι, ἐμεῖο δὲ σύνθεο μῦθον·
> νημερτέως γάρ τοι μυθήσομαι οὐδ' ἐπικεύσω,
> ὡς ἤδη Ὀδυσῆος ἐγὼ περὶ νόστου ἄκουσα
> ἀγχοῦ, Θεσπρωτῶν ἀνδρῶν ἐν πίονι δήμῳ,
> ζωοῦ·

> *(Odyssey* 19.268–272)

> But stop crying, and listen to my words,
> for I will tell you unerringly and will not conceal
> that I have already heard about the return of Odysseus,
> who is nearby, in the fertile territory of Thesprotians,
> and alive.

In the next moments, Penelope hears that Odysseus is alive and is now in Thesprotia, gathering gifts. He is bringing home much wealth, and returning alone, all his companions lost. The beggar mentions the episode on Thrinakia where Odysseus' men perform a perverted sacrifice and eat the cattle of the sun, their subsequent death at sea, and Odysseus' own escape to Phaeacia, details that are in agreement with the macro-narrative of the *Odyssey* (19.273–282). In this version of the story, the Phaeacians apparently do not give Odysseus sufficient gifts, for he decides to wander and gather more, even

---

[6] On this point see Clayton 2004:72.

though he could have been home earlier. At the moment, the beggar claims, Odysseus is in Dodona, consulting the oracle of Zeus as to whether he should return openly or secretly (19.283–299).

Penelope, then, learns that Odysseus may come back secretly, that he is alone, and, strikingly, that he is now engaged in begging. This last detail has obvious suggestiveness to it, coming as it does from the mouth of a beggar, and it deserves further attention. Penelope's mysterious interlocutor describes Odysseus' accumulation of wealth in terms that leave no doubt about its nature:

αὐτὰρ ἄγει κειμήλια πολλὰ καὶ ἐσθλά,
αἰτίζων ἀνὰ δῆμον.

(*Odyssey* 19.272–273)

But he is bringing treasures, many and excellent ones,
begging throughout the land.

The verb αἰτίζω, which describes Odysseus begging *as himself* in this passage, is used to describe the beggar-Odysseus in Ithaca.[7] Eleven verses later, at 11.284, the verb is ἀγυρτάζω. The latter verb is highly appropriate since elsewhere it tends to denote not strictly speaking beggars, but vagabond priests and musicians, who are paid for their services. A begging priest of Cybele is called ἀγύρτης (*Anthologia Palatina* 6.218), and Orpheus is described by Strabo as a man who started his career by soliciting money (ἀγυρτεύοντα) in exchange for music and prophecy (ἀπὸ μουσικῆς ἅμα καὶ μαντικῆς).[8] In Sophocles' *Oedipus Tyrannus*, Teiresias is called ἀγύρτης when he is accused of both trickery and an excessive desire for possessions (388–389). Thus when Aithon refers to Odysseus' activity as ἀγυρτάζειν, he describes adequately the way Odysseus does in fact acquire his possessions at the court of Alkinoos – both as a king among kings, and also, even primarily, as an *aoidos*.[9] When the Phaeacians send Odysseus home with lavish gifts, it is certainly not in any expectation of reciprocity. Commenting on the relationship between Odysseus and Phaeacians, Redfield observes: "Such unreciprocated reception of gifts is really

---

[7] Odysseus: 17.222, 228, 346, 351, 502, 558; 20.180, 182.

[8] Strabo 7 fr. 18.

[9] For a discussion of the reciprocal relationship between poet and patron, see Watkins 1994a:536–543. For comments on *aoidoi* and beggars within the social scale, see Nagy 1990:56–7. Begging for objects of value rather than food is mentioned in a taunt directed at Odysseus by Melanthios, *Odyssey* 17.222.

a form of begging, but on a heroic scale."[10]

The imaginary Odysseus in Thesprotia also begs on a heroic scale. Penelope's guest repeatedly mentions that Odysseus is bringing home wealth, and attributes its quantity to Odysseus' unmatched mastery of gainful cunning. In fact, Penelope is even told that Odysseus could have come back home long ago, had he not chosen to enlarge his fortune instead:

> καί κεν πάλαι ἐνθάδ᾽ Ὀδυσσεὺς
> ἦην· ἀλλ᾽ ἄρα οἱ τό γε κέρδιον εἴσατο θυμῷ,
> χρήματ᾽ ἀγυρτάζειν πολλὴν ἐπὶ γαῖαν ἰόντι.
>
> *(Odyssey* 19.282–284)

Odysseus could have been here long ago.
But he thought in his heart that it would be more profitable
to collect possessions, roaming over much land.

This is a strange thing to say to a grieving wife about an absent husband, especially considering the pressure on Penelope to resolve the situation on Ithaca in one way or another. Yet this too is consistent with Odysseus' actual behavior among the Phaeacians, where he says that, eager though he is to be home, he is willing to stay even for another year if that will bring more gifts:

> Ἀλκίνοε κρεῖον, πάντων ἀριδείκετε λαῶν,
> εἴ με καὶ εἰς ἐνιαυτὸν ἀνώγοιτ᾽ αὐτόθι μίμνειν
> πομπήν τ᾽ ὀτρύνοιτε καὶ ἀγλαὰ δῶρα διδοῖτε,
> καί κε τὸ βουλοίμην, καί κεν πολὺ κέρδιον εἴη
> πλειοτέρῃ σὺν χειρὶ φίλην ἐς πατρίδ᾽ ἱκέσθαι,
> καί κ᾽ αἰδοιότερος καὶ φίλτερος ἀνδράσιν εἴην
> πᾶσιν, ὅσοι μ᾽ Ἰθάκηνδε ἰδοίατο νοστήσαντα.
>
> *(Odyssey* 11.355–361)

Lord Alkinoos, most exalted of men,
even if you should urge me to stay here for a year,
and arrange a send-off and give me splendid gifts,
even to that I would agree. It would be much more profitable
to return to my dear native land with a fuller hand.
I would be more respected and dearer
to all men who should see me upon my return to Ithaca.

---

[10] Redfield 1983:234.

The beggar's claim that Odysseus is begging – and on a grand scale – and that he is delaying his return home in order to accumulate more wealth, fits into the context of Odysseus' deliberate self-revelation and Penelope's understanding of his implicit messages. It may be understood as a veiled conversation between husband and wife, though a wife who has not yet accepted her husband's claims – which is quite distinct from not understanding or even not believing them. In the words of Kurke, "the *Odyssey* reveals a culture pattern centered on the *oikos* and structured as a repeating loop of departure and return."[11] The household is sustained by its individual representatives and their achievements. Fame, prestige, and wealth as their material manifestation belong to the household, and the household's individual representatives have to leave in search of glory and then return with reports of their achievement and 'treasures', *keimelia*, to be added to the household's store.[12] Part of this pattern, however, is the inherent risk to the household of abandonment by the best of its members.[13] If Odysseus disappears without a trace, the household is deprived of both his presence and the *kleos* and booty that were the hoped-for results of his quest. Both Penelope and Telemachus bemoan the diminution of their household, in livelihood as well as in prestige.[14] This throws light on why Odysseus assigns such importance to not arriving home empty-handed. His expedition has gone astray and his absence has become inordinately long – long enough to put the household in danger of ruin. Only by coming back with extraordinary fame and wealth can Odysseus hope to "make right" his dangerously long absence. If a longer absence means a more glorious return, the risk may be worth taking. At the palace of Alkinoos Odysseus is ready to take that risk, even though he must know that each additional year makes Penelope's task of guarding the house in his absence harder. Yet it is this very concern for the house, which Penelope expresses repeatedly, that also makes accumulation of wealth an acceptable justification for Odysseus' delay. When she envisages marrying one of the suitors, it is the house that is foremost on her mind, a house that is full of life-sustaining wealth:

> τῷ κεν ἅμ' ἑσποίμην, νοσφισσαμένη τόδε δῶμα
> κουρίδιον, μάλα καλόν, ἐνίπλειον βιότοιο,

---

[11] Kurke 1991:19, cf. Redfield 1983.

[12] On the significance and value of precious objects in pre-monetary society, see Gernet 1981.

[13] Kurke 1991:17–19.

[14] E.g., at *Odyssey* 1.232–243, 2.40–49, 19.124–135.

τοῦ ποτε μεμνήσεσθαι ὀΐομαι ἔν περ ὀνείρῳ.

(Odyssey 19.579–581)

> Him I would follow, leaving behind this house,
> the house of my marriage, a very fine one, full of livelihood,
> the house I think I will remember in my dreams.

The stranger is speaking Penelope's own language when he explains Odysseus' long absence in economic terms. He appears to have a heightened awareness both of the problems faced by Odysseus' household and of the means Odysseus will use to resolve these problems. Unromantic as this may sound, it may be important for Penelope to know that her husband is bringing home much wealth and also that it is his desire to increase the loot that has so prolonged his absence.

The beggar-Odysseus concludes his words with an oath, a detail no less telling than his references to begging:

> ἴστω νῦν Ζεὺς πρῶτα, θεῶν ὕπατος καὶ ἄριστος,
> ἱστίη τ' Ὀδυσῆος ἀμύμονος, ἣν ἀφικάνω·
> ἦ μέν τοι τάδε πάντα τελείεται ὡς ἀγορεύω.
> τοῦδ' αὐτοῦ λυκάβαντος ἐλεύσεται ἐνθάδ' Ὀδυσσεύς,
> τοῦ μὲν φθίνοντος μηνός, τοῦ δ' ἱσταμένοιο.

(Odyssey 19.303–307)

> First of all, let Zeus be my witness, the highest and best
>   of the gods,
> and then the hearth of flawless Odysseus, to which
>   I have come:
> all the things I proclaim will come true.
> Odysseus will come back here within this very *lukabas*,
> with one month waning and the next one beginning.

The fact that Odysseus utters such an oath is remarkable in itself and argues strongly in favor of the notion that Odysseus is not attempting to conceal his identity from Penelope but rather to reveal it indirectly. An actual beggar could be expected to swear that all he told is true (for example, that he actually did meet Odysseus on Crete or hear his story in Thesprotia), but he would hardly be likely to utter an oath regarding the precise timing of Odysseus return. Yet this is what the beggar-Odysseus does when he says that Odysseus will come back during 'this very *lukabas*'. The *lukabas* itself is an obscure word, but it seems to denote the *interlunium*, the dark period of several nights when no moon is visible; luckily the temporal reference is somewhat clarified by the context.[15] Odysseus connects the *lukabas* with waning of the old moon and rising of the new. This has long been seen as a reference to Apollo's festival, on the model of the celebrations of Apollo Neomenios ('of the new moon').[16] In other words, the beggar predicts that Odysseus will come back on the day of Apollo's festival. Penelope presumably can observe the phases of the moon, and she certainly knows when the festival of Apollo is taking place. In the course of the narrative, it will become apparent that the very next day is in fact the day of the festival. At the end of Book 19, when Penelope announces her decision to set the bow contest for tomorrow, Odysseus responds by actually

---

[15] Scholia explain *lukabas* as 'year', and Wilamowitz accordingly interpreted the expression τοῦδ' αὐτοῦ λυκάβαντος to mean 'within this year'. Suggested etymologies connect the word with light, (root **leuk-* as in λύχνος, λεύσσω, Latin *lux*), and βαίνω (Leumann 1950:212n4, Stanford 1965:222 ad loc., Ameis and Hentze 1895 ad loc.) Koller 1973:29–33 suggested **λύκα βάντα*, 'the light having gone'. Others seek pre-Greek origins connecting the word with the name of the Attic mountain Λυκαβηττός (Ruijgh 1957:147, 1979:559–60), or suggest a Semitic connection (Szemerenyi 1974:144–57), see also Hoekstra 1992:204 (on *Odyssey* 14.161) and Russo 1992:91 (on *Odyssey*19.306) and Chantraine 1999 s.v. The idea that *lukabas* is a festival of Apollo Lykeios or Lykios was put forth by van Windekens 1954:31–4. Whether this is actually the meaning of *lukabas* seems doubtful, but a connection with the festival of Apollo is clear in the context of the *Odyssey* (see Russo 1992:92 on *Odyssey* 19.306–7). Austin (1975:244–246) argues that the word signifies the 'dark of the moon', a period of a few days when the old moon has waned but the new one is not yet clearly visible. He is followed on this point by the recent commentaries (Rutherford 1992:175, Russo 1992:92, both on *Odyssey* 19.306–307). In Book 19, therefore, *lukabas* denotes "the interlunar period about to end with the new moon festival of the god" (Russo 1992.92).

[16] Russo 1992:91–92 on *Odyssey* 306–307. Herodotus (6.57) mentions monthly celebrations of Νεομηνία, and Apollo Neomēnios is also mentioned by scholia on the *Odyssey* 20.155. Several sources mention that the first day of every month, as well as the seventh, is sacred to Apollo (Scholia on Pindar *Nemean* 3.1, Scholia on Aristophanes *Wealth* 1126). See the *Herodotean Life of Homer* 462-465 on Samian Neomenia, for which Homer supposedly composed the *eiresione*-song, sung for a long time afterwards by *paides* when they gathered for the festival of Apollo. There is no indication that the festival of Apollo in the *Odyssey* is a monthly occurrence, and it is hardly possible to equate it with *Neomenia*, but if the transition from one month to the next was sacred to Apollo, then it seems unsurprising that his festival, monthly or not, would fall on that day. See Roscher 1884–1891:423–425 for a discussion of Apolline calendar points. It has been pointed out (Robertson 1991:46) that the appearance of a new moon is often hard to detect and so it may be impractical to hold a festival on the very day of a new moon, whereas the seventh day of a new month is a more practical marker, so that the festival may not literally coincide with the first of the month. Apollo is associated with the seventh day of the month no less than with the new moon. In Sparta the kings sacrificed to Apollo not only on the first but also on the seventh day of each month (Herodotus 6.57) and at Olbia there were even two priestly colleges, one of Neomeniastai and one of Hebdomiastai, one for the first and one for the seventh day (Graf 1974:210–215). It seems that Odysseus arrives on Ithaca during the dark interlunar period which lasts for several days, and kills the suitors on the day of Apollo's feast, which may be the seventh, but in any case is the day of the moon's clear return.

predicting that Odysseus will come back in time to string the bow.[17] It appears, therefore, that the *lukabas* is coming to an end on the very next day, with the end of one month and the beginning of the new one. This would be consistent with the other calendar signs in the *Odyssey*. For example, the wintry night Odysseus spends with Eumaeus is described as σκοτομήνιος, 'moonless', or 'in the dark part of the month' (*Odyssey* 14.457), so that the new moon is expected shortly.

To return to the dialogue, the beggar then utters an oath promising that Odysseus will come back on the very next day, an oath that seems to contradict what he himself said about Odysseus' being in Dodona and the plans of the Thesprotian king, Pheidon, to send him home by ship. The oath seems absurd on the assumption that Odysseus wants to preserve any verisimilitude in his disguise, but it does make sense in the mouth of Odysseus himself. He is indeed in a position to know that Odysseus will be back tomorrow, and at this point in the dialogue he is no longer concerned with sustaining the disguise.[18]

It seems fitting that the final remarkable claim by the beggar (that Odysseus will come back tomorrow) leads to a marked change of pace in the dialogue. For the moment, Odysseus has gone as far as he can, and now Penelope in effect calls for an intermission, a time for her to assess the situation perhaps. After that, she will come back and, in effect, announce her decision. For now, however, she does not call into question the stranger's extravagant oath, but simply responds in the same way as she did earlier when Theoklymenos predicted Odysseus' imminent return, by expressing her wish that the prediction may come to pass:

> αἲ γὰρ τοῦτο, ξεῖνε, ἔπος τετελεσμένον εἴη·
> τῶ κε τάχα γνοίης φιλότητά τε πολλά τε δῶρα
> ἐξ ἐμεῦ, ὡς ἄν τίς σε συναντόμενος μακαρίζοι.
> ἀλλά μοι ὧδ' ἀνὰ θυμὸν ὀΐεται, ὡς ἔσεταί περ·
> οὔτ' Ὀδυσεὺς ἔτι οἶκον ἐλεύσεται, οὔτε σὺ πομπῆς
> τεύξῃ.

(Odyssey 19.309–314)[19]

> If only your words may come true, stranger.
> Then you would quickly come to know my friendship and
> receive many gifts

---

[17] See below, p250-251.
[18] See further below, p251.
[19] Cf. Penelope's response to Theoklymenos, 17.163–165 = 19.309–311.

from me, so that a person meeting you would say how
  blessed you are.
But this is how it seems to me in my heart, and how it will be:
neither will Odysseus come back home, nor will you receive
  your send-off.

Penelope's reaction is subtly different from that of Eumaeus, who hears
the same oath earlier and who does call it into question (14.166–173). Both
Penelope and Eumaeus express pessimism regarding Odysseus' return, but
Eumaeus also says that the oath is a falsehood, futile and unworthy of his
guest: τί σε χρὴ τοῖον ἐόντα/μαψιδίως ψεύδεσθαι; 'Why should you, such as you
are, tell lies idly?' (*Odyssey* 14.364–365).[20] Penelope, on the other hand, does not
call the oath false or express any indignation at her guest for pronouncing
it, but rather makes her own prediction, that Odysseus will never come
back. Russo observes that this is an instance of "a psychological pattern that
Homer has consistently used in his portrait of Penelope: she lets hopes buoy
her up briefly, then sinks into pessimism."[21] There is indeed a psychological
dimension to Penelope's reaction, but her immediately renewed pessimism
may also be strategic. It is Penelope's protection against false hopes, but it
could be a signal to Odysseus that more will need to be said and done before
his wife falls into his embrace. An emphatic denial also protects her from
the maids who are within earshot and whom she immediately addresses.
Penelope's pessimistic words could serve to diffuse any suspicions on their
part that something unusual has gone on between Penelope and the beggar,
for example, that she has received any unusually trustworthy information
regarding her husband's return. Penelope does not need to put up such a
defense earlier in her conversation with Theoklymenos, even though the seer
also utters an oath no less remarkable than that of Odysseus: he tells Penelope
that Odysseus is already on Ithaca, (something that she can be presumed to
remember in Book 19). On that occasion Telemachus is present, but the suitors
are not, nor are the maids mentioned as being in the immediate proximity,
and Penelope does not react to the astonishing prophecy by denial, but
simply expresses her wish that it may come to pass and promises the prophet
a reward if it does, using exactly the same words as she later addresses to
Odysseus (17.163–165 = 19.309–311). The same formulae are used in the oaths
on all three occasions: when Penelope talks to Theoklymenos, in conversation
between Odysseus and Eumaeus, and in the interaction between Odysseus

[20] Cf. 14.387: μήτε τί μοι ψεύδεσσι χαρίζεο μήτε τι θέλγε.
[21] Russo 1992:92.

and Penelope in Book 19. A dictional link between these three scenes is thus established.[22] All of this suggests that Penelope's professed pessimism is conditioned by its conversational context.

It has been argued that Odysseus' oaths are only offered, but not actually sworn, because they lack certain elements present in other Homeric oaths, namely the spelling out of the oath's conditions, (for example, what will happen to the swearer if he lies), or a depiction of the actual swearing, or an authorial assertion that the oath has been sworn.[23] The reason that the oaths are not sworn, the argument goes, is their rejection by the addressees, Eumaeus, Penelope, and Philoitios. The fact that the oaths are not accepted may then be seen as an indication of how desperate Odysseus' supporters are and how hard it will be for Odysseus to convince them that he is back when not a single person believes that he is still alive.[24] According to this scenario, the fact that she does not accept Odysseus' oath indicates that Penelope is far from any suspicion of his identity. There is indeed irony in the fact that Odysseus, who is not prone to statements of fact, is offering, for once, to swear to something that is actually true, and no one will accept his oath. At the same time, the question of acceptance is a complicated one. Eumaeus does explicitly refuse to enter into a pact by which Odysseus proposes that Eumaeus reward him if his words come true or kill him if they do not. The pact, however, is distinct from the oath, and the word used to designate it, *rhetra* (*Odyssey* 14.393), appears nowhere else in Homer in connection with oaths. The fact that a separate pact is needed to augment the oath, and the fact that all Odysseus' oaths remain unsworn underscores their unusual nature, namely the fact that they contain not a promise, but a prediction of the future and a prediction of something supposedly beyond the swearer's control. In this, they are distinctly unlike the actually sworn oaths elsewhere in Homer and it is not clear whether they need to be, or can be, accepted. When Circe swears not to harm Odysseus, or Achilles swears not to return to fighting until the Achaeans recognize his worth, their oaths have to do with actions the swearers can control. The beggar-Odysseus' oaths are different and present a puzzle to their audiences: how can this beggar know exactly when Odysseus will come back?

---

[22] Another oath is offered to the cowherd Philoitios at *Odyssey* 20.229–235.

[23] See Callaway (1998), who offers Circe' oath to Odysseus (*Odyssey* 10.343–347) as an example of a basic oath pattern. Odysseus requests the oath and then describes its execution: ὡς ἐφάμην, ἡ δ' αὐτίκ' ἀπώμνυεν, ὡς ἐκέλευον | αὐτὰρ ἐπεί ῥ' ὄμοσέν τε τελεύτησέν τε τὸν ὅρκον (*Odyssey* 10.345–346). The same formula occurs at 14.280 = 2.378 = 10.346, and cf. *Iliad* 19.113, where again the completion of the oath is explicit (ὄμοσεν μέγαν ὅρκον).

[24] Callaway 1998:167–168.

Theoklymenos' oath, phrased in the same way as those of Odysseus, is also a prediction, or rather a profession of the seer's superior vision.[25] By offering the oath Theoklymenos is not taking on any obligation, but rather emphasizing his confidence in his powers as a seer and in the knowledge he gains through them. The effect of these oaths, both that of Theoklymenos and those of Odysseus, does not depend on whether they are accepted or not, and there would in any case be little benefit for the addressee in acceptance of such an oath. This, too, is unusual. When Circe swears not to harm Odysseus, this is of distinct benefit to him because it affects Circe's behavior. But whether the beggar's words are true or not, it is (at least ostensibly) not up to him to accomplish Odysseus' return. These prediction-oaths do not function like other oaths do, but they do have meaning beyond the actual prediction they contain. They raise the question that is immediately voiced by Eumaeus, namely why should the beggar utter them at all? Theoklymenos utters his because he is a seer and through his art can know what is concealed from others. The beggar, by uttering his, lays claim to similar knowledge, which, not being a seer, he can only possess because he is Odysseus himself.

Penelope's reaction to the oath is as complex as the oath itself. The difference in her response to the similar oaths by Theoklymenos and Odysseus suggests what is perhaps obvious, namely that her words should not be taken as simple expressions of her thoughts and feelings, but rather should be seen in their conversational contexts as part of her strategies, which are different on different occasions. Nowhere does Penelope deny the possibility of Odysseus' return more frequently and emphatically than in the conversation in Book 19, precisely when the signs of that return are coming thick and fast and when she herself gives indications of understanding them. In this setting, Penelope's insistence that Odysseus will not come back suggests not that she is hopeless and in the dark about her guest's identity, but rather the opposite. The more Penelope inclines towards believing the beggar, the more urgently she needs to be sure, and expressions of pessimism about Odysseus' return are both a way of drawing more information from the beggar and a way of letting him know that words alone will not suffice. Besides, now that the return is finally in the making, stronger than usual defenses are needed to safeguard it. Just as Odysseus refuses to make himself at home in his house before his vengeance on the suitors is complete, so Penelope will not admit

---

[25] Callaway (1998) unfortunately does not consider Theoklymenos' utterance in her discussion of Odyssseus' three oaths.

her husband's return until it is as certain as it can ever be. Anticipation of the desired end is psychologically risky and fraught with the real danger of jeopardizing their ultimate success.

Penelope's protestations are not born of obliviousness to the beggar's hints, however, and she lets him know as much by pointing out, in her last words before the intermission, that Odysseus himself might now look like her guest:

> ἀλλ' ἄγε νῦν ἀνστᾶσα, περίφρων Εὐρύκλεια,
> νίψον σοῖο ἄνακτος ὁμήλικα· καί που 'Οδυσσεὺς
> ἤδη τοιόσδ' ἐστὶ πόδας τοιόσδε τε χεῖρας·
> αἶψα γὰρ ἐν κακότητι βροτοὶ καταγηράσκουσιν.
>
> (*Odyssey* 19.357–361)

> But come now, wise Eurykleia, rise
> and wash your master's age-mate. Odysseus'
> feet and hands look like this now probably,
> for mortals age quickly in hard times.

Eurykleia immediately echoes these words by saying that she has never seen anyone so like Odysseus:

> πολλοὶ δὴ ξεῖνοι ταλαπείριοι ἐνθάδ' ἵκοντο,
> ἀλλ' οὔ πώ τινά φημι ἐοικότα ὧδε ἰδέσθαι
> ὡς σὺ δέμας φωνήν τε πόδας τ' 'Οδυσῆϊ ἔοικας.
>
> (*Odyssey* 19.379–381)

> Many sorely-tried strangers come here,
> but I think I have never seen anyone so like Odysseus,
> the way you resemble him in your looks, your voice,
>   and your feet.

The first part of the dialogue thus ends with clear hints not only of the beggar's true identity, but also of the fact the Penelope is aware of it. The words Eurykleia utters before the footbath presage her actual assertion that the beggar is Odysseus (19.474–475), and the two utterances by the nurse constitute a ring composition that encloses the narrative of Odysseus' naming and of his boar hunt, full as it is of premonitions of his return.

The only thing that seems to go against the flow amidst these accumulating signs of Odysseus' imminent return is Penelope's failure to look at him precisely at the moment Eurykleia recognizes her master. Instead,

Penelope is famously distracted, oblivious to the winking of the old nurse: ἡ δ' οὔτ' ἀθρῆσαι δύνατ' ἀντίη οὔτε νοῆσαι, 'she could neither see nor clearly perceive' (19.478). I do not think, however, that these lines constitute an argument against recognition. Penelope's failure to look at Odysseus may be an obstacle to complete certainty on her part, but it does not prevent her from guessing who the stranger is. She has plenty of evidence apart from the scar. The verb νοέω, used here to indicate what Penelope is unable to do, conveys the idea of sharp vision, both physical and mental.[26] For example, in a scene from Book 16 Athena appears in Eumaeus' tent and Odysseus sees her (νόησε 16.164) while Telemachus does not.[27] The phrase used in the scene is reminiscent of Penelope's failure to see the scar: οὐδ' ἄρα Τηλέμαχος ἴδεν ἀντίον οὐδ' ἐνόησεν, 'but Telemachus did not see her in front of him nor clearly perceive her' (16.160). Still, Telemachus can perceive Athena's presence indirectly, and does so. He sees Odysseus' transformation and concludes that either the stranger is a god himself or that a deity is present. Odysseus then explains that Athena is at hand (16.207). In the same way, Penelope is prevented from experiencing the full *enargeia* of Odysseus' identity, but she is not prevented from deducing it.[28]

Moreover, quite apart from Athena's intervention, an argument can be made that averting her eyes is a sensible thing for Penelope to do. The nurse's attempt to attract Penelope's attention is dangerous, or at least it is so seen by Odysseus, and surely not only because he may be recognized by Penelope, but because he may be discovered by the maids and therefore the suitors. Odysseus quickly plugs the opening gap in his disguise by grasping his old nurse by the throat and imposing silence on her under the threat of death. This gap would be considerably larger if the nurse succeeded in exchanging glances with Penelope. Further, the whole interaction between Penelope and Odysseus at this point is based on communicating indirectly, and it is in their mutual interest to keep it that way. Among other things, it allows them to probe and test each other's mind before reuniting. The same kind of probing would be awkward or offensive if Odysseus' revelation were complete. In Book 23, although Penelope does not accept Odysseus immediately, she also does not engage in the kind of testing that goes on in Book 19, but rather sits silently looking at her husband for a long time. On that occasion, even

---

[26] Snell 1931:77, von Fritz 1945:223, Ruijgh 1967:371–72, Frame 1978:28–33, Bakker 2002:76–80; see especially Nagy 1990:202–222, esp.205–12, for a discussion of νοέω in archaic Greek poetry.

[27] Bakker 2002:78.

[28] Interestingly, Eurykleia herself also does not see the scar, but rather feels it by touch (19.468, 475). See Clayton 2004.74–78 for a discussion of the significance of this detail.

though Odysseus understands that Penelope wants to test him (πειράζειν, *Odyssey* 23.114), she in fact asks not a single question. The final test of the bed is administered under the guise of an order given to Eurykleia to make up Odysseus' bed outside his bedroom. The kind of questioning and doubting that takes place before the bow contest is evidently out of place in its aftermath, perhaps because of the inequality between them, which is doubtless a part of this marriage, and which Penelope seems to accept, much to the chagrin of many a feminist reader of the poem.[29] Before the contest the balance of power is different, and it is not to Penelope's advantage to accept Odysseus as himself until he has proven his worth by killing the suitors. Faced with the scar, however, she may be unable to postpone such acceptance, especially considering Eurykleia's open recognition of her master. Both for Penelope and for Odysseus it is better that Penelope not look.

While Eurykleia discovers the scar Penelope recedes into the background and when the conversation is resumed it is not the same as before. It has been observed that the first part of the dialogue is full of emotion and characterized by elaborate speech frames, such as the comparison of Penelope to the melting snow, or the description of Odysseus keeping his eyes dry and firm like horn or iron.[30] The second, shorter, part of the conversation contains some remarkable *muthoi* but no elaborate speech frames and considerably less emphasis on outward emotion.[31] In my opinion, the high emotional pitch of their first exchange is consistent with recognition, though perhaps not in the way this term is usually understood.[32] Penelope's emotion suggests that she understands the stranger's hinted self-revelation and is inclined to believe it. The question of her certainty or lack thereof will never be answered, but

---

[29] The famous *homophrosune* of the couple does not presuppose equality but rather mutual agreement about each other's roles. On the question of *homophrosune*, the inequality and domination it involves (or conceals, depending on one's perspective) and the unequal roles Odysseus and Penelope play in the poem, see Doherty 1995, Wohl 1993, Holmberg 1995 and Nieto Hernández 2008:39–62.

[30] Beck 2005:100–107.

[31] Beck 2005:105–107.

[32] Beck (2005), to whom I am indebted for her useful discussion of speech frames, emotion in the dialogue, and distinctions between its two parts, has a different explanation for this change, namely that the focus of the episode is on its first emotional part and the "ironic and moving gulf between the sorrowing Penelope, ignorant of the stranger's identity and mourning her husband's supposed absence, and the ease and skill with which Odysseus conceals his identity from her." (107) The shorter frames of the second part signal that it has less to tell us about Penelope: "at this point in the story, the narrator is not particularly interested in Penelope's decision to hold the bow contest, her motivation in doing so, the effect of her statement to this effect on Odysseus, etc." (107) As will be clear from what follows, I have a different assessment of the second part.

in the second part of the dialogue Penelope proceeds, in my opinion, on the assumption that her guest is Odysseus. Her withdrawal from action and the interlude with the boar hunt provide a pause that makes this change all the more visible. The almost melodramatic recognition by Eurykleia, the recollections of how Odysseus acquired his name and with it the identity he is now in the process of regaining, and the boar hunt with all its connotations of furious virility – all these parts of the intermission are in harmony with the developments between Odysseus and Penelope. The interlude enlarges upon the theme of recognition and points to Odysseus' Autolycus-like cunning and the boar-like force with which he will take vengeance on his foes and regain his wife. Notionally, this process is already in motion, but not yet in practical terms. The second part of the conversation is, among other things, about the practicalities of Odysseus' return. In what follows I will suggest that Penelope at the end of Book 19 in effect proposes a course of action for Odysseus, but that the practical subtext does not exhaust the complexity of her performance, or rather, several sequential performances which constitute the second part of her conversation with Odysseus. It is to these performances, rich with mythological allusion, that I now turn. I will begin with the myth of Aedon and Penelope's dream and then come back, briefly, to consider her most famous tale, which is actually told in the first part of the dialogue, namely the tale of weaving and unweaving the shroud for Laertes.

CHAPTER TWELVE

AEDON

PENELOPE BEGINS IN A STRIKING WAY, with an extended comparison between herself and the nightingale – Aedon, the daughter of Pandareos. Although technically a simile, the comparison is so extensive as to amount to a mythological exemplum, and this is a noteworthy fact since Penelope's previous narratives were all about herself and her present and her immediate past. This, by contrast, is a story about the events and people of the remote past, such as a poet might tell. It is an unprecedented move on Penelope's part, and it commands attention:

αὐτὰρ ἐπὴν νὺξ ἔλθῃ, ἕλῃσί τε κοῖτος ἅπαντας,
κεῖμαι ἐνὶ λέκτρῳ, πυκιναὶ δέ μοι ἀμφ' ἁδινὸν κῆρ
ὀξεῖαι μελεδῶναι ὀδυρομένην ἐρέθουσιν.
ὡς δ' ὅτε Πανδαρέου κούρη, χλωρηῒς ἀηδών,
καλὸν ἀείδησιν ἔαρος νέον ἱσταμένοιο,
δενδρέων ἐν πετάλοισι καθεζομένη πυκινοῖσιν,
ἥ τε θαμὰ τρωπῶσα χέει πολυδευκέα φωνήν,
παῖδ' ὀλοφυρομένη Ἴτυλον φίλον, ὅν ποτε χαλκῷ
κτεῖνε δι' ἀφραδίας, κοῦρον Ζήθοιο ἄνακτος·
ὡς καὶ ἐμοὶ δίχα θυμὸς ὀρώρεται ἔνθα καὶ ἔνθα,
ἠὲ μένω παρὰ παιδὶ καὶ ἔμπεδα πάντα φυλάσσω,
κτῆσιν ἐμήν, δμῳάς τε καὶ ὑψερεφὲς μέγα δῶμα,
εὐνήν τ' αἰδομένη πόσιος δήμοιό τε φῆμιν,
ἦ ἤδη ἅμ' ἕπωμαι, Ἀχαιῶν ὅς τις ἄριστος
μνᾶται ἐνὶ μεγάροισι, πορὼν ἀπερείσια ἕδνα.
παῖς δ' ἐμὸς εἷος ἔην ἔτι νήπιος ἠδὲ χαλίφρων,
γήμασθ' οὔ μ' εἴα πόσιος κατὰ δῶμα λιποῦσαν·
νῦν δ' ὅτε δὴ μέγας ἐστὶ καὶ ἥβης μέτρον ἱκάνει,

καὶ δή μ' ἀρᾶται πάλιν ἐλθέμεν ἐκ μεγάροιο,
κτήσιος ἀσχαλόων, τήν οἱ κατέδουσιν Ἀχαιοί.

(Odyssey 19.515–534)

But when the night comes and sleep takes all others,
I lie in my bed and bitter cares, swarming around my heart,
give me no peace as I grieve.
As when the daughter of Pandareos, the tremulous[1]
    nightingale,
sings beautifully when the spring has just began,
perching in the thick of the tree leaves;
she, frequently varying the strains of her voice, pours out
    varied melody,
mourning the son of Lord Zethos, her own son Itylos,
whom she once killed with bronze in her *aphradia*.[2]
Just so my mind is stirred this way and that,
whether I should stay with my son and keep everything
    in place,
my possessions, servants and the high-roofed great house,
respecting the marriage bed of my husband and the talk of
    the people,
or whether I should follow, finally, one of the Achaeans,
    whoever is best
of those who woo me in the halls and provides a countless
    bride-price.
My son, while he was still innocent and soft in his mind,
did not let me marry and leave my husband's house.
But now that he has grown up and reached the stage of youth,
he begs me to retreat from the household,
vexed over his property which Achaeans devour.

The simile has a deceptive immediacy about it. Penelope's grief and lamentation invite the poetic trope of the nightingale,[3] and the varied sound of the bird's song echoes the back-and-forth of Penelope's indecision. The transparency of the comparison, however, is undercut by the *myth* of Aedon,

---

[1] For the translation of χλωρηΐς see Irwin 1974:68–75.

[2] On the meaning of ἀφραδίη see below.

[3] Even the name of Penelope signals the theme of lament, being derived from *penelops*, a bird that is associated in poetry with such typical birds of lament as the nightingale and halcyon. See Levaniouk 1999 and below.

a mother who killed her own son, since the connection between the myth and the narrative is far from obvious.[4]

The myth of Aedon survives in two versions. The first version is the familiar one about Prokne and Philomela (or Aedon and Khelidon), made canonical by Athenian tragedy, Ovid, and the mythological handbook ascribed to Apollodorus.[5] Prokne's husband, Tereus, rapes her sister, Philomela, who contrives to let Prokne know what happened by weaving her story into a fabric. In anger, Prokne kills her own and Tereus' son, Itys, and serves the boy's flesh to his father. It is important to note the logic of this action: being left both childless and incurably polluted is the ultimate punishment for the offender, whose *genos* is thus cut short.[6] Prokne loves her son and will forever lament him as a bird, but she uses her control over him to irrevocably harm her husband in the same way as Medea harms hers in Euripides' play.

The second version is given by the scholia and Eustathius with a reference to Pherecydes, and runs as follows: Aedon is married to Zethos, the fortifier of Thebes, and they have only one son, Itylos. Zethos' twin, Amphion, is married to Niobe and they have many children. Aedon becomes jealous of this and attempts to kill Niobe's eldest son, but makes a mistake in the darkness of

---

[4] Discussions of the comparison include: Austin 1975:228–9, Russo 1982 and 1992.100–101, Marquardt 1985:40, Katz 1991:145, Felson 1994:31–32, Papadopoulou-Belmehdi 1994:153–160, Nagy 1996a:7–58, McDonald 1997, Anhalt 2001–2. Anhalt (2001–2:145) characterizes the comparison as "powerful but puzzling, the analogy's precise relevance to Penelope's own situation inexplicit and unclear."

[5] The names Aedon and Khelidon, attested first on the seventh-century temple at Thermos (see n6 below) are surely traditional and early. In what follows I will refer to this version of the myth as the Prokne-Philomela story, to make it easily distinguishable from the other version in which the heroine's name is Aedon.

[6] This version of the plot seems to appear for the first time in Aeschylus' *Hiketides* (60–68), but the account that later became standard seems to derive from Sophocles' *Tereus* (certainly if P.Oxy. 42.3013 is the hypothesis of that play). Of the unfragmentary sources, the story is told by Apollodorus (3.14.8) and later by Ovid *Metamorphoses* 6.427–674. Other attestations include: Aeschylus *Agamemnon* 1140–1145, Sophocles *Electra* 147–149, Euripides *Heracles* 1020, Aristophanes *Birds* 200–210, Thucydides 2.29.3, Demosthenes *Funeral Oration* 28, Pausanias 1.5.4, 1.24.3, 1.41.8, 10.49, and Strabo 9.3.13. For an exhaustive discussion of the myth and its variants see Cazzaniga 1950.27–93, Mihailov 1995:167–168, 174–175, 180–182. Aedon and Khelidon (Χελιδϝων) are depicted on a metope from the seventh-century temple of Apollo at Thermos: see Sotiriadis 1903:74, 90 and p.5, Cazzaniga 1950:21, Antonetti 1990:178–181 and 386 (pl.11), Mihailov 1995:150–151. The metope from Thermos is sufficient evidence that Aedon *could* be used as a proper name, *pace* Russo who thinks that the scholia misunderstood ἀηδών in 19.518 in this way (Russo 1992:100). Aedon and Khelidon are so called in Boios (ap. Antoninus Liberalis 11).

the children's bedroom and kills her own.[7] In the version told by Eustathius, Aedon instructs Itylos to sleep separately that night, or to sleep at the back of the room, but the boy either forgets or disobeys, and is unwittingly killed by his mother.[8]

Both versions of the myth have played their part in modern interpretations of Penelope's *exemplum*, but when a deeper connection is sought between the narrative and the simile, the story of Prokne tends to predominate. Interpreted in the light of this myth, the simile has been taken to indicate suspicion or submerged hostility towards Odysseus, (who is cast in the role of Tereus),[9] or at least some wavering in Penelope's commitment to him. Some see in the nightingale comparison a "Klytemnestra-paradigm," which involves a woman breaking apart from her husband and consequently from his offspring, like Prokne.[10] Most recently, Anhalt has suggested that Penelope's reference to Aedon "may reveal apprehensions concerning Odysseus' actions during his absence and uncertainty about the constancy of his attachment to herself."[11]

Aedon's *aphradia* (*Odyssey* 19.523) is often understood, on the basis of Prokne's story, as 'madness' that reflects Penelope's mental turmoil. For example, Austin comments that "like the nightingale, Penelope is distraught to the point of madness – note her word *aphradia* in verse 523."[12] Interpreting the myth in the same vein, Russo argues that Penelope alludes to a story "quite similar to the tale of Tereus, Prokne, and Itys" and accordingly concludes: "From her admission that her heart is divided, 524, we may read into her account of Pandareos' daughter the implication that the nightingale

---

[7] Scholia to the *Odyssey* (V1, V2, B2) 19.518, Pherecydes FGrH 3 F 124. The Scholion B1 is the briefest of all and states simply that Aedon killed a son of Amphion, and then out of fear of revenge killed her own.

[8] Eustathius on 19.51. Russo (1992:100) writes: "This story may be an earlier variant of the Attic tale, or perhaps a fiction largely invented by the scholia, which misunderstood ἀηδών of 518 as a proper name." I regard the latter hypothesis as highly improbable. If the Theban myth did not already exist, the scholiasts, familiar with the Attic version, would no doubt have transplanted it into the Theban setting, with Zethos in place of Tereus, instead of inventing a completely different tale. The independence of the scholia's version is further confirmed by the fact that in it Aedon and Zethos have a daughter, Neis, who is not mentioned in Homer. The scholia are also independent of the Hesiodic *Catalogue of Women*, where Amphion had either twenty or nineteen children (fr. 183 MW).

[9] Ahl and Roisman 1996:235, and, more generally, 229–242 on Penelope's reluctance to accept Odysseus as he is in place of her fantasy of Odysseus as he was twenty years earlier.

[10] Austin 1975:228–229, Papadopoulou-Belmehdi 1994:137–160, Katz 1991:128–154 and 54, 80, 85. Cf. Russo 1992:100.

[11] Anhalt 2001–2:155–156.

[12] Austin 1975:229

killed her own son not by mistake, as in the scholia's explanation, but 'in her senseless folly,' like Prokne, which is a better meaning of δι' ἀφραδίης in 523."[13] Penelope's anxiety and apparent agitation facilitate this understanding of *aphradia*. In a recent study, McDonald cites the Theban version of the myth where Aedon is not afflicted by any mental disturbance, but still understands *aphradia* as madness, because it "keeps continuity with the intensified mental suffering . . . that Penelope evokes in the passage."[14] By contrast, those who have the Theban plot in mind, tend to translate δι' ἀφραδίης as 'by mistake' or 'unwittingly'.[15]

The most troublesome and much disputed part of the comparison is doubtless Aedon's murder of her son. Since the myth is generally understood as a confession, the murder of Itylos is often interpreted psychologically.[16] Austin sees the myth as Penelope's way "to adumbrate some of the ambivalence in her own emotions" and express "the ambiguity of a mother's position"; Marquardt suggests that "Penelope's own son is in some way dead to her too"; and Anhalt sees in the nightingale Penelope's pain at the "regrettable consequences" of her own actions, including her decision to consider remarriage.[17] Others have seen in Penelope's myth a veiled threat against Telemachus.[18] More often, however, the myth is thought to express Penelope's fear of causing her son's death. Those who see Prokne in the background connect this fear with a conflict between Telemachus and his mother, who is pursuing her own goals.[19] Those who have the Theban plot in mind tend to see in the myth Penelope's fear of harming her son by mistake.[20] Behind this fear, and mixed with it, McDonald detects an "inadmissible but powerful wish to slay the son, flee the husband, and be free, alone, singing a beautiful song of grief."[21] I agree with some of the views mentioned so far and disagree with others, but it would be cumbersome to list such agreements and

---

[13] Russo 1992:100. Katz (1991:145) agrees with Russo in translating it as "in her senseless folly."

[14] McDonald 1997:9.

[15] Stanford (1965:336 *ad* 19.518), Felson (1994:31, "inattentiveness"). Rutherford (1992:192) takes it to imply that the killing is accidental.

[16] This approach seems to owe much to Austin's study of the *Odyssey* (1975).

[17] Austin 1975:223–229, Marquardt 1985:40, Anhalt 2001–2:151.

[18] Ahl and Roisman 1996:234–235.

[19] Katz 1991:54, 80, 85, 128–54, Papadopoulou-Belmehdi 1994:137–151, Ahl and Roisman 1996:235, Anhalt 2001–2.

[20] E.g., Felson (1994:31), Rutherford (1992:192). Marquardt (1985:40) suggests (rightly, in my opinion) that Penelope "must question whether her encouragement of the suitors did not unintentionally create the painful situation which prevails in Ithaca," and thus endanger Telemachus.

[21] McDonald 1997:18.

disagreements on each point. Instead, I will simply present my interpretation of the Aedon myth in the *Odyssey*. The crucial element of this presentation focuses on the peculiarities and implications of the specific version of the myth as told by Penelope.

Although it is standard practice for interpreters to rely on both versions,[22] the *Odyssey* refers explicitly not to the Prokne-Philomela myth, but to the Theban story of Aedon, the wife of Zethos, and I think the *variance* between the two versions should be taken seriously in interpreting the simile. In the *Odyssey*, Aedon's father is not Pandion but Pandareos, her husband not Tereus, but Zethos. These details and differences are not trivial: there is not a single attested version of the myth in which Zethos simply substitutes for Tereus in the Prokne and Philomela plot. While the existence of two versions has, of course, been noticed, and even led to differences in interpretation, the fact of variation itself has remained in the footnotes. And yet it is likely that both versions of the myth were known to some poets and to at least some of their audiences, and the choice of one (the lesser known) of them is a deliberate move. In the highly traditional medium of Homeric poetry mythological variation is an interpretive clue to the audience. This is not to say, of course, that Penelope's words are incomprehensible to those who are not familiar with a specific version of the myth. The very fact that many modern scholars found the story of Prokne and Philomela helpful is testimony to the contrary, and even someone who has never heard of Aedon before, in any version, could make some sense of Penelope's words since she does state the main facts of the myth. Still, the version of the myth that is actually signaled by the poem is obviously relevant in a very different sense from the version that is not so signaled. On a more general level, such distinctions may indeed be neutralized, but they are crucial for the meaning of the myth in its immediate context. Fuller precision and deeper resonance is achieved by understanding Penelope's words in the light of the version she signals.

---

[22] Anhalt (2001–2:148) expresses the prevailing opinion that "we can never know for certain which version of the nightingale story Penelope evokes." Austin (1975) leaves the matter without comment; Russo (1982, 1992.100), Katz (1991), Papadopoulou-Belmehdi (1994), and Ahl and Roisman (1996) cite Prokne's tale; Marquardt (1985:40) lists both versions, labeling the Theban one as "later," with unclear implications for the *Odyssey*. Rutherford (1992:192–93) acknowledges that the *Odyssey* refers to the Theban version but does not examine its implications. McDonald (1997:16) exceptionally observes that the Prokne-Philomela story is *not* told in the *Odyssey*, but in his interpretation focuses, in the first instance, on features shared by both versions, and secondarily on the Prokne-Philomela myth, which, he argues, is present "in the fabric" of the two Odysssean Pandareid stories.

In spite of the multiple echoes, the story of Prokne fits Penelope only loosely. Prokne negates her marriage and kills her son, but Penelope's supposed ambivalence towards Telemachus and Odysseus is hard to find in the rest of the poem,[23] and there appears to be no plausible motive for the disclosure of such feelings to her guest, be he Odysseus or not.[24] While both women suffer, their suffering is not the same: Prokne's agony stems from the fact that the son she loves belongs also to the man she hates, but Penelope is spared that predicament. Penelope's divided heart finds only a questionable parallel in Prokne, who is tormented (in the surviving sources) not by coming to a decision, but *after* the murder, by the consequences of her action.[25] And even Prokne's frenzy is hardly reminiscent of Penelope's anxiety: Penelope is torn, but she weighs her options again and again, a far cry from acting in a fit of passion.

The Theban myth, on the other hand, fits the *Odyssey* very well. There is no unmarried sister involved, no misdeed on the part of the husband, and no madness. Most importantly, this Aedon has no negative feelings either towards her son or towards her husband. On the contrary, she is full of envy because the *genos* of Amphion is flourishing while her Itylos has to compete, all alone, against his multiple cousins. By plotting against the eldest son of Niobe she is trying to weaken the competition. But she is not good at plotting, and kills her own son – her plan is a miscalculation. The expression δι' ἀφραδίης captures her fault exactly, without indicating any kind of madness, for it regularly refers to a lapse in planning or attention.[26] This Aedon kills not in a frenzy but literally because of 'non-thinking', a failure to plan carefully enough.[27] Her miscalculation is fatal and leaves both herself and Zethos without offspring – quite the opposite of what she intended to do. Penelope, too, is plotting and taking

---

[23] Anhalt (2001–2:149–150) observes that prior to the simile "Penelope has shown no ambivalence toward Telemachos."

[24] The idea that the reserved and cunning Penelope confesses freely to a stranger is far from self-evident, yet Austin saw in Penelope's words "the inner resources of her thought" (1975:228) and the simile is still analyzed on this assumption. A notable exception is Ahl and Roisman 1996:215–272.

[25] The early sources are all fragmentary, and it is quite possible that there were Proknes, lost to us, who agonized prior to the murder, like the Euripidean Medea. Such a Prokne, however, could no longer be said to kill her son in a fury or madness.

[26] Cf. *Odyssey* 14.480, where "Odysseus" thoughtlessly leaves his cloak behind (ἀφραδίης) and *Iliad* 16.354, where some sheep are attacked by wolves due to inattentiveness (ἀφραδίῃσι) of the shepherd. In reading *aphradia* in this way I am in agreement with Marquardt 1985:40, Felson 1994:31, Rutherford 1992:192.

[27] Ahl and Roisman (1996:234) object to the translations that imply a simple accident. This does not mean, however, that 'madness' is the correct translation.

risks in order to 'preserve everything intact' (19.525); one misstep, and she might leave herself without a son and cut short the *genos* of Odysseus – the opposite of her intentions.

Penelope's dilemma is not between her husband and son but between waiting for a perfect solution at the risk of losing everything, or settling for something much worse but also perhaps slightly less dangerous.[28] It is sometimes assumed that because Penelope's continued presence in the house is dangerous for her son, her removal through marriage to one of the suitors would solve Telemachus' problems. This is, however, far from obvious. Penelope nowhere describes her remarriage as an action of loyalty to Telemachus, and it is doubtful that her departure would indeed improve his position: Athena-Mentes, at any rate, seems to think that in order to claim his proper place in Ithaca he would have to kill the suitors *even after* Penelope remarries (*Odyssey* 1.290–96).[29]

The Theban story is obviously related to the Prokne-Philomela one, but their variance is as significant as their relatedness, and on one crucial point the two are diametrically opposed: the wife of Tereus deliberately stamps out her husband's lineage; the wife of Zethos aims at *advancing* it, although she achieves quite the opposite. Penelope names Zethos and not Tereus as Aedon's husband to signal that she implies a Theban-like plot and to leave no room for uncertainty about her aims. The myth does indeed point to Penelope's fear of causing her son's death inadvertently, but she is not simply afraid: she makes a specific claim that what she *hopes* to do is the opposite – to safeguard Telemachus' fortunes, to hold out for the best possible outcome, for him as well as for herself.

The myth of the nightingale leads Penelope to tell the beggar that Telemachus has grown up. There is a connection here: while Telemachus was younger, it was safer. Now he loudly claims to be master of the house, sends Penelope upstairs, and puts himself in danger by attracting the unfriendly attention of the suitors.[30] Like Itylos who does not go to sleep where he was

---

[28] See below and Murnaghan 1987:155–166. Anhalt articulates the view that Penelope's choice is that between Telemachus and Odysseus: "if Penelope remains faithful to Odysseus she must therefore perpetuate the tense situation in the palace and even, possibly, endanger Telemachos' life; if she remains loyal to Telemachos (and chooses a new husband), she must therefore consider Odysseus dead." A similar view is held by Ahl and Roisman (1996:235). Scodel 2001.324 describes Penelope's strategy as "consistently trying to avoid the worst outcomes."

[29] Penelope is well aware that she may be a crucial link in legitimizing Telemachus' succession (1.215–216).

[30] E.g., *Odyssey* 1.345–387.

told to, Telemachus is now independent and, for Penelope, no longer reliable.[31] While Penelope still thinks that it is best for Telemachus to wait, Telemachus himself is no longer sure of this, and begins to follow his own course of action.[32]

In Penelope's simile, Itylos is both the *philos* child of Aedon (19.522), and the son of *Lord* Zethos (Ζήθοιο ἄνακτος 19.523). This double characterization captures the dual aspects of Penelope's worry, both for her child and for the son and heir to Odysseus. Penelope herself talks of Telemachus in both these ways at the moment when her worry for him is at its highest, not in Book 19 but in Book 4, when she discovers that he has left for Pylos. At first, as soon as she can control her tears enough to speak, Penelope laments the disappearance of her beloved son (παῖδ' ἀγαπητὸν, 4.727), but almost in the same breath she is already thinking of what to do and hoping that perhaps old Laertes may find some way of saving the offspring of Odysseus (Ὀδυσσῆος γόνον ἀντιθέοιο 4.741). The perpetuation of the *genos* of Laertes is an important theme in the poem from Athena-Mentes' visit at the beginning, when she predicts that Telemachus' stock will not become nameless (1.222–223), to Laertes' expression of joy at his son and grandson competing in prowess (24.514–515). Penelope's commitment to Telemachus *is* commitment to Odysseus, since without Telemachus there would be no continuation for Odysseus' *genos*.

The fact that Aedon has only one son adds to the comparison, since for Penelope too everything is at stake, and the fact that Telemachus is the only son is emphasized by the *Odyssey*.[33] Granted, Aedon has one son in all versions of the story, but this fact is peripheral for Prokne, while in the Theban version it is the fact that Aedon has only one son that sets the plot in action, and it is the same fact that makes the mistake so devastating.

Opposed to the only child Itylos are the numerous children of Niobe, opposed to the only child Telemachus are his age-mates and competitors, the suitors.[34] By marrying Penelope the lucky suitor would step, at least in part, into Odysseus' place: μητέρ ἐμὴν γαμέειν καὶ Ὀδυσσῆος γέρας ἕξειν, 'to marry my mother and have the position of Odysseus' (15.522), is how Telemachus

---

[31] E.g., *Odyssey* 4.696–710.

[32] Cf. Finley's formulation of Penelope's strategy (1978:5): "If she gained nothing final, she lost nothing final and meanwhile, though at a loss of property, maintained a kind of order and kept the future open for Telemachus and for herself." See also Marquardt 1985:35 and Murnaghan 1987:155–166.

[33] *Odyssey* 2.365 (μοῦνος ἐὼν ἀγαπητός), 11.68, 16.19, 16.117–120.

[34] Penelope addresses her suitors as κοῦροι, e.g. 19.141. They are obviously a little older than Telemachus, but comparable in age.

describes their goal.[35] Having Odysseus' *geras* should be Telemachus' prerogative, and thus the suitors in effect compete with him for inheritance from Odysseus. When Telemachus explains his troubles to the disguised Odysseus in Book 16, he points out precisely that he has no brothers to rely on (16.115–116), and attributes the presence of the suitors in the house to his position as the only son:

> μοῦνον δ' αὖτ' Ὀδυσῆα πατὴρ τέκεν· αὐτὰρ Ὀδυσσεὺς
> μοῦνον ἔμ' ἐν μεγάροισι τεκὼν λίπεν, οὐδ' ἀπόνητο.
> τῶ νῦν δυσμενέες μάλα μυρίοι εἴσ' ἐνὶ οἴκῳ.
>
> *(Odyssey 16.119–121)*

> The father of Odysseus had only one son. And Odysseus too
> had only me, and had no joy of it, but left me alone in
>   his halls.
> That is why so many enemies are now in the household.

Just as Aedon wishes to destroy her son's eldest cousin, so Penelope wishes rather unsentimentally for the suitors' death:

> τῶ κε καὶ οὐκ ἀτελὴς θάνατος μνηστῆρσι γένοιτο
> πᾶσι μάλ', οὐδέ κέ τις θάνατον καὶ κῆρας ἀλύξει.
>
> *(Odyssey 17.546–547)*

> May death be accomplished for the suitors,
> all of them, and let not a single one escape death
>   and destruction.

As suggested by Marquardt, Penelope's decision to encourage many suitors at once is itself a defensive stratagem, a plan that makes them keep each other at bay.[36] The purpose of this plan is surely to buy time for Odysseus to return, but the dangers are obvious. Like Aedon, Penelope risks losing her son through a scheme that was meant to trap his competitors.

---

[35] Telemachus is here speaking specifically of Eurymachus, but there is little doubt that others, certainly Antinoos, share his goal at least initially, though their chances are not as good and accordingly they seem to give up this goal while Eurymachus still persists in it. See Scodel 2001 for an illuminating discussion of the suitors' motives at each stage in the development of events. The question of what would happen to Odysseus' property if Penelope married one of the suitors is too complex to be addressed here, but to a certain extent Penelope herself is part of Odysseus' *geras*, and having her as wife would in and of itself put her future husband in Odysseus' place.

[36] Marquardt 1985:32–48. See *Odyssey* 13.379–381.

As Murnaghan has convincingly argued, Penelope is holding out for a perfect solution, the "miracle" of Odysseus' return, while Telemachus is ready to settle for something less and tries only to create "the conditions that will allow him to take his father's place"[37] – or at least some part of that place. Aedon in the Theban myth refuses to accept the weaker position of her Itylos in comparison with Niobe's larger brood. Second best is not enough for Aedon, and the myth lets Penelope's guest know that it is not enough for Penelope either. In the end, Penelope succeeds where Aedon failed: she furthers the suitors' demise, while her own son is safe. Aedon's plan miscarries because of her *aphradia*, in contrast to Penelope, who is *periphron*.[38] In the meanwhile, however, Penelope has to combine and balance two strategies: trying to achieve the best outcome while avoiding the worst. The latter strategy does not preclude the former, but it does come first, if Aedon's mistake is to be avoided.[39]

Turned into the nightingale, Aedon now sings a changing melody, frequently 'turning' her voice (θαμὰ τρωπῶσα χέει πολυηχέα φωνήν, 19.521), and the nightingale (the bird as opposed to the woman) has its own role to play in Penelope's simile. Like Penelope, the nightingale is above all a figure of lament, and a further point of contact is established between them by their shared tendency to cry, or sing, at night. Penelope may cry by day, but it seems that at night her grief finds its freest and deepest expression: again and again, she cries in bed until Athena sends her sleep (e.g.1.363, 16.450, 19.603, 21.357). Nightingales, of course, sing at night, and the sleepless nightingale is a *topos* in Greek poetry. The bird is called ἄμορος ὕπνου, 'having no share of sleep',[40] and the expression ὕπνος ἀηδόνειος, 'nightingale sleep', came to mean a very short sleep.[41] Like the sleepless bird, Penelope has been spending her night in thought and worry, her mental process as varied and fluid as the bird's voice. In comparing her indecision to the bird's song, Penelope points to the variation in her own thought and action – much needed, before it is too late.

---

[37] Murnaghan 1987:157 and, more generally, 155–66.

[38] Penelope's ruthlessness in eliminating competition is a trait she may have also possessed outside of the *Odyssey*: Sophocles' *Euryalus* probably dramatized Penelope luring Odysseus into killing his own son by another woman, an Epirote princess Euippe (Parthenius, *Erotica* 3, see Sutton 1984:46).

[39] Cf. Scodel 2001:324, who argues that in order to understand Penelope's decision to set up the bow contest it is not necessary to consider her psychology at all "except to see her as consistently trying to avoid the worst outcomes."

[40] Aelian *Varia Historia* 12.20.

[41] Nikokhares fr. 16 (Koch). Cf. Nonnus *Dionysiaca* 5.411, Lucian *Halcyon* 2, and Ovid *Metamorphoses* 11.410. Cf. also Dionysius *De Avibus* 2.7.

The exact quality of the nightingale's voice is captured by two variant epithets: πολυηχέα in verse 521, and πολυδευκέα, preserved in its place by Aelian.[42] The two adjectives are synonymous to an extent, but πολυδευκέα brings to the surface an aspect of meaning that is present but not singled out in the more general πολυηχέα. Arguing that these variants "stem ultimately from variant performances in oral poetry,"[43] Nagy has examined the archaic semantics of πολυδευκής. This word, he suggests, should be understood as "having much continuity" or "having continuity in many different ways." The πολυδευκής song of the nightingale is, then, variable but uninterrupted, in sharp contrast to Aedon's performance in life, rudely interrupted by her own fatal mistake. Variation with its "turns" is what enables continuity.[44] Throughout the *Odyssey*, Penelope is praised for just that. The main metaphor for her cunning, the weaving and unweaving of Laertes' shroud, involves both continuity and a back-and-forth movement.[45] This trick Penelope describes as δόλους τολυπεύω (19.137) with the verb τολυπεύω, (to 'carry through' or 'wind on' and hence 'achieve'), conveying the idea of continuity.[46] Continuity through variation is thus a hallmark of Penelope's cunning as it is of her wool working. It is also, as much as variation, a distinctive feature of the nightingale's song. Aristotle specifically mentions that its song is continuous: ἀηδὼν ᾄδει μὲν συνεχῶς, 'the nightingale sings without interruptions'.[47]

Penelope begins the comparison with the worries that crowd on her mind, thick (πυκιναί, 516) like the leaves in which the nightingale perches (πυκινοῖσιν, 520). The nightingale sings the way Penelope thinks, with frequent turns, in a setting full of vitality, accentuated by the mention of early spring and the epithet of the nightingale – χλωρηΐς, a word that connotes, as Irwin has argued, not color, but the throbbing fluidity of the bird's voice.[48] The mention of Aedon's deed comes as a harsh interruption, momentarily slid into this description through a relative clause. The break is marked by the change

---

[42] Aelian *De natura animalium* 5.38. See Nagy 1996a:8 on this variant.

[43] Nagy 1996a:9.

[44] Nagy 1996a:55–58 on *mimesis* as "continuity through variety."

[45] In fact, the back and forth movement is doubled in this case, since any kind of weaving involves moving back and forth in front of the loom as, e.g., in Pindar *Pythian* 9.18: ἁ μὲν οὔθ' ἱστῶν παλιμβάμους ἐφίλησεν ὁδούς, "she [Kyrene] did not love the back-and-forth paths of the loom."

[46] Cf. Nagy 1996a:49–52 on the parallel semantics of Latin *ducere* in the expression *filum deducere* 'draw out a thread'. For more on the implications of this verb, see below.

[47] Aristotle, *Historia Animalium* 632b21. I am indebted to Nagy (1996:49) for these references as well as a Latin parallel: Pliny (*Natural History* 10.81) describes the nightingale's song as *garrulus sine intermissu cantus*.

[48] Irwin 1974:72–73.

in the sound of the verses, which are in general imitative of the nightingale's song: with the death of Itylos a harsh alliteration of *k* and *kh* sounds intrudes, taking the place of *p-ph* and *t-th* sounds in the previous verses. The *p-ph* alliteration (interspersed with nasals) returns in 525.[49] Just as the sound of this verse resumes what came before the mention of Itylos' death, so too does the meaning of Penelope's words: she starts with her worries and the nightingale's song, then sharply alters both her subject and her sound to tell of the murder of Itylos, and then completes the ring composition by returning again to her own roused *thumos*. This seamless inclusion of a discordant note is a pointed "turn" in Penelope's performance for Odysseus.

Besieged by a throng of young men in her own house, Penelope reminds Odysseus, through the nightingale comparison, that sometimes flexibility and variation is a requirement of continuity. She reminds him also that her foremost goal has been to guard the fortunes of Telemachus, and here the choice of the myth is critical: the comparison with the Theban Aedon places Penelope firmly on her son's and husband's side. She has held out, even in her grief and anxiety, but the risk of repeating Aedon's mistake weighs heavily on her. The implication that she has not abandoned all hope of Odysseus' return must be pleasing to him, but it also means that now it is up to him to deliver the perfect solution she has waited for. The myth not only presents Penelope's aims in a favorable light, but puts pressure on Odysseus to justify the risks she had to take because of his absence.[50] The discordant note of Itylos' murder makes starkly clear both the costs of his delay and the urgent need for his action.

The diction that introduces the myth of Aedon is reminiscent of an episode in Book 4, already mentioned above, and a comparison of these two sequences can serve as a test for my proposed interpretation. There are several structural similarities between the two episodes: in both cases, Penelope laments and fears for Telemachus, searches for a useful course of action, and finds consolation in a dream. In Book 4 Penelope is vexed by cares at night, as she confesses, in a dream, to her sister's image:

---

[49] See the quotation at the beginning of this section. The alliteration may be schematically depicted as follows: 521: *d-dr-p-p*, 522: *th-tr-p-p-ph*, 523: *p-ph-ph-p* (and 522: *lon-lon-hon*), 525: *m-p-p-d-mp-d-p-nt-ph*. Cf. end of 522 and 523: *kh-k-kt-k-kt*.

[50] Telemachus certainly is in danger, but the suitors are not decisive about killing him: δεινὸν δὲ γένος βασιλήϊόν ἐστι κτείνειν, "it is dangerous to kill the royal stock," says Amphinomos (16.401–402). At 20.240–247 they give up their plans (at least for the moment) because of a bad omen.

καί με κέλεαι παύσασθαι ὀϊζύος ἠδ' ὀδυνάων
πολλέων, αἵ μ' ἐρέθουσι κατὰ φρένα καὶ κατὰ θυμόν.

(*Odyssey* 4.812–813)

And you urge me to cease from my suffering and from
the many pains which trouble me in my mind.

The cares that trouble her on that occasion are much the same as those in
Book 19: worries about Telemachus, whose secret departure for Pylos has just
become known to her. The image of her sister, sent by kindly Athena, promises
that Telemachus will return. In Book 19, and nowhere else, what Penelope's
troubles do to her is also conveyed by the verb ἐρέθω:

κεῖμαι ἐνὶ λέκτρῳ, πυκιναὶ δέ μοι ἀμφ' ἁδινὸν κῆρ
ὀξεῖαι μελεδῶναι ὀδυρομένην ἐρέθουσιν.

(*Odyssey* 19.516–517)

I lie in my bed and bitter cares, swarming around my heart,
vex me as I grieve.

This verb is usually translated in these passages as 'to trouble'. Lattimore
renders it as 'torment', Fitzgerald has bitter thoughts 'crowding' on Penelope,
Cunliffe has a separate gloss for the two passages in question, 'to keep from
rest, trouble', and LSJ lists 'disquiet' as an Odyssean meaning, again citing only
these two passages. But elsewhere this verb and the related ἐρεθίζω mean not
only to trouble, but to provoke – to anger or to fighting, mostly. For example,
in the *Iliad* Aphrodite threatens to abandon Helen saying: μή μ' ἔρεθε σχετλίη,
μὴ χωσαμένη σε μεθείω, 'Do not provoke me, wretch, or I may abandon you in
anger' (3.414). The 'cares' do not simply trouble Penelope: they goad her on
and compel her to act.

In Book 4, Penelope is 'provoked' because she has just learned that
Telemachus is away from Ithaca. She grieves for her son more than she does
for her husband and is desperately afraid for him:

τοῦ δὴ ἐγὼ καὶ μᾶλλον ὀδύρομαι ἤ περ ἐκείνου.
τοῦ δ' ἀμφιτρομέω καὶ δείδια μή τι πάθησιν.

(*Odyssey* 4.819–820)

I grieve for him even more than for that other man.
I am afraid for him and fear that something may happen
            to him.

Although there is little Penelope can do while Telemachus is away, her frantic search for some useful plan of action is captured in a striking comparison:

> ὅσσα δὲ μερμήριξε λέων ἀνδρῶν ἐν ὁμίλῳ
> δείσας, ὁππότε μιν δόλιον περὶ κύκλον ἄγωσι,
> τόσσα μιν ὁρμαίνουσαν ἐπήλυθε νήδυμος ὕπνος.

> (*Odyssey* 4.791–793)

> As much as a lion ponders, caught in a crowd of men,
> in fear, when they draw their treacherous circle around him,
> so much she was anxiously pondering when sweet sleep
>   came over her.

Homeric women are not typically compared to lions, but, as Foley puts it, "Penelope . . . has come remarkably close to enacting the role of a besieged warrior."[51] The simile captures Penelope's valiant effort to defend her son, to do what her husband might be expected to do, were he present. It also captures her limitations: the lion is cornered. Still, Penelope does not give up and consent to marriage with one of her suitors, but rather does what she can to diminish the risk to her son, and continues to hold out.[52] In fact, the lion in Book 4 is even reminiscent of the nightingale in Book 19 in one respect. This is the only Homeric lion whose action is described by μερμηρίζω. This verb often refers to deciding between two options, and this makes the strategizing lion of Book 4 all the more similar to the wavering Penelope of Book 19. A typical formula involving this verb is διάνδιχα μερμήριξεν, 'ponder this way and that', and the verb is frequently followed by a construction expressing two alternatives (e.g. *Odyssey* 16.73–76). In the same way, Penelope describes herself as torn between two options in her self-comparison to Aedon:

> ὣς καὶ ἐμοὶ δίχα θυμὸς ὀρώρεται ἔνθα καὶ ἔνθα.

> (*Odyssey* 19.524)

> In the same way my heart is roused this way and that.

---

[51] Foley 1978:10.

[52] Penelope's consent to marry would presumably save Telemachus' life for the moment, though arguably it would not completely guarantee his safety in the future. If Scodel's (2001) assessment of the suitors' motives and chances is right, then marriage at this point would also likely lead to a loss of Telemachus' fortune.

In Book 4 Penelope decides to send Dolios with a message to Laertes, hoping that the old king can instill some shame into the Ithacans and prevent them from 'destroying his offspring and that of godlike Odysseus' (ὅν καὶ Ὀδυσσῆος φθῖσαι γόνον ἀντιθέοιο, 4.741). Specifically, Penelope hopes that Laertes can devise some cunning way (μῆτιν ὑφήνας, 4.739) to appeal and complain to the people (λαοῖσιν ὀδύρεται 4.740), and the diction of her request makes Laertes into a figure very much like Penelope herself, characterized by weeping and cunning. Unlike Penelope, Laertes can appear at the male gathering of the λαός, but his old age and the absence of his son has reduced him to having more or less the same resources as a woman. In the absence of Odysseus, a woman and an elder have to do their best to fill the void. They would not be in this position had Odysseus been there – but he, of course, is absent. By contrast, in Book 19 there is no more need to call on Laertes: Odysseus himself can fulfill his proper role, and Penelope in effect challenges him to do so.

CHAPTER THIRTEEN
THE DREAM

A CTION BY ODYSSEUS is just what Penelope envisages next, immediately after the Aedon comparison, in her dream about the eagle and the geese – or rather her message in the form of the dream.[1] The transition is abrupt, and Anhalt comments that Penelope seems to "deflect interest away from the simile."[2] The abruptness certainly seems deliberate, but in my opinion it is not because the simile is meant to recede quickly from the audience's mind. Rather, the dream narrative builds on the simile and presents Penelope's conclusions derived from it while giving Odysseus no chance to comment on his wife's dilemma, as he might be expected to do. By plunging into the dream, Penelope lets the beggar know that she is not asking for advice: something entirely different is going on. Far from waiting for Odysseus to propose a solution, Penelope presents her guest with her own vision of how her predicament will end: if he is indeed Odysseus and wants to avoid her remarriage, he will kill the suitors. Although at the resumption of their conversation Penelope says that she will question her guest (εἰρήσομαι, 19.509), she asks no direct questions and only requests that he interpret the dream, which already contains its own interpretation. Towards the end of the conversation, far from asking his opinion, Penelope is emphatic that he should pay attention to what she says: ἄλλο δέ τοι ἐρέω, σὺ δ' ἐνὶ φρεσὶ βάλλεο σῇσιν, 'I will tell you another thing, and you put it away in your mind' (19.570). If Penelope does also question the beggar, it is only in an indirect way, by observing his reaction to the dream.

In the dream, Penelope's domestic geese are destroyed by an eagle and Odysseus makes a remarkable appearance in person:

> ἀλλ' ἄγε μοι τὸν ὄνειρον ὑπόκριναι καὶ ἄκουσον.
> χῆνές μοι κατὰ οἶκον ἐείκοσι πυρὸν ἔδουσιν

---

[1] See Winkler 1990:153–54 and Felson 1994:32 on this point. Cf. Book 4, where Penelope's first crisis over Telemachus is also followed by a dream (*Odyssey* 4.795–840).

[2] Anhalt 2001–2.145.

ἐξ ὕδατος, καί τέ σφιν ἰαίνομαι εἰσορόωσα·
ἐλθὼν δ' ἐξ ὄρεος μέγας αἰετὸς ἀγκυλοχήλης
πᾶσι κατ' αὐχένας ἧξε καὶ ἔκτανεν· οἱ δ' ἐκέχυντο
ἀθρόοι ἐν μεγάροισ', ὁ δ' ἐς αἰθέρα δῖαν ἀέρθη.
αὐτὰρ ἐγὼ κλαῖον καὶ ἐκώκυον ἔν περ ὀνείρῳ,
ἀμφὶ δέ μ' ἠγερέθοντο ἐϋπλοκαμῖδες Ἀχαιαί,
οἴκτρ' ὀλοφυρομένην, ὅ μοι αἰετὸς ἔκτανε χῆνας.
ἂψ δ' ἐλθὼν κατ' ἄρ' ἕζετ' ἐπὶ προὔχοντι μελάθρῳ,
φωνῇ δὲ βροτέῃ κατερήτυε φώνησέν τε·
'θάρσει, Ἰκαρίου κούρη τηλεκλειτοῖο·
οὐκ ὄναρ, ἀλλ' ὕπαρ ἐσθλόν, ὅ τοι τετελεσμένον ἔσται.
χῆνες μὲν μνηστῆρες, ἐγὼ δέ τοι αἰετὸς ὄρνις
ἦα πάρος, νῦν αὖτε τεὸς πόσις εἰλήλουθα,
ὃς πᾶσι μνηστῆρσιν ἀεικέα πότμον ἐφήσω.'

(*Odyssey* 19.535–550)

But come, respond to a dream for me and listen to it.
I have twenty geese at home, they eat wheat
out of the water, and I delight in looking at them.
But a great eagle with a curved beak came from
    the mountain
and broke each one's neck and killed all of them. And they
    lay in a heap
in the house, while the eagle rose up high into the shining
    ether.
But I cried and wailed, though in a dream,
and Achaean women with beautiful hair gathered
    around me
as I was bitterly lamenting that the eagle killed my geese.
But the eagle came back and settled on a projecting
    roof-beam,
and in a human voice consoled me and spoke to me:
"Take heart, daughter of far-famed Ikarios.
This is not a dream, but a true waking vision, and it will
    come to fulfillment.
The geese are the suitors, and I was an eagle before,
but now I have come back and I am your husband,
and I will bring an ugly death upon all of the suitors."

According to a popular interpretation, the geese in the dream are the suitors from the very beginning and Penelope's crying over them conveys her secret (or subconscious) disappointment at the loss of their courtship.[3] Such an understanding of the dream, however, underrates both the precision and resonance of its details and its role as a crucial step in the unfolding dialogue. It is true that within the dream itself the eagle equates the geese with the suitors, but that internal interpretation is presented as a *reversal* and therefore *cannot* apply to the first part of the dream. The shift in the symbolism of the geese is supported by the distinction drawn between ὄναρ and ὕπαρ and by the explicit now-then contrast in the eagle's speech:

χῆνες μὲν μνηστῆρες, ἐγὼ δέ τοι αἰετὸς ὄρνις
ἦα πάρος, νῦν αὖτε τεὸς πόσις εἰλήλουθα.

(Odyssey 19.548–549)

The geese are the suitors, and I was an eagle before,
but now I come back and I am your husband.

The implication is that Penelope at first did not think the eagle was Odysseus, nor that the geese were suitors. What are the geese before they are reinterpreted as suitors? A answer has been proposed by Pratt, who argues that the twenty geese, symbols of conjugal fidelity and good guardians of the house, stand for the twenty years that Penelope herself has been such a

---

[3] E.g., Austin 1975.229–31, Katz 1991:146–147, Felson 1994:32, Ahl and Roisman 1996:235–36, McDonald 1997:16. The dream has been also seen as reflective of an unconscious and/or mixed pleasure in the suitors' presence and attachment to them (Devereux 1957:382, Rankin 1962:622, Russo 1982:8–10, 1992.102, Murnaghan 1987:130, Felson-Rubin 1987:71–74). Devereux's (1957.382) opinion is illustrative: "It is hard to understand how literary critics could have overlooked the fact that a rapidly aging woman, denied for some twenty years the pleasures of sex and the company and support of her husband, would inevitably be unconsciously flattered by the attention of young men and highly eligible suitors, which is precisely what the chief suitor accuses her of in public." This, to my mind, overly realistic view is not based on anything in the *Odyssey* but rather on general assumptions regarding the behavior of women. On the dream as a form of divination see Amory 1963:106 and Allione 1963:90–91. On the dream as Penelope's creation, see Büchner 1940:149n1, Harsch 1950:16, and Winkler 1990:154. See also Clayton 2004:45–46 on the dream as a self-referential text "centered on self-interpretation and generation of meaning," which, however, can generate meaning endlessly, thus ultimately eluding interpretation.

guardian.[4] Pratt's interpretation follows, with more precision, the general direction of Finley's earlier suggestion that the geese do not signify the suitors but the "state of half-orderliness" Penelope has maintained.[5] Equating the suitors with the geese in the first part of the dream fails to explain why Penelope chooses to mention their number, especially since the suitors are far more numerous than twenty and indeed we are told that they are 'neither ten nor twenty':

> μνηστήρων δ' οὔτ' ἄρ δεκὰς ἀτρεκὲς οὔτε δύ' οἶαι,
> ἀλλὰ πολὺ πλέονες.
>
> (*Odyssey* 16.245–246)

> The suitors are not ten exactly, nor only twenty,
> but many more.

By contrast, the fact that Odysseus comes home in the twentieth year is repeatedly emphasized: ἤλυθον εἰκοστῷ ἔτεϊ ἐς πατρίδα γαῖαν, 'he came in the twentieth year back to his native land' (16.206 = 19.484 = 21.208 = 24.322).[6] The fact that Penelope chooses this number for her geese is a vital clue to their significance. Penelope's mention of Achaean women who cry along with her (19.543–544) is also hard to comprehend on the assumption that the geese are

---

[4] Pratt 1994. For more on Penelope and water birds, see Bader 1998 and Levaniouk 1999. McDonald (1997:10) notes the excess of Penelope's grief at the loss of her geese and sees in it an argument against a "literal" interpretation and in favor of equating the geese with the suitors. But if the geese are not "literally" the geese, but instead stand for Penelope's long effort at preserving the household of Odysseus, then her excessive grief at the devastation makes perfect sense. On analogies to the dream in later (and modern) Greek poetry, see Athanassakis 1994.

[5] Finley 1978.247. There have been objections to this line of thought: in Katz's opinion, Finley "disregards the obvious meaning of the text," (Katz 1991:146) and a similar criticism has been voiced à propos Pratt's argument by Rozokoki (2001:n6), who claims that it goes against "the interpretation provided within the dream itself (19.548–50)." The latter criticism does not take into account the reversal that is taking place within the dream. As for "the obvious meaning of the text" there is, of course, no such thing. What is clear is that scholars disagree about the interpretation of the dream, which is one of the most complex utterances in Homer. It is also clear is that we are culturally ill-equipped to understand such utterances by virtue of our being outsiders to the song culture of Homeric poetry.

[6] Cf. 2.175, 5.34. Rozokoki's argument (2001:2) that twenty in the *Odyssey* means simply "a significant number" is not persuasive: at 14.98 it is ξυνεείκοσι that has that function, its exaggerated meaning emphasized by ξυν-, at 22.57 it is another standard expression, ἐεικοσάβοιον, and at 20.158 ἐείκοσι might well be the exact number. The fact that twenty can be used to mean 'many' does not, in any case, override the emphasis the *Odyssey* places on the fact that Odysseus comes home in the twentieth year. Athanassakis (1987:263) suggests that twenty is the number of Penelope's favorite suitors, but there is nothing in the poem to support this.

suitors, since from the beginning of the poem public opinion seems to be in favor of Penelope's remaining in the house, however difficult that is (2.136–137, cf. 16.75, 19.527). It is hard to imagine Penelope wailing over the death of the suitors, or other Achaean women joining her in this questionable lament, and it is even harder to imagine Penelope confessing such a fantasy, especially to a man she at least suspects of being Odysseus, let alone to any stranger. Moreover, Penelope is not simply weeping, but indeed lamenting, and the words used, in particular the verb κωκύω, 'wail', and the expression οἴκτρ' ὀλοφυρομένην, 'bitterly lamenting', are especially associated with laments for family members.[7] If she grieves over the loss of her marriage and household with all its hopes, then the language is understandable and the other women may indeed be expected to join her.

Penelope's initial reaction, then, is grief at the sight of her twenty-year effort gone to waste. The second part of the dream, however, is a sudden reversal. The eagle turns out to be on Penelope's side, the geese are in fact suitors: it is not the household that is gone, but the suitors who are dead. And the author of this metamorphosis is Odysseus. Penelope has conveyed to her guest what she has accomplished in the twenty years of his absence, the magnitude of the devastation she expects any minute, and the solution that Odysseus must now achieve. In effect, Penelope takes him up on his claim to be Odysseus – the perfect king. And after describing in her dream-narrative the kind of resolution she expects from the "real" Odysseus, Penelope pointedly remarks that this task still lies ahead:

> ὣς ἔφατ', αὐτὰρ ἐμὲ μελιηδὴς ὕπνος ἀνῆκε·
> παπτήνασα δὲ χῆνας ἐνὶ μεγάροισι νόησα
> πυρὸν ἐρεπτομένους παρὰ πύελον, ἧχι πάρος περ.
>
> (*Odyssey* 19.552–554)

Thus he spoke, and honey-sweet sleep released me.
And looking around I saw the geese in my house,
eating wheat at the water trough, as before.

In the course of the "dream" the geese stood first for Penelope's twenty years of guardianship and then for the suitors, and now they are equally capable of both meanings: the *oikos* still perseveres, but the suitors are still at the trough.[8]

---

[7] Pratt 1994:152 and n17.

[8] Cf. Felson-Rubin (1987:82n34) who sees unresolved ambiguity in 552–553. I agree that the meaning of these lines is not overdetermined, but see them as polyvalent rather than ambiguous.

Polyvalent and shifting in its symbolic values, the dream is equally complex in its genre. It seems to intertwine the themes and conventions of several genres in such a way that they coalesce into a performance most finely attuned to its occasion. Of course, the occasion, a meeting between a wife and her disguised husband on the eve of their momentous reunion, is itself multi-faceted, complex, and certainly unusual.

The very appearance of Odysseus as an eagle is an element rich in conno-tation, and not only because the eagle is Zeus' bird and the largest winged predator of Homeric similes. In Modern Greek oral poetry, the eagle often stands both for a warrior and for an aggressive lover or bridegroom, whose bride is usually a partridge or dove. For example, the eagle and the dove are newlyweds in widely used verses from a wedding song:

> Σήμερα λάμπει ὁ οὐρανός, σήμερα λάμπει ἡ μέρα,
> Σήμερα στεφανώνεται ἀετός τὴν περιστέρα.

> Today the sky is shining, today the day is shining,
> Today the eagle and the dove exchange their wedding
> crowns.[9]

There is a good possibility that such imagery goes back to antiquity, and indeed there is an instance where it seems to surface in the *Odyssey*. In Book 20, the suitors are plotting Telemachus' murder, when they are stopped by an inauspicious omen. An eagle appears on the left, the inauspicious side, carrying a trembling dove. Athanassakis comments: "As a potential bride-groom, each suitor is an eagle, and to each suitor Penelope is a dove. Therefore, the allegorical 'ideogram' before them bodes failure for each one of them, and success for the eagle of Penelope's dream, who is none other than Odysseus."[10] If the eagle as bridegroom is a conventional metaphor already in the Homeric song culture, then perhaps, like today, it was used in wedding songs. This opens up the possibility that Penelope uses the diction of wedding songs to create her dream tale.

And indeed the very notion of a bride's dream before wedding or meeting her future husband may be traditional, in which case Penelope is surely tapping into that tradition. In the *Odyssey*, Nausikaa's dream before she meets Odysseus may be an example of this, although their marriage, of course, fails to take place. There is, moreover, a curious parallel to Penelope's dream in an epic poem far removed from Homer geographically, chronologi-

---

[9] Cited by Athanassakis 1994:124.
[10] Athanassakis 1994:124.

cally, and linguistically. In a version of the Uzbek epic poem *Alpamysh* recorded between 1922 and 1939 from performances of Fazil Yuldash-ogly, Alpamysh and his betrothed Barchin are separated when their fathers quarrel and her own migrates to a remote land with all his people.[11] When the time comes for Barchin to marry, a large number of suitors wish to compete for her hand, but she wants to marry Alpamysh alone. She sends a secret message asking him to come to her rescue and in the meanwhile persuades the suitors to postpone their advances for six months. Alpamysh undertakes the long journey, arrives on the last day of the reprieve, is victorious in the contests, and, of course, marries Barchin. There are many interesting parallels between the *Alpamysh* and the *Odyssey*, including Barchin's refusal to choose Alpamysh right away and her insistence that, though her mind is made up, the contests will go on as planned. Although she spends six months longing for Alpamysh and worrying that he will not come, once a messenger tells her that her future husband has finally arrived she responds with something close to, "Arrived, so what of it?"[12] The parallel that concerns me here, however, has to do with the dream Barchin sees on the eve of Alpamysh's arrival. In that complicated dream she sees a huge eagle, which alights next to her and touches her head with his wing. She also dreams that the top circle of her yurt collapses. When she wakes up Barchin tells her dream to the forty girls who are her attendants, and one of them interprets it. The interpreter begins by saying that Barchin should not fear the dream because it is actually an auspicious one: it signifies that her betrothed will arrive on the next day. She identifies the eagle with Alpamysh, and sees even the damage to the yurt as a positive sign: the number of the poles supporting the yurt is the same as the number of Barchin's suitors, so that the dream predicts their destruction.[13]

The tale of the Returning Husband is immense if not worldwide in its spread, and virtually inexhaustible in the number of permutations that are wrought on its basic elements. The complex task of grouping its variants (for example, into Western and Eastern groups) and distinguishing between typological and genetic relationships goes far beyond my present concerns. The possibility that the *Odyssey* and *Alpamysh* share some of their origins should

[11] Alimjan 1939. This version, which is about 14,000 lines long and which later appeared in Russian translation (Penkovsky 1982) is currently the best-known version of the story. The influential studies of Zhirmunsky are based on it; a different version was translated into German by Reichl (Reichl 2001). The story of Alpamysh is attested in prosaic form and in epic song (*dastan*) over a huge territory inhabited by Turkic peoples, and multiple versions of it are recorded (Tajik, Kazakh, Karakalpak, Kirghiz, Turkmen etc.).

[12] Penkovsky 1982:142.

[13] Penkovsky 1982:122–123.

not be excluded and has indeed been suggested, but it is the typological dimension of the comparison that is of interest to me here.[14] Another variation on this theme occurs in Ovid's *Metamorphoses*, where Alkyone waits for her husband Ceyx, who has gone on a sea voyage and drowned. One night he appears to her in a dream, naked and wet, and tells her of his death. The next day his body is washed ashore.[15] While Barchin's dream is much more similar to Penelope's than that of Alkyone, the latter heroine has nevertheless much in common with Penelope,[16] and structurally her dream occurs at a similar point in the plot as that of Penelope and of Barchin, on the eve of the (future) husband's return, even if Ceyx does not return alive.

Barchin's dream, however, is a particularly striking parallel to Penelope's because it contains the crucial element of reversal in interpretation. While Barchin is disturbed by the dream, her friend interprets it as a positive sign. Both Barchin and Penelope see something that at first seems to be destructive to the dreamer (the damaged yurt, the dead geese) but is actually destructive to her enemies (vanquished suitors). In both cases, numbers are important for the correct interpretation and in both cases the successful suitor is identified with the eagle, which alights in proximity of the dreamer.

The examples of Barchin, Alkyone, and even Nausikaa suggest that Penelope's dream is a traditional element in a sense that it may be typical for a waiting wife or bride in songs to see a prophetic dream on the eve of her husband's arrival. The parallel with Barchin opens the possibility that the particular dream Penelope sees, with its eagle and emotional reversal, belongs to a certain traditional type. Penelope's audience, including Odysseus, might have heard other songs with a woman waiting for her husband or bridegroom and seeing such a dream just before his arrival. In this case, Penelope alludes to such songs in performing for Odysseus her dream-tale about her husband's return.

The "eve-of-arrival" dreams, such as those seen by Alkyone or Barchin, are always prophetic, and Penelope's dream is no exception. The *Odyssey* plays in a rather mind-bending way with the notion of prophetic dream (more on this below), but the fact that Penelope's dream is in fact mantic poetry is signaled by its diction, in particular by her use of the verb *hupokrinesthai* when she asks Odysseus to respond to her dream: ἀλλ' ἄγε μοι τὸν ὄνειρον ὑπόκριναι καὶ ἄκουσον, 'But come, respond to a dream for me, and listen to it' (19.535).

---

[14] Zhirmunsky 1967.
[15] Ovid *Metamorphoses* 11.616–735.
[16] See below.

As Nagy has shown, this verb *hupokrinesthai* refers to "responding by way of performing," the way a seer would perform oracular poetry "in responding to questions about omens."[17] There is a related and parallel example of mantic poetry in Book 15 of the *Odyssey*, where Helen interprets an actual portent similar to Penelope's dream. Here Telemachus, still in Lacedaimon, prays to find his father at home, and as he prays an omen appears on the right, an eagle carrying off a domestic goose. As in Penelope's dream, the wild eagle 'from the mountain' (15.175) is contrasted with birds of entirely different nature, pampered domestic geese (15.176). As is typical for oracular poetry, the starting point is visual, the portent, the sight of the eagle and the goose. This sight then prompts a question from Peisistratos to Menelaos:

> φράζεο δή, Μενέλαε διοτρεφές, ὄρχαμε λαῶν,
> ἦ νῶϊν τόδ᾽ ἔφηνε θεὸς τέρας ἦε σοὶ αὐτῷ.

> (*Odyssey* 15.167–168)[18]

Consider now, Zeus-nourished Menelaos, leader of men,
  whether the gods showed this portent to the two of us
    or to you.

Menelaos ponders how to perform a fitting response (ὅππως οἱ κατὰ μοῖραν ὑποκρίναιτο νοήσας, 15.170), but never does so because Helen anticipates him, and claims for herself the role of a *mantis*:

> τὸν δ᾽ Ἑλένη τανύπεπλος ὑποφθαμένη φάτο μῦθον·
> κλῦτέ μευ· αὐτὰρ ἐγὼ μαντεύσομαι, ὡς ἐνὶ θυμῷ
> ἀθάνατοι βάλλουσι καὶ ὡς τελέεσθαι ὀΐω.
> ὡς ὅδε χῆν᾽ ἥρπαξ᾽ ἀτιταλλομένην ἐνὶ οἴκῳ
> ἐλθὼν ἐξ ὄρεος, ὅθι οἱ γενεή τε τόκος τε,
> ὣς Ὀδυσεὺς κακὰ πολλὰ παθὼν καὶ πόλλ᾽ ἐπαληθεὶς
> οἴκαδε νοστήσει καὶ τείσεται· ἠὲ καὶ ἤδη
> οἴκοι, ἀτὰρ μνηστῆρσι κακὸν πάντεσσι φυτεύει.

> (*Odyssey* 15.171–178)

Helen of the long robes anticipated him and made
  a pronouncement:

---

[17] Nagy 2002:141.

[18] Hollmann shows that the verb φράζεσθαι, especially in the imperative, is used in oracular contexts to describe the process of decoding of a coded message. The use of this verb is thus itself a signal that the message being considered is coded. See Hollmann 3.1.4, forthcoming.

> "Hear me! I shall prophesy, the way the immortals put
>   it in my heart
> and the way I think it will come to fulfillment:
> just as this eagle snatched a goose reared in the house,
> having come from the mountain, where he has his origins
>   and parents,
> so Odysseus, after suffering much and wandering much,
> will come home and take revenge
> – or he is already at home and prepares evil for all the
>   suitors."

Relying on this and other examples, Nagy points out two important features of these oracular performances: "the words of such an oracular performance are based on the actual vision of the given omen that is seen 'in real life' or in a dream" and "the vision has to be performed first as a question – either by a character in the narration or simply by the narrative itself – before its meaning can be performed as a response."[19]

Helen's prophetic episode in Book 15 is helpful in several ways for understanding Penelope's prophetic performance in Book 19. In both cases there is an omen, a vision (as Nagy points out, in Book 19, "the dream is the omen"), a question prompted by it, and a response to the question. But what is a relatively linear structure in Book 15, (a vision, told by the narrator and actually seen by several characters, followed by Peisistratos' question, followed by Helen's response), is woven in Book 19 into a remarkably complex knot. The vision is not told by the narrator, but only by Penelope, so that the possibility is open for the audience to question whether there was ever such a dream "in real life."[20] We witness, in any case, only a verbal performance of a vision, and Penelope takes on the role of the narrator in performing it. She also poses a direct question to the beggar, asking him to interpret the dream. And then, as expected, there is a response to the question, but who is giving it?

Famously and uniquely, Penelope's dream contains its own interpretation, the one offered by the eagle-Odysseus himself. This is highly unusual and certainly does not fit into an *Alpamysh*-like scenario where the woman wakes up distressed by a dream and really is in need of an interpretation. The speaking eagle is all the more remarkable because the dream, even without his speech, would not have been hard to interpret. Helen succeeds in interpreting the eagle and goose omen in Book 15, and no doubt the "real" Odysseus could

---

[19] Nagy 2002:143.
[20] See more on this below.

have equally well interpreted the dream in Book 19 without assistance, that is, without its last element. Penelope, apparently, does not require this service of her guest and gives him no opportunity to render it. The communication that takes place here between Penelope and Odysseus is evidently not a consultation regarding an omen, but something different, and this brings me back to the question whether the dream is in fact a dream.

Both the setting and the content of the dream immediately inspire suspicions about the dream's genuineness as an actual vision. Winkler states simply that, "Penelope is here inventing a dream as a way of further safe communication with this fascinating stranger."[21] There is some evidence to support this assessment. Penelope's dream is one of three Homeric dreams that are narrated in the context of loyalty testing, and the other two are false. In Book 14, within his own story about acquiring a cloak in an ambush at Troy, Odysseus produces a dream on the spot to save his freezing companion. The dream is introduced by the same formula that Agamemnon uses to tell his false dream to the Achaean kings: κλῦτε φίλοι· θεῖός μοι ἐνύπνιον ἦλθεν ὄνειρος, 'Hear me, friends, for a divine dream came to me in my sleep' (*Iliad* 2.56 = *Odyssey* 14.495). When Agamemnon uses his dream to test the spirit of his men, he misrepresents it by adding a layer of his own deception to that of Zeus. He does, however, actually see the dream, and that event is narrated in the poetic voice of the *Iliad*, not that of Agamemnon. In the case of Odysseus in Book 14 and Penelope in Book 19, however, we are never told in the poet's voice that the dreams actually took place, and these are the only two dreams in Homer to lack such external confirmation. Odysseus' dream in the cloak narrative is represented as a clever device for achieving his ends and has nothing to do with anyone's nighttime visions: if there were no need for a cloak, there would have been no dream. The same is true for Penelope's dream: it depends on what has happened so far in the conversation between Odysseus and Penelope, and although one could, of course, assume that Penelope saw this dream at some unknown point in the past and has kept quiet about it, nothing in the *Odyssey* warrants such an assumption and nothing, in my opinion, is gained by it. My suggestion is that in the *Odyssey*, rather than seeing the dream, Penelope performs for Odysseus a *muthos*, a prophetic dream narrative, and her performance represents a complex and self-conscious variation on a sequence not unlike the episode with Barchin's dream in the *Alpamysh*. Penelope performs her prophetic dream-song for Odysseus just as she performs the myth of

---

[21] Winkler 1990:154. On the dream as Penelope's creation see also Büchner 1940:149n1, Harsh 1950:16, Newton 1998:144–145.

Aedon, like an *aoidos*, relying on familiar associations and introducing striking variations to fulfill the demands of her particular performance.

As before, Penelope is engaged in myth-making, and in this case her myth-making has particularly far-reaching implications for her communication with Odysseus and her own role in the *Odyssey*. To a certain extent, Penelope's dream is a covert test of Odysseus, an invitation to confirm his wife's thoughts and plans. Penelope conveys to the beggar that if he is indeed Odysseus then her despair will turn into a triumph over the suitors. If he is Odysseus he will kill them all. Her request for an interpretation is a covert question: is this indeed his intention? Does he claim to be able to do it? Winkler remarked that a dream containing its own interpretation, such as Penelope's, is "a unique event in the annals of oneirokrisy," and explained this peculiarity as follows: "She [Penelope] has in effect given the beggar both the allegory and its interpretation and is asking him whether she is right."[22]

I agree with the substance of this assessment, but it does not entirely explain Penelope's choice to incorporate interpretation into the dream instead of letting the beggar-Odysseus produce his own. Penelope is not simply asking a question, but uttering a prophecy, and it has been observed that in Homer prophecies predict the plot of the narrative, so that their fulfillment is equivalent to the unfolding of the plot.[23] In Book 15, Helen predicts that her prophecy will come to fulfillment (ὡς τελέεσθαι ὀΐω, 'the way I think it will come to fulfillment', 15.173) and so does the eagle in Penelope's dream (ὅ τοι τετελεσμένον ἔσται, 'which will come to fulfillment', 19.547). The *telos*, or 'fulfillment', of these prophecies is also the *telos* of the *Odyssey*, namely the return of Odysseus. There is an important difference, however, between the prophetic stance and technique of Helen and Penelope: Helen is an outsider to the plot who utters a prophecy based on an external sign, the way a professional seer would (and the seer Theoklymenos does, for example, at *Odyssey* 15.530–534). Penelope's prophecy, on the other hand, is akin to the oaths disguised Odysseus utters regarding his own return, which are based on Odysseus' own knowledge, concealed from others. In a similar way, Penelope's dream is prophetic, but also based on the understanding she has reached with the beggar and her opinion (perhaps uncertain) that he is Odysseus. Penelope creates for herself a prophetic dream of the kind she would be likely to see if she were in a song where her husband comes back on the next day. By doing so she in effect makes the next day into the day of her husband's return and,

---

[22] Winkler 1990:153.
[23] Nagy 2002:145–146.

in a typically Odyssean twist, extends her myth-making into the making of the *Odyssey* itself.[24]

And, of course, Penelope does this in a conversation with the very husband who is the subject of her dream. Next to internal self-interpretation, the most unusual feature of Penelope's dream-narrative is surely the fact that the supposedly absent husband is present and moreover asked to interpret the dream. The latter fact allows for an entirely new level of signification and communication to be activated. On the one hand, the request for an interpretation of a self-interpreting dream may be an agonistic move on the part of Penelope. As if in a poetic *agon*, her performance determines the shape of Odysseus' reply and preempts any changes. Odysseus seems to acknowledge as much when he says that no other explanation of the dream is possible, since 'Odysseus himself' told her how it will come to pass:

> τὴν δ' ἀπαμειβόμενος προσέφη πολύμητις Ὀδυσσεύς·
> "ὦ γύναι, οὔ πως ἔστιν ὑποκρίνασθαι ὄνειρον
> ἄλλῃ ἀποκλίναντ', ἐπεὶ ἦ ῥά τοι αὐτὸς Ὀδυσσεὺς
> πέφραδ', ὅπως τελέει· μνηστῆρσι δὲ φαίνετ' ὄλεθρος
> πᾶσι μάλ', οὐδέ κέ τις θάνατον καὶ κῆρας ἀλύξει.

> *(Odyssey 19.554–558)*

> Responding to her much-devising Odysseus spoke:
> "Lady, there is no way to respond to the dream
> by turning it another way, since Odysseus himself
> told you how it will come to fulfillment. Doom is apparent
>   for the suitors,
> all of them, and not one of them will escape death and
>   destruction."

There is irony in this confirmation, since this 'Odysseus himself' is a creation of Penelope, a character in her tale. On the other hand, by calling the speaking eagle of Penelope's dream 'Odysseus himself' the real Odysseus is confirming the veracity of Penelope's prophecy: there is indeed only one way to respond to the vision she has performed, the one contained in her dream. In discussing the semantics of *hupokrinesthai*, Nagy remarks on the notion of unchangeability and quotability built into it.[25] Although, from the point of an outside observer, oral poetry may differ from one performance to the next,

---

[24] See below, with references, on Odysseus and Penelope as authorial figures.
[25] Nagy 2002:141–142.

notionally when Homeric poetry "quotes" the words of a hero, those words are always the original words, exactly the same. In this way, Homeric poetry is like mantic poetry, which also has to be "quoted" exactly because it predicts the future just as it will be. Nagy comments: "It seems that in this case there can be only one way for Odysseus to respond, that is, to repeat the words already quoted by Penelope. For the meaning to be clarified, the quoted words would have to be quoted again, that is, performed. We see here at work the poetic mentality of unchangeability: once the words of response have been performed as a speech act, they are ready to be quoted again as a fixed and unchangeable saying."[26] Nagy further suggests that the "recurring sameness" of Homeric quotations, ("responses" signaled by *hupokrinesthai*), corresponds to the "recurring sameness" of visions, which prompt the responses.[27] The strangeness of the oracular episode in Book 19 is that the vision is created by Penelope, who steps into the role of "Homer," and the response is also performed by her, quoting eagle-Odysseus. At first, this unusual performance seems to correspond to the external reality of the *Odyssey* no more than Odysseus's dream in an ambush at Troy does, a never-seen dream, presented as a clever trick within Odysseus' tale for Eumaeus (14.462–506), which is itself not a "true" tale from the standpoint of the *Odyssey*, but an *ainos* aimed at getting a cloak. The words of the self-interpreting eagle, himself both the vision and the seer, within a telling of a never-seen dream, might be expected to have an equally tenuous relationship to any potential reality. But authenticated by Odysseus and fulfilled by the *Odyssey*, these words turn out to be a true prophecy and the kind of permanent and definitive response that is signaled by *hupokrinesthai* in Homer. Correspondingly, the dream created by Penelope becomes a real oracular vision, which demands to be interpreted, turned into a speech act, in an unchangeable and definitive way, as done by the eagle "quoted" by Penelope.[28] Penelope performs Odysseus for Odysseus, and the Odysseus of Penelope's performance turns out to be the real one, according to Odysseus himself, and the *Odyssey*.

By "authenticating" the words of the eagle, the beggar also, yet again, confirms his identity, or at least his claim to this identity. As one scholar puts it, "[Odysseus'] assurance is so peculiarly explicit that Penelope must realize

---

[26] Nagy 2002:144.

[27] Nagy 2002:147.

[28] Nagy 2002.147. I draw here also on Nagy's formulation that "to interpret is really to formalize the speech-act that is radiating from the dream or the omen." (Nagy 1990:168 n95).

that Odysseus himself is speaking."[29] Through her dream, Penelope conveys to the beggar that if he is indeed Odysseus he will kill the suitors. The beggar responds that death is what awaits them and even adds that not a single one will escape, thus asserting that he is able to accomplish the deed. In this way, 'Odysseus himself' conveys this message to Penelope both in her own dream-narrative and, in disguise, in the macro-narrative of the *Odyssey*.

I hasten to add that this does not remove from Penelope the burden of her decision. The beggar's acceptance of her prophecy in fact re-imposes on her the task of making choices and taking actions to bring it to fulfillment. The beggar defers to the eagle-Odysseus of the dream as the only true interpreter of Penelope's vision, but for the moment this 'Odysseus himself' remains her own creation. Her myth-making will merge with that of the *Odyssey* in the end, but that end is still far from being accomplished, at least from Penelope's point of view. And if at this stage Penelope has indeed made up her mind about her guest and has decided on a course of action for tomorrow, this would make her worry of being deceived or mistaken, a worry to which she confesses in Book 23 (215–217), all the more acute. The stranger lets her know that he is Odysseus, and she believes him, but, for all that, a successful accomplishment of Odysseus' return still remains to be seen. If indeed this is the real Odysseus in front of Penelope, then there is no possibility of holding out just a little longer and no room for more hope if he fails. The time for holding tight and avoiding the worst outcomes has passed and the decisive moment is at hand. As Odysseus himself says to Telemachus, 'no other Odysseus will yet arrive' (*Odyssey* 16.204).

The shifting polyvalence of the expression 'Odysseus himself' is an indication of the strange permutations that reality undergoes in this conversation, and the strange mixture of certainty and suspense this produces. Another is a phrase that the eagle utters in the dream: οὐκ ὄναρ, ἀλλ' ὕπαρ ἐσθλόν, ὅ τοι τετελεσμένον ἔσται, 'not a dream but a true waking reality, which will come to fulfillment' (19.547). The eagle denies that he is a dream, and claims that Penelope sees what she sees in actuality. Moreover, Penelope is the one who composes these words in her performance, perhaps hinting that this dream is not really a dream but is happening before her waking eyes. But, of course,

---

[29] Amory (1963:105–106). I agree with Amory on this and several other points about the dream, although I disagree with her opinion on the recognition question, and consequently on the supposed difficulties faced by "the poet" in this scene. According to Amory, Odysseus' explicit and essentially self-revealing assurance "leaves the poet, who has decided to postpone his recognition scene until after the contest, with the problem of preventing an immediate acknowledgement of Penelope's recognition."

the eagle, who claims to be not a dream, remains a part of Penelope's dream-performance. In response to the beggar's upholding of her prophecy, Penelope will famously deny the reliability of dreams, and claim that hers will not come true (19.560–569). Her protests, however, raise another question pertinent to the situation: what about the reliability of waking sight? It is perhaps the uniqueness of this situation that explains the strange usage of *hupar* by the eagle: ὕπαρ ἐσθλόν, ὅ τοι τετελεσμένον ἔσται, 'a true waking vision which will come to fulfillment'. It would seem that a prophecy could be fulfilled in the future, or a prophetic dream, but a *hupar*, the actual reality, is by definition something already come to pass. Indeed, the dictionary of Liddell and Scott even creates a unique translation for *hupar* in this passage: "no illusive dream, but a (vision of) reality." The fact remains, however, that elsewhere *hupar* is not used to designate true prophetic visions as opposed to deceptive ones, but in direct opposition to *onar*, denotes the state of being awake and actually seeing something with one's eyes. Used adverbially, *hupar* means 'actually, in reality'.[30] Penelope's unexpected use of *hupar* underscores, perhaps, the peculiarity of what happens in Book 19: Odysseus is right here before her, and yet, unless and until he can kill the suitors, his return cannot reach its fulfillment.

The collocation οὐκ . . . ὄναρ . . . ἀλλ' ὕπαρ recurs in Book 20, when Penelope does indeed see a dream, and in her dream Odysseus lies next to her in bed, looking just as he was when he departed for Troy:

> τῇδε γὰρ αὖ μοι νυκτὶ παρέδραθεν εἴκελος αὐτῷ,
> τοῖος ἐών, οἷος ἦεν ἅμα στρατῷ· αὐτὰρ ἐμὸν κῆρ
> χαῖρ', ἐπεὶ οὐκ ἐφάμην ὄναρ ἔμμεναι, ἀλλ' ὕπαρ ἤδη.
>
> (*Odyssey* 20.88–90)

> And again this night someone slept with me who looked like
>   him [Odysseus],
> such as he was when he left with the army. And my heart
> rejoiced, since I did not think it was a dream, but a waking
>   reality already.

Penelope thinks (ἐφάμην) this is a reality already (ἤδη), but it is not: once awake she has to remind herself that the archery trial with all its horrible potentialities is still ahead. And yet the dream is an intimation of hope. It is even *too* hopeful, and cautious Penelope is afraid of getting ahead of the events:

---

[30] Cf. Aeschylus, *Prometheus Bound* 486, Plato, *Republic* 520c. Cunliffe's gloss on *hupar* makes no exceptions for *Odyssey* 19.547 and reads "a waking reality, the actual sight of something."

the dream is, in her words, one of those 'bad dreams', κακὰ ὀνείρατα, 'bad' presumably because it is so tempting yet potentially deceptive.[31] At night, with her self-control relaxed, Penelope is presented with just the vision she has been trying not to indulge in for fear of bitter disappointment. The variation between ὕπαρ ἐσθλόν, 'a true waking reality', in Book 19 and ὕπαρ ἤδη, 'waking reality already', in Book 20, where the other expression is metrically possible, underscores the implications of ἤδη, 'already': in her dream Penelope is getting ahead of herself, anticipating reunion with Odysseus all too vividly. The return to reality is wrenching and Penelope greets the dawn in tears (20.58).

There are the only two occurrences of the word *hupar* in Homer, and it seems that in both cases they express Penelope's sense that Odysseus' return is really underway. At the same time the contexts in which these visions occur make this long-awaited reality as yet intangible, like a dream. Penelope's use of the word *hupar* in her dream-tale seems to convey both the immediacy of Odysseus' presence for her and the distance between them, the impossibility of direct communication before the return is indeed accomplished. In Book 19, this effect is augmented by the eagle's human speech: the eagle is a bird, yet speaks with a human voice; he is Odysseus himself, yet not. The expression φωνῇ βροτέῃ, 'with a human voice', unique in Homer, finds many parallels in Modern Greek folk songs, and in fact the whole two lines introducing the eagle's words are semantically, and even poetically, very close to their Modern Greek parallels. Athanassakis, who has studied these similarities, offers the following relatively older example from Moni Iviron:

> κι ἔνα πουλὶ καθέ[ζετο] κι ἐμένα παρηγόρα
> ἔλεγεν μὲ [τὸ στόμα] του ἀνθρώπινη λαλίτσα.

> And a bird perched and spoke to me,
> uttered a human speech with its mouth.

Equally close to the Odyssean lines is another, relatively more recent, folk song from Thessaly:

> πουλάκι ἐδιάβη κι ἔκατσε//στὴ σέλλα στὸ καλτάκι
> (δέν κελαηδοῦσε σὰν πουλί, σάν τ' ἄλλα τὰ πουλάκια)
> μόν' κελαηδοῦσε κι ἔλεγε//ἀνθρώπινη λαλίτσα.[32]

---

[31] And arguably, it is deceptive to some extent: Odysseus is no longer the way he used to be. Nevertheless, the vision of youthful Odysseus and correspondingly youthful Penelope suggests the resumption of marriage. For a different, and fuller, discussion of the dream in connection to the prayer, see McDonald 1997:12–16.

[32] Athanassakis 1994:128–129.

> A bird came down and settled on my saddle
> (it did not speak like a bird, like all the other birds),
> but it sung and spoke with human speech.

In these modern songs, the birds speaking with a human voice often represent long absent or dead relatives who return in this way to their loved ones and offer consolation. For example, in the song from Moni Iviron quoted above the bird says ὑπόμενε τά θλίβεσαι, 'Endure your grief', and Athanassakis compares that with the way the eagle in the *Odyssey* checks Penelope's tears (κατερήτυε, 545) and consoles her (θάρσει, 546). Athanassakis attributes the long survival of these lines to "their being an integral part of a theme deeply embedded in Greek culture, that of the return of someone who has been away from hearth and kin for many years, either alive and in person, or imagined and metamorphosed, if he is still away from home, or dead."[33]

In the *Odyssey*, the speaking eagle appears in Penelope's own performance. Not only does she create a unique self-interpreting variant of a pre-return/pre-marriage dream-tale, she might be adopting an element from another kind of song, a song about a dear one returning in the guise of a speaking bird, incorporating into her performance yet another genre that resonates with the macro-narrative of the *Odyssey*.[34] Odysseus does not come back to Penelope in the shape of a bird, yet he does come back in disguise, and thus not completely. He does offer her consolation when he promises that Odysseus' return is imminent, but this too is only a promise, not yet a reality. In this sense, as he sits across from his wife, Odysseus both has and has not come back. Penelope's famous words about the uncertainty of dreams accentuate the tantalizing reality, but not-yet reality, of her *hupar*.

---

[33] Athanassakis 1994:130.

[34] Incidentally, this is another telling divergence between her dream and that of Barchin in the *Alpamysh*. While the eagle stands for the bridegroom or husband in both cases, it does not speak in the Uzbek epic.

CHAPTER FOURTEEN
THE DECISION

I N RESPONSE TO THE DREAM TALE, Odysseus implicitly asserts that he will do just what Penelope expects, and Penelope is by no means blind to this assurance. She does act accordingly, even though her verbal response is skeptical. The scenario she described is a dream, and dreams, she reminds Odysseus, are not always fulfilled (*Odyssey* 19.560). Much has been said about Penelope's famous gates of dreams, and the punning wordplay on ἐλέφαντος (564) and ἐλεφαίρονται (565), κεράων (566), κραίνουσι (567), and ἀκράαντα (565). I do not have much to add to the previous scholarship on this matter, but one thing that is important to note is that Penelope does not question the interpretation of the dream.[1] The meaning of the dream is not in doubt, but only whether it will come to pass. A comment on the baffling nature of dreams might be expected to be about the difficulty of understanding what dreams mean, but that is not what Penelope says. In her words the only difference between the two kinds of dreams has to do with whether or not they turn out to be true.[2] There is no reason to conclude from Penelope's pessimism that she has no inkling of the beggar's identity. The feat of killing all the suitors is, after all, something miraculous and possible only with active divine help, given their sheer number. Penelope has reason to doubt that it can ever be accomplished, even if the beggar is indeed Odysseus. In her desire to believe his hints she may also, of course, worry about being deceived by this stranger who seems to be Odysseus but who might even be a god in disguise. Still, in spite of the inevitable risks, proceeding on the assumption that the beggar is Odysseus is Penelope's best strategy and best hope. And so she announces to Odysseus her well-considered and motivated decision: she will provide him with a chance to accomplish his return by staging the bow contest.[3]

---

[1] As observed by Winkler 1990:54.

[2] Winkler 1990.54.

[3] The bibliography on Penelope's decision is immense. Many scholars have argued that Penelope's decision is opaque and her behavior ambivalent and contradictory, and meant to

The decision to hold the contest makes sense as an outcome of the dialogue in Book 19. It is true, as has been suggested, that the contest may make sense for Penelope whether or not she suspects the beggar of being Odysseus. For one thing, she can expect that none of the suitors will be able to string Odysseus' bow, and if all suitors lose, Penelope would at least gain another delay.[4] As Marquart puts it, "The proposal of the contest of the bow, suggested to her by talk of Odysseus' apparel (19.218–42), is another example of her cunning, a desperate, final attempt to put off the suitors forever, with any luck."[5] She would also damage the suitors' standing on Ithaca, something that could be advantageous to Telemachus.[6] Scodel suggests further that the suitors begin by hoping to gain not only Penelope but also Odysseus' property, (which could happen if Telemachus is immature and can be pushed aside or else murdered), but shift their attention to competing just for Penelope as their original goal becomes less and less realistic.[7] Scodel sees Penelope's alluring appearance in front of the suitors in Book 18 as a turning point, an attempt to seduce them into competing only for herself and leaving Telemachus alone.[8] The staging of the contest is then the continuation of the same strategy, since "she will have emphasized that she is the only prize and

---

be so (Murnaghan 1986 and 1987, Felson-Rubin 1987 and 1994, Katz 1991). Others see her decision as the result of an unconscious recognition (e.g. Amory 1963, Austin 1975) or an intuitive response to the beggar's presence (Russo 1982). Finally, some see Penelope's decision as fully rational, but taken in ignorance of the beggar's identity because her situation is such that she simply cannot wait any longer. The fact that she takes this decision in Odysseus' presence is, on that view, a coincidence and a source of narrative irony (Foley 1995, Heitman 2005).

[4] Combellack 1973:39–40 seems to have been the first to suggest this. See especially Scodel 2001:323–324.

[5] Marquardt 1985:41.

[6] Scodel 2001:323–324. Eurymachus, at least, fears public disgrace if the beggar succeeds in the contest after the suitors have failed (*Odyssey* 21.230–229).

[7] Russo 1992 on *Odyssey* 20.336–337 offers a similar, though not identical, interpretation of the change in suitors' strategy. Russo seems to take Eurymachus' assertion at 1.402–404 that Telemachus will have his inheritance at face value, while Scodel sees it as a ploy (2001:310).

[8] Scodel presents this as part of Athena's rather than Penelope's strategy: Athena is intent on death for the suitors, and therefore wants them to compete in the bow contests. This requires that "the suitors be so bedazzled by Penelope that they will be willing to compete in the bow contest." Accordingly, Athena renders Penelope irresistibly beautiful (18.190–196), and Penelope succeeds in dazzling the suitors: their knees go slack and their thoughts at once turn to sharing her bed (18.212–213). This is in contrast to their earlier designs on Odysseus' property. Thus Penelope's strategy succeeds, but it is distasteful to her and could be seen as improper. Accordingly, Scodel suggests, Penelope is distanced from her own actions, and instead Athena manipulates her (2001:319–320). The distancing, of course, is only partial. Athena beautifies unwilling Penelope in her sleep, but the decision to show herself to the suitors is Penelope's own, even if inspired by the goddess (18.158–196).

distracted them from Telemachus."[9] Indeed, by soliciting gifts from the suitors Penelope signals that she will marry soon, and therefore seems to be moving towards remarriage even before her dialogue with Odysseus, though this is hardly conclusive: Penelope has encouraged the suitors before, and always delayed. She could solicit gifts, and even promise to set up a contest, and continue to delay. Still, there is a theoretical possibility that Penelope could free herself from the suitors by staging a contest in which they would all lose. Scodel accordingly suggests that there is no need "to collapse various possible outcomes into a single gamble and say either that she gambles that no suitor can succeed or that she gambles that the beggar is Odysseus."[10] By contrast, I do not see Penelope's two possible gambles as equal, though they are perfectly compatible. The hope that all suitors will lose may be real, but it is not clear what would happen in this case. Could the suitors request a different contest? There do not seem to be any mythological parallels that could help answer this question. Though there is much comparative evidence for bow contests, including some in cognate Indic epic, that share telling details with the *Odyssey*, I do not know of an example where such a contest would be lost by all. In the absence of any parallels, it is hard to know how much weight can be assigned to this possibility.

In the end, however, what tips the scale in favor of gambling "that the beggar is Odysseus" are not considerations of potential scenarios, but the totality of Book 19, in particular the timing and the setting, rather than the mere fact of Penelope's decision.[11] While Penelope cannot wait long, there is nothing in the *Odyssey*, except the presence of the beggar, that compels her to have the contest on the very next day. Those who argue against recognition, yet justify Penelope's decision to stage the contest, would say that she has finally just reached the point beyond which she will not go, that the risks have simply become too high, or that it would be irresponsible for her to wait any longer. That she has reached this point just when Odysseus finally arrives is, then, the supreme irony of the poem. It is impossible to disprove this position because it depends on a subjective assessment of what the responsible thing for Penelope to do is, and what is too much and too long. It can only be said that Penelope's situation in Book 19 does not seem to be more dangerous than in Book 4 and that there is nothing in the poem to indicate that she could not wait even a few more days. There is also no obvious reason for Penelope

---

[9] Scodel 2001:324.
[10] Scodel 2001:324.
[11] Cf. Foley 1995:102–103 on this point.

to announce the decision first to the beggar (rather than, for example, to Telemachus) unless Penelope thinks the beggar is her husband.

The particular way Penelope presents her decision and the way Odysseus reacts are consistent with this interpretation. It seems to be the pattern in this part of the conversation for Penelope to dazzle her audience and then move on to the next step without letting them (and him) come up for air. She ends her dream tale by saying that she does not expect it to come true, though that would be a welcome joy for her and her son (19.569). This line marks yet another change of pace in the conversation, one that Penelope accomplishes on her own, while Odysseus is silent.

It is time to move on to the stratagem for completing Odysseus' return, the contest of the bow. Penelope announces her decision and then describes the set-up of the contest – for the benefit of this beggar – in every detail down to the number of the axes through which the competitors will have to shoot an arrow.[12] Penelope does not invite any questions, but simply asks her guest to 'put it into his mind', fittingly enough, since it is important for Odysseus to know the logistics of her plan. If the beginning of their conversation was marked by an overflow of emotion, its end contains a concise statement of practicalities. Odysseus' response makes it clear that he stands by his claims and yet again reasserts his identity:

τὴν δ' ἀπαμειβόμενος προσέφη πολύμητις Ὀδυσσεύς·
ὦ γύναι αἰδοίη Λαερτιάδεω Ὀδυσῆος,
μηκέτι νῦν ἀνάβαλλε δόμοισ' ἔνι τοῦτον ἄεθλον·
πρὶν γάρ τοι πολύμητις ἐλεύσεται ἐνθάδ' Ὀδυσσεύς,
πρὶν τούτους τόδε τόξον ἐΰξοον ἀμφαφόωντας
νευρήν τ' ἐντανύσαι διοϊστεῦσαί τε σιδήρου.

(*Odyssey* 19.582–587)

And responding to her much-devising Odysseus spoke:
"Respected wife of Odysseus, son of Laertes,
do not postpone this contest in your house any longer.
For much-devising Odysseus will come back beforehand,
before these men can handle the polished bow
and string it and shoot through the iron."

---

[12] 19.572–575. The details might be insufficient for us to picture the set-up, but it is surely enough for Odysseus.

There is no question any more of Odysseus' being in Thesprotia. Penelope makes no mention of it, even though the beggar who gave her that information has proven his reliability by describing Odysseus' clothes and even though she has never accused him of lying. The beggar, for his part, does not pretend to sustain the verisimilitude of his Thesprotian story. He does not ask Penelope to wait until Pheidon sends Odysseus to Ithaca, nor at least inquire about her apparently illogical haste with the contest. The Thesprotian story has done its service and is now abandoned.[13] Instead, her guest assures Penelope that Odysseus will be back before the suitors can string the bow, an assurance that seems preposterous in the mouth of anyone but Odysseus himself, and which nevertheless elicits no skepticism from Penelope. She does not suggest that the stranger not stoop to lies, as Eumaeus does earlier. She does not even treat Odysseus' statement as a prediction of a prophetic type by responding in a conventional way along the lines of "I wish that may come to pass, but it will not." That she has done before. Now Penelope simply says that she wishes she could stay with her guest all night and not go to sleep:

> εἴ κ᾽ ἐθέλοις μοι, ξεῖνε, παρήμενος ἐν μεγάροισι
> τέρπειν, οὔ κέ μοι ὕπνος ἐπὶ βλεφάροισι χυθείη.

> (*Odyssey* 19.589–590)

> If only you were willing, stranger, to keep delighting me,
> sitting by me in the house, sleep would not flow over
> my eyes.

That, of course, cannot be. Penelope quickly adds that sleep they must, and that she will now retire to her sorrowful bed, wetted by tears ever since Odysseus' departure, while the beggar should also go to sleep, on the ground or in bed, as he chooses:

> ἀλλ᾽ οὐ γάρ πως ἔστιν ἀΰπνους ἔμμεναι αἰὲν
> ἀνθρώπους· ἐπὶ γάρ τοι ἑκάστῳ μοῖραν ἔθηκαν
> ἀθάνατοι θνητοῖσιν ἐπὶ ζείδωρον ἄρουραν.
> ἀλλ᾽ ἦ τοι μὲν ἐγὼν ὑπερώϊον εἰσαναβᾶσα
> λέξομαι εἰς εὐνήν, ἥ μοι στονόεσσα τέτυκται,
> αἰεὶ δάκρυσ᾽ ἐμοῖσι πεφυρμένη, ἐξ οὗ Ὀδυσσεὺς
> ᾤχετ᾽ ἐποψόμενος Κακοΐλιον οὐκ ὀνομαστήν.

---

[13] This is, of course, not to say that the Thesprotian story is non-traditional and does not have its own resonances in the *Odyssey*. On the Odyssean engagement with local traditions of Thesprotia and Epirus see Malkin 1998:120–155.

ἔνθα κε λεξαίμην· σὺ δὲ λέξεο τῷδ᾽ ἐνὶ οἴκῳ,
ἢ χαμάδις στορέσας, ἤ τοι κατὰ δέμνια θέντων.

(Odyssey 19.591–599)

But it is impossible for people to remain forever
    without sleep.
For in everything immortals set up a proper measure
for mortals on the life-giving earth.
But I will go to the bedroom upstairs
and lie in my bed, which has become sorrowful for me,
always stained with my tears, since that time when Odysseus
left for that accursed Troy, not to be named.
There I shall lie, and you lie down in this part of the house.
Either spread bedding on the ground, or let the maids make
    a bed for you.

The deadly contest is still in the future, and yet the mention of her bed at the end of the conversation in Book 19 seems like a glimpse of affection already now proffered to Odysseus. It is, needless to say, camouflaged, and directed not to the beggar but to the supposedly absent Odysseus. Still, Penelope first mentions the pleasure she derives from the beggar's presence and then describes her lonely bed. She asserts her fidelity to Odysseus, whose departure turned her bed into a place of sorrow, and draws his attention to the fact that for all these years she sleeps alone in the same bed in the same room. In contrast to Penelope's nightly confinement to the bed, the beggar can sleep where he chooses: he has no sleeping place that is his own. This contrast emphasizes the permanence of the bed but also draws attention to the fact that Odysseus has no access to it yet. Penelope devotes four lines to the bed, and this focus on it at the very end of the dialogue inevitably resonates with what is still in the future in the unfolding plot, but what was surely known to most audiences of the poem, namely her famous final test of Odysseus by means of this very bed.[14] For the moment, the bed remains empty and stained by tears, but it offers to Odysseus a vision of constancy in his house. This vision will make the test in Book 24 all the more effective because it fosters in Odysseus expectations that the test will suddenly undermine. Paradoxically, it is after the contest, when Odysseus does gain access to the bed and when

---

[14] There is vast bibliography on the test of the bed. I find Zeitlin 1995 and Heitman 2001:98–100 most relevant for my purposes.

so much uncertainty is removed and resolved, that the bed suddenly appears uprooted. The mention of the bed on the eve of the contest is striking in itself, but it is also marked by verbal symmetry. Penelope puts two forms of the verb λέγω, 'to lie down', in the same line, one before and one after the caesura, one referring to herself and one to the beggar:

> ἔνθα κε λεξαίμην· σὺ δὲ λέξεο τῷδ' ἐνὶ οἴκῳ.

(Odyssey 19.598)

> There I shall lie, and you lie down in this part of
> the house.

These final words both underscore the separation between herself and her guest and bring them together. Moreover, this connection between husband and wife reappears again at the beginning of Book 20 when Odysseus wakes up (in his improvised bed, 20.95) to the sound of Penelope's crying (in her bed, 20.58). Her crying is described as a reaction to her dream, mentioned above, in which Odysseus sleeps next to her. For his part, Odysseus wakes and thinks for a moment that Penelope is next to him (20.91–94). At the end of their dialogue Penelope establishes a symmetry and nighttime connection between herself and her guest, and this theme is continued in Book 20.

At the very end of Book 19 Penelope retreats to her room accompanied by the maids (*Odyssey* 19.600–601). It seems that no part of the conversation in Book 19 is free of witnesses, and the brief and quiet mention of ἀμφίπολοι, 'maids', at the end echoes the much louder and larger scene of the maids taunting Odysseus at the beginning of the book. In the very last line, Penelope, as usual, cries for Odysseus until Athena puts her to sleep: a formulaic ending endowed by its context with a special meaning.

Penelope's tears at the end establish a symmetry with the beginning of the dialogue. There, Odysseus frames his perfect-king utterance not only as a praise for Penelope but also as a contrast to his own misfortune. As an expert performer, Odysseus begins with a *captatio benevolentiae* of sorts and refuses at first to recollect his native land because it is too painful:

> τῶ ἐμὲ νῦν τὰ μὲν ἄλλα μετάλλα σῷ ἐνὶ οἴκῳ,
> μηδέ μοι ἐξερέεινε γένος καὶ πατρίδα γαῖαν,
> μή μοι μᾶλλον θυμὸν ἐνιπλήσῃς ὀδυνάων
> μνησαμένῳ· μάλα δ' εἰμὶ πολύστονος· οὐδέ τί με χρὴ
> οἴκῳ ἐν ἀλλοτρίῳ γοόωντά τε μυρόμενόν τε
> ἧσθαι, ἐπεὶ κάκιον πενθήμεναι ἄκριτον αἰεί·

μή τίς μοι δμῳῶν νεμεσήσεται ἠὲ σύ γ' αὐτή,
φῇ δὲ δάκρυπλώειν βεβαρηότα με φρένας οἴνῳ.

(*Odyssey* 19.115–122)

Therefore question me now in your house about all the
   other things,
but do not ask about my family and my native land,
lest you fill my heart with pains even more
as I recollect. For I am full of grief, and it is not fitting for me
to sit in another's house wailing and crying,
since it is bad to mourn incessantly forever.
And there is a danger that one of your maids, or you yourself,
   may become indignant with me
and say that I flow with tears because my brain is heavy
   with wine.

This preemptive apology for tears contrasts sharply with what follows. When Odysseus does in fact tell his tale he demonstrates prodigious feats of memory and precise selection of detail rather than any excessive emotion: Penelope is the one who cries, while his own eyes remain dry. But Odysseus' mention of tears establishes yet another level of connection between himself and his wife, since it frames his whole performance as a kind of lament. Odysseus speaks of tears as unseemly in another's house and mentions the nemesis that would fall on him for crying and howling like a drunk (19.122). By virtue of saying all this, however, Odysseus associates his performance with lament, as he makes clear that he is kept from lamenting only by the external circumstances. This motion towards lament comes immediately after the "perfect king" comparison, and is connected to it by a causal τῷ (19.155), leaving Penelope in no doubt about the reason for her guest's grief: his lost home, where he is the perfect king.

When Penelope begins the second part of the conversation she echoes Odysseus' hints at lament by talking of her own tears. Although she responds to the perfect king comparison at once, with her loom tale, she now reciprocates Odysseus' original performance on a different level, taking into account everything that has happened in the meantime. By comparing herself to the nightingale, she in effect begins with a lament, a genre proper to her, and the main genre of public discourse available to a woman.[15] Like the lamentations

---

[15] The nightingale is above all a bird of lament, described in poetry as δακρυόεσσα, 'tearful' (Euripides *Helen* 1109), βαρύδακρυς, 'weeping grievously' (IBID., 1110), and ὀδυρομένη,

of Helen and Hecuba in the *Iliad* (22.430–443 and 476–515), it is a *muthos* in the full sense of the word, a powerful "act of self-presentation with an emphasis on extension and detail."[16] The story of Aedon is a finely tuned instrument for achieving this self-presentation, and it is also what Martin calls a "narrative from memory," the most difficult and important genre which becomes a part of every other kind of discourse, when practiced by a master.[17] Penelope uses both lament and narrative from memory as a poet would, varying and recombining the tales to convey her emotions, tell her story, and exert influence on her audience. Further, in her dialogue with Odysseus Penelope emerges not only as a self-conscious and adroit performer, but also as a performer who, like Odysseus elsewhere, crosses over into the poet's territory. Odysseus' tendency to take control of his own narrative has not gone unremarked. As one scholar observes, "Odysseus' power to create the narrative, the plot, of his own life, both verbally and in action, is one of the crucial elements in his likeness to an *aoidos*."[18] In Book 19, Penelope does the same, though on a smaller scale: in her dialogue with her disguised husband she simultaneously composes, in performance, both her sad song and the plot of her life, and displays awareness of her own composition.[19]

The lament of the nightingale becomes part of Penelope's performance in Book 19, but it is also emblematic more broadly of her bardic role in the *Odyssey*. It has been suggested that by comparing herself to the nightingale, Penelope draws attention to her own song. The word ἀηδών, 'nightingale', whether or not it in fact derives from ἀείδω, 'to sing', would have been perceived as related to this verb.[20] Because of its beautiful song, the nightingale can stand for the poet, as, for example, when Bacchylides (3.98) refers to himself as '*aedon* from Ceos', in spite of the strong association the bird has with lamenting women.[21]

'lamenting' (Moschus 3.9). The song of the nightingale is called μινύρισμα, 'warbling' (Theocritus *Epigrammata* 4. 11), πολύθρηνος, 'much-wailing' (Euripides *Phaethon* fr. 773.23), and πολύδακρυς, 'of many tears' (Aristophanes *Birds* 211).

[16] Martin 1989:88.

[17] Martin 1989:44 and 77–88. On the conventions of Greek laments, some of which persist from antiquity to modern times, see Alexiou 1974. On the social function of lament in a modern Greek context, see Herzfeld 1993:244.

[18] Holmberg 1995:117.

[19] All of this is not to say that Penelope is equal to Odysseus in the *Odyssey*, only that they mirror each other in many respects.

[20] Chantraine 1968–1980, s.v. See also Nieto Hernández 2008:39–62, on the relevance of this etymology in the *Odyssey*.

[21] For more on the implication of the fact that "Penelope's song" is a lament see Nieto Hernández 2008:39–62.

In conclusion, I come back to Nagy's argument that the nightingale's song is distinguished both by its rich vocal modulations, its variety, and also by its duration and continuity, and that "the continuity is implicit in the variety."[22] Being also a lament, an everlasting expression of grief, the nightingale's song seems quintessentially Odyssean. It is described by epithets beginning with *polu-* (*poluekhes, poludeukes*), it is said to last without interruption, and it is characterized by 'frequent turns', thus recalling not only Penelope's performance, but the personality of the poem's protagonist, the *polutropos* Odysseus, himself much given to grief. The same qualities belong also to Penelope's weaving, with its repeated reweavings and returns, each reweaving being both a repetition and different from the preceding ones, and to oral poetry. The fact that the nightingale's song seems so Odyssean is hardly separable from the fact that the *Odyssey* is so self-reflective about its own oral poetics. This poetics, in turn, and with it the song of the nightingale, resonate with the fundamental Odyssean idea, the idea of return. Citing a study of actual nightingale songs Nagy observes that the bird is capable of complex patterns of interplay between combination and selection, a way of manipulating the combinations of sounds similar to poetic sequences. To quote Nagy: "The idea of re-selecting, that is, selecting again the same combination in order to make another combination, fits the image of coming around, turning, re-turning."[23] The variant epithet of the nightingale in Book 19, *poludeukes,* is particularly telling in this regard, since this adjective is also the derivational source for the noun Polydeukes, the name of one of the Divine Twins. As Nagy suggests, the Divine Twins are a model of "consistency, perseverance and reliability" but their myth also has deep links to astral and solar lore.[24] By virtue of being equated, from the Indo-European standpoint, with the evening and morning star, the Divine Twins rise again and again, in a cyclical pattern of eternal return. In Vedic, their epithet is Nasatyau, the 'retrievers' or 'returners', because they bring back the light of the sun.[25] While the solar aspect of the Dioskouroi is attenuated in Greek, their role as saviors who can bring one back to life is well attested.[26] This theme of return to life, and specifically its solar manifestation, is obviously central to the *Odyssey*. Significantly, Odysseus arrives on Ithaca just as the morning star announces dawn:

---

[22] Nagy 1996:36.
[23] Nagy 1996:41.
[24] Nagy 1996:51.
[25] Frame 1978:134–152, Nagy 1990:258–259.
[26] They are called σωτῆρας in their *Homeric Hymn* 33.6. See Burkert 1985:213 with further references.

εὖτ' ἀστὴρ ὑπερέσχε φαάντατος, ὅς τε μάλιστα
ἔρχεται ἀγγέλλων φάος Ἠοῦς ἠριγενείης,
τῆμος δὴ νήσῳ προσεπίλνατο ποντοπόρος νηῦς.

(*Odyssey* 13.93–95)

When the brightest star is in the sky, the one that especially
comes announcing the light of the early-born Dawn,
at that time the seafaring ship put in to the island.

It seems possible that an allusion to this idea of return is present in Penelope's description of the nightingale, especially considering that the nightingale sings at the beginning of spring and that, since it sings at night, dawn puts an end to its laments. I will have more to say about Penelope's connectedness to the idea of return specifically in connection with the solar myth when I come to the broader context and resonance of her *muthoi*. For now, suffice it to say that the poetics of variation and continuity, the poetics of return, so essential to the *Odyssey*, is fully engaged in the first, longest and most virtuosic of verbal exchanges between Penelope and Odysseus.[27]

---

[27] Cf. Felson's comments on fluidity vs. stability in the *Odyssey*: "The paradox underlying the return of Odysseus – that two fluid polytropes, or figures of many turns will return to the fixity of their steadfast marriage, symbolized by their steadfast bed – matches the paradox underlying Homeric epos in general: that the freshest and newest and most spontaneous is rooted in the most abiding, most traditional, and indeed, most formulaic of genres." (1994:144)

CHAPTER FIFTEEN
BACK TO THE LOOM

BEFORE TURNING TO THE QUESTION of larger context, it is necessary to consider one more *muthos* Penelope tells in Book 19: the tale of her weaving and unweaving of Laertes' shroud. I have left Penelope's most famous tale aside until now because it occupies a unique position in the dialogue. In general, Odysseus dominates the first part of the conversation, Penelope the second, but the tale of Laertes' shroud is an exception: it is Penelope's longest continuous narrative and it happens near the beginning of the book. In a sense, as much as Odysseus' initial performance, it determines, or at least makes possible, the rest of the dialogue.

Looking back over the entire book, the exchange between Penelope and Odysseus is, in a paradoxical way, agonistic even as it leads to a degree of harmony between the speakers. Each performer has challenged the other to understand the hidden message and respond in kind, and each has engaged in what Martin terms "powerful self-presentation," a fixture of agonistic speech.[1] Odysseus achieves such self-presentation by means of his "perfect king" comparison, his Cretan lie, his report about Odysseus in Thesprotia; Penelope achieves it through the myth of Aedon and her dream, but initially through the tale of her weaving. In terms of genre, the "conversation" of Odysseus and Penelope can be seen both as a performative dialogue and as a performa-

---

[1] Martin 1989.87. Odysseus makes an open claim to be a king and a veiled claim to be Odysseus. His claim that Odysseus is bringing home great wealth is, I have argued elsewhere (Levaniouk 2000a), offered to Penelope almost by way of justification for his long absence. In her turn, as Marquardt (1985, esp.45–46) has argued, Penelope also engages in this kind of apologetic discourse, explaining to Odysseus why his house is full of suitors.

tive *agon*.[2] It is designated as *muthoi* (19.103), and here this word is used in its proper Homeric sense of authoritative speech acts.[3]

At the very beginning, in response to Penelope's conventional question about his origins, the beggar compares her to a perfect king, offering her a mini-performance in the genre of the "ruler's truth." Martin argues that this performance is self-referential, and I have followed him in my discussion of this utterance as it applies to Odysseus. It is, however, equally extraordinary in its application to Penelope since Odysseus does a remarkable thing: he frames this comparison as praise for Penelope, in effect representing her as his surrogate. On the surface of his words, it is Penelope, not Odysseus who is the perfect king. Even the mention of Penelope's *kleos* reaching the sky resonates with Odysseus' proclamation of his own *kleos* reaching the sky in Book 9.19–20, (which is also a self-revelation, though not a veiled one).[4]

And yet in the mouth of Odysseus this consummate compliment is also a test. Odysseus' *muthos* points indirectly to Penelope's loss: Ithaca is manifestly not the flourishing kingdom Odysseus describes. It also points to Penelope's problematic position as an independent woman, involuntary though it is.[5] It is a challenge, yet a challenge of praise, and as such it may be seen as the mirror-image of *neikos*, which Martin defines, in its Iliadic context, as the verbal duel between two warriors.[6] Odysseus begins with saying as much:

> ὦ γύναι, οὐκ ἄν τίς σε βροτῶν ἐπ' ἀπείρονα γαῖαν
> νεικέοι.
>
> *(Odyssey 19.107–108)*
>
> Lady, no mortal on the boundless earth
> would reproach you.

Penelope is quick to understand and avert any suspicion by defining her role in feminine terms:

> ξεῖν', ἦ τοι μὲν ἐμὴν ἀρετὴν εἶδός τε δέμας τε
> ὤλεσαν ἀθάνατοι, ὅτε Ἴλιον εἰσανέβαινον

---

[2] Oral-traditional societies tend to have developed traditions of agonistic discourse: see Ong 1981 and Martin 1989:66–67 with further references. Martin discusses such discourses in the *Iliad* as a subgroup of *muthoi*, which he defines as authoritative speech acts mimetic of actual performances (Martin 1989:22–42 and 65–77, building on earlier findings of Nagy 1979:222–242).

[3] Martin 1989:22–42 and 65–77, Nagy 1979:222–242.

[4] Cf. *Odyssey* 8.74.

[5] See Nagler 1990, Jamison 1999.

[6] Martin 1989:22–42 and 65–77, Nagy 1979:222–242.

Ἀργεῖοι, μετὰ τοῖσι δ' ἐμὸς πόσις ἦεν Ὀδυσσεύς.
εἰ κεῖνός γ' ἐλθὼν τὸν ἐμὸν βίον ἀμφιπολεύοι,
μεῖζον κε κλέος εἴη ἐμὸν καὶ κάλλιον οὕτω.

(Odyssey 19.124–128)

Stranger, the immortals ruined my excellence, my beauty
and stature,
when the Argives boarded for Troy,
and among them was my husband Odysseus.
If he returned and took care of my life,
my glory would be greater and better in this way.

Penelope has been self-sufficient for twenty years, but she claims to be in need of her husband's management. Her unusual independence is presented as a misfortune, which only detracts from her *kleos*. Thus begins the mutual renegotiation of their positions between Odysseus and Penelope, the re-establishment of their famous *homophrosune*. This like-mindedness, which should not be sentimentalized, involves a mutual agreement on the proper roles of husband and wife.[7] In response to Odysseus' provocation, Penelope proceeds in earnest with her self-presentation, the narrative of her weaving ruse. It is a tale not of a king, but of a faithful and resourceful wife.[8]

This tale, and Penelope's weaving in general, has probably received more scholarly attention than anything else about Penelope, and it has justly been discussed in connection with speech and song. Weaving is a metaphor for the making of poetry, and Penelope's work has been seen as emblematic of song in general and Odyssean poetics in particular.[9] It has been also seen as a peculiarly feminine mode of communication: for Penelope, who does not have access to the male world of public speaking, weaving itself becomes a silent

---

[7] The fact that what emerges as their proper roles is not to the liking of many modern readers of the poem is a different matter. Penelope has high demands for her husband, as she amply demonstrates in Book 19, but once he is fully back he sends her upstairs to weave, and she leaves silently, disappearing from the poem. Much has been said about Penelope and the difficult question of a woman's power and powerlessness in Homer. See, e.g, Papadopoulou-Belmehdi 1994:79–86, Foley 2001:126–144, Nieto Hernández 2008:39–62. Cf. Ferrari's observation à propos an entirely different (and non-Odyssean) episode in Penelope's story: "From the start and in all ways, Penelope knows her place." (2002:55).

[8] For a survey of scholarship on the shroud tale, see Bona 1966:107–22, Heubeck 1992:374–375, Goldhill 1988:1–3.

[9] On the Indo-European association between poetry and weaving see Schmitt 1967:298–301. On Greek archaic poetry see Snyder 1980–1981:193–196. Papadopoulou-Belmehdi 1994 and Clayton 2004 are two very different treatments of Penelope's weaving in relation to song, speech, and the poetics of the *Odyssey*. See also e.g. Felson 1994:15–42, Slatkin 1996:234–237.

kind of speech. The plotting, the reversal, the repetition and variation, and the self-reflexiveness of Penelope's work represents a manipulation of time and narrative typical of the distinctively Odyssean poetic technique. Indeed, Penelope the weaver has been seen, along with Odysseus, as "a figure of the poet, quietly working behind the scene."[10] From that point of view, Penelope's walking back and forth at her loom emerges as a key not only to Odyssean poetics, but specifically to what is perhaps its most distinctive feature, namely its pervasive and multi-layered self-referentiality.[11] The magnitude and intricacy of issues involved is immense and I will not attempt to do them justice here. My focus will be on her telling of the ruse to Odysseus in Book 19, and specifically on this telling in relation to her other *muthoi* in the dialogue. Although she may use her weaving as a silent language, and although she is indeed excluded from the masculine world of public discourse, Penelope, unlike Philomela, can use not only her loom, but also her words, which in her conversation with beggar-Odysseus constitute an actual poetic performance, albeit addressed to an internal audience of one.

In the first instance, the tale of her weaving is Penelope's answer to Odysseus' praise. Penelope reacts to the description of a perfect king by immediately focusing on Odysseus, leaving no doubt who is the perfect king on Ithaca. The return of Odysseus as the king is the underlying theme of the conversation in Book 19, and the "ruler's truth" thus serves to highlight this dominant theme, much as the proem to an epic poem might do. Penelope's performances in the second part of the conversation, the myth of Aedon and the dream, are also, to a certain extent, a response to the "perfect king" comparison, since they are all concerned with Odysseus' regaining of that role and Penelope's regaining of her own role as Odysseus' wife.

In her initial response, Penelope does not entirely decline the beggar's praise, but rather offers a corrective to it by means of the weaving tale. Indeed, it has been suggested that Penelope does not even entirely disown the role of king, because she, alone among the feminine characters in Homer, claims

---

[10] Winkler 1990:156.

[11] Clayton 1994 goes a step further to suggest that the poetics of the *Odyssey* exhibit a particular affinity with the feminine, that is, those aspects of it that can be seen as Penelopean, (emphasis on process over product, ambiguity, variation, etc.), can also be seen as specifically feminine. The difficulty I see with this argument is that, as Clayton herself says, "Penelope's web models oral poetic performance in general, and not just the *Odyssey*" and therefore all oral poetry "shows affinity with the feminine, or Penelopean, narrative process" (82). This seems overly general and hard to justify. In any case, if all oral poetry shares Penelopean qualities, the argument that Odyssean poetics has something distinctively feminine about it is weakened.

to weave not only fabric, but also stratagems.[12] In general, Homeric women are confined to literal weaving, while the metaphorical weaving of wiles is done by men. Penelope is the only character whose weaving is both literal and metaphoric, and in this way she breaks through the gender boundary. As one scholar observes, this is just one of the ways in which the *Odyssey* signals Penelope's exceptional position among women: she has indeed occupied the position of a surrogate king, and like a king, she is compared to lion, though a lion in dire straits.[13] Penelope's *kleos* is also exceptional, even if it is not of the same kind as that of warrior heroes like her husband.[14] Together, the perfect king comparison and the loom tale reflect both Penelope's exceptional position, a position too large for gender boundaries to contain, and her firm insistence on knowing her place all the same. In contrast to the *muthoi* she will tell in the second part of the dialogue, the narrative of the loom is much less private: it is told not only by Penelope but, with variation, by two of the suitors, so that it appears for the first time in the *Odyssey* long before Penelope sits down to talk with the beggar. The weaving story, therefore, constitutes public knowledge. In a sense, it is Penelope's identifying story, her public face,[15] and it is no surprise that it is the first thing she tells the beggar about herself and that her telling is prompted by mention of *kleos*.

In fact, the theme of *kleos* is signaled every time this tale is told. In Book 2, when the loom tale is told for the first time, Antinoos claims that Penelope increases her *kleos* by postponing remarriage (2.125–126). In Book 24, when the tale is told for the last time, the shade of Agamemnon reacts to Amphimedon's narrative by predicting immortal *kleos* for Penelope (24.196–197). In Book 19 Odysseus elicits the tale by talking of Penelope's *kleos*, and she implicitly corrects him by declining the kind of *kleos* he offers her and instead laying claim to her proper kind, not that of a king, but that of his wife. The very repetition of the weaving tale makes it seem like a set piece, a song in its own right, so that in effect the tale *is* her *kleos*. We see it within the *Odyssey* itself spreading both into this world and the next as it is told first on Ithaca and

---

[12] As Clayton 1994:24 points out, the verb ὑφαίνω, 'to weave', is used as often with a metaphorical object (*metis, dolos*) as with the literal one. In the metaphorical instances the subject is invariably male. On literal vs. metaphorical weaving of wiles see also Clayton 1994:21–52.

[13] I am indebted to Papadopoulou-Belmehdi's (1994:82–84) discussion of literal and metaphorical weaving in Homer and of Penelope's unique position among women. See further Papadopoulou-Belmehdi 1994.85–86 (with reference to 1992:195–233) on metaphorical connections been weaving and good royal governance.

[14] On the problematic nature of Penelope's *kleos* see, e.g., Loraux 1987:2, Foley 2001:138–143.

[15] *Odyssey* 2.93–110, 19.137–156, 24.129–148. The differences between these tellings are examined by Lowenstam (2000), to whom I am much indebted.

then in the underworld. It is an interesting detail that the tale is told twice by Penelope's suitors, who benefit least from Penelope's *kleos*, yet become its unwilling conveyers. In the first instance, Antinoos even compares Penelope to the famed women of old and finds none of them a match for her:

εἰ δ' ἔτ' ἀνιήσει γε πολὺν χρόνον υἷας Ἀχαιῶν,
τὰ φρονέουσ' ἀνὰ θυμόν, ἅ οἱ περὶ δῶκεν Ἀθήνη,
ἔργα τ' ἐπίστασθαι περικαλλέα καὶ φρένας ἐσθλὰς
κέρδεά θ', οἷ' οὔ πώ τιν' ἀκούομεν οὐδὲ παλαιῶν,
τάων αἳ πάρος ἦσαν ἐϋπλοκαμῖδες Ἀχαιαί,
Τυρώ τ' Ἀλκμήνη τε ἐϋστέφανός τε Μυκήνη·
τάων οὔ τις ὁμοῖα νοήματα Πηνελοπείῃ
ᾔδη· ἀτὰρ μὲν τοῦτό γ' ἐναίσιμον οὐκ ἐνόησε.

(Odyssey 2.115–122)

> But if for a long time still she continues to torment the sons
>   of Achaeans,
> occupied in her mind with those gifts which Athena grants her,
> to be an expert in beautiful handwork and have an excellent
>   mind,
> and clever thoughts, such as we have never heard of, not
>   even about the women of old,
> those well-tressed Achaean women who lived long ago,
> Tyro and Alcmene, and Mycene with fine garlands.
> Not one of them knew thoughts similar to those of Penelope.
> But in this instance she did not think right.

Antinoos, of course, means what he says negatively, but he cannot quite pull it off. He first says Penelope excels over other women both in her work (no doubt her weaving is meant) and excellent mind. Then come the *kerdea*, her acts of cunning, in emphatically enjambed position, then another declaration that not even the women of old could compare to Penelope in their designs, and finally his only overtly negative claim, namely that Penelope did not think well enough about the damage to Telemachus' property when she made her plans. Is this praise or blame? In the mouth of Antinoos, the reference to *kerdea* is ambiguous: he complains about Penelope's cunning employed against himself but his words still constitute praise, since it is clear that his internal audience, the assembled Ithacans, will not find fault with Penelope's trick. Unable to deny that Penelope's cunning is worthy of *kleos*, Antinoos attempts to at least dampen her success by claiming that it comes at Telemachus' expense. There is some truth to his words, but only for the moment. Odysseus' return, with much wealth, will more than make up for the temporary decrease of Telemachus' patrimony, so that in the end Penelope's *kleos* will be to Telemachus' advantage. In any case Telemachus is a separate subject, and in the meanwhile it is clear that Penelope is creating a surpassing *kleos* for herself, and that Antinoos chafes at the thought that she is doing so at the suitors', above all his own, expense.

When the weaving tale is told for the last time by Amphimedon in Book 24, the suitors are dead and lie unburied in the courtyard of Odysseus' house (24.186–187). Now, if Laertes is buried in the shroud Penelope wove for him, it will be as a happy father and grandfather, whose male descendants are left behind to carry on his line. This is in sharp contrast to the Laertes we see for much of the *Odyssey*. The old man's condition seems to be directly dependent on his male offspring, so that he serves as a barometer of sorts for the state of the *genos*. When Odysseus fails to return, he retreats to the countryside and grieves for his son, but still eats, drinks, and supervises his servants, leading a modest but sustainable life, as long as Telemachus is not in danger. When Telemachus leaves for Pylos, he stops eating and drinking and caring for his orchards, but only weeps, a picture of ultimate wretchedness (*Odyssey* 16.137–145). In this he is like Penelope, who says in Book 4 that she grieves for Telemachus even more than she does for Odysseus. Odysseus' disappearance is a heavy blow to the family, but not its utter ruin. If Telemachus dies, then the devastation is complete. Conversely, when both his son and his grandson return safe and sound, the old man revives and, with Athena's help, regains some of his former strength (*Odyssey* 24.265–282).

Penelope's shroud, which seemed at first to signify the death of Laertes and the end of his line's flourishing, comes to signify the opposite: the restoration of Laertes as the proud elder of an idealized male line, a sharp contrast to the suitors' own inglorious and for a time, at least, shroudless death.[16] A shade in the underworld, Amphimedon recalls Laertes' shroud that shone like the sun and the moon, a deadly symbol for the suitors, but a sign of wealth and pride for Laertes' household (*Odyssey* 24.145–147).

Amphimedon's telling of the shroud tale is distinct from that of Antinoos in a telling temporal detail: Antinoos seems to imply that Penelope has

---

[16] Lowenstam 2000:341–342. As he points out, Penelope wove the shroud during the day, in the light of the sun, and undid her work at night; but the web, ironically, represents death and night in its completion, while its undoing connotes day and life. Lowenstam concludes: "This reversal is what the suitors did not understand, pressing Penelope during the day to finish her deathly task."

finished the shroud some time ago and therefore some time before Odysseus arrives on Ithaca. In Amphimedon's tale, Odysseus' arrival seems to follow immediately upon the end of Penelope's weaving:

εὖθ' ἡ φᾶρος ἔδειξεν, ὑφήνασα μέγαν ἱστόν,
πλύνασ', ἠελίῳ ἐναλίγκιον ἠὲ σελήνῃ,
καὶ τότε δή ῥ' Ὀδυσῆα κακός ποθεν ἤγαγε δαίμων
ἀγροῦ ἐπ' ἐσχατιήν, ὅθι δώματα ναῖε συβώτης.

(*Odyssey* 24.147–150)

Then she displayed her fabric, having woven a great piece of
weaving
and washed it, and it was like the sun and moon.
It was then that some evil spirit brought Odysseus
from somewhere to the edge of his estate, where the
swineherd lived.

This discrepancy has not gone without scholarly comment, and this is no place to restate the possible explanations, though it seems reasonable for Amphimedon, looking as he is at the totality of the suitors' courtship, to omit details of timing that are still important for Antinoos. The salient fact remains that this telling brings the completion of the web and the arrival of Odysseus into contact, so that in retrospect the two events seem linked. Amphimedon also believes that Penelope and Odysseus colluded and that it was Odysseus' cunning idea to set up the archery contest. He is mistaken on the latter point, but the gist of his guess is not far from the truth. Though there is no direct collusion, Odysseus and Penelope do come to an understanding in Book 19. In contrast to Antinoos, Amphimedon acknowledges in retrospect that marriage to the suitors was a hateful prospect for Penelope, and that she was planning death for the suitors all along, her web a manifestation of this plotting:

μνώμεθ' Ὀδυσσῆος δὴν οἰχομένοιο δάμαρτα·
ἡ δ' οὔτ' ἠρνεῖτο στυγερὸν γάμον οὔτε τελεύτα,
ἡμῖν φραζομένη θάνατον καὶ κῆρα μέλαιναν.

(*Odyssey* 24.125–127)

We were wooing the wife of Odysseus, who was long-absent,
but she would neither reject hateful marriage, nor
accomplish it,
devising for us death and black destruction.

265

Penelope's own telling of the shroud tale is subtly distinguished from the other two, even though the main part of it is repeated verbatim on each occasion. For example, both Antinoos and Amphimedon report that the truth was revealed to them by one of the maids, 'who knew it clearly' (2.108). Penelope apparently does not know which of the maids betrayed her to the suitors, for she blames them collectively, and, naturally enough, she lays emphasis not on their knowledge but on their treachery (19.154–155).[17] But the greatest change is effected not within the tale itself, but by the way it is framed. Against the background of the other two tellings, the theme of Penelope's *kleos* stands out all the more clearly, though Penelope never makes it explicit. By telling the shroud tale when she does, right after Odysseus says that her *kleos* reaches heaven, she implicitly agrees with the others that her *kleos* is epitomized by that tale. At the moment of the telling, however, Penelope finds that *kleos* wanting, and claims that it would have been both greater and better if Odysseus were there. And indeed though Penelope's *kleos* does not require Odysseus to never absent himself from Ithaca, (in fact it is hardly compatible with such a scenario), it does require him to return, and Penelope here recognizes the ultimate dependence of her reputation on Odysseus.[18] Her achievements in his absence may be exceptional, and she may indeed surpass other women, but if Odysseus fails to come back and she is forced to marry one of the suitors, then surely her *kleos* will be much diminished and her achievement destroyed. Conversely, Odysseus' *kleos* depends to some extent on Penelope, because coming back to Ithaca to find his wife gone to another's house would be a sad outcome of his long effort. Granted, it would not be as dreadful a blow as Agamemnon suffers on his return, but it would hardly be glorious. Perhaps Odysseus' cross-gender comparison of Penelope to a king implies, on his part, a recognition of their mutual dependency.[19] Nagy observes that Penelope is the "key not only to the *nostos* but also to the *kleos* of Odysseus" and that the

---

[17] See Lowenstam 2000 for a detailed discussion of the timing indications in all three tellings of the tale and for differences in detail between them.

[18] As has been remarked. See, e.g., Loraux 1987:2, Foley 2001:138–143.

[19] On their mutual dependency and on the relationship between Penelope's weaving and the notion of a just king see Papadopoulou-Belmehdi 1994:79–86.

shade Agamemnon in Book 24 foresees that Odysseus will have *kleos* because of his wife.[20]

The notion of comparing and almost equating Penelope and Odysseus, the king and the weaver, may even be reflected in Penelope's diction.[21] The verb Penelope uses to describe her weaving of wiles is not the expected ὑφαίνω, 'to weave', but τολυπεύω, which also means 'to bring to an end, complete', and words conveying the notion of completion occur both at the beginning and end of the tale, marking it off in a ring composition: Penelope asks the suitors to wait until she completes the shroud (ἐκτελέσω, 19.143) and is forced to do so at the end (ἐξετέλεσσα, 19.156).[22] Unlike ὑφαίνω, which is frequently used of both plotting and weaving, τολυπεύω literally means to wind up wool into a clew and is used metaphorically of deception only here. This unusual choice of word requires a better explanation than the simple avoidance of repeating ὑφαίνω twice. The effect of τολυπεύω is to establish a parallel between Penelope and Odysseus and thus to augment the theme of their mutually dependent *kleos*.[23] It can do so because in the *Odyssey* this verb is used primarily in the meaning 'to bring to an end, complete' and twice about Odysseus' accomplishment of the Trojan war (ἐπεὶ πόλεμον τολύπευσε, 1.238, 14.368). Moreover, the accomplishing of war, designated by τολυπεύω, is specifically connected with the kind of *kleos* one gets or does not get in *Odyssey* 24. Just before the suitors arrive in the underworld with the tale of their own death, the theme of *kleos* is activated in a dialogue between the shades of

---

[20] Nagy 1979:36–38 (see also 38–39 for a discussion of the Odyssean equation of the "best of the Achaeans theme" to the question of who will marry Penelope, all leading to the "incontrovertible conclusion" that Odysseus is the best of the Achaeans). Nagy's interpretation of Agamemnon's words in the underworld is based in part on understanding as masculine the pronoun οἱ at *Odyssey* 24.194-198: ὡς ἀγαθαὶ φρένες ἦσαν ἀμύμονι Πηνελοπείῃ, | κούρῃ Ἰκαρίου, ὡς εὖ μέμνητ' Ὀδυσῆος, | ἀνδρὸς κουριδίου. τῶ οἱ κλέος οὔ ποτ' ὀλεῖται | ἧς ἀρετῆς, τεύξουσι δ' ἐπιχθονίοισιν ἀοιδὴν | ἀθάνατοι χαρίεσσαν ἐχέφρονι Πηνελοπείῃ. Nagy (1979/1999:37–38) translates the lines in question as "Thus the *kleos* of his *arete* shall never perish, and the immortals shall fashion for humans a song that is pleasing for sensible Penelope." On this interpretation, the 'merit' (*arete*) of Odyseus is "to have won a Penelope (rather than a Clytemnestra)." Others have taken the pronoun as referring to Penelope (Schein 1995:23, who also comments on the dependence of Odysseus' *nostos* and *kleos* on Penelope, and Foley 2001:127). There is no certain way of resolving the question: the preceding clause refers to Penelope, weighing perhaps in favor of the feminine pronoun and Penelope's *kleos*, but the passage as a whole is a praise for Odysseus, (beginning with Agamemnon's first words, ὄλβιε Λαέρταο πάϊ, πολυμήχαν' Ὀδυσσεῦ, 24.192), opening the possibility of the masculine pronoun.

[21] See Papadopoulou-Belmehdi 1994:79–86 for a discussion of this equation.

[22] Lowenstam 2000:341.

[23] On the effects of τολυπεύω, including blurring of gender-differences and the interplay of literal and figurative in Penelope's use of it, see Clayton 2004.32–33.

Achilles and Agamemnon. The latter hero is, of course, consistently contrasted with Odysseus throughout the poem, as is Clytemnestra with Penelope. On this occasion too, after hearing Amphimedon's report, Agamemnon will famously praise Penelope's *arete* and claim that immortals will make a pleasant song for (and about) her, while that of Clytemnestra will be hateful (24.196–202). Before the suitors' arrival, however, Agamemnon compares himself not to Odysseus, but to another Achaean more fortunate than himself in *kleos*, Achilles:

> ὡς σὺ μὲν οὐδὲ θανὼν ὄνομ' ὤλεσας, ἀλλά τοι αἰεὶ
> πάντας ἐπ' ἀνθρώπους κλέος ἔσσεται ἐσθλόν, Ἀχιλλεῦ·
> αὐτὰρ ἐμοὶ τί τόδ' ἦδος, ἐπεὶ πόλεμον τολύπευσα;
> ἐν νόστῳ γάρ μοι Ζεὺς μήσατο λυγρὸν ὄλεθρον
> Αἰγίσθου ὑπὸ χερσὶ καὶ οὐλομένης ἀλόχοιο.
>
> (*Odyssey* 24.93–97)

> But even in death you have not lost your name, but forever
> you will have noble glory among all men, Achilles.
> But for me what pleasure was it that I brought the war to
>   conclusion?
> On my return Zeus devised a dismal death for me,
> at the hands of Aegisthos and my accursed wife.

Although Agamemnon does not say that Achilles has *kleos*, 'glory', while he himself does not, the implication is there that his accomplishing (τολύπευσα) of war did not bring him the kind of *kleos* that Achilles has, or the kind he would like to have, and the reason for that is his terrible *nostos*, 'return'. He might have *kleos* indeed, but like that of Clytemnestra, it can hardly be called *esthlon*, 'good'. There is no further use of τολυπεύω, 'to carry through, accomplish', in the *Odyssey*, so that the parallel between the masculine task of bringing the war to conclusion and Penelope's task of completing her guiles stands out clearly, as does the connection of both accomplishments to *kleos*. When Penelope and Odysseus meet in Book 19, he has accomplished the war, and she has accomplished her weaving, yet neither is able to have the kind of *kleos* they desire. Both have *kleos* in the making, suspended and incomplete. Penelope is compared to the women of old, known no doubt through song, and the songs about Odysseus have already reached Phaeacia and indeed Ithaca, if Phemios' performance of the *nostos* of the Achaeans in Book 1 includes him. And yet Penelope in Book 1 wants Phemios to stop singing, and it has been suggested that it is precisely because she is dissatisfied with what the song says about Odysseus, which at that point can only be that he disappeared. For

Penelope the *nostos* of the Achaeans is not a finished matter, because she is still hoping for a different song about Odysseus.[24] That Odysseus' *kleos* is bound up with his *nostos* has been argued in detail and hardly needs restating, but Penelope's *kleos* is bound up with his *nostos* too, and that she makes clear to her guest at the beginning of their conversation in Book 19.[25]

The shroud tale, like the rest of the conversation in Book 19, raises the question of Penelope's limits, but gives no definite answer to it. Exactly how desperate is she and does she ever intend to marry one of the suitors? The dramatic dynamics of the *Odyssey* require Odysseus to appear "in the nick of time," yet in the *Odyssey* that last moment is hard to pin down as it expands and contracts depending on the circumstances.[26] The last minute reversal, moreover, is foreseen and indeed staged by its protagonists, not only Odysseus but Penelope as well. This, too, is in contrast to the more widespread version of this tale-type where the hero arrives to rescue his bride when her wedding to another is already in progress, in the middle of the celebration.[27] In the *Odyssey*, instead, there is a mock, not a real, celebration, and when it happens the suitors are already dead. This, I suspect, is partly the result of Penelope's participation in Odysseus' return, which is also in contrast to the more customary passivity of the heroine of the "nick of time" tales. In a self-consciously Odyssean way, Penelope seems to be aware of the timing of her own rescue.

When Antinoos tells the assembly of Ithacans about Penelope's ruse of the shroud, the completion of her work seems like a victory for the suitors because it is their assumption that the finished shroud brings the new marriage closer. The victory is small and short-lived, however, for Penelope, although she herself links remarriage to the completion of the shroud, shows no immediate intention to choose a new husband even after her weaving is over. And indeed Penelope never actually promises to marry when she finishes the shroud but only requests that the suitors stop pressing her to remarry while she weaves (2.97 = 19.142 = 24.132). When in Book 19 Penelope says that her heart is still divided whether to remarry or to continue waiting, this is often taken as a sign of her despair, but the very fact that she continues to

---

[24] Nieto Hernández 2008:39–62, with references.

[25] See Nagy1979/1999.26–39 on Odysseus' *kleos* and *nostos* and the contrast between him and Achilles, who can only have *kleos* if he gives up *nostos*.

[26] For a different opinion, see Foley 1995.102–103, Heitman 2005. 63–84.

[27] As, for example, in the Uzbek *Alpamysh*. There is a large number of tales in which the husband comes back on the day of the rival's wedding to his abducted wife (Aarne and Thompson 1928: 301, 531, 555). This subject is discussed in detail by Zhirmunsky 1966, esp. 281.

see waiting as an option at all at this point is remarkable, and suggests that for Penelope the game continues. For Antinoos, Penelope's ruse of the loom appears to be one of several. He recalls that Penelope used to give hopes to the suitors and to send messages to them, but in retrospect he sees that she was not sincere, and this seems to be Penelope's first strategy. The weaving is "another deception" that she has devised:

ἤδη γὰρ τρίτον ἐστὶν ἔτος, τάχα δ' εἶσι τέταρτον,
ἐξ οὗ ἀτέμβει θυμὸν ἐνὶ στήθεσσιν Ἀχαιῶν.
πάντας μέν ῥ' ἔλπει, καὶ ὑπίσχεται ἀνδρὶ ἑκάστῳ,
ἀγγελίας προϊεῖσα· νόος δέ οἱ ἄλλα μενοινᾷ.
ἡ δὲ δόλον τόνδ' ἄλλον ἐνὶ φρεσὶ μερμήριξε·
στησαμένη μέγαν ἱστὸν ἐνὶ μεγάροισιν ὕφαινε.

(Odyssey 2.90–94)

It is already the third year, and soon will be the fourth,
since she has been thwarting the desire in the hearts of
    Achaeans.
She gives hope to all, and makes promises to each one,
sending out messages, but her mind has other intentions.
Here is another trick she devised in her mind:
setting up a great loom in her house, she started to weave.

Like the first tactic, the ruse is exposed as such, but there is no telling whether or not it is the last one. Of course, from the point of view of the external audience it has to be, because it is such a climactic and striking one, and because we know that it succeeds. From an internal point of view, however, the possibility of further tricks has to be entertained. After all, Penelope presents her last strategy, the ruse of the loom, as a result of divine inspiration (19.138) and who can tell whether or not it may come again?[28] Moreover, Penelope's narrative of her weaving makes it clear that she can secretly hope for Odysseus' return while openly denying it. Within her story, Penelope quotes herself telling the suitors that Odysseus is dead:

---

[28] One of the subtle differences between Penelope's and Antinoos' version of the story is the fact that Penelope presents her weaving deception as the first one (πρῶτον, 19.138), Antinoos as the second (ἄλλον, 2.93). Possibly Penelope is less keen to tell the beggar of her first stratagem, that of sending encouraging messages to the suitors. In any case, the use of πρῶτον sets up an expectation that more is to come, but instead Penelope denies that she will devise any more ways of postponing a new marriage.

κοῦροι, ἐμοὶ μνηστῆρες, ἐπεὶ θάνε δῖος Ὀδυσσεύς,
μίμνετ᾽ ἐπειγόμενοι τὸν ἐμὸν γάμον, εἰς ὅ κε φᾶρος
ἐκτελέσω, μή μοι μεταμώνια νήματ᾽ ὄληται.

(Odyssey 19.141–143)

Young men, my suitors, since godlike Odysues died,
hold off pressing for my marriage until I finish
this robe, so that my weaving is not wasted in vain.

As Penelope herself admits to her guest, what she told the suitors was not sincere: it was a *dolos* (19.137). She claimed that Odysseus was dead, and continued, for three years, to weave and unweave the fabric, giving him time to return. Later in the dialogue Penelope will again deny that Odysseus will come back, but the possibility that she can utter such denials without believing them has been strengthened by her own account of her past tactics.

The story of Penelope's weaving appears strikingly different in its different re-tellings in the *Odyssey*, in spite of the almost verbatim repetition of its main narrative. In fact, it appears so different in part precisely because of the repetition. When the tale is told for the first time, the fabric is the shroud of Laertes and the completion of Penelope's work seems to presage Penelope's separation from the house of Odysseus. At the last tale, new details emerge: the fabric is compared to the sun and moon simultaneously and we are told that Penelope washed it (24.146–147). These details have been connected specifically to wedding preparations, since Penelope's washing recalls the only extended laundry scene in the *Odyssey*, that of Nausikaa, whose sudden decision to wash clothes is overtly presented as preparation for marriage (*Odyssey* 6.25–67).[29] The fact that Penelope's fabric shines like the sun and moon has invited similar thoughts, since "the conjunction of sun and moon is a particularly propitious time for marriage."[30] In the *Odyssey*, the comparison to sun and moon occurs two more times, in an identical verse describing the houses of Menelaos and of Alkinoos respectively (4.45 = 7.84).[31] In the first of these houses, a double wedding is being celebrated as Telemachus arrives. In the second, Odysseus is offered Nausikaa's hand. Odysseus' arrival on Ithaca may itself take place under the conjunction of sun and moon, since the festival of Apollo marks the end of one month and the beginning of another (in accordance

---

[29] Clayton 2004:47.

[30] Austin 1975:283 (with references) and 251. On this point see also Bieber 1949:33 and Papadopoulou-Belmehdi 1994:117–119.

[31] On further implications of the two houses see Clayton 2004:47–49.

with the rhythm of the moon) and at the same time Odysseus' return is corre-lated with the return of the sun, perhaps with the winter solstice.[32] In retro-spect, from the vantage point of Amphimedon in the underworld, Penelope's work does not seem like a shroud for Laertes at all, but instead like a splendid accoutrement of her remarriage to Odysseus. Penelope claimed, of course, that it was a shroud for Laertes, but Penelope does not always tell the suitors the truth. Her weaving, ever recurrent and itself subject to the celestial rhythm (woven by day, unwoven by night) is too polysemic to be so easily classified. What seemed at one point to be preparation for Laertes' death now emerges as a preparation for marriage. It has always seemed like a virginal weaving since Penelope, married woman though she is, is put in a position of a marriageable maiden. This kind of weaving stops once marriage begins, and conversely the marriage is in the future while the weaving goes on. Wool-working may be the main occupation of a good Homeric wife, but it is also true that both literary and pictorial representations feature it predominantly as an emblem of maid-enhood. Ferrari observes that scenes of wool-working on vases "show that spinning is the mark of females who are maidenly" and that "signs of wool-working are primarily attached to pretty girls" and that in literary representa-tions as well "wool-work is predominantly an emblem of maidens."[33] Penelope may be making clothes all the time as part of her wifely duties, but the weaving she undertakes to trap the suitors is specially marked since she sets up a 'great loom', (μέγαν ἱστόν, 2.94 = 19.139 = 24.129, 2.104 = 19.149 = 24.139), for it, something that is evidently not always there and needs to be constructed for the occasion. Like Odysseus himself she is thrown back in time, becoming a *parthenos* again, her weaving a lead-up to marriage. In retrospect, it leads up to marriage specifically to Odysseus, and that is how Amphimedon pres-ents it in the underworld: as soon as the weaving is done, Odysseus appears on the scene.

When Penelope tells her weaving tale to the beggar in Book 19, this retro-spective view is not yet possible in terms of the plot, but in the manner of oral poetry, Penelope's telling refers to all other occurrences of her tale, including the one in the underworld that is chronologically still in the future.[34] Talking to the disguised Odysseus, Penelope concludes her tale despondently, saying that she cannot find another ruse and her son and parents are pressing her to remarry. The virginal weaving is finished, and now it is time for marriage. At

---

[32] Papadopoulou-Belmehdi 1994:118. See above, p106-107, on the signs of spring correlating with Odysseus' return.

[33] Ferrari 2002:57.

[34] See Nagy 1996:50 on this point.

this moment, the meaning of Penelope's work seems evenly split, balanced on the cusp between the two poles represented by the two other tellings of the loom tale, the shroud of Laertes and the splendid wedding tapestry. There is irony in the way these words lead Penelope directly back to inquiring who the stranger is, and doing so in a marked way. Penelope augments the customary formulaic question regarding her guest's identity by adding 'since you are not from an old-renowned tree or rock'.

> ἀλλὰ καὶ ὣς μοι εἰπὲ τεὸν γένος, ὁππόθεν ἐσσί·
> οὐ γὰρ ἀπὸ δρυός ἐσσι παλαιφάτου οὐδ' ἀπὸ πέτρης.
>
> (Odyssey 19.157–163)
>
> But even so tell me your origins, where you are from,
> for you were not born from an old-renowned tree, or a rock.

The form of her request suggests that she has a more than usual interest in this beggar, who is, already at this point, no ordinary stranger to her and who will, as we know and she might already suspect, will give her weaving its happier meaning and bring her *kleos* to completion.[35]

---

[35] On implications of the phrase 'tree and rock' see above, p90-91.

CHAPTER SIXTEEN

THE PANDAREIDS AND THE FESTIVAL OF APOLLO

I HAVE SUGGESTED above that to a certain extent the myths Odysseus and Penelope tell each other in *Odyssey* 19 are related to their own story as a myth might be related to a ritual or a festival, both in the sense that there are parallel thought structures involved, and that the myth is often tragic or negative, whereas the festival or ritual is not. In other words, though the return of Odysseus is not a ritual in any literal sense, it interacts in a ritual-like way with the stories told within it: the macronarrative enacts a festival, while the micronarratives narrate myths associated with it. At the same time, once the events of the *Odyssey* have run their course, the story of Odysseus' return itself emerges as a myth associated with the festival of Apollo. In effect, the *Odyssey* becomes the myth associated with the festival that is internal to itself. There is a certain displacement of categories involved here, so that the story of the *Odyssey* appears both as a myth and a ritualized action.

There is a similar displacement involved in the comparisons of Odysseus or Penelope to an *aoidos*. In one sense, Odysseus is like one because he creates a poetic tale, but in another sense he is unlike one, because his poetic tale is also his own life, which is not the case with a real *aoidos*. Just as Odysseus and Penelope become both makers of their own tale and characters within it, self-conscious epic heroes who partake of the poetic awareness of themselves, so the return of Odysseus during a festival becomes a self-conscious myth, a myth which incorporates its own ritual setting and internalizes its own occasion. I have argued that what Odysseus says to Penelope in Book 19 is congruent with its setting, the eve of Apollo's festival, and the same can be said about Penelope's words. In order to make this point, however, it will be necessary to leave Book 19 for the moment and take a look at its echoes in the beginning of Book 20.

Penelope's Aedon is daughter of Pandareos, not of Pandion as in other versions of the myth, and the daughters of Pandareos also appear at the beginning of Book 20. The expression 'the daughters of Pandareos' occupies the same position in the line as the 'the daughter of Pandareos' in Book 19, establishing a strong connection between the two instances (19.518, 20.66). This repeated occurrence of the little-known daughters of Pandareos is striking and hardly accidental. Their myth, as told in the *Odyssey*, matches and complements both the myth of Aedon and the setting in which both myths are told: the daughters of Pandareos appear in the *Odyssey* on the morning of the contest day, the festival of Apollo.

The myth about the Pandareids is poorly known, the *Odyssey* itself being our main source. In the Odyssean account, the orphaned daughters of Pandareos are brought up by the gods and hold out a promise of perfect marriage. Hera gives them beauty, Athena teaches them crafts, and Aphrodite seeks marriage for them. And then, at the last moment, for incomprehensible reasons, the girls are simply carried away from life by *thuellai*.[1] Penelope prays to Artemis and asks for escape, to be killed suddenly by the goddess's arrow or to be whisked away, like the Pandareids:

> Ἄρτεμι, πότνα θεά, θύγατερ Διός, αἴθε μοι ἤδη
> ἰὸν ἐνὶ στήθεσσι βαλοῦσ' ἐκ θυμὸν ἔλοιο
> αὐτίκα νῦν, ἢ ἔπειτά μ' ἀναρπάξασα θύελλα
> οἴχοιτο προφέρουσα κατ' ἠερόεντα κέλευθα,
> ἐν προχοῇς δὲ βάλοι ἀψορρόου Ὠκεανοῖο.
> ὡς δ' ὅτε Πανδαρέου κούρας ἀνέλοντο θύελλαι·
> τῇσι τοκῆας μὲν φθῖσαν θεοί, αἱ δ' ἐλίποντο
> ὀρφαναὶ ἐν μεγάροισι, κόμισσε δὲ δῖ ' Ἀφροδίτη
> τυρῷ καὶ μέλιτι γλυκερῷ καὶ ἡδέϊ οἴνῳ·
> Ἥρη δ' αὐτῇσιν περὶ πασέων δῶκε γυναικῶν
> εἶδος καὶ πινυτήν, μῆκος δ' ἔπορ' Ἄρτεμις ἁγνή,
> ἔργα δ' Ἀθηναίη δέδαε κλυτὰ ἐργάζεσθαι.
> εὖτ' Ἀφροδίτη δῖα προσέστιχε μακρὸν Ὄλυμπον,
> κούρης αἰτήσουσα τέλος θαλεροῖο γάμοιο,
> ἐς Δία τερπικέραυνον - ὁ γάρ τ' εὖ οἶδεν απαντα,
> μοῖράν τ' ἀμμορίην τε καταθνητῶν ἀνθρώπων -
> τόφρα δὲ τὰς κούρας ἅρπυιαι ἀνηρείψαντο
> καί ῥ' ἔδοσαν στυγερῇσιν ἐρινύσιν ἀμφιπολεύειν·
> ὣς ἔμ' ἀϊστώσειαν Ὀλύμπια δώματ' ἔχοντες,
> ἠέ μ' ἐϋπλόκαμος βάλοι Ἄρτεμις, ὄφρ' Ὀδυσῆα

---

[1] On *thuellai* see Nagy 1979/99:194–95, 204 and 1990:243–251.

ὀσσομένη καὶ γαῖαν ὕπο στυγερὴν ἀφικοίμην,
μηδέ τι χείρονος ἀνδρὸς ἐϋφραίνοιμι νόημα.

(Odyssey 20.61–82)

Artemis, mistress and goddess, daughter of Zeus,
    if only you would
hit me with your arrow and take the breath out of
    my breast
right now, or if only a snatching wind would pick
    me up
and carry me over the misty paths
to cast me down where the back-flowing Okeanos
    pours forth its stream,
as when the snatching winds took the daughters
    of Pandareos.
The gods had destroyed their parents,
    and they were left
orphans in the house, and the luminous Aphrodite
    brought them up
on cheese and sweet honey and wine.
And Hera gave them looks and intelligence above
    all women,
the pure Artemis granted them stature,
and Athena taught them glorious crafts.
But when luminous Aphrodite came to great
    Olympus,
to ask the thunderbolt-hurler Zeus for the
    accomplishment of flourishing marriage
for the girls, for he knew everything,
fortune and misfortune for mortal men,
then the snatching winds carried the girls off
and gave them as attendants to the grim Erinyes.
Just like that, I wish the dwellers on Olympus would
    hide me from sight,
or may the beautiful-haired Artemis strike me,
    so that I may
go under the earth to see Odysseus
and not delight the heart of a lesser man.

Penelope's apparent despair in this scene has been taken as incompatible with recognition of Odysseus, but that does not follow.[2] Rather, an argument can be made that the escapist and ardent tone of the prayer is better accounted for precisely on the assumption that Penelope has recognized Odysseus. If Penelope suspects that the beggar is her husband, then the suspense is justified: all will be gained or lost on this day. The tension of the moment is signaled by the urgency in Penelope's request, to escape αὐτίκα νῦν, 'immediately'. If she has mistaken an imposter for Odysseus, then she has needlessly destroyed the fruit of her own long effort. If she is right and the beggar is Odysseus, there is still the very real danger of his being killed by the suitors.[3] Worse still, Telemachus may be killed with him. On the other hand, if her strategy is successful and Odysseus' promises come true, then Penelope will gain what she wanted, the death of all the suitors, and intactness of her family. Penelope's request to die rather than 'gladden' the heart of an inferior husband is hardly compatible with the idea that she is reconciled to the prospect of marrying one of the suitors, and suggests instead that she has no intention of ever entering into such a marriage.[4]

The question, then, remains: is the prayer nothing but a complaint? This question is tied to another, namely: what went wrong with the Pandareids? It is not that the Pandareids were unfit for a better fate, since the gods gifted them generously. The Pandareids never come to fertility because such was their *moira*, 'fortune', or rather ἀμμορίη, 'ill fortune' (20.76). Their 'luck', their circumstances are at fault, and the *Odyssey* makes these circumstances clear.

---

[2] Russo (1992:113), followed by Katz 1991:149. Russo takes line 82 to indicate that Penelope is "willing, finally, to face the possibility of marrying one of the suitors" and that "her complaint confirms the fact that she has no suspicion that her husband is already returned in the disguise of the beggar" (1982:113). But Penelope's wish to die rather than 'gladden the heart of a lesser man' should surely not be taken as precisely the opposite, namely coming to terms with that prospect.

[3] A possibility rarely taken seriously in modern criticism, but certainly envisaged by the *Odyssey* (2.246–251).

[4] Logically, Penelope might be hoping that all the suitors will lose and she will not have to marry any of them (see above, p248-249). Scodel (2001) argues that to stage the contest of the bow is a reasonable choice for Penelope whether or not the beggar is Odysseus. If he is, the contest "offers him an opportunity to act" (323). If he is not, the suitors are likely to fail and perhaps "leave simply in embarrassment" (324). Of course, as Scodel observes (324), it is not clear whether the losers of the contest must abandon "the larger game" of wooing Penelope. Scodel's argument that a contest of the bow in which all the suitors lose does not worsen Penelope's situation seems persuasive. The details of Book 19, however, suggest that Penelope does think that the beggar is Odysseus, and the urgency of her prayer itself is better understandable if Penelope thinks the contest is a decisive moment, not one ruse among many.

The Pandareids are called ὀρφαναὶ ἐν μεγάροισι 'orphans in the house', and Eustathius sees in this bereavement the source of their demise:

περικαλεῖς μὲν οὖσαι δι' ὀρφανίαν δὲ δυσπραγοῦσαι καὶ εἰς ὑποδύσκολον καὶ ὡς οἷον εἰπεῖν ἐρινυῶδες ἦθος μεταβληθεῖσαι τῇ λύπῃ ᾤχοντο, καὶ δία τοῦτο καὶ ἀνέμοις ἐπαχθῆναι καί Ἐρινύσι παραδοθῆναι μυθεύονται.

(Eustathius on *Odyssey* 19.518)

Extremely beautiful but having the misfortune to be orphaned, they underwent a transformation and became irksome and so to say Erinyes-like in character, and were destroyed by grief, and because of this it is said that they were carried off by winds and handed over to the Erinyes.

Penelope too is orphaned in a sense, and Pandareids come to mind when she says that she would have had both beauty and fame, had it all not perished when Odysseus left for Troy (*Odyssey* 19.124–126).

Snatched away by the winds, the Pandareids are taken to the streams of Okeanos and become servants to the 'grim Erinyes' (στυγερῇσιν ἐρινύσιν, 20.78). It is a fitting fate for those who have left life too early, having had neither marriage nor offspring.[5] Like the Erinyes, such souls can be vengeful: they were cheated of life and demand revenge. Johnston has argued that the Erinyes belong to a group of what she calls "reproductive demons," forces that are dangerous to children and pregnant or parturient women. I will not here repeat her arguments in favor of her assertion that beliefs in such forces were current among the Greeks long before the Hellenistic period. What is important to reiterate here is that the "reproductive demons" were often transformed women who failed precisely at reproduction.[6] It is to this group, Johnston argues, that the Pandareids belong. Their connection with the Erinyes follows the same principle: fate is so unfair to them that they literally lose their human face and turn into terrible, vengeful creatures. Something like this is likely to be Eustathius' meaning when he says that the Pandareids

---

[5] Roscher 1886–1903:1501, Rohde 1925:292 n1, 373 n1, 680, 651, Bremmer 1983:101–105, Henrichs 1991: part IV. On *aoroi* see Brashear 1990:53–55. See Johnston 1994:153 n7 for further bibliography on the subject. Cf. what Penelope says about Telemachus when she learns that he has left for Pylos (4.727–728): νῦν αὖ παῖδ' ἀγαπητὸν ἀνηρείψαντο θύελλαι | ἀκλέα ἐκ μεγάρων, οὐδ' ὁρμηθέντος ἄκουσα, "and now the snatching winds carried my beloved child from the house without glory, and I did not even hear that he left."

[6] Johnston 1994:140–148.

became "so to say" Erinys-like, δι' ὀρφανίαν δυσπραγοῦσαι, 'being unlucky on account of being orphaned'.

The Pandareids were denied family life; Penelope's may now come to nothing. Like them, Penelope had all that was necessary to succeed: beauty, stature, skills, intelligence. But if her husband and her son perish together on this day, Penelope's quest for a 'flourishing marriage' will have been in vain.[7] And *if* this has to be so, she would rather vanish out of sight like they did, and (the implication is) turn into a 'follower' of Erinyes, barren and horrible 'because of grief'.

As Penelope prays for an arrow of Artemis she makes clear the conditions under which she wants her prayer fulfilled: she does not wish to 'gladden the heart of a lesser man'. But by setting up this condition, Penelope opens up another possibility: what if she does *not* have to marry one of the suitors? The implication is that *in that case* Penelope would not like to become like the daughters of Pandareos nor to be killed by Artemis' arrow. What would she like, then? I suggest that what Penelope is in effect asking for is the renewal of her marriage to Odysseus. Penelope does not need to formulate her most intimate desire openly, because it is implicit in her prayer and also in the choice of the prayer's addressee. Artemis is a goddess whose domain is not only virginal youth but also the transition, ever unsafe, to the next stage of life. It is a commonplace that the dancing circle of Artemis is the place from which girls get snatched away to become mothers.[8] To make the transition into married life a girl has to have Artemis on her side, and offerings were made to the goddess both before and after the wedding. As Burkert puts it, "her arrow threatens every girl who fulfills her womanly destiny."[9]

Penelope's vivid dream about Odysseus sleeping at her side, looking exactly as he did when he left for Troy, follows immediately upon her prayer, and if the prayer is in fact about the resumption of their marriage, then it leads naturally into the dream, which dramatizes this very resumption (20.87–90).

In contrast to this dream, the myth about the daughters of Pandareos is a negative version of Penelope's future, but it is not simply a cry of despair. The dream and the prayer articulate the same wish, but uttering it would be too presumptuous: Penelope is almost superstitiously reluctant to affirm anything until she is absolutely certain it will not slip away. She presents her prayer

---

[7] Only in Penelope's case it is not she, but her husband who is snatched away: νῦν δέ μιν ἀκλειῶς ἅρπυιαι ἀνηρείψαντο (*Odyssey* 1.241).

[8] A classic example is Nausikaa, who is ready for marriage and is herself compared to Artemis as she is playing with her friends (*Odyssey* 6.102-104, 151).

[9] Burkert 1985:151.

as a negative mirror-image of her wish, but the opposition of marriage and the arrows of Artemis is a traditional one, and by elaborating on the negative part of it while making it conditional Penelope suggests the positive part. The escapist tenor of the prayer only makes this psychological strategy more effective: the most ardent desire is left unspoken.

In Book 19, Penelope compares herself to a daughter of Pandareos and does so as a mother, through the myth of Aedon. In Book 20 she speaks as a *nymphe* thinking of marriage, and here she imagines her future through the model of Pandareos' never-married daughters.[10] On the basis of the two Pandareid myths Penelope emerges both a mother and a *nymphe* who stands alone as a female counterpart to the differentiated team of father and son, Odysseus and Telemachus.[11] Both myths fit not only Penelope's situation, but also the setting in which they are told, namely the festival of Apollo.

In the *Odyssey*, the festival marks the end of a period of dissolution and reversal, at least as far as the household of Odysseus is concerned.[12] In his discussion of dissolution and reversal festivals, Burkert analyzes several myths, some of them with clearer ritual ties than others, but all having to do with abnormal behavior of women.[13] For example, there are the Lemnian women polluted by their sickening body smell, who kill all the males on the island, except for the king.[14] The period of darkness is marked by women losing their attractiveness (foul smell) and turning against men (murder). The daughters of Proitos, too, suffer from both ills in different versions of their myth. In Hesiod, the Proitids are infected with revolting ugliness:

> καὶ γάρ σφιν κεφαλῇσι κατὰ κνύος αἰνὸν ἔχευεν·
> ἀλφὸς γὰρ χρόα πάντα κατέσχεθεν, αἱ δέ νυ χαῖται
> ἔρρεον ἐκ κεφαλέων, ψίλωτο δὲ καλὰ κάρηνα.[15]

(fr. 133.3–5 MW)

And he [Dionysus] poured a terrible itch over their heads,
and leprosy covered all of their skin, and their hair
fell out and their fair heads became bald.

---

[10] For Penelope as *nymphe* see, e.g. the extended discussion by Papadopoulou-Belmehdi 1994:95–107.

[11] See Ferrari 2002:177–178 for a discussion of the lack of differentiation between maidens and matrons, reflected both in the female initiation rites and in their depictions on pottery.

[12] See Bierl 2009:75 and 249–265 on dissolution as an integral part of the polis and its ritual practices, representing the marginal period in the transition of youths to adulthood.

[13] Burkert 1983:135–212.

[14] For more on the Lemnian myth and its relation to the *Odyssey*, see above, p122–135.

[15] Other mentions of Proitids in the *Catalogue of Women* are: fr. 37.10–15 MW, fr. 130–132 MW.

The girls roam the countryside 'with every kind of indecency', according to Apollodorus, until they are cured by the prophet Melampous.[16] And once they are cured, they marry: in fact, Melampous himself marries a daughter of Proitos, and, notably, becomes a king through this marriage.[17]

The Hesiodic version of the Proitid myth focuses on nubile women, but in others the whole female population of the Argolid joins the Proitids. In their frenzy, the women kill their own children and run off into the wild (Apollodorus 2.28.1). The myth seems to unfold along two tracks, one involving maidens, the other mothers. Hesychius associates the Proitids with the Argive festival of the Agrania, certainly a festival of dissolution and also a festival of the dead, νεκύσια.[18] Elements of such a festival are also present in the *Odyssey*, where Theoklymenos sees shades around the house of Odysseus:

> εἰδώλων δὲ πλέον πρόθυρον, πλείη δὲ καὶ αὐλή,
> ἱεμένων Ἔρεβόσδε ὑπὸ ζόφον· ἠέλιος δέ
> οὐρανοῦ ἐξαπόλωλε, κακὴ δ' ἐπιδέδρομεν ἀχλύς.
>
> (*Odyssey* 20.355–357)

> The entryway is full of ghosts, and so is the yard,
> ghosts going down to Erebus, into the darkness. The sun
> has perished from the sky, and an evil mist has spread.

Burkert classes the myth of the nightingale, in all its versions, together with that of the Proitids.[19] Here too there is a mother who kills her child, invariably a male child, whether in a frenzy or not. The motivation for the killing is a matter of myth: anger, in the case of Lemnian women, madness in the case of the Proitids, both in the case of Prokne, and mental blindness in the case of Aedon. The fact of the killing is fundamental and remains unchanged. But if Aedon, daughter of Pandareos, can be compared to the murderous Argive mothers who follow the Proitids, so the youthful and unmarried daughters of Pandareos can be compared to the Proitids themselves, also on the verge of marriage and also suddenly and shockingly unmarriageable.

---

[16] Apollodorus 2.27 (μετ' ἀκοσμίας ἁπάσης), cf. Aelian *Varia Historia* 3.42 (γυμναί).

[17] Apollodorus 2.29.1.

[18] Hesychius s.v Ἀγράνια· ἑορτὴ ἐν Ἄργει ἐπὶ μιᾷ τῶν Προίτου θυγατέρων. Ἀγράνια· νεκύσια παρὰ Ἀργείοις καὶ ἀγῶνες ἐν Θήβαις. Plutarch (*Greek Questions* 299e-f) describes a rite of flight and pursuit that was part of Agrionia at Orkhomenos. For a discussion of the festival see Nilsson 1906:271–276, Burkert 1983:168–179. On the Agrionia in Orkhomenos see Schachter 1981:180–81.

[19] Burkert 1983:179–184.

Ugliness, infertility and lewdness are all part of the dissolution, and present in the *Odyssey*. The specter of infertility looms over Penelope, and while no ugliness affects her in the eyes of others, she does say repeatedly that her beauty is destroyed (18.251, 19.124). I am not suggesting, however, that the dissolution affects Penelope: rather, it threatens her. It is the maids who represent the dissolution. Just as the suitors are opposed to Telemachus and Odysseus, so the maids are opposed to Penelope and repeatedly disparaged by herself and Eurykleia as 'shameless dogs'.[20] It is noteworthy that both myths of the Pandareids in the *Odyssey* are offset by a mention of the maids. In Book 19 the dialogue between Odysseus and Penelope is preceded by a confrontation with the arrogant maids. Upbraiding one of the maids before she turns to Odysseus, Penelope calls her a 'shameless dog', κύον ἀδεές (19.91). Book 20 begins before dawn on the festival day with Odysseus witnessing the maids as they go out to lie with the suitors. Furious, Odysseus famously addresses his own heart, urging it to bear this insult, just as it bore an even 'more dog-like' thing, the cannibalism of the Cyclops: τέτλαθι δή, κραδίη· καὶ κύντερον ἄλλο ποτ' ἔτλης (20.18). This scene, in which the themes of abnormal sexuality and abnormal eating intersect, forms both a prelude and a contrast to Penelope's prayer to Artemis in which she mentions the Pandareids. Opposed to the maids' lewdness is Penelope's desire for a resumption of her marriage. Curiously, the scholia hint that when the Pandareids underwent their horrible transformation they were afflicted by a disease that disfigured them, and the disease is called κύων, the dog.[21]

The myths of the Pandareids convey the dangers (perversion of motherhood and failure to marry) that are inherent in the murky period leading up to the festival of Apollo. These myths present only the negative side of the coin, but it is quite likely that in their local contexts festival and ritual would have articulated a positive alternative. The local contexts for the myth of Pandareids are lost, but it is not hard to imagine them being associated in a local setting with a ritual or a festival, an association that would be similar in most general terms to the relationship between the Agrania and the myth of the Proitids. In the *Odyssey*, of course, the positive alternative is to be found in the macro-narrative of the poem itself and the ultimate success of Odysseus and Penelope.

---

[20] E.g., 19.154, 372. Cf. the use of adjective κυνῶπις about Helen (4.145), Aphrodite when she is caught *in flagrante delicto* with Ares (8.319), and Klytemnestra (11.424).

[21] Scholia on the *Odyssey* 20.66.

The very existence of two variant Pandareid myths, one about a mother and the other about unmarried girls, reflects a traditional pattern of myth-making: the example of the Proitids suggests that myths of this kind may tend to become two-pronged, with variants involving girls and mothers. In fact, this kind of thinking is reflected in the famous Attic/panhellenic version of the Aedon myth, where the married Aedon and unmarried Khelidon, or the married Prokne and unmarried Philomela, become partners in the murder of Itys.

The traditional background of the Pandareid myths is probably unrecoverable and nothing is known of any ritual ties that these myths might have.[22] Still, there are glimpses of that background that point to possible answers to the question: why the Pandareids? There are links, however tenuous, that connect the Pandareids to Apollo. In the Theban version of Aedon's story, the sister-in-law whom Aedon envies and whose children she tries to kill is Niobe. In the end, Niobe's children are killed, but by Apollo and Artemis.[23] Niobe's myth is in a certain sense parallel to that of Aedon: both have to do with female fertility, and in both it is undercut in an unexpected way, through the fault of the woman herself. Apollo and Artemis are the powers that destroy, and therefore could have protected, Niobe's offspring. The same gods preside over Penelope's family in the second half of the *Odyssey*.[24]

But the connections between Aedon and Niobe go deeper. Niobe and her father Tantalos hail from Anatolia, and so does Pandareos, associated as he is with the neighborhood of Sipylos and with Ephesos.[25] Like Niobe's father Tantalos, Pandareos is a transgressive figure who overreaches in his dealings with the gods, and indeed he interacts with Tantalos in myth. His main

---

[22] Van der Valk (1949:236) supposes the myth to be Ionic (and "otherwise unknown").

[23] *Iliad* 24.602–617, Aeschylus fr. 152a R, Sophocles, *Niobe* fr. 441a R. The myth appeared in the *Catalogue of Women* (Hesiod fr. 183 MW), and was known to Alcman (PMG 75), Sappho fr. 205 Voigt, Mimnermus (fr. 19 W), Pindar (fr. 64), and Bacchylides (fr. 20 D).

[24] The arrows of Apollo and Artemis seem also to be on the mind of Ithacans as the festival approaches. Apart from Penelope's prayer to Artemis, Melanthios would like to see Telemachus struck down by Apollo's arrow (17.251–252), while Penelope wishes the same fate on Antinoos (17.494).

[25] In most of our sources, Niobe comes from Lydia, and in some she returns home after the death of her children (*Iliad* 24.615, Pherecydes FGrH 3 F 38, Scholia T on *Iliad* 24.602, Hyginus *Fabulae* 9). Niobe probably also goes home in Aeschylus' play, since Tantalos appears on stage (fr. 159 R). Tantalos is described as living at Sipylos in Pindar *Olympian* 1.38. In some versions of his myth Zeus punishes him by putting Mt. Sipylos on top of him (which seems to be a variation on "the rock of Tantalos" theme): Scholia to *Odyssey* 19.518, 20.66.

action in myth is the theft of Zeus' golden dog from Crete. He gives the dog to Tantalos, but the latter eventually denies ever having received it and swears a false oath to that effect.[26] In one version of the myth, the roles of the two transgressors are reversed: Tantalos steals the dog, and Pandareos swears falsely to conceal it.[27] The similarity between Pandareos and Tantalos gives the Theban myths about Aedon and Niobe a very symmetrical structure: two Anatolian transgressors, Tantalos and Pandareos, marry their two daughters, Niobe and Aedon, to two fortifiers of Thebes, Amphion and Zethos. Both families are in the end left childless.

Curiously, Pandareos also has an Iliadic namesake, who is himself a trickster: Pandaros, whose name is an alternate form of Pandareos. In the *Iliad*, Pandaros is the archer who breaks the truce between the Achaeans and Trojans by shooting and wounding Menelaos.[28] He is a treacherous character, famous for his skill with the bow, and he shoots unexpectedly from afar. Craftiness and a knack for breaking oaths seems to be a trait that goes with the name, and this suggests that a mythmaking tradition now lost to us is at work. Pandaros comes from Lycia, (Apollo's territory, wherever it is imagined to be).[29] His bow comes from Apollo himself: Πάνδαρος, ᾧ καὶ τόξον Ἀπόλλων αὐτὸς ἔδωκεν, 'Pandaros, to whom Apollo himself gave the bow' (*Iliad* 2.827). Incidentally, Odysseus also shares a proclivity for trickery with Pandaros and Pandareos and he also has a notable bow: his comes from Eurytos, an archer who rivaled Apollo.[30]

The Iliadic archer Pandaros and the crafty Pandareos both come from the Anatolian coast, an area which is very likely to have contributed to the evolution of the Homeric poems. The name Pandaros or Pandareos is probably

---

[26] Scholia to *Odyssey* 19.518, 20.66, scholia to Pindar, *Olympian* 1.91, Antoninus Liberalis 36.

[27] Scholia on Pindar, *Olympian* 1.91.

[28] *Iliad* 4.86–127. Athena, who urges Pandaros to shoot the treacherous arrow also instructs him to pray to Apollo: εὔχεο δ' Ἀπόλλωνι Λυκηγενέϊ κλυτοτόξῳ (4.101).

[29] *Iliad* 5.105, 171–173. This Lycia is apparently not the same as Sarpedon's Lycia in South-Western Anatolia, since Pandaros' contingent is said to come from Zeleia in the foothills of Mount Ida (*Iliad* 2.824–227). The problem has not been convincingly solved, but it seems impossible to divorce Pandaros' Lycia from Apollo Λυκηγενής: see Kirk 1985:254 (on *Iliad* 2.826–827). Pandaros is also son of Lykaon, ('Lycia dweller'), *Iliad* 2.826, 4.89 etc. Sthenelos "introduces" Pandaros to Diomedes as follows: ὃ μὲν τόξων ἐῢ εἰδὼς | Πάνδαρος, υἱὸς δ' αὖτε Λυκάονος εὔχεται εἶναι (*Iliad* 5.245–246).

[30] *Odyssey* 21.31–33. Eurytos' rivalry with Apollo: *Odyssey* 8.223–228.

Anatolian in origin.[31] If so, it might be related to a place named Pandai near Mount Sipylos, right in the center of Pandareos' activities. Sadly, Pandai for us is not much more than a dot on the map. But one thing is known about the place: it had a cult of Apollo. In a third-century BCE inscription of an agreement between the citizens of Smyrna and Magnesia, one of the gods who is called upon to witness the oath is "Apollo in Pandai."[32] Further south, the places where Pandareos is said to come from, in various versions of his myth, Ephesos and Miletos, are near some of the greatest of Apollo's oracles, Klaros and Didyma, part of the string of Apolline oracular shrines all along the coast. One might look somewhere in this area, if more remained, for a traditional background to the Pandareids' myth. Finally, Pausanias describes the two Pandareids named Kameiro and Klytie, as depicted in Polygnotos' *Nekyia* on the walls of the Cnidian Leskhe.[33] This might be entirely accidental, but in this lost image the sisters appear in an Odyssean context of *nekyia*, at Apollo's sanctuary, and in a building belonging to an Anatolian city.[34]

There are obvious points of contact between the Pandareid myths and the *Odyssey*: there is trickery, transgression, and violation of oaths; in the case of Pandaros the latter trait is combined with the skill at archery, bestowed by Apollo; there is the death of children, both of Aedon's son and of Niobe's large brood, and again Apollo is involved, along with Artemis; there is the notion of unmarried and childless, and therefore unfulfilled, life in the story of the younger Pandareids. In sum, it seems entirely possible that the myths of the Pandareids are particularly suited to appear in the context of Apollo's festival in the *Odyssey* because in their local forms they were associated with some similar or related settings. It may be that these myths themselves were once connected to rituals of dissolution and reversal followed by re-establishment of order, perhaps even a festival of Apollo, or it may be that their relatedness to the *Odyssey* is much less direct. In either case, the fit between these myths and their context may be due to the fact that they are drawn from traditional settings in some way related or parallel to the poetic settings where they

---

[31] Von Kamptz 1982:361, who suggests that names of this form tend to derive from toponyms, cf. Ἀμισώδαρος, a Lycian king in the *Iliad* (16.328), and Amisos, a place in Pontos mentioned by Strabo (12.543). However, there seem to be Carian toponyms where -dar- is present in the toponym itself, e.g. Ταρκόνδαρα, CIG 2694, 2607, Βρυγίνδαρα (Kretschmer 1896:328).

[32] Ἀπόλλω τὸν ἐμ Πάνδοις (*Orientis Graecae Inscriptiones Selectae* 229).

[33] Pausanias 10.30.1–3

[34] Robert (1892:81–82) suggested that Kameiro might be an eponym of the Kameiros in Rhodes.

feature in Homer.[35] The ritual of Apollo in the *Odyssey* is not only mentioned, but evoked by Penelope's myths, just as it is also evoked by myths of Odysseus. These myths, in return, acquire resonance from the festival setting they themselves help create.

---

[35] See Nagy 1996b:113–146 on the traditional nature of Homeric mythological *exempla* and cf. the views exemplified by Wilcock 1964 and 1977 to which Nagy reacts. Lang (1983, esp. 149) offers a convincing argument against the notion of invention and drastic innovation in Homeric myths, showing that such invention would in fact deprive *paradeigmata* of their effectiveness.

CHAPTER SEVENTEEN
PENELOPE AND THE *PENELOPS*

S O FAR I HAVE ARGUED that Penelope's myths, above all the Pandareid myths, have special affinity to their poetic environment in the *Odyssey*, namely a crisis and a turning point from dissolution to "light and life," which in the *Odyssey* is marked by the festival of Apollo. In this chapter, I am pulling even further back to an even larger frame, to look at Penelope's own intrinsic relatedness to just such a transition. By virtue of being concerned with questions both fundamental and overarching, the observations that follow will not apply directly to the dialogue in Book 19. They are relevant, however, in a more general way because they are about the mythological persona of Penelope, and this persona reaches its fullest manifestation in the *Odyssey* in Books 19 to 23, beginning with the dialogue between Penelope and disguised Odysseus and ending with their open embrace and a night together. What follows is one way of trying to reconstruct some of Penelope's mythological background, not in a sense of origins, of something left in the past, but in a sense of something present and active in the *Odyssey* as we know it. I will not make any claims regarding the antecedents of Penelope as a mythological figure, or try to imagine what she might have been before the *Odyssey* took its familiar shape. I will instead attempt to uncover a set of affiliations that describes Penelope as a particular kind of mythological character. I do think this kind of figure is likely to have substantial and deep roots, but my main point is that her qualities are palpably present in the *Odyssey*. In other words, what follows is primarily about the diachronic (rather than historical) dimensions of Penelope, and my suggestion is that these dimensions are also synchronically active in the *Odyssey*.

A good point to begin looking for Penelope's diachronic dimension is her name, which, I suggest, is a *nom parlant*. When Penelope compares herself to Aedon, she compares herself both to a woman with a bird name, and to a bird. Penelope's own name is also derived from that of a bird, and it signals her belonging to a thematically related group of bird-women in myth. Penelope's belonging to this group, however, is not entirely obvious, and its elucidation requires a certain amount of reconstruction.

Among several folk etymologies of the name Penelope, which are mostly concerned with weaving (and which may also be operative in the *Odyssey*), Eustathius cites on the authority of Didymus a derivation from the name of a water bird, πηνέλοψ, the *penelops*. This derivation is linguistically unobjectionable, but it has enjoyed little popularity. The reason is a perceived lack of relevance for the *Odyssey*: as Farnell put it, "some of us felt when we were informed that Queen Penelope had been discovered to be a wild duck, that the discovery of origins darkens rather then enlightens our understanding of the evolution of myth."[1] In contrast with the folk etymologies related to weaving, (involving, for example πήνη, 'woof'), there is no immediately apparent link between Penelope and water birds.[2]

Eustathius himself addresses the problem of relevance by relating Didymus's explanation: Penelope used to have a different name, but on one occasion she was thrown into the sea by Palamedes and saved by the πηνέλοπες, hence the change of her name.[3] More will be said about this story later, but for now it is simply important to mention that it takes us beyond the Homeric *Odyssey*. My argument, on the other hand, is that the etymological connection with the πηνέλοψ is relevant for Penelope as we know her in *Homer*.[4]

The main difficulty in interpreting Penelope's name lies in the scarcity of information provided by the Greek sources about the *penelops*: less than ten lines is all that we have by way of description, and even a certain identification of the bird is lacking. It is generally accepted that the *penelops* is some species

---

[1] Farnell 1921:62.

[2] For an interpretation of Penelope's name different from the one suggested in this study, see Bader 1998. In Bader's opinion Penelope's name results from a wordplay: the *p*- of πήνη is substituted for the initial *kh*- of χηνέλοψ or χηνάλοψ, a name of a bird. According to Bader, χηνέλοψ was reinterpreted and "mutated" to give χηναλώπηξ, a combination of χήν, 'goose' and ἀλώπηξ, 'fox'. Bader thus argues for an identification of πηνέλοψ with χηναλώπηξ, with πηνέλοψ being at first only a poetic formation based on Penelope's name. Thus, according to Bader, Penelope's name is based not on πηνέλοψ (which post-dates the name) but instead on χηνέλοψ/χηναλώπηξ, which fits Penelope's behavior: 'goose' corresponds to her fidelity, while 'fox' symbolizes her cunning. See also Bader 1997a, 1197b.141–142. I find it very hard, however, to reconcile poetic usage of πηνέλοψ outside of Homer with the theory that it is dependent on Penelope's name. The fact that πηνέλοψ is not even mentioned in Homer seems to me to argue against this theory.

[3] Scholia to *Odyssey* 4.797.

[4] I have made this point elsewhere (Levaniouk 1999), and what follows is an abridged and re-thought version of that argument.

of wild duck or goose, but evidence connecting it to both is tenuous, since no ancient source actually identifies the *penelops* with either. The idea that the *penelops* is a duck seems to be based on one confusing passage in the scholia to Aristophanes, and the identification with geese on the fact that the *penelops* appears in various lists of birds next to several species of goose and sheldrake.[5] All that is actually clear from these references is that the *penelops* is a smallish water bird, and Aristotle mentions additionally that it lives at sea.[6]

Since the *penelops* is consistently mentioned in the company of geese, it must have had something in common with them, and several scholars have explored a connection between the *penelops*, Penelope, and geese. Penelope's delight in her geese (in her dream tale) and the extraordinary grief she displays at their destruction have long been noticed,[7] and Kretschmer has connected Penelope's affection for her geese with the *penelops*.[8] He argues that geese are traditionally regarded as faithful and loving mates, and it is this quality that connects them to Penelope, the proverbial faithful wife. This connection is signaled by the derivation of her name from *penelops*. Further, Pratt points out that geese were known for their vigilance and prudence, especially in guarding their nest: Aristotle speaks of their ἤθεα αἰσχυντηλὰ καὶ φυλακτικά, 'prudent and vigilant habits', and, in a Hellenistic epigram, a goose on a woman's tomb is said to be a sign of δόμων φυλακὰν μελεδήμονα, 'careful guardianship of the house'.[9] Both prudence and guardianship of the house are, of course, two of Penelope's most prominent qualities.[10]

As will be clear from what follows, fidelity is in fact a likely point of contact between the *penelops* and the geese, and it is therefore likely that Penelope's name signals, among other sings, her fidelity to Odysseus. No textual links, however, have been noticed between the descriptions of the *penelops* and those of geese as faithful guardians; the connection here is based entirely on the assumption that the *penelops* is a type of goose. Such an

---

[5] According to the scholia to Aristophanes *Birds* 1302 the *penelops* is similar to a duck (νήττῃ μέν ἐστιν ὅμοιον), but larger, though the same scholia claim that it is about the size of a pigeon (περιστερή). Penelops is listed with geese and sheldrake by Aristotle in *Historia Animalium* 593b23. The sheldrake (χηναλώπηξ) is a species of duck, but it is goose-like in appearance and was seen as a goose by the Greeks. Aristophanes (*Birds* 1302) also lists it next to the goose.

[6] *Historia Animalium* 593b23.

[7] For several divergent interpretations, all of which agree on the importance of Penelope's grief, see e.g, Rankin 1962: 617–624, Russo 1992:103, Pratt 1994:149–151, Heitman 2005:73–75, Rozokoki 2001:2–3.

[8] Kretschmer 1945:80–93.

[9] Aristotle, *Historia Animalium* 488b23, *Anthologia Palatina* 7.425.7.

[10] In discussing the poetic relevance of Penelope's geese I rely on Pratt 1994.

assumption is not justified: the *penelops* shares a trait or perhaps several traits with geese, (both are water birds, for example), but that is not the same as being one.

Poetic references to the *penelops* are as scarce as prosaic ones, but they are also interestingly different and more useful for interpreting Penelope's name. Of particular interest are two fragments of lyric poetry, which I cite in full:

> ὄρνιθες τίνες οἴδ' Ὠκεάνω γᾶς ἀπὺ πειράτων
> ἦλθον πανέλοπες ποικιλόδειροι τανυσίπτεροι;
>
> (Alcaeus 345 LP)[11]

What are these birds that came from the ends of the earth,
long-winged *penelopes* with varied song?

> τοῦ μὲν πετάλοσιν ἐπ' ἀκροτάτοις
> ἵζάνοισι ποικίλαι αἰολόδειροι
> πανέλοπες ἁλιπορφυρίδες <τε> καὶ
> ἀλκυόνες τανυσίπτεροι.
>
> (Ibycus PMG 317a)[12]

On its topmost branches
perch many-colored glittering-voiced
penelopes, gleaming like the sea,
and long-winged halcyons.

The Ibycus fragment comes from a corrupt and obscure passage in Athenaeus's *Deipnosophistae*, where it is cited in unmetrical form.[13] The meter can be corrected without significantly altering the syntax of the passage; the resulting word order, accepted in most modern editions, is the one cited here. But the most difficult problem of the fragment is the manuscript reading αδοιπορφυρίδες, which seems to the editors to be meaningless. Here I choose the reconstructed reading ἁλιπορφυρίδες, 'gleaming or flashing like (or in?)

---

[11] For a justification of 'with varied-[sounding] throat' as a translation of ποικιλόδειρος see Nagy 1996:59 n1, following Irwin 1974:72–73.

[12] For a remark on the translation of αἰολόδειρος see below, p294.

[13] Athenaeus 9.388d. The manuscript reading of the fragment is: τοῦ μὲν πετάλοισιν ἐπ' ἀκροτάτοις (Π ἐπακροτάτοισι) ξανθοῖσι (B ξανθίαι) ποικίλαι πανέλοπες αἰολόδειροι αδοιπορφυρίδες (B ἀδ.) καὶ ἀλκύονες τανυσίπτεροι.

the sea', suggested by Schneidewin (and accepted by Hermann and by D'Arcy Thompson).[14]

In the Ibycus fragment *penelopes* are mentioned together with halcyons, and the two birds also come together in Aristophanes' *Birds*:

οὑτοσὶ δὲ πηνέλοψ· ἐκεινοσὶ δέ γ' ἀλκυών.

(*Birds* 298)

This one here is a *penelops*, that one there is a halcyon.

Given the scarcity of references to the *penelops*, it is important that in two of them it is mentioned together with the halcyon. If the *penelops* has traits in common with the goose, it also appears to have something in common with the halcyon. And in fact while dictional links between the *penelops* and geese seem lacking, it does share with the halcyon the epithets ποικίλος, 'of varied color', τανυσίπτερος, 'long-winged', and ἀλιπορφυρίς – if this reading should be restored in Ibycus. This restoration is important because ἀλιπόρφυρος is a fairly rare adjective that is, however, consistently used of the halcyon and birds closely related to it, for example the κηρύλος, whose name Thompson defines as "a doubtful, perhaps foreign, word, sometimes applied to the Halcyon, sometimes compared with it."[15] Sometimes the *kerulos* is regarded as the male counterpart of the halcyon, as seems to be the case in the following fragment of Alcman:

οὔ μ' ἔτι, παρσενικαὶ μελιγάρυες ἱαρόφωνοι,
γυῖα φέρην δύναται· βάλε δή, βάλε κηρύλος εἴην
ὅς τ' ἐπὶ κύματος ἄνθος ἅμ' ἀλκυόνεσσι ποτῆται
ἀδεὲς ἦτορ ἔχων ἀλιπόρφυρος εἴαρος ὄρνις.[16]

(Alcman PMG 26)

---

[14] Schneidewin, 128–131 and Hermann as quoted by Bergk *Poetae Lyrici Graeci* 239 (on Ibycus 8 [13]), Thompson 1936:46.

[15] Thompson 1936:139. In the list of birds in Aristophanes' *Birds*, quoted above, *kerulos* is mentioned immediately after the halcyon (*Birds* 299): Πε. τίς γάρ ἐσθ' οὔπισθεν αὐτῆς; | Ευ. ὅστις ἐστί; κηρύλος. Note also that the halcyon is female in this passage.

[16] I retain the reading εἴαρος in the last line although most modern editions, including the PMG, adopt Hecker's emendation to ἱαρός, 'sacred'. The halcyon, however, is specifically associated with winter solstice, which may be regarded as the beginning of spring (see below), and it seems reasonable that *kerulos* should share this association. The reading εἴαρος is attested unanimously by the three ancient sources to quote the verse: Antigonus of Carystus *Historia Mirabilium* 23.1, Athenaeus 9.16 and Photius (*Lexicon* s.v. ὄρνις). In the beginning of the same line Photius has ἀδεὲς, Antigonus νηλεές. I opt for the former, because it is easier to understand, though the latter is perhaps to be seen as the *lectio difficilior*. I am puzzled by the

291

No longer, o honey-toned holy-voiced maidens,
can my limbs carry me. If only I could be a *kerulos*,
who flies over the bloom of the waves together with the
halcyons, having a fearless heart, the sea-shining bird of
spring.

Identified with *kerulos* as a male halcyon is another seabird, κῆυξ or κῆξ, whose name, clearly onomatopoeic, also imitates the cry of the female halcyon.[17] The *keux* is a seagull or tern, according to D'Arcy Thompson,[18] who describes the name as a "vague, poetic, and even legendary word . . . hardly used as a concrete and specific bird-name." I suggest that, as a poetic concept, the *penelops* belongs to the same group of birds as the *kerulos*, the *keux*, and the halcyon. The *penelops* appears alongside the halcyon in poetry (as opposed to natural history), shares epithets with it, and, like the halcyon, lives at sea. This last bit of information about the *penelops*, the only specific thing Aristotle says about it, is confirmed by Alcaeus 345, where the *penelopes* come not simply from the sea, but from the very ends of the earth and the Okeanos. Here, the *penelopes* seem to be envisaged as a kind of seabird that flies far over the water and rarely sees shore, and in that too it is similar to the halcyon. Not only does the halcyon fly over the waves, as in Alcman, but it famously even nests at sea.[19]

Among the fabulous birds of Greek mythology the halcyon has a fair claim to first place, so much legendary and mysterious information is associated with it, but for the moment I will only point out two features that are relevant for discussion of the *penelops* and the *Odyssey*. First, halcyons are known for their mournful song, often described as a lament (θρῆνος): a song of a female who has lost her mate. For example, here is how the halcyon is described by Dionysius:

---

editorial preference (Page, PMG 26) for the conjectural νηδεές (Boissonade), since this is not a word attested elsewhere, while both ἀδεές, and νηλεές are metrically unobjectionable and make sense.

[17] Scholia on Lucian 1.178.

[18] Thompson 1936.22.

[19] The main sources on the halcyon's nest are Aristotle *Historia Animalium* 524b4, Aelian 9.17, Dionysius *De Avibus* 2.7 and Plutarch *On the intelligence of animals* 35 (959a–985c). For further references and comments see Thompson 1966:48. Plutarch's description of the halcyon's nest is especially relevant for what follows because he reports that the nest is constructed of artfully interwoven thorns without any binding materials, and compares the process to weaving and the result to Apollo's famous horn altar on Delos, also constructed without any binding.

ἀλκυών· εἰ τὸν ἄρρενα τελευτῆσαι συμβαίη, βορᾶς ἀπεχόμεναι
καὶ ποτοῦ ἐπὶ πολὺ θρηνοῦσι καὶ διαφθείρονται, καὶ τὰς ᾠδὰς δ' εἰ
καταπαύειν μέλλοιεν, κήυξ κήυξ συνεχῶς ἐπειποῦσαι σιγῶσιν.

(Dionysius *De Avibus* 2.7)

Halcyon: if the male chances to die, the females lament for a long
time and perish, abstaining from food and drink. And if they are
about to leave off singing, they utter "keux, keux" at frequent inter-
vals and then fall silent.

Second, because of this song as well as other features, the halcyon is often
compared to the nightingale. In fact, D'Arcy Thompson observes that ἀλκυών
and ἀηδών are easily confused.[20] For example, different manuscripts of
Aristotle's *Historia Animalium* 8.593b9 give either ἀλκυών or ἀηδών. The Suda
lists ἀλκυών between ἀηδών and κήυξ as θαλάσσια ζῷα, 'marine animals'.[21]
And, most strikingly, there is a version of the Itylus-myth, recorded by Boios,
where the mother of Aedon-nightingale is transformed into a halcyon.[22]

The voice of the halcyon is often described in the same terms as the
voice of the nightingale, as sweet (ἡδύς), as shrill or clear (λιγύς), and also
by a variety of adjectives with the underlying meaning 'mourning', (e.g.
πολύθρηνος, πολύδακρυς), as in the following passages:

τῶν ἀλκυόνων δ' οὐκ εἴποι τις εἰς φωνὴν ὄρνεον ἥδιον.

(Dionysius *De Avibus* 2.7)

No one could name a bird with a sweeter voice than the halcyon.

πάντη δ' ὀρνίθων γενεὴ λιγύφωνον ἀείδει,
ἀλκυόνες περὶ κῦμα, χελιδόνες ἀμφὶ μέλαθρα,
κύκνος ἐπ' ὄχθαισιν ποταμοῦ, καὶ ὑπ' ἄλσος ἀηδών.

(*Anthologia Palatina* 9.363.16–18)

---

[20] Thompson 1936.22.
[21] Suda s.v. Ἡμερινὰ ζῷα.
[22] Antoninus Liberalis 11. According to Antoninus Liberalis and Athenaeus (9.49), Boios is the
author of the Ὀρνιθογονία, '*Origin of Birds*', but there is some confusion about his identity. Some
scholars think that the name is a re-interpretation of Boio, the name of an ancient Delphic
priestess, to whom the Ὀρνιθογονία is apparently attributed by the antiquarian Philochorus
(4-3 century BCE). See RE s.v. Boio.

The whole race of birds sings in clear voices,
halcyons over the waves, swallows around houses,
swans on the river banks, and the nightingale in groves.

θαλαττία τις ὄρνις . . . πολύθρηνος καὶ πολύδακρυς, περὶ ἧς
    δὴ παλαιὸς
ἀνθρώποις μεμύθευται λόγος.

(Lucian *Halcyon* 1)

A kind of sea bird . . . much-lamenting and of many tears, about
which there is an old story among men.

In descriptions of the nightingale, epithets referring to the bird's song
often merge with those referring to its appearance. For example, in *Works
and Days* (203) it is called ποικιλόδειρος, 'with varied throat', and Nagy has
argued that this word refers not to the color of the bird's neck but to its
variegated (ποικίλος) song, in this sense being synonymous with another
epithet ποικιλόγηρυς, 'with varied voice', which is given by the scholia
to the same passage.[23] Another interesting epithet of the nightingale is
αἰολόδειρος (Nonnus 47.33), which probably stands in the same relation-
ship to αἰολόφωνος, 'shifting in sound', as ποικιλόδειρος to ποικιλόγηρυς.
Liddell and Scott translate αἰολόδειρος as 'with sheeny neck', but there is
more to the epithet: αἰόλος means 'swift, rapid, changeable', and by exten-
sion 'changeful of hue, glittering', so that the word could refer not only to
the bird's color, but also to its voice, which in the case of the nightingale is
more justifiable.

It is through these characteristic epithets that the nightingale is linked
not only with the halcyon, but, more interestingly, with the *penelops*. The
penelops is described as ποικιλόδειρος in Alcaeus' fragment and αἰολόδειρος
in that of Ibycus, where it is also ποικίλος – yet another epithet connecting it
with the halcyon.[24]

Moreover, in Ibycus' fragment *penelopes* and halcyons are represented
as sitting πετάλοισιν ἐπ' ἀκροτάτοις, 'on the topmost leaves', literally 'petals',
a *topos* about the nightingale, who sings δενδρέων ἐν πετάλοισι καθεζομένη
πυκινοῖσι, 'sitting in the dense leaves (petals) of the trees' in the *Odyssey*
(19.520). This might seem unremarkable, since many birds sit in trees, but in
fact only particular creatures sit 'on the petals'. In the whole of Greek poetry

---

[23] Nagy 1996:59 n1.
[24] Simonides PMG 508 = Aristotle *Historia Animalium* 542b4.

outside of the Ibycus fragment, this expression is applied only to the nightingale, the swallow, the sparrow, the cuckoo and the cicada, and only about the nightingale is it used repeatedly.[25] In every case, the image is that of a small and fragile creature, whose delicacy is matched by the delicacy of petals in which it hides.[26] And without exception, the creatures who sit 'in the petals' sing in a voice that is like the nightingale's in its mournful tone. The swallow in Aristophanes' *Frogs* (682) 'twitters the tearful nightingale song' (τρύζει δ' ἐπίκλαυτον ἀηδόνιον νόμον), the cicada in Alcaeus 347a LP 'laments out of the petals' (ἄχει δ' ἐκ πετάλων), and the sparrow in the *Iliad* (2.315) flies around her nest 'bewailing her dear children' (ὀδυρομένη φίλα τέκνα), reminding one of the nightingale in the *Odyssey* (19.522), who sings 'mourning her dear son Itylos' (παῖδ' ὀλοφυρομένη Ἴτυλον φίλον). The nightingale, about whom the expression ἐν πετάλοισι, 'among the leaves/petals', is used most often, is *par excellence* the tiny bird with a musical voice, the main manifestation of a poetic figure of which the sparrow, the swallow, and even the cicada can be seen as variations.[27] The *penelopes* and the halcyons who sit πετάλοισι ἐπ' ἀκροτάτοις, 'on the topmost petals', in the Ibycus fragment are presented in the light of the same theme. Here, then, we see the nightingale, the halcyon, and the *penelops* linked by poetic associations. It would be contrary to the poetic diction of the Ibycus fragment to see the *penelops* here as a duck or a goose: in Greek poetry as much as in actuality, it is unusual for many ducks or geese to sit even on trees, not to mention leaves or petals.

It is probably not an accident, however, that the kingfisher, identified early on with the halcyon, is an exception among the water birds: only slightly larger than the sparrow, this bird lives on tree-covered banks of rivers and lakes and has a habit of sitting on the tips of slender branches which project over the water, and diving off them.[28] On the other hand, if the *penelops* is indeed similar to the halcyon, it is not entirely surprising that sometimes it

---

[25] *Odyssey* 19.520, *Homeric Hymn* 19.17–18, *Anthologia Palatina* 12.2.3, 12.136.3.

[26] The only bird noticeably larger than a nightingale or a sparrow who is said to sit ἐν πετάλοισι is the cuckoo in *Works and Days* 486, and it is interesting that only here the expression is qualified: δρυὸς ἐν πετάλοισι, 'in oak leaves': a larger bird calls for sturdier 'petals'. Note also that the cuckoo is also a bird with a remarkable voice, sometimes seen as a voice of lament in the Greek poetic tradition. Cf. Alexiou's list of birds who join the lamentation in Greek folk songs: cuckoo, halcyon, nightingale, swallow, turtledove (Alexiou 1974:93–97).

[27] That the creatures who can sit in the petals do form a recognizable group is confirmed, for example, by the corresponding perception of Joannes Chrysostomus (In *Acta Apostolorum* 60.61.16): εἴ τις δὲ καὶ ἠχὴ γένοιτο, λιγυρὰ καὶ πολλὴν καταχέουσα τῶν ἀκουόντων τὴν ἡδονήν. Ἡ γὰρ ὄρνιθες ᾠδικοὶ ἄκροις τῶν δένδρων ἐφιζάνουσι τοῖς πετάλοις, καὶ τέττιγες, καὶ ἀηδόνες, καὶ χελιδόνες, συμφώνως μίαν τινὰ ἀποτελοῦσι μουσικήν ...

[28] Thompson 1936:46–47.

should be grouped with geese. The halcyon is both a water bird and a bird of lament. As a bird of lament, it is similar to the nightingale. But as a water bird, the halcyon can be grouped with geese, perhaps especially because of its proverbial faithfulness. Water birds in general are often seen as faithful and affectionate mates – a perception based on their actual behavior. If the same two possibilities were open to the *penelops,* this may explain why this bird, nightingale-like in poetry, is listed among geese in Aristotle.

From the meager evidence we have it appears that the *penelops* shares most of its features with the halcyon. This may be an impression created by the scarcity of our information. On the other hand, the halcyon also gives its name to several female mythological characters, and the remarkable fact is that the best known of these Alkyones is quite similar to Penelope. The story of Alkyone and her husband Keyx was told in the Hesiodic *Ehoiai,* but the papyrus evidence is so fragmentary that virtually only the names are left. Later sources, however, are unanimous on two points: that Keyx is either lost or dead, and that Alkyone remains faithful, waits for a long time, and laments for her husband until both are transformed into birds. In other words, the central fact of the Alkyone and Keyx myth is their unwavering loyalty to each other, very much reminiscent of Odysseus and Penelope.

Moreover, in both cases there is a negative side effect to this loyalty, namely its tendency to provoke jealousy in the gods. In early versions of the Alkyone and Keyx myth, the couple grows too proud of their harmonious union and this becomes their undoing: they boast that they love each other more than Zeus and Hera, are punished for that, and finally are turned into birds.[29] There is, needless to say, no such impious boast in the *Odyssey,* since that would be incompatible with the eventual happy reunion of the couple. But there is a hint at the same theme. Penelope does at one point remark to Odysseus that the gods were jealous of their happiness as a married couple:

> θεοὶ δ' ὤπαζον ὀϊζύν,
> οἳ νῶϊν ἀγάσαντο παρ' ἀλλήλοισι μένοντε
> ἥβης ταρπῆναι καὶ γήραος οὐδὸν ἱκέσθαι.

> (*Odyssey* 23.210–212)

> But the gods gave us sorrow,
> they begrudged us enjoyment of our youth by each other's side,
> and reaching the threshold of old age.

---

[29] Hesiod fr. 10d MW.

Like Alkyone and Keyx, Penelope and Odysseus are a perfect match and content with each other, perhaps too content, Penelope seems to say, enough to arouse the jealousy of the gods. In both cases the happy couple is separated, the husband goes away and disappears, (temporarily in one myth, forever in the other), and the lonely wife, ever faithful, laments in his absence. The similarity between the two myths and the two women with bird-names indicates that the similarity between the birds who give them these names is also not an illusion. Each parallel is interesting in itself but they acquire a different weight in combination, and it is the combination that suggests that cognate myth-making patterns are here at work.

Further, there is an echo of the divine jealousy theme in a version of the Aedon story, thus bringing together all three related bird-women. This version, told only by Antoninus Liberalis (11), has been largely excluded from the discussion of the myth on the grounds that it is late, possibly Hellenistic, and composite. And so it is no doubt, but it is interesting nevertheless to observe what this story is composed of. The main elements of the story are largely the same as in the Attic myth: two sisters (named Aedon and Khelidon), the rape of Khelidon by Aedon's husband, the killing of the child. The husband, however, is not Tereus as in the Athenian version, but one Polytekhnos, the father is Pandareos rather than Pandion (as in the *Odyssey*); the setting is Asia Minor, and there are several features of the story that are unique. Aedon and Polytekhnos commit the same mistake as Alkyone and Keyx did: they claim that they love each other more than Zeus and Hera. Angry Hera takes vengeance by inciting the couple to a competition as to who will finish first, Aedon weaving a fabric or Polytekhnos making a chariot. When Aedon wins, Polytekhnos retaliates by raping her sister. The two women then plan the usual revenge: they kill Itys, cook him, and serve his flesh to Polytekhnos before their flight. Then they flee back to their parents in Ephesos. When Polytekhnos pursues them, he is captured by Pandareos and his attendants and bound and subjected to a strange punishment: his body is smeared with honey and he is tied to a tree to be tormented by flies. Aedon, however, pities him – a feature completely absent from all versions of the Athenian story – and chases away the flies. In the end, of course, the whole family is turned into birds. It may be that the Ephesian Aedon story in Antoninus Liberalis is influenced by the story of Alkyone and Keyx, but even if so, the very fact that the two myths are susceptible to such a combination is noteworthy because it confirms the long-standing connectedness of Alkyone and Aedon, halcyon and nightingale, and also their mutual connection to Penelope, a character reminiscent of Alkyone who compares herself to Aedon. Or it may be that in Aedon and Polytekhnos we have yet another independent but cognate couple to add to Alkyone and Keyx and Penelope and Odysseus. In any case, it seems that, different though they are, all these myths in some way belong together, just as the two versions of the Aedon myth belong together.

In what may or may not be a strange coincidence, one detail of Liberalis' myth is actually reminiscent not only of the other versions of the Aedon myth, or of Alkyone and Keyx, but rather of Penelope and Odysseus. Like Penelope, this Aedon is a weaver, and like Odysseus who builds a raft to sail from Kalypso's island and a house on Ithaca with its tree-bed, Polytekhnos is a master-carpenter, whose very name brings to mind Odysseus' characteristic epithets such as *polutropos* and *polumetis*.

This detail suggests that the story of Aedon and Polytekhnos is not just a mixture of Alkyone and Keyx with the better known Aedon myth, but contains features not attributable to either, which makes it look very much like an independent myth. The fact that a myth with such a mixture of features could exist and that some of its idiosyncrasies are reminiscent of Odysseus and Penelope suggests yet again that all three mythological couples are in some way related. An extreme fidelity is always a part of the Alkyone and Keyx story (as it is of the halcyon myth) and it is also the cardinal feature for Penelope, but it is optional for Aedon. Penelope and Alkyone are thus closer to each other than to Aedon, though all three share important features, and can influence each other. In all three myths, there is a disruption or a breakdown of marriage, and in all cases the women, and birds, lament. Alkyone is left without a husband (and consequently offspring), Aedon without a son, and Penelope is threatened with losing both.

By the same token, it seems that the *penelops* and halcyon are more similar to each other than to the nightingale, yet here too there are persistent associations linking all three birds.

Furthermore, the association between the *penelops* and the halcyon goes beyond the themes of fidelity and lament. To follow its ramifications it is necessary to consider a striking feature of the *penelopes* in the Alcaeus fragment, the fact that they come from the banks of the Okeanos and the ends of the earth (Ὠκεάνω γᾶς ἀπὺ πειράτων). This detail does not seem to be accidental, since Pliny mentions the *penelopes* in a similar near-Oceanic habitat:

> Mnases Africae locum Sicyonem appellat et Crathin amnem in
> oceanum effluentem e lacu, in quo aves, quas meleagridas et penel-

opas vocat, vivere; ibi nasci [sc. electrum] ratione eadem qua supra dictum est.

(Pliny *Natural History* 37.11)

Mnases mentions Sicyon, a place in Africa, and the river Crathis, which flows into the Ocean out of a lake, in which there live birds, called *meleagrides* and *penelopes*. It is said that amber arises there in the same way as described above.

Although the lake in Pliny's passage is in Africa, it is connected by a water-way to the Ocean, and bears amber, a substance generally associated with the sun and consequently with places such as the edges of the Ocean, where the sun sets and rises. In the same chapter Pliny mentions another lake where amber drips from poplar trees into the water, and this lake is situated in the extreme West, near the garden of the Hesperides. Pliny also mentions the myth of the sisters of Phaethon, who, after their brother is struck down by Zeus, are turned into poplars and forever mourn his death, dropping their tears into the waters of the Eridanos, (which is mythologically identified with Okeanos).[30] The tears become amber. According to Pliny, this tale of amber's origins is first mentioned by Aeschylus, who calls the river not Eridanos, but Rhodanos, and places it in Spain.[31] The same myth is alluded to by Euripides in the *Hippolytus*:

ἠλιβάτοις ὑπὸ κευθμῶσι γενοίμαν
ἵνα με πτερούσαν ὄρνιν
θεὸς ἐν ποταναῖς
    ἀγέλαις θείη·
ἀρθείην δ' ἐπὶ πόντιον
κύμα τᾶς Ἀδριηνᾶς
ἀκτᾶς Ἠριδανοῦ θ' ὕδωρ
ἔνθα πορφύρεον σταλάσ-
    σουσ' εἰς οἶδμα τάλαιναι
κόραι Φαέθοντος οἴκτῳ δακρύων
τὰς ἠλεκτροφαεῖς αὐγάς.

(Euripides, *Hippolytus* 732–740)

---

[30] Nagy 1992:236–239.

[31] Pliny is quick to debunk the Greek notion that amber is to be found in the Eridanus, or that there are islands in the Adriatic known as "Electrides" because the amber is carried there by the water. He concludes that the Greek poets are terribly ignorant both of amber and of geography (*Natural History* 37.11).

If only I were in the hidden hollows of the rocks,
where a god might turn me into
a winged bird among the flying flocks.
If only I could fly over the
waves of the Adriatic coast
and over the water of the Eridanos,
where the unhappy girls lament for Phaethon and
drip the amber-gleaming rays of their tears
into the glittering swell of water.

The myth of Phaethon is, of course, full of solar themes since Phaethon is Helios' son, and is driving his father's chariot when he dies and falls into the streams of Eridanos, (an image that seems to be a parallel to the sun's setting into Okeanos). In keeping with the solar theme, Phaethon's sisters are turned into amber-producing trees. In Sophocles, a similar fate befalls Meleager's sisters: according to Pliny, Sophocles located them in countries beyond India, in other words, in the far East rather than the far West, and instead of turning into trees they are turned into birds, but like Phaethon's sisters they eternally shed tears, which become amber.[32] Meleager's sisters are turned into *meleagrides*, the birds that share Mnases' amber-bearing lake with *penelopes*. *Meleagrides*, in other words, have a reason for swimming in the amber lake, and presumably so do *penelopes*. If *penelopes* come from the ends of the earth in Alcaeus and are set in a typical ends-of-the-earth solar landscape in Mnases, this suggests that there was an association between the *penelops* and the ends of the earth, and this association probably had something to do with the sun. If so, a connection to this bird would not be amiss for a heroine of the *Odyssey*.

It hardly needs pointing out that solar themes occupy an important place in the *Odyssey*. Indeed, it has been argued, convincingly in my opinion, that Odysseus' return as a whole follows a solar model, complete with travel across the waters of Okeanos to the land of the dead, and back. Nagy puts it as follows:

---

[32] It is noteworthy that the solar theme is present in both cases, since the life of Meleager himself is inextricably joined with fire of the hearth, and thus with the theme of the celestial fire. Nagy (1992:148–150) suggests that Greek words for dawn (Ionic ἠώς/Aeolic αὔως) and for hearth (ἑστία) ultimately go back to the same root meaning 'shine' and observes that "the semantic connection between the macrocosm of dawn and the microcosm of the sacrificial fireplace is explicit in the *Rig-Veda*, where the coming of the dawn is treated as an event parallel to the simultaneous kindling of the sacrificial fire." Pliny (*Natural History* 37.11) is amusingly outraged by the notion that so respectable a character as Sophocles could entertain a notion that amber is produced (and in large quantities) from birds' tears.

In fact, the entire plot of Odysseus' travels is interlaced with diction that otherwise denotes the theme of sunset followed by sunrise. To put it more bluntly, the epic plot of the *Odyssey* operates on an extended solar metaphor.[33]

This solar metaphor has as its foundation the basic notion of death and rebirth of the sun, sunset and sunrise. Sunset is described as plunging into the waters of Okeanos (*Iliad* 8.485, *Odyssey* 20.63–65) and also as going underneath the earth to the land of the dead, sunrise as rising from the Okeanos (*Iliad* 7.421–423, *Odyssey* 19.433–434). Moreover, it seems that sun symbolism even played a role in the etymological development of the root *nes- and its derivatives, including *nostos*, a word which arguably captures the central theme of the *Odyssey*. As Frame has shown, this word means fundamentally a "return to light and life," in other words a return that is simultaneously a rebirth, such as that of the sun.[34] Solar symbolism is to be found in many episodes of Odysseus' *apologoi*, including the Cyclops, Circe, Kikones and Laestrygonians, and also, of course, the crucial episode on the island of Helios. This episode, moreover, was felt to be thematically so important as to be mentioned in the proem, alone of all Odysseus' adventures at sea. There is no need to elaborate further on this point.[35]

The Oceanic regions, apparently frequented by *penelopes*, also play an important role in the *Odyssey*, and not only in Odysseus' wanderings. In *Odyssey* 24, the souls of the suitors are led by Hermes to the underworld and pass the stream of Okeanos, a landmark called Leukas Petre, 'the white rock', the gates of the sun, and the district of dreams. The mythical Leukas Petre has its topographical equivalent in a number of places in Greece: prominent rocks on the coastline that are called by the same name, Leukas. The most famous of them, Cape Leukas (Strabo 10.2.9), had a ritual connected with it: leaping from its top into the sea was believed to be a cure for love. According to Menander, Sappho jumped off it for the love of Phaon.[36] But the first to jump was Aphrodite herself, out of love for Adonis.[37] Nagy argues that the rock at Cape Leukas is a topographical analogue to the mythical white rock in *Odyssey* 24, and the

---

[33] Nagy 1990:225, and more generally 223–262.

[34] Frame 1978:1–33.

[35] See Frame 1978:34–80, and Cook 1995:15–48 on the proem and the role of the episode of the Cattle of the Sun in it.

[36] Menander F 258 K. The concept of the White Rock is discussed in detail by Nagy 1990:224–235. On Phaon's solar aspect see Nagy 1990:235 (like Phaethon, the name Phaon means 'bright'). See also below for more on this point.

[37] According to Ptolemaios Chennos, in Photius, *Bibliotheca* 152–153.

plunge from it is related to the sun's plunge into the Okeanos. This plunge is symbolic of leaving the realm of the day. Taken to the extreme, this plunge means death, but can also mean unconsciousness, forgetfulness, and sexual release.[38] Symbolic implications of death and rebirth are present both in the myths associated with Cape Leukas and in the ritual associated with it, about which more will be said later. For now, suffice it to say that the white rock, in the *Odyssey* and elsewhere, marks the boundary between life and death envisaged specifically in terms of the solar plunge into the waters of Okeanos.

All of this brings me back to the halcyon and one of its most distinctive features, namely its habit of vertical diving. I am not the first to suspect that the vertical plunge of diving birds such as the halcyon is thematically parallel not only to jumping off the white rock, but also to the solar plunge into the waters of Okeanos.[39] Birds had a role to play in the yearly ritual at Cape Leukas, as described by Strabo,[40] since every year a criminal would be cast off the rock 'for the aversion of evil', (ἀποτροπῆς χάριν), and wings and even birds would be tied to him. In myth, bird-transformations often go together with leaps into the sea. In a myth reported by the Suda, for example, seven daughters of the giant Alkyoneus after their father's death throw themselves into the sea off a headland. Out of pity, Amphitrite turns them into birds and calls them, in memory of their father, Ἀλκυόνες, 'the halcyons'.[41] Alkyone, the wife of Keyx, leaps off a jetty and is also transformed into a halcyon. In Boios, Aedon's mother, after turning into a halcyon, immediately wants to dive into the sea.[42]

The halcyon, moreover, has much to do with notions of death and rebirth and with solar symbolism. Alkyone was the principal star in the constellation of Pleiades, whose rising movement ancient astronomers connected with the increase of daylight in spring, and which had special significance as indicators of seasonal change, especially times of planting, harvesting, and sailing.[43] The Suda says that the Pleiades were called Ἀλκυόνες.[44] But the central part of the halcyon lore is, of course, the ancient notion of the "halcyon days," during which the halcyon supposedly builds its nest and lays its eggs at sea. Aristotle says that the halcyon reproduces at the time of the winter solstice, and that

---

[38] For relations between love, sleep and death in Greek poetics see Vermeule 1979:145–178.
[39] Gresseth 1964:95 (quoted below).
[40] Strabo 10.2.9.
[41] Suda, s.v. Ἀλκυονίδες ἡμέραι.
[42] In Antoninus Liberalis 11.
[43] West 1978:253-255 with references.
[44] s.v. Ἀλκυονίδες ἡμέραι.

the "halcyon days" consists of seven days of calm weather before the solstice, when the mother bird makes her nest, and seven days after the solstice, when she lays the eggs and sees them hatch.[45] Simonides, quoted by Aristotle, also refers to fourteen days of calm, a sacred period when the halcyon rears her young:

> ὡς ὁπόταν
> χειμέριον κατὰ μῆνα πινύσκηι
> Ζεὺς ἤματα τέσσερα καὶ δέκα,
> λαθάνεμον δέ μιν ὥραν
> καλέουσιν ἐπιχθόνιοι
> ἱερὰν παιδοτρόφον ποικίλας
> ἀλκυόνος.

(PMG 508)

> as when,
> in a winter month,
> Zeus makes a calm for a fortnight,
> the season that knows not wind
> the earth-dwellers call it,
> the sacred season of child-rearing for the variegated
> halcyon.

The mysterious period when the halcyon builds her nest, which is supposed to be floating at sea, is preceded by equally mysterious interaction between the male and female birds. In the fragment of Alcman quoted further above (Alcman PMG 26), the poet wishes to be like a *kerulos* who flies above the waves with the halcyons. Antigonus of Carystus, who quotes these lines in his *Historia mirabilium*, explains that the *kerylos* is a male halcyon and that when he becomes old and weak the female supports and carries him on her wings.[46] This is, of course, an example of the famous devotion of the female to her mate, a feature that is closely tied to her lament once the male is dead. Plutarch, commenting on the halcyon's *philandria*, says that the female remains with the male throughout the year like a wedded wife, and when he becomes too weak to fly, carries him, feeds him, and remains with him to the end:

---

[45] *Historia Animalium* 8.542b4.
[46] *Historia Mirabilium* 23.8.

φίλανδρος μὲν οὕτως ἐστίν, ὥστε μὴ καθ' ἕνα καιρὸν ἀλλὰ δι'
ἔτους συνεῖναι καὶ προσδέχεσθαι τὴν τοῦ ἄρρενος ὁμιλίαν, οὐ
διὰ τὸ ἀκόλαστον (ἄλλῳ γὰρ οὐ μίγνυται τὸ παράπαν) ἀλλ' ὑπ'
εὐνοίας ὥσπερ γυνὴ γαμετὴ καὶ φιλοφροσύνης· ὅταν δὲ διὰ
γῆρας ἀσθενὴς ὁ ἄρρην γένηται συνέπεσθαι καὶ βαρύς, ὑπολαβοῦσα
γηροφορεῖ καὶ γηροτροφεῖ, μηδαμοῦ προϊεμένη μηδὲ καταλείπουσα
χωρίς, ἀλλὰ τοῖς ὤμοις ἐκεῖνον ἀναθεμένη καὶ κομίζει πανταχόσε
καὶ θεραπεύει καὶ σύνεστιν ἄχρι τελευτῆς.

(Plutarch *On the intelligence of animals* 983a)

She is so devoted to her mate that she stays with him and accepts
his company not only for the breeding season but throughout the
year, not on account of intemperance (for she has no intercourse at
all with any other), but out of love and friendliness, like a married
wife. And when the male becomes too weak and heavy to fly with
her because of old age, she picks him up and carries and feeds him
in his old age, never letting him fall or leaving him behind, but
instead she puts him on her shoulders and takes him everywhere
and attends to him and stays with him until the end.

Immediately after this comment, Plutarch turns from the halcyon's wifely
loyalty to her care for her offspring, saying that as soon as the female halcyon
perceives that she is pregnant she constructs her remarkable floating nest,
woven out of spikes so tightly and perfectly fitted together that it can hardly
be destroyed, even by stone or iron. The male is never mentioned again, and
the impression is created that it is only after his death that the female turns
to nest-building, since the mates are apparently inseparable in life, and yet
the male is nowhere to be seen when it comes to raising the young. Gresseth
summarizes the order of events described in Plutarch, as follows: "The male
and female halcyon are constantly together through the course of a year; then
mysteriously but apparently quite regularly and in the natural course of their
lives the male, who has another name, grows weak, is fed and carried by his
mate, and finally dies. The female then turns her entire care to the birth and
protection of her offspring."[47] The male halcyon grows weak, but the female
does not, and the loving birds, instead of ageing together, seems to have vastly
different biological clocks. Nothing is said of the death of the female halcyon.

---

[47] Gresseth 1964:91.

Guessing what a myth is about is a hazardous activity, but it is possible to shed some light on its workings without attempting to unduly confine its meaning. To my mind, Gresseth's interpretation of the halcyon myth is the best one to date, and it does account for its major aspects and idiosyncrasies in a systematic way. Gresseth points out that in many cultures the sun is symbolized by a bird, and that birds in myth sometimes have the ability to renew themselves.[48] Relying both on the internal logic of the Greek myth and on comparative evidence, he suggests that the myth of the halcyon has to do with the rebirth of the sun at the time of the winter solstice. The equation of the halcyon with kingfisher would be easily understandable in this case, as Gresseth observes: "The kingfisher has bright sky-colored markings, for one thing; moreover, a further correspondence, which I think applies to my interpretation of this myth, is that the kingfisher plunges almost vertically into the sea and rises again, as mythologically does Helios in Ocean."[49]

This solar symbolism would also explain the strange, apparently yearly, weakening and death of the male halcyon, which would correspond to the weakening of the sun. Gresseth points out that there is an inconsistency here, since the sun, though weakened, cannot be said to die during winter, though it can be said to die at night. His suggestion is that perhaps the two cycles are somehow combined in the halcyon myth. Further, citing example of myths in which birds renew themselves, sometimes through contact with water, Gresseth suggest that in the pattern of the halcyon myth, (the death of male, followed by the female's laying of the egg), we have "a story of rebirth rather than one of death and birth."[50] He points out that the nest of the halcyon, which floats at sea unlike any actual bird's nest, means that the young halcyons will rise like the sun out of the water and concludes that the myth of the halcyon emerges, at least in part, as a "story of the birth or rebirth of the sun, symbolized as a bird, from his nest or floating island somewhere in the sea."[51] It seems that there is certainly some truth to this interpretation. The idea that the offspring of the halcyon are somehow the reborn husband, whom she will again mourn when he dies and bear again in a year's time, is remarkably reminiscent of the sun myth. In the *Rig Veda* the dawn-goddess Uṣas is both the wife or bride of the sun god and his mother.[52] As Nagy observes, the incestuous aspect of this arrangement is partially attenuated in Indic by

---

[48] Gresseth 1964:93–94 with references.
[49] Gresseth 1964:95.
[50] Gresseth 1964:98.
[51] Gresseth 1964:98.
[52] *Rig Veda* 1.115.1, 7.75.5, 7.63.3, 7.78.3. See Nagy 1990:246–247 on this point.

putting the dawn-goddess in the plural, so that each Dawn is the wife of the previous Dawn's son rather than her own. The attenuation is partial, however, because the husband and son is always the same, Surya, the sun. Gresseth was apparently unaware of the Indic evidence when he formulated his theory regarding the halcyon myth, but that makes the fact that he detected the same pattern all the more salient. Some of this pattern, of course, may be due to the naturalistic logic of the myth. In Nagy's words, "In the logic of the myth, it appears that the setting sun mates with the goddess of regeneration so that the rising sun may be reborn. If the setting sun is the same as the rising sun, then the goddess of regeneration may be viewed as both mate and mother."[53]

Such an overtly incestuous myth is nowhere to be found in Greek sources, but what can be found, and even in abundance, are myths that can be seen as derivatives of, and variations on, the fundamental solar pattern. The halcyon myth is only one example, but there are others that are of relevance to the *Odyssey*, and are indeed mentioned in the poem. Of particular interest is Nagy's investigation of the myth of Phaethon and its cognates, the myths in which a hero is abducted by a goddess.[54] In such myths, the hero is envisaged as carried away by a gust of wind (with the goddess being the ultimate agent of the action) and taken to the ends of the earth, where his fate can be alternatively imagined as death, immortalization, or both. The dynamics of the solar myth are often discernible in such abductions, and the goddesses who perform them can be said to continue in a function that, on the basis of Vedic comparative evidence, can be assigned to the dawn goddess. One victim of such abduction is none other than Phaethon, a hero with overt solar associations, who is the son of Helios in the best-known version of his myth and whose name is in fact an epithet of the sun.[55] In Hesiod's *Theogony*, however, Phaethon is not the son of Helios but rather of Eos, the dawn goddess, and instead of dying by falling into the Eridanos with his father's burning chariot, he is abducted by Aphrodite:

> τόν ῥα νέον τέρεν ἄνθος ἔχοντ' ἐρικυδέος ἥβης
> παῖδ' ἀταλὰ φρονέοντα φιλομμειδὴς Ἀφροδίτη

---

[53] Nagy 1990:246.

[54] Nagy 1990:242–255.

[55] Nagy 1990:235. φαέθων, meaning 'bright, shining' is an epithet of sun in Homer, part of the formulaic expression ἠέλιος φαέθων (*Iliad* 11.735, *Odyssey* 5.479, 11.16, 19.441, 22.388). Phaethon's story was probably told in the Hesiodic *Catalogue of Women* (Hyginus *Fabulae* 154 = Hesiod fr. 311 MW) and was dramatized by Aeschylus (*Heliades* fr. 68–73 R) and Euripides (*Phaethon* fr. 773–781 N). A version of the story is also preserved in the Scholia to *Odyssey* 17.208, with reference to unspecified tragedians.

ὦρτ' ἀνερειψαμένη, καί μιν ζαθέοις ἐνὶ νηοῖς
νηοπόλον μύχιον ποιήσατο, δαίμονα δῖον.

(*Theogony* 988–991)

When the tender flower of splendid youth was on him,
a child with tender thoughts, the smile-loving Aphrodite
snatched and carried him away and in her sacred shrine
made him a hidden temple attendant, a divine spirit.

Nagy suggests that the two different myths about Phaethon, one more overtly solar than the other, are nevertheless cognate and both center on "the inherited personification of a solar child and consort."[56] In the Hesiodic myth Aphrodite plays an ambiguous role. On the one hand, death is implied by her abduction of Phaethon, in particular by the use of the participle ἀνερειψαμένη (990), a verb used of abduction by the snatching winds, such as is envisaged by Penelope when she ostensibly prays for death in *Odyssey* 20 (ἀναρπάξασα θύελλα, 63). Similarly, Phaethon's epithet *mukhios*, 'hidden, innermost', implies the notion of death and the underworld, since Tartaros is described as hidden in the *mukhos*, 'the innermost place', of the earth at *Theogony* 119. On the other hand, in the Hesiodic myth Phaethon becomes a *daimon*, and that implies immortalization, and moreover the notion of preservation beyond death is implicit in his birth from the dawn goddess.

Nagy compares the combined role of Eos and Aphrodite in the Hesiodic Phaethon myth to the function of the Vedic Uṣas, who is both the mother and the consort of the sun, suggesting that, "the Hesiodic tradition seems to have split the earlier fused role of mother and consort and divided them between Eos and Aphrodite respectively."[57] Another similar abduction is that of Kleitos, who is abducted by Eos herself (*Odyssey* 15.250), and who, like Phaethon, has a genetic affinity to a solar figure, being the grandson of the seer Melampous.[58] As shown by Frame, the myth of Melampous centers on the theme of the cattle of the sun.[59] The myth of Kleitos, like that of Melampous, appears in the *Odyssey*, and surely not by accident, given Odysseus' own involvement with the cattle of the sun theme. Nagy analyzes the myth as follows:

The wording *herpasen* for the abduction of Kleitos at *Odyssey* 15.251 implies that he was taken by a maleficent Harpy and dropped into

---

[56] Nagy 1990:255.
[57] Nagy 1990:248–249.
[58] Melampous' story is told twice in the *Odyssey*: 15.225–255 and 11.287–297.
[59] Frame 1978:91–92.

Okeanos. This theme of death is parallel to sunset. On the other hand, the subject of *herpasen* is Eos herself, and the theme of sunrise is parallel to rebirth. Since the abductor of Kleitos is represented as the Dawn, it is at least implicit that Kleitos is to be reborn like the Sun and thus preserved.[60]

Aphrodite comes to share the function of Eos as both the abductor and preserver not only in the myth of Phaethon but also in that of Adonis, who is also said to be hidden by the goddess. It is out of love for Adonis that Aphrodite is said to leap off the White Rock, and Nagy argues that the idea of plunging Aphrodite may have been inspired by the Near Eastern association of the goddess with the planet Venus, also known as Hesperos, 'the evening star', and Heosphoros, 'the dawn-bearer'. In the evening, Venus (Hesperos) sets after the sun, appearing to follow it, and in the morning it rises before dawn (Heosphoros), appearing to lead the sun back. Nagy suggests that a similar logic governs Aphrodite's leap off the White Rock, in effect to bring back her lover. Certainly this is how the scholia to Hesiod imagine Aphrodite's function in the Phaethon myth: ὁ ἑῷος ἀστὴρ ὁ ἀνάγων τὴν ἡμέραν καὶ τὸν Φαέθοντα ἡ Ἀφροδίτη ἐστίν, 'Aphrodite is the dawn star which leads up the day and the Phaethon [Sun]'.[61]

Furthermore, Nagy argues that the same themes are expressed in the tale, presumably derived from Sappho's poetry, in which she too jumped off the White Rock, out of love for Phaon. In Nagy's words, "The 'I' of Sappho's poetry is vicariously projecting her identity into the goddess Aphrodite, who loves the native Lesbian hypostasis of the Sun-God himself."[62] Like Phaethon, Phaon attains a solar-like preservation, or rather rejuvenation in a myth attested in Sappho's poetry (Sappho fr. 211 Voigt): as an old man, Phaon ferries Aphrodite in the guise of an old woman across a strait of water and in gratitude the goddess restores to him youth and beauty.

It amounts to pointing out the obvious to say that the same themes find expression in the *Odyssey*. The poem is our earliest source for two of the abduction stories, that of Kleitos by Eos (*Odyssey* 15.250) and that of Orion, also by Eos (*Odyssey* 5.121). The latter story is told by Kalypso explicitly as a precedent for her own detention of Odysseus, and while Odysseus is not literally abducted, his relatives on Ithaca speak of him as if he is, using the verb ἀνερείπομαι, 'to snatch up and carry off', and imagining him blown away by the snatching

---

[60] Nagy 1990:252.
[61] Scholia to Hesiod *Theogony* 990.
[62] Nagy 1990:259.

winds.[63] Like the heroes who are in fact abducted, Odysseus is both hidden by Kalypso on her remote island and offered preservation, since the nymph plans to make him immortal (5.135–136). And arguably Odysseus does in the end achieve preservation, though not of the kind promised by Kalypso, because he, following the solar model, returns from the underworld to the land of the living. It has been argued, though certainty is hardly possible, that Arete, the queen of the Phaeacians whom Odysseus petitions for protection, can be seen as a female figure, in effect a surrogate mother, presiding over Odysseus' rebirth.[64]

Be that as it may, one point that can be derived from a survey of the solar myth and heroic abductions by the dawn goddess is the very notion of the solar consort who has a role to play in solar or solar-like return. Aphrodite's jump off the White Rock following Phaethon, or Sappho's following Phaon, can be seen as an act of despair or, alternatively, it can be seen, in effect, as a mission of rescue driven by love. In its starkest form, the logic of the myth is that the female consort brings back the solar hero by mating with him and allowing him to be reborn. In its literal form this scheme may apply only to the sun god himself, but its modification takes a parallel course. In the *Theogony*, Phaethon is not literally reborn, but, as Nagy observes, his preservation as Aphrodite's attendant and a *daimon* is expressed in terms of hero cult. As Nagy puts it, "If the hero is situated in a sacred precinct and if he is propitiated at set times, then he is being treated like a god and it follows that he must be like a god; thus he must be in some sense alive. From the standpoint of myth, he is explicitly dead, but from the standpoint of cult, he is implicitly reborn and thus alive."[65]

To return to the myth of Alkyone and the halcyon, I suggest that Alkyone's jump off the jetty to follow her drowned husband is parallel to Aphrodite's and Sappho's jumps off the White Rock. Just like the myth of Phaethon who crashed his father's solar chariot, that of Keyx is tragic: Keyx dies and Alkyone follows her beloved husband in death. And just as Phaethon is forever lamented by his sisters who turned into trees, so Keyx is forever lamented by his wife who turned into a bird. Both myths are entirely pessimistic in their firm focus on death and give no direct intimation of rebirth at all, except for the general presence of the solar theme. And yet notions of

---

[63] Telemachus at 1.241 and Eumaeus at 14.371 utter the same words: νῦν δέ μιν ἀκλειῶς Ἅρπυιαι ἀνηρέψαντο. Cf. Penelope speaking of Telemachus: νῦν αὖ παῖδ' ἀγαπητὸν ἀνηρέψαντο θύελλαι (2.727).

[64] Newton 1984.

[65] Nagy 1990:254.

rebirth, in both cases, are intimated outside of the main myth. In the case of Phaethon, the correlative notion of rebirth is implicit in the Hesiodic version of the myth, while in the case of Keyx and Alkyone the clearer hints at rebirth are to be found not in the myth about humans but in that about birds, though it is noteworthy that both in Ovid and in Apollodorus Keyx is in fact the son of Eosphoros, the morning star.[66]

The connection between the tale of Alkyone, the human wife of a human husband, and the halcyon myth is not universally recognized. Gresseth regarded their combination as secondary, an accident perhaps based on the similarity of their names, but I think such an *ad hoc* explanation is unnecessary.[67] Even in the case of the halcyon, the solar symbolism is not always overt: sometimes, the focus is only on the grief and mournful song of the female. And yet there is a meaningful connection between the two myths, one of death and the other of rebirth. Alkyone is deprived of her husband and cannot renew his life through a son, but the bird halcyon does just that, on a solar model. The thematic connections between Alkyone and the mythic halcyon go beyond lament and involve a vertical leap into the sea – out of love, like Aphrodite and Sappho. There is no rebirth in the human story, only death, yet the form of this death establishes a link with the myth about the bird, which may also involve rebirth.

This brings me finally to my main suggestion, namely that just as Odysseus' return operates on a solar metaphor and Odysseus himself, in one part of his complex identity, can be seen as a solar hero, so Penelope in her prayer to Artemis hints at the role of a solar consort. When Penelope prays to Artemis she addresses the goddess as 'daughter of Zeus', an epithet that is applied to Aphrodite in her abducting function and that has an exact cognate in Vedic, where it applies exclusively to the dawn-goddess Uṣas. While the epithet is much less restricted in Homer and applies to a number of goddesses, this is the only instance of its use about Artemis.[68] Praying to a thus markedly characterized Artemis, Penelope expresses a wish to follow her husband into the underworld, precisely by being carried away by the snatching winds and falling into Okeanos, like the heroes abducted by Dawn. Most importantly, Penelope wishes not simply for death, but specifically to follow Odysseus underneath the earth (20.80–81), and in this desire for an Oceanic

---

[66] Ovid *Metamorphoses* 11.271, Apollodorus 1.7.4. Here, however, Eosphoros is not identified with Aphrodite, and is accordingly imagined as Keyx's father.

[67] Gresseth 1964:98.

[68] See Nagy 1990:246–251 for a detailed examination of this epithet and its two variants (*diva(s) duhitar* and *duhitar- divas* in Vedic, Διὸς θυγάτηρ and θυγάτηρ Διός in Greek).

leap after her husband, she emerges as a figure similar not only to Alkyone, but to Aphrodite and Sappho with their leaps off the White Rock for love of their solar partners. Penelope's prayer with its references to the fate of the Pandareids evokes the solar regions, and the twin themes of falling into the Okeanos and going beneath the earth recall the movements of the sun.

In this way, while Penelope speaks only of death, the solar themes hint at rebirth as well, and this is confirmed by the context of the prayer. Book 20 opens at night, when Odysseus, unable to sleep and consumed with desire for revenge, is comforted by Athena. The goddess promises victory and puts her protégé to sleep, as she has often done for Penelope.[69] But just as Odysseus falls asleep, Penelope wakes up. It is at this moment that she utters her prayer, and so soon as she speaks her last word, the dawn comes:

Ὣς ἔφατ'· αὐτίκα δὲ χρυσόθρονος ἤλυθεν Ἠώς.

(*Odyssey* 20.91)

So she spoke, and the golden-throned Eos came at once.

While Penelope speaks of disappearance and loss, her diction and the context of her prayer hint that there is a possibility of re-emergence and return. The day of the contest is Penelope's chance to regain what she has lost or to lose it forever, and the two possibilities are reflected in Penelope's prayer, signaled by the fruitless Pandareids on the one hand, and a suddenly vivid recollection of Odysseus on the other. At the moment, both possibilities are open, though the solar theme implicit in the scene presages, at least for the external audience, the outcome of the coming trial.

Penelope may have good mythological reasons for assuming the role of a solar consort to Odysseus: it is not an *ad hoc* equation. This role may even be signaled in her connection to the *penelops*, just as Alkyone is expressed through her identification with the halcyon. We know nothing of the *penelops'* diving habits, but at the very least we are told that it lives at sea and frequents the Oceanic regions, and this, in conjunction with its similarities to the halcyon, makes vertical diving a distinct possibility. More remarkable is the fact that there are at least two different myths in which Penelope herself is cast into the sea and rescued by birds, *penelopes*. Both versions of Penelope's plunge are mentioned by various scholia and Eustathius as a way of explaining her name. According to one myth, Penelope is cast into the sea by her parents and saved

---

[69] *Odyssey* 20.44–55.

by the birds. There is no explanation for her parents' strange action, and once she is rescued they take her back, now with two names:

λέγεται γὰρ Ἀρναία πρότερον καλουμένη παρὰ τῶν φύντων εἰς τὴν θάλασσαν ἐκριφῆναι, εἶτα ὑπό τινων ὄρνεων πηνελόπων λεγομένων εἰς τὴν χέρσον ἐξενεχθῆναι, καὶ οὕτως ἀναληφθεῖσαν ὑπὸ τῶν γεννησάντων ὀνομασθῆναι Πηνελόπην ἀπὸ τῆς τῶν ὀρνίθων ὁμωνυμίας, καὶ τραφεῖσαν διώνυμον εἶναι τὸ λοιπόν.[70]

(Scholia vetera to Pindar, *Olympian* 9.85, scholion 79d)

It is said that she was first called Arnaia and was thrown into the sea by her parents, and then carried to shore by some birds called *penelopes*. And in this way she was recovered by her parents and named Penelope, by the same name as the birds, and when she grew up she had two names for the rest of her life.

In the second version of Penelope's sea adventure the explanation is different, as is her initial name. She is first called either Ameirake or Arnakia but then receives the name Penelope after Nauplios throws her into the sea as a vengeance for Odysseus' treatment of his son Palamedes. Again, she is brought to shore by *penelopes*.[71] The version with Penelope's parents is both more mysterious and in some sense more logical, since in the other story Penelope would only get her name after Palamedes' death at Troy. The existence of the two versions, however, is important because it shows what is the most salient and therefore the least variable feature of the myth: that Penelope falls into the sea but returns to shore, thanks to her avian namesakes.

The plunge into the sea is yet another link between Penelope and Alkyone, and for both of them it has to do with birds. If that is so, then it seems that Penelope has deep ties to the theme of solar-like disappearance and re-emergence that is so prominent in the *Odyssey*. There is, in other words, a diachronic dimension to her complexity and her very name signals not only her fidelity to her husband, but her intrinsic connectedness to the cyclic sequence of darkness, disappearance, and lament, followed by light, return, and rebirth. The effects of this diachronic depth are felt synchronically in the *Odyssey* as we have it, where Penelope is both a figure of lament and a figure of return to light and life. Her tears are more visible than her links to the

---

[70] The same story is told by Tzetzes on Lycophron, scholion 792.
[71] Eustathius 1.64 on *Odyssey* 1.344 with reference to Didymus.

theme of rebirth, but both aspects of her mythic personality are active in the *Odyssey*.[72]

Finally, Penelope's mythic background may have its own links with the festival of Apollo. I have tried above to tease out possible pointers to a connection between Apollo and the Pandareids, suggesting that their myths are suited to appear in the context of Apollo's festival in the *Odyssey* and may derive from cognate local settings. If that is so, then Penelope, of course, connects herself to the festival through the Pandareids. But there may be an even deeper connection too, because the whole complex of ideas that seems to be encapsulated by Penelope's name may also intersect with mythological themes clustering around Apollo and his female counterpart and sister, Artemis, the addressee of Penelope's prayer. It is an accident that leaps off the White Rock at Cape Leucas, discussed above, are in fact associated with Apollo. According to Strabo, the temple of Apollo Leucatas stood on the very rock from which Sappho and others jumped for love, and the yearly flinging of a criminal off the same rock took place at a festival of Apollo.[73]

For her part, Artemis also has ties to the themes important in the mythology of the halcyon and, in all likelihood, of the *penelops*, themes that are certainly prominent in the *Odyssey*: the Oceanic regions, the solar cycle, abduction, and a deadly plunge into the sea conceptualized through the image of a diving or falling bird. Twice in the *Odyssey* there is a mention of an island called Ortygia, a word derived from the Greek name for a quail, *ortyx*. The place-name is most strongly connected to Artemis, who is often said to be born on the island, and who is even herself called Ortygia in Sophocles' *Trachiniae* (213).[74] Several historical places bore that name, and some of them had a cult of Artemis or claimed to be her birthplace. The most prominent of these locations is Delos itself, also said to be called Ortygia, according to one explanation because quails landed on it during their migrations, carried from the sea by winds.[75] The birth of Artemis is not mentioned in the *Odyssey*, but her connection to Ortygia is present in a different way. Kalypso tells the story of Orion's death, by an arrow of Artemis at Ortygia:

---

[72] It could be argued that there is a notion, clear in the *Odyssey*, that a woman provides a link between the generations of males, and in that sense assures her husband's continuation into the future. Telemachus is not Odysseus reborn, but his survival is one of the several different ways in which Odysseus returns to life. From that point of view, a wife's devotion to her husband goes hand in hand with her ability to give birth to his sons.

[73] Strabo 10.2.9.

[74] Artemis is born on Ortygia according to, e.g., *Homeric Hymn to Apollo* 16.

[75] Phanodemos (FHG I 366), cited by Athenaeus 9.47.

ὣς μὲν ὅτ’ Ὠρίων’ ἕλετο ῥοδοδάκτυλος Ἠώς,
τόφρα οἱ ἠγάασθε θεοὶ ῥεῖα ζώοντες,
ἧος ἐν Ὀρτυγίῃ χρυσόθρονος Ἄρτεμις ἁγνὴ
οἷς ἀγανοῖς βελέεσσιν ἐποιχομένη κατέπεφνεν.

(Odyssey 5.123–126)

Just as when rose-fingered Dawn took Orion for herself,
you, the easy-living gods, were resentful then,
until on Ortygia the pure golden-throned Artemis
came and killed him with her gentle arrows.

Here Ortygia seems to be the place where Orion is taken by Eos, a place therefore associated with sunrise and sunset and presumably located near Okeanos. The collocation of abduction to the ends of the earth and of death by Artemis' arrows is certainly reminiscent of Penelope's prayer in Book 20. Ortygia is mentioned for the second time by Eumaeus, in description of his native land:

νῆσός τις Συρίη κεκλήσκεται, εἴ που ἀκούεις.
Ὀρτυγίης καθύπερθεν, ὅθι τροπαὶ ἠελίοιο,
οὔτι περιπληθὴς λίην τόσον, ἀλλ’ ἀγαθὴ μέν,
εὔβοτος, εὔμηλος, οἰνοπληθής, πολύπυρος·
πείνη δ’ οὔποτε δῆμον ἐσέρχεται, οὐδέ τις ἄλλη
νοῦσος ἐπὶ στυγερὴ πέλεται δειλοῖσι βροτοῖσι·
ἀλλ’ ὅτε γηράσκωσι πόλιν κάτα φῦλ’ ἀνθρώπων,
ἐλθὼν ἀργυρότοξος Ἀπόλλων Ἀρτέμιδι ξύν,
οἷς ἀγανοῖς βελέεσσιν ἐποιχόμενος κατέπεφνεν.

(Odyssey 15.403–411)

There is an island called Syria, perhaps you have heard of it,
above Ortygia, where the turns of the sun are.
It is not very populous, but good,
suitable for cattle and sheep, full of vineyards, rich in wheat.
Hunger never visits people there, nor is there any other
dreadful illness for poor mortals,
but, when people in the city grow old,
Apollo of the golden bow comes along with Artemis
and approaches and kills them with his gentle arrows.

The description of Eumaeus' Syria fits its location at the ends of the earth: it is reminiscent of blissful golden age lands like that of the Phaeacians or

Hyperboreans. One aspect of the inhabitants' charmed existence is a gentle death by the arrows of Artemis and Apollo, comparable with *Odyssey* 5.123–126, where Orion is the victim of the goddess's shafts. Ortygia evidently belongs to this environment. Moreover, the island is again associated specifically with the solar theme, since it is located near the 'turning places of the sun', presumably a reference to the solstices.[76]

What happens to Eumaeus in this setting is abduction by a Sidonian woman. She dies shortly after, and the manner of her death is significant:

> τὴν μὲν ἔπειτα γυναῖκα βάλ' Ἄρτεμις ἰοχέαιρα,
> ἄντλῳ δ' ἐνδούπησε πεσοῦσ' ὡς εἰναλίη κήξ.

> (*Odyssey* 15.478–479)

> And then Artemis of the arrows struck down the woman,
> and she fell with a thud into the bilge, like a diving sea
> bird [*kex*].

Eumaeus' story presents a non-fabulous version of abduction and also a realistic, even comic, version of the plunge into Okeanos. These details are part of Eumaeus' supposed biography, but they are also a variation on an already familiar theme, and again Artemis' arrow is combined with a watery fall and the fall is compared to the dive of a sea bird (*kex*).

If Artemis wields her deadly arrows in such solar contexts, then so does Apollo. It is perhaps noteworthy that our earliest evidence for the linking of the sun with Apollo comes from Euripides' *Phaethon*: when the hero's mother, Klymene, laments her dead son she says that he was destroyed by Helios, 'whom men rightly call Apollo', referring to the folk etymology of Apollo as 'destroyer' (224–226). But suggestive as this testimony is of Apollo's solar proclivities, it is relatively late and very complex. More directly applicable to the *Odyssey* is Apollo's role in an undoubtedly early myth of Idas and Marpessa as told by Simonides. The myth, uprooted and incomplete as we have it, is hard to interpret, but it is clear that it involves a number of themes and elements paralleled in the *Odyssey*, including archery, abduction, death by falling into water, and even Ortygia. In Simonides (PMG 563), Idas abducts his bride

---

[76] The expression τροπὰς ἠελίοιο is used of solstices in Hesiod (*Works and Days* 564, 663). The ends-of-the-earth characteristic of Eumaeus' native land need not contradict Hoekstra's suggestion that the swineherd's description is "in accord with the normal meaning of Συρίη." Hoekstra suggests that in Eumaeus' account this phrase signifies "the place on the horizon where the sun was seen to rise on midwinter day," which would in fact point to Syria (Hoekstra 1990:257 with references).

Marpessa from Ortygia, (the one located in Chalcis, on the island of Euboea). Her father, Euenos, pursues them up to the river Lykormas in Aitolia, where he commits suicide by casting himself down into the river, which henceforth is called Euenos. Next, Apollo appears and takes hold of Marpessa, but Idas resists and lifts his bow against the god. The duel is judged by Zeus, who gives the choice to Marpessa, and she chooses Idas.

The first thing to observe about this myth is its striking structural similarity to the story of Odysseus and Penelope, if the latter story is considered as a chronological whole, including parts that are not mentioned in the *Odyssey*. In both cases, the hero has to win his bride not once, but twice. When Idas abducts Alkyone from her father that is not the end of the story because he still has to face Apollo. Similarly, Odysseus first has to win Penelope's hand in marriage and then to regain her with his bow.[77] Interestingly, Pausanias reports that Odysseus and Penelope were pursued by her father Ikarios as they drove off from Lacedaemon, a detail reminiscent of Idas and Marpessa being followed by her father Euenos, even if Ikarios seems to have a less hostile intent and the situation is resolved without the loss of life. According to Pausanias, upon giving his daughter to Odysseus, Ikarios tried to make his new son-in-law settle in Lacedaemon instead of returning to Ithaca. When that failed, he attempted to keep Penelope from going with Odysseus and followed them in his chariot, imploring her to stay. Odysseus finally asked Penelope either to come willingly with him or go back to her father, and in response she said nothing but veiled her face, this being a sufficient sign for Ikarios that she wished to go with her husband.[78]

In both myths, then, there is a first part in which a daughter is separated from her reluctant father and taken away by her new husband, and a second part in which the husband has to compete for her with his bow against a challenger or challengers.[79] The role of Apollo in the story of Idas and Marpessa

[77] There are no early sources on the marriage of Odysseus and Penelope. Apollodorus reports that Odysseus gave Tyndareus the idea of binding Helen's suitors by an oath in order to enlist his help in procuring Penelope's hand from Ikarios. Pausanias mentions that Ikarios proposed a footrace for the suitors of Penelope, and that Odysseus dedicated an image of Athena Keleuthea and set up three sanctuaries to her along the Aphetaid road, the course of the race (3.12.1–5).

[78] Pausanias 3.20.10–11.

[79] This double plot belongs to a very widespread type, though the similarities between the two myths in question are closer than those they share with other such tales. Zhirmunsky (1967:281) discusses a large number of tales consisting of two successive parts, the "heroic wooing" and the "return of the husband." In all these tales the hero wins, after several feats, a beautiful bride but is then separated from her, usually when the other competitors for her hand treacherously attempt to kill or imprison him and abduct the bride. The hero returns, after more adventures, on the day of the rival's wedding with his abducted bride, usually in

is also to some extent parallel to his role in the *Odyssey*. The god threatens the marriage of Idas and Marpessa, though in the end Idas succeeds in withstanding the challenge. In the *Odyssey* there is no such evident hostility on the god's part, but the crisis point of Odysseus' return falls on his festival and Odysseus attributes his success at archery to the god's favor (*Odyssey* 22.5–7). This suggests that Apollo is indeed the power that controls the way to Odysseus' reunion with Penelope, a power whose challenge has to be met if the resumption of their marriage is to be achieved. There is a point of contact and a morphological similarity between the way in which Apollo is involved in each myth. The threat to the marriage of Odysseus and Penelope that is implicit in the figure of Apollo can also perhaps be compared to the deadly threat that Artemis, also as an archer, presents to the union of Eos and Orion. When it is a question of males abducting and competing for a female, the threat comes from Apollo, but when it is female Eos who abducts the male Orion the threat correspondingly comes from Artemis.[80]

Furthermore, an additional element can be added to Simonides' presentation of the myth of Idas and Marpessa on the basis of the *Iliad*, and it is a telling one. In the *Iliad*, Meleager's wife, Kleopatre, a figure of lament and the daughter of Idas and Marpessa, is said to be nicknamed Alkyone:

> τὴν δὴ τότ' ἐν μεγάροισι πατὴρ καὶ πότνια μήτηρ
> Ἀλκυόνην καλέεσκον ἐπώνυμον, οὕνεκ' ἄρ' αὐτῆς
> μήτηρ ἀλκυόνος πολυπενθέος οἶτον ἔχουσα
> κλαῖεν ὅ μιν ἑκάεργος ἀνήρπασε Φοῖβος Ἀπόλλων.

(Iliad 9.561)

> At that time in their house her father and her lady mother
> called her by the nickname Alkyone, because her
> mother wept, having the fate of the sorrowful halcyon,
> when Apollo the far-shooter stole her.

---

disguise, and in many tales a bow contest becomes the means both of his recognition and his vengeance. Along with many fairy tales, the Uzbek epic *Alpamysh* follows this pattern, and Zhirmunsky concludes that the two parts of that epic are not joined accidentally, but rather form two parts of the single plot. Zhirmunsky further compares the *Odyssey* to *Alpamysh* and suggests that the *Odyssey* in effect excluded the "heroic wooing" part of the plot and represents only the "second round" of Odysseus' tale, but the first part nevertheless exists in the story of Odysseus' wooing of Penelope as attested in Apollodorus and Pausanias: Zhirmunsky 1967:281–283. For more on the *Odyssey* and the *Alpamysh*, see above pp235–236.

[80] The symmetry here is not complete, of course, since Artemis challenges Eos only implicitly, by killing Orion.

Here the central theme is once more the separation of the devoted couple, Marpessa and Idas, which will be ended by way of the bow. Here the halcyon finds its place in the story, both as a bird of lament, and as a source of Kleopatre's nickname. Like Penelope, Marpessa seems to be firmly attached to her husband, whom she chooses over Apollo in Simonides' telling of the myth, and her lament is reminiscent not only of the halcyon but also of Penelope.

When Penelope laments and prays to Artemis on the day of Apollo's festival and when she mentions abduction by the snatching winds, a fall into Okeanos, death by an arrow of Artemis, separation from Odysseus, and the daughters of Pandareos, it seems that she does much more than simply re-enact her role as a bride. Rather, she gives voice to the themes that are constituent of her own mythic persona, some of them even signaled by her very name. The same themes turn out to be not only appropriate for the festival of Apollo, but essential to it, so that both Penelope and Odysseus seem inseparable from the festival, not in the sense that there could never be an *Odyssey* without the festival of Apollo, but in the sense that in the *Odyssey* as we have it the festival brings together and positions within a larger system of mythic and religious thought the very themes that are fundamental to Penelope and Odysseus. The festival is a match for its protagonists, and, conversely, almost everything they say and do as it approaches is attuned to its workings. Penelope's myths in Book 19 and her prayer in Book 20 are exquisitely integrated into their contexts, immediate and broad, precisely by virtue of being to a striking extent not *ad hoc*. They belong to a particular nexus in a rich and living system of myth-making, a system that includes Homer and that is at work in the creation of Odysseus' return and of Apollo's festival. The very character who utters these speeches, Penelope herself, is part of the same nexus, and it is this factor that allows her words to have such resonance and fit in such a complex and intricate way both with their setting and with her own poetic and mythic personality.

CONCLUSION

MY GOAL HAS BEEN TO CONTRIBUTE to the understanding of the dialogue between Penelope and Odysseus in Book 19 by looking at its mythic aspects. In Homeric poetry, evocation of myth is a diachronic phenomenon: it can accumulate in a poem, or rather, evolve with the poem, so that there are layers of evocation in the dialogue that are likely to represent a span of its development but that nevertheless constitute an organic whole. Homeric references to myth are also, synchronically, a poetic instrument of great range, flexibility, and precision. Mythological variation, selection between versions, genre appropriation, and evocation of myth and ritual are only some of the ways in which myths are used in Homer, both by the narrative voice and by the characters who speak in myths to each other. It seems most likely that the poets who performed epic poetry lived in a world of divergent, conflicting, competing, and evolving local mythologies, and that their experience with this world, which they helped create, is reflected in the way myth behaves in Homer. Some stylized reflection of this world may be seen in the way Odysseus and Penelope converse through myth in *Odyssey* 19.

I have argued that in the dialogue the myths can evoke not only other poetic but also other ritual contexts to which they are related. By becoming part of panhellenic poetry, these myths need not lose all ties to ritual, but rather can transform these ties into a register of poetic language. Indeed, a complex relationship between myth and ritual may even be enacted in the *Odyssey*, with Apollo's festival becoming a focal point that notionally brings together various myths told and alluded to in the poem. The festival of Apollo in the *Odyssey* is the only festival of a god mentioned in Homer, and while its importance has long been recognized, its far-reaching effects are still not fully explored.[1] The festival places Apollo in a role quite unlike that of Athena, Hermes, Zeus, or Poseidon, the gods who appear as characters in the poem. Apollo himself is conspicuously absent, and this physical absence

---

[1] For a recent overall analysis of the festival see Detienne 1998:41–61. The festival is commented upon by Wilamowitz 1884:53–55, 1927:91–92, and Otto 1981 [1929]:93. See also Austin 1975:238–253.

paradoxically makes him into a particularly powerful divine presence in the *Odyssey*. Odysseus relates to Athena in a way that presumably no member of the audience could recognize from personal experience: Athena ordinarily does not come down to sit and talk with mortals under olive trees. Apollo, on the other hand, is present in the poem in a way much more recognizable as an actual religious experience, through manifestations of his power and through being worshipped at a festival.

The festival has loomed large in my discussion of the dialogue, but one could go much further. In these concluding remarks I touch on a few of these possibilities. It may be possible to establish more correspondences between the festival in the *Odyssey* and such information as we have about the actual festivals of Apollo, though this would be a task of great complexity, since there is epigraphic, archaeological, prosaic, and poetic evidence for such festivals, early and late, and its different pieces come from such diverse times and places as to make any generalization hazardous, if not pointless.

We have seen that the dialogue between Penelope and Odysseus is deeply connected with the timing of the festival, since it is here that Odysseus predicts his own return at the end of the current *lukabas*, which coincides with the festival, and here that Penelope makes her decision to announce the bow contest. There is also a larger rhythm than the transition from one month to the next, though less directly indicated. Signs of spring accumulate in the poem as the festival of Apollo approaches, and one of the signs is Penelope's mention of the nightingale, who sings 'when the spring has just begun' (*Odyssey* 19.519)

The darkness that precedes the festival is not only celestial, but also social, and as I have noted above the festival in the *Odyssey* perhaps shares something with the festivals of dissolution and inversion that tend to mark the beginning of the new year. Apollo tends to be associated with the first months of the year, which are often named after the god.[2]

Relations between sexes are a large a part of the inversion and dissolution on Ithaca, and these relations, including those of Odysseus and Penelope (and therefore their dialogue), may in fact resonate strongly with the festival of Apollo. A suggestive poetic example pointing in this direction is a description in Apollonius' *Argonautica* of the festival of Apollo celebrated by the

---

[2] E.g. Apellaios in Delphi, Apellonios in Elis, Apellaion on Tenos etc. See Versnel 1993:297 with references. On Delos, the beginning of the local calendar was marked by a new-moon festival of the month Lenaion, (roughly, last half of January and the first half of February), a festival in honor of Leto, Apollo, and Artemis: Bruneau 1970:91–93. On ritual activity associated with the Leto and the birth of Apollo and Artemis at Ortygia near Ephesos see Versnel 1993:298 and n31.

Argonauts on the tiny island of Anaphe (4.1711–30), in which it is possible to discern similarities to a New Year celebration.[3] I have already drawn some connections between the Lemnian New Year festival and the *Odyssey*, and the Anaphiote episode of the *Argonautica* can be added to the picture. One conspicuous feature of the Lemnian festival is the disturbed relationship between sexes and the presence of ridicule as part of its expression. In Pindar's account, one Erginos is mocked by women for having gray hair, and I have compared him to Odysseus, mocked by the Phaecians for his apparent lack of athletic abilities and mocked again by the maids in disguise as an aged beggar.[4] The Anaphiote festival of Apollo is similarly marked by mockery and banter between the Argonauts and Medea's Phoenician servants, and this is presented as an aetiology for a local custom, the conflict (δηριόωνται, 4.1728) between local women and men at Apollo's festival.

In the *Odyssey* too, the relations between sexes are altered as the festival approaches. In the *Argonautica* the jeers exchanged by the Argonauts and the women are accompanied with laughter and described as sweet by Apollonius (γλυκερὴ . . . κερτομίη, 4.1725–26). There is little sweet in the abuse exchanged between Odysseus and the maids on Ithaca, and yet this may be a difference between more or less mythic versus more or less ritual perspectives. Certainly, an abusive exchange between Odysseus and the women precedes his victory at Apollo's festival and his reunion with Penelope.

On Lemnos the proceedings end in sex between the Argonauts and the women, and it seems safe to assume that on Anaphe the sexes also reconcile in the end. In the *Odyssey*, Penelope and the maids seem to represent two different manifestations of the feminine, two separate sides that elsewhere can be combined. This notion would fit well here: Odysseus exchanges abuse with the maids, but makes love to Penelope. On the other hand, though it is a far cry from merry festival banter, the very dialogue between Odysseus and Penelope fits, in its own way, into the same structure. The dialogue is antagonistic, but also results in growing proximity between Penelope and Odysseus and constitutes a large first step on the way to their marital bed. As I have argued, the dialogue may even contain echoes of wedding songs and pre-wedding themes.

The dialogue between Penelope and Odysseus is thus a prelude to the resumption of their marriage, and this too is consonant with the festival of

---

[3] See Bremmer 2005.

[4] Erginos: Pindar *Olympian* 4.18-21 and Scholia on 4.19 (scholion 32c), Callimachus fr. 669 Pf. See Burkert 1970 and Bremmer 2005:30 for interpretation. Odysseus: *Odyssey* 8.158–164, 18.321–336, 19.65–69, and 369–375. On ridicule in the *Odyssey*, and especially on ridicule as an aspect of blame poetry, see Nagy 1979:256–264.

Apollo. Apollo's best-known aspect is his concern with the transition of male youths to full adulthood, and marriage is a consequence of this transition. There are some indications that prospects of weddings are in the air at various festivals of Apollo. A Hellenistic epigram by Phaidimos urges Apollo not to aim his bow at giants or wolves, but to shoot a shaft of love at the young unmarried men of Skhoinos, so that they may defend their fatherland emboldened by their love.[5] It has been suggested that a festival of Apollo is presupposed by the epigram, and may be even a local custom of arranging marriages at this festival.[6] This connection between love and Apollo can be viewed in conjunction with a recurrent mythic story-pattern, in which boy meets girl and falls in love at a festival of the god. The most famous example is the story of Acontius and Cydippe as told by Callimachus: Acontius falls in love with Cydippe when both attend a festival of Apollo and Artemis on Delos, and Acontius in the end gains her hand in marriage by a trick.[7] Antoninus Liberalis preserves a similar story about Ctesylla and Hermochares, who meet at a festival of Apollo on Ceos, and here again the boy falls in love with the girl and finds a way to compel her father to arrange their marriage.[8] Hermochares sees Ctesylla as she dances by the altar of Apollo in Karthaia, while Acontius and Cydippe meet at Delos. In both cases Artemis is also involved: the girl is tricked into an oath to marry the boy and swears by the goddess or in her sanctuary.

The conjunction of themes here is reminiscent of the *Odyssey*, where Odysseus meets Nausikaa in a scene resonant with premonitions of wedding, and compares her both to Artemis and to a young palm he saw by the altar of Apollo at Delos. The Apollo who appears in Demodokos' song of Ares and Aphrodite is certainly an Apollo with love on his mind, since he asks Hermes what he would give to lie next to Aphrodite. No wedding happens on Skheria, but there are suitors vying for Nausikaa's hand and her father offers her to Odysseus. Much of what happens between Odysseus and Nausikaa is echoed on Ithaca, so that the Phaeacian princess acquires a surprising connection to Penelope, as if she is playing a role that vitally concerns Penelope, but which Odysseus' wedded wife cannot play. And there are hints of Nausikaa in Penelope, for example, when the latter is compared to Artemis and Aphrodite as she impresses the suitors and Odysseus on the eve of Apollo's festival

---

[5] *Anthologia Palatina* 13.22. See Robertson 1991:33, with references. Although I do not agree with all of the conclusions, I am much indebted to this work for its discussion of parallels to the Odyssean Apollo festival, which Robertson regards as an instance of the "betrothal symposium."

[6] Robertson 1991:33.

[7] Callimachus *Aetia* 3 frs. 66–75.

[8] Antoninus Liberalis 41, with reference to the third book of Nicander's *Heteroeumena*.

(*Odyssey* 17.37). The comparison seems to put her in the role of a *parthenos*, transitioning from the realm of Artemis to that of Aphrodite, and it is repeated exactly when Penelope comes out in Book 19 to talk to Odysseus (19.54). The two episodes involving Nausikaa and Penelope respectively are linked by a striking transformation of Odysseus into a youthful man with hyacinth-like hair tumbling down his shoulders (6.231, 23.158), a sign, it has been argued, of sexual attractiveness, and also perhaps a detail evocative of Apollo.[9] In this setting, the dialogue in Book 19 emerges as an interaction that is, along with everything else it is, a clandestine courtship, an *agon* between sexes, a meeting that leads to marriage. The eve of Apollo's festival is not only a superbly fitting, but also most likely a traditional setting for such a meeting.

Also consonant with a festival setting is the fact that the hunt plays an unexpectedly large role in the dialogue. Within the dialogue itself there is a description of Odysseus' pin that depicts a hunting scene and in the same book a flashback to the most extensive hunting narrative in Homer, Odysseus' boar hunt on Mount Parnassus. Hunting, especially the kind of hunting that has to do with transition to adulthood, is easily connected with Apollo. Indeed, hunting can fit into the same structural position as a contest or games on a young man's way to marriage.[10]

Two beasts play a dominant role in several myths of these hunts, the boar and the lion, and there are examples that suggest a connection between the hunt, marriage, and festival of Apollo. Statius (*Thebaid* 1.557–668) may preserve just such a myth: Tydeus and Polyneices arrive at Argos during a celebration of Apollo's festival, compete in wrestling, and are recognized by Adrastus by the emblems on their shields as the lion and the boar who are supposed to

---

[9] See above pp67-68.

[10] For example, in a myth recorded by Pausanias (1.41.3–4, Dieukhidas FGrH 485 F 10) a Megarian king gives his daughter's hand to the man who can kill a lion, which has previously killed the king's son. The successful suitor, Alcathous, then dedicates a shrine to Artemis Agrotera and Apollo Agraios, two deities of the hunt. The hunter/suitor Alcathous, is in fact strongly connected to Apollo: cf. Pausanias' report of a local story in which Apollo helped Alcathous build the wall of Megara's citadel. Megarian Apollo may have something to do with transition from one generation to the next, and continuity or lack thereof in such transitions. Alcathous becomes the king of Megara by marriage, because the previous kings' two sons are killed, one by the lion and another by Theseus. Alcathous hunts down the lion and becomes king, but then goes on to repeat the fate of his father-in-law. His elder son is slain by the Calydonian boar. The younger one runs to tell the father the grim news just as Alcathous prepares to sacrifice to Apollo, and the son flings the logs from the sacrificial fire before speaking. Not knowing the reason for this son's action, the angry father kills him on the spot by striking him with one of the logs. Cf. the prospect of failed generational transition from Odysseus to Telemachus (though it is not Odysseus who endangers Telemachus' life) and its prominence in the dialogue in Book 19.

marry his two daughters according to Apollo's prophecy. It has been suggested that the arrival of two de facto suitors makes Statius' Apollo festival into a "betrothal banquet," and that such banquets regularly take place at Apollo's festivals, the suitors' feasting included.[11] The setting, in Statius at least, is a festival in early spring, since everyone is wearing crowns of laurel, and, as in the *Odyssey*, the weather is bad.[12] Inclement weather is also part of Manses' telling of the story, where the two heroes fight for the hides of boar and lion that are dedicated at Apollo's temple, a detail that emphasizes their identification with the animals.[13] A spring festival of Apollo, stormy weather, and marriage is a nexus of themes certainly reminiscent of the *Odyssey*, and it may not be a coincidence that there too both the lion and the boar make appearances. As he approaches Nausikaa on Skheria, Odysseus is compared to the lion (6.130–134), uniquely in the *Odyssey*, while on Ithaca the dialogue between him and Penelope is split in two by recollection of his identity-forming boar-hunt. In all accounts, the identity of the hero and the beast is strongly felt, and so is Apollo's presence. The place where Odysseus hunts is none other than the setting to Apollo's Delphic shrine, Mount Parnassus, and the place where he received his wound was shown at Delphi in Pausanias' time.[14]

Perhaps the best known and most studied aspect of Apollo's festival is the promotion of youths to manhood, which is pertinent not only to Telemachus but also to Odysseus, and Penelope of course talks about her son's growing up. Finally, her decision to stage the bow contest is not to be separated from the festival, especially given the decidedly Apolline pedigree of Odysseus' bow. These are large subjects, however, which demand fuller treatment than can be given here.[15]

I have kept closer to the dialogue itself while trying to trace its mythology in some detail. It is a truism to say that the conversation in Book 19 is only comprehensible in its context. The question is rather what constitutes the context. My contention is that along with the immediate dramatic context of the *Odyssey* the dialogue is also taking place in a complex mythic context, in a landscape of tradition, or rather, of many cooperating and competing traditions that contribute to the formation of the Homeric epic. These include not

---

[11] Robertson 1991:29–30.

[12] Statius, *Thebaid* 1.554–555, 342–389, 403–407, 454–456. See Robertson 1991:29–30 for discussion and comparison with the Odyssean festival.

[13] Mnases fr. 48 Müller, Scholia to Euripides *Phoenician Women* 409.

[14] Pausanias 10.8.8.

[15] Odysseus' bow comes from Eurytos, who is said to have challenged Apollo in archery with dire results for himself (8.226–228). On the bow, see Griffin 1989, Detienne 1998:60–61, Russo 2004.

only strictly speaking the traditions of epic poetry, but more generally those of myth and cult, because myths can bring into Homeric poetry their ritual associations and their power as special speech, which is more evident in local contexts.

There is no gap between the two contexts: it is not that the sophisticated verbal exchange of the poem's protagonists only happens on one level, while the diachronic dimension of the Odyssean myths are confined to another. Instead, I argue that there is a complete interpenetration of these layers, if indeed they are layers at all. There is consequently no gap between studying the *Odyssey* in its relations to myth and cult and the kind of analysis that centers on the poem itself, the actions and characters, their manner of speaking, and the verbal subtleties of their conversations. It is not the case that the dialogue between Odysseus and Penelope is simply highly artful poetry superimposed on the bare bones of mythological background. On the contrary, there is no way to dissociate the dialogue from its mythological resonances: part of its artfulness in fact consists of the poetic treatment of the myths, most clearly manifested by choosing between different versions, but also by evocative detail that brings certain myths to mind. Penelope and Odysseus talk in a mythic setting and they talk in myths; these myths resonate in turn with their present context, evoking still others, and the meaning of the dialogue is inseparable from this process.

BIBLIOGRAPHY

Aarne, A. and Thompson, S. 1964. *The Types of the Folktale: A Classification and Bibliography*. Helsinki.

Adrados, F. R. 1972. "Les institutions religieuses mycéniennes." *Minos* n.s. 11:170–203.

Ahl, F. and Roisman, H. M. 1996. *The Odyssey Re-Formed*. Ithaca.

Alden, M. J. 1997. "The Resonances of the Song of Ares and Aphrodite." *Mnemosyne* 50:513–529.

Alexiou, M. 1974. *The Ritual Lament in Greek Tradition*. Cambridge, MA.

Ali, M. A. and Lees, W. N. 1864–5. *Wís o Rámín: A Romance of Ancient Persia*. Calcutta.

Alimjan, Kh. 1939. *Alpamysh*. Tashkent.

Allione, L. 1963. *Telemaco e Penelope nell'Odissea*. Turin.

Ameis, K. F. and Hentze, C. 1895. *Homers Odyssee*. Leipzig.

Amory, A. 1963. "The Reunion of Odysseus and Penelope." In Taylor 1963:100–136.

———. 1966. "The Gates of Horn and Ivory." *Yale Classical Studies* 20:3–57.

Amyx, D. 1988. *Corinthian Vase-Painting of the Archaic Period*. Berkeley.

Anhalt, E. K. 2001–2. "A Matter of Perspective: Penelope and the Nightingale in *Odyssey* 19.512–534." *Classical Journal* 97:145–159.

Antonetti, C. 1990. *Les Etoliens: image et religion*. Paris.

Arrigoni, G. 1977. "Atalanta e il cinghiale bianco." *Scripta Philologa* 1:9–47.

Arthur, M. 1983. "The Dream of a World Without Women: Poetics and the Circles of Order in the *Theogony* Prooemium." *Arethusa* 16:97–116.

Athanassakis, A. 1994. "The Eagle of Penelope's Dream through the Millennia of the Greek Poetic Tradition." *The Ancient World* 25.121–133.

Auffarth, C. 1991. *Der drohende Untergang: "Schöpfung" in Mythos und Ritual im Alten Orient und in Griechenland*. Berlin.

Austin, N. 1975. *Archery at the Dark of the Moon: Poetic Problems in Homer's Odyssey*. Berkeley.

Bader, F. 1998. "Le nom de Pénélope, tadorne à la πήνη." In Isebaert and Lebrun 1998:1–41.

Bakker, E. 1997. *Poetry in Speech: Orality and Homeric Discourse*. Ithaca.

————. 2002. "Remembering the God's Arrival." *Arethusa* 35:63–81.

————. 2003. "Archery in the Light of the Sun: Apollo in the *Odyssey*." Presented at the conference "Apolline Politics and Poetics," Delphi, July 9, 2003.

Barringer, J. M. 2001. *The Hunt in Ancient Greece*. Baltimore.

Beck, D. 2005. *Homeric Conversation*. Hellenic Studies 14. Washington, D.C.

Bérard, C. et al. 1989. *A City of Images: Iconography and Society in Ancient Greece*. Translated by D. Lyons. Princeton.

Bieber, M. 1949. "Eros and Dionysos on Kerch Vases." *Hesperia Supplements* 8:31-38 and 440-441.

Bierl, A. et al., eds. 2004. *Antike Literatur in neuer Deutung*. München.

————. 2009. *Ritual and Performativity. The Chorus of Old Comedy*. Translated by A. Hollmann. Hellenic Studies 20. Washington, D.C.

Block, E. 1985. "Clothing Makes the Man: A Pattern in the *Odyssey*." *Transactions of the American Philological Association* 115:1–11.

Bona, G. 1966. *Studi sull'Odissea*. Turin.

Borthwick, E. 1988. "Odysseus and the Return of the Swallow." *Greece and Rome* 35:14–22.

Bowra, C. M. 1961. *Greek Lyric Poetry from Alcman to Simonides*. Oxford.

Brashear, W. M. 1990. "Zauberformular." *Archiv für Papyrusforschung* 36:49–74.

Braswell, B. K. 1982. "The Song of Ares and Aphrodite: Theme and Relevance to *Odyssey* 8." *Hermes* 110:129–137.

Braun, K. and Haevernick, T. E. 1981. *Bemalte Keramik und Glas aus dem Kabirenheiligtum bei Theben*. Das Kabirenheiligtum bei Theben IV, Berlin.

Breed, B. W. 1999. "Odysseus Back Home and Back from the Dead." In Carlisle and Levaniouk 1999:137–161.

Bremer, J. M., de Jong, I. J. F., and Kalff, J., eds. 1987. *Homer, Beyond Oral Poetry: Recent Trends in Homeric Interpretation*. Amsterdam.

Bremmer, J. N. 1983a. *The Early Greek Concept of the Soul*. Princeton.

————. 1983b. "The Importance of the Maternal Uncle and Grandfather in Archaic and Classical Greece and Early Byzantium." *Zeitschrift für Papyrologie und Epigraphik* 50:173–186.

————. 1988. "La plasticité du mythe: Méléagre dans la poésie homerique." In Calame, ed. 1988:37–56.

————. 2005. "Anaphe, Aeschrology and Apollo Aiglêtês: Apollonius Rhodius 4.1711-1730." In Hader and Cuypers 2005:18-34.

Brennan, T. C. 1987. "An Ethnic Joke in Homer?" *Harvard Studies in Classical Philology* 91:1–3.

Brown, C. G. 1989. "Ares, Aphrodite, and the Laughter of the Gods." *Phoenix* 43:283–293.

Bruneau, P. 1970. *Recherches sur les cultes de Délos à l'époque hellénistique et à l'époque impériale*. Paris.

Büchner, W. 1940. "Die Penelopeszenen in der Odyssee." *Hermes* 75:129–167.

Bundy, E. L. 1962. *Studia Pindarica.* Vol. 1. Berkeley.

Burkert, W. 1960. "Das Lied von Ares und Aphrodite." *Rheinisches Museum* 103:130–144.

———. 1966. "Kekropidensage und Arrhephoria." *Hermes* 94:1–25.

———. 1970. "Jason, Hypsipyle, and New Fire at Lemnos: A Study in Myth and Ritual." *Classical Quarterly* 20:1–16.

———. 1975. "Apellai und Apollo." *Rheinisches Museum* 118:1–21.

———. 1979. *Structure and History in Greek Mythology and Ritual.* Berkeley.

———. 1980. "Griechische Mythologie und Geistgeschichte der Moderne." In den Boer, ed. 1980:159–199. Geneva.

———. 1983. *Homo Necans: The Anthropology of Ancient Greek Sacrificial Ritual and Myth.* Berkeley.

———. 1985. *Greek Religion.* Cambridge, MA.

Cairns, D. L., ed. 2001. *Oxford Readings in Homer's Iliad.* Oxford.

Calame, C., ed. 1988. *Métamorphoses du mythe en Grèce antique.* Paris.

———. 1996. *Thésée et l'imaginaire athénien: légende et culte en Grèce antique.* Lausanne.

Callaway, C. 1998. "Odysseus' Three Unsworn Oaths." *American Journal of Philology* 119:159–170.

Carlisle, M. and Levaniouk, O., eds. 1999. *Nine Essays on Homer.* Lanham.

Carter, J. B. and Morris, S. P., eds. 1995. *The Ages of Homer: A Tribute to Emily Townsend Vermeule.* Austin.

Casanova, A. 1969. "Il mito di Atteone nel Catalogo Esiodeo." *Rivista di Filologia e di Istruzione Classica* 97:31–46.

Cassin, B. and Labarrière J.-L., eds. 1997. *L'animal dans l'antiquité.* Paris.

Càssola, F. 1975. *Inni Omerici.* Milano.

Cazzaniga, I. 1950. *La saga di Itis nella tradizione letteraria e mitografica greco-romana.* Milan.

Chadwick, J. and Baumbach, L. 1963. "The Mycenaean Greek Vocabulary" *Glotta* 41:157–271.

Chaniotis, A. 1988. "Zu den Inschriften von Amnisos." *Zeitschrift für Papyrologie und Epigraphik* 71:157–160.

———. 1992. "Amnisos von Homer bis zum Ende der Antike: Die antiken Ortsnamen, Siedlungswesen, Seefahrt, Wirtschaft, Kulte." In Schäfer 1992:51–127.

Chantraine, P. 1968/1999. *Dictionnaire étymologique de la langue grecque.* Paris.

Clay, J. S. 1983. *The Wrath of Athena: Gods and Men in the Odyssey.* Princeton.

———. 1989. *The Politics of Olympus. Form and Meaning in the Major Homeric Hymns.* Princeton.

Clayton, B. 2004. *A Penelopean Poetics: Reweaving the Feminine in Homer's Odyssey.* Lanham.

Cohen, B., ed. 1995. *The Distaff Side: Representing the Female in Homer's Odyssey.* New York.

Combellack, F. M. 1973. "Three Odyssean Problems." *University of California Studies in Classical Antiquity* 6:17–46.

Condoléon-Bolanacchi, E. 1989. "Géranos." *Horos* 7:145–166.

Cook, A. B. 1914, 1924, 1940. *Zeus: A Study in Ancient Religion.* 3 vols. Cambridge.

Cook, E. 1995. *The Odyssey in Athens: Myths of Cultural Origins.* Ithaca.

Coughanowr, E. 1979. "The meaning of *MOLOBROS* in Homer." *Classical Quarterly* 29:229–230.

Cuypers, M. 2001. *pepnumenos.* In B. Snell, W.A. Beck, M. Meier-Brügger, *Lexikon des frühgriechischen Epos*, 3.19 s.v.

Cunliffe, R. J. 1977. *A Lexicon of the Homeric Dialect.* Norman.

Danek, G. 2002. "Traditional Referentiality and Homeric Intertextuality." In Montanari and Ascheri 2002:3–20.

Davies, M. 2001. "The Boar-Hunt in Greek Myth." *Prometheus* 27:1–8.

Delavaud-Roux, M.-H. 1992. "La géranos en Grèce antique." *Connaissance Hellénique* 53:39–47.

den Boer, W., ed. 1980. *Les Études classiques aux XIXe et XXe siècles: Leur place dans l'histoire des idées.* Geneva.

Detienne, M. 1973. "L'olivier: un mythe politico-religieux." In Finley, ed. 1973:293–306.

———. 1998. *Apollon le couteau à la main.* Paris.

Detienne, M. and Vernant, J.-P. 1978. *Cunning Intelligence in Greek Culture and Society.* Translated by J. Lloyd. Atlantic Highlands, NJ.

Devereux, G. 1957. "Penelope's Character." *Psychoanalytic Quarterly* 26:378–86.

Dickinson, O. T. P. K. 1994. *The Aegean Bronze Age.* Cambridge.

Dillon, M. 1947. "The Hindu Act of Truth in Celtic Tradition." *Modern Philology* 44:137–140.

Dimock, G. 1965. "The Name of Odysseus." *Hudson Review* 9:52-70

Dodd, D. 2003. "Adolescent Initiation in Myth and Tragedy: Rethinking the Black Hunter." In Dodd and Faraone 2003:71–84.

Dodd, D. and Faraone, C. A., eds. 2003. *Initiation in Ancient Greek Rituals and Narratives: New Critical Perspectives.* London.

Doherty, L. E. 1995. *Siren Songs: Gender, Audiences, and Narrators in the Odyssey.* Ann Arbor.

Donlan, W. 1993. "Dueling with Gifts in the *Iliad*: As the Audience Saw It." *Colby Quarterly* 29:155–172.

Dué, C. 2002. *Homeric Variations on a Lament by Briseis.* Lanham.

Durand, J.-L. and Schnapp, A. 1989. "Sacrificial Slaughter and Initiatory Hunt." In Bérard 1989:53–70.

Edmunds, L., ed. 1990. *Approaches to Greek Myth.* Baltimore.

Edwards, M. W. 1991. *The Iliad: A Commentary.* Vol. 5, *Books 17–20.* Cambridge

Emlyn-Jones, C. 1984. "The Reunion of Penelope and Odysseus." *Greece and Rome* 31:1–18.

———. 1986. "True and Lying Tales in the Odyssey." *Greece and Rome* 33:1–10.

Erbse, H. 1972. *Beiträge zum Verständnis der Odysse*. Berlin.

Falkner, T. 1989. "Ἐπὶ γήραος οὐδῷ: Homeric Heroism, Old Age and the End of the *Odyssey*." In Falkner and de Luce 1989:21–67.

Falkner, T. and de Luce, J., eds. 1989. *Old Age in Greek and Latin Literature*. Albany.

Farnell, L. R. 1907. *The Cults of the Greek States*. Vol. 4. Oxford.

———. 1921. *Greek Hero Cults and Ideas of Immortality*. Oxford.

Faure, P. 1964. *Fonctions des Cavernes Crétoises*. Paris.

Felson, N. 1994. *Regarding Penelope: From Character to Poetics*. Princeton.

Felson-Rubin, N. 1987. "Penelope's Perspective: Character from Plot." In Bremer, de Jong, and Kalff 1987:61–83.

Felson-Rubin, N. and Sale, W. M. 1983. "Meleager and Odysseus: A Structural and Cultural Study of the Greek Hunting-Maturation Myth." *Arethusa* 16:137–171.

———. 1984. "Meleager and the Motifemic Analysis of Myth: A Response." *Arethusa* 17:211–23.

Felson-Rubin, N. and Deal, H. M. 1994. "Some Functions of the Demophoön Episode in the *Homeric Hymn to Demeter*." In Foley 1994:190–197.

Ferrari, G. 2002. *Figures of Speech: Men and Maidens in Ancient Greece*. Chicago.

Figueira, T. J. and Nagy, G. eds. 1985. *Theognis of Megara: Poetry and the Polis*. Baltimore.

Finley, J. H. 1978. *Homer's Odyssey*. Cambridge, MA.

Finley, M. I., ed. 1973. *Problèmes de la terre en Grèce ancienne*. Paris.

Foley, H. P. 1978. "Reverse Similes and Sex Roles in the *Odyssey*." *Arethusa* 11:7–26.

———. 1994. *The Homeric Hymn to Demeter: Translation, Commentary, and Interpretive Essays*. Princeton.

———. 1995. "Penelope as Moral Agent." In Cohen 1995:93–115.

———. 2001. *Female Acts in Greek Tragedy*. Princeton.

Foley, J. M. 1991. *Immanent Art: From Structure to Meaning in Traditional Oral Epic*. Bloomington.

———. 1999. *Homer's Traditional Art*. University Park, PA.

———., ed. 2005. *A Companion to Ancient Epic*. Malden, MA.

Forsyth, P. Y. 1984. "Lemnos Reconsidered." *Echos du monde classique* 28:3–14.

Frame, D. 1978. *The Myth of Return in Early Greek Epic*. New Haven.

———. 2009. *Hippota Nestor*. Hellenic Studies 37. Washington, D.C.

Franco, C. 2003. *Senza ritegno: il cane e la donna nell'immaginario della Grecia antica*. Bologna.

Frazer, J. G. 1890. *The Golden Bough: A Study in Comparative Religion*. 2 vols. London.

Frisk, H. 1960–73. *Griechisches etymologisches Wörterbuch*. Heidelberg.

Fritz, K. von. 1943. "*NOUS* and *NOEIN* in the Homeric Poems." *Classical Philology* 38:79–93.

———. "ΝΟΥΣ, NOEIN and Their Derivatives in Pre-Socratic Philosophy (Excluding Anaxagoras): Part I. From Beginning to Parmenides." *Classical Philology* 40:223-242.

Frontisi-Ducroux, F. 1997. "Actéon, ses chiens et leur maître." In Cassin and Labarrière, eds. 1997:435-454.

Furley, W. D. and Bremer, J. M. 2001. *Greek Hymns: Selected Cult Songs from the Archaic to the Hellenistic Period*. Vol. 1, *The Texts in Translation*; Vol. 2, *Greek Texts and Commentary*. Tübingen.

Gallavotti, C. 1969. "I cani di Atteone in Ovidio e Igino e nell'epica greca." *Bollettino del Comitato per la preparazione dell'edizione nazionale dei classici greci e latini* 17:81–91.

Gennep, A. van. 1960. *The Rites of Passage*. Translated by M. B. Vizedom and G. L. Caffee. Chicago.

Gérard-Rousseau, M. 1968. *Les mentions religieuses dans les tablettes mycéniennes*. Rome.

Gernet, L. 1981. *The Anthropology of Ancient Greece*. Translated by J. D. B. Hamilton and B. Nagy. Baltimore.

Gigon, O. et al. 1946. *Phyllobolia für Peter von der Mühll zum 60. Geburtstag am 1. August 1945*. Basel.

Goldhill, S. 1988. "Reading Differences: The *Odyssey* and Juxtaposition." *Ramus* 17:1–31.

Graf, F. 1979. "Apollo Delphinios." *Museum Helveticum* 36:2–22.

———. 1974. "Das Kollegium der *MOLPOI* von Olbia." *Museum Helveticum* 31:209–215.

———. 1993. *Greek Mythology: An Introduction*. Translated by T. Marier. Baltimore.

———. 2003. "Initiation: A Concept with a Troubled History." In Dodd and Faraone 2003:3–24.

Graziosi, B. and Haubold, J. 2005. *Homer: The Resonance of Epic*. London.

Gresseth, G. K. 1964. "The Myth of Alcyone." *Transactions of the American Philological Association* 95:88–98.

Griffin, R. 1989. "Community and its Ritual Orders in *Odyssey* 21." *Res Publica Litterarum* 12:69–76.

Griffith, M. and Mastronarde, D. J., eds. 1990. *The Cabinet of the Muses: Essays on Classical and Comparative Literature in Honor of Thomas G. Rosenmeyer*. Atlanta.

Guarducci, M. 1974. "Ancora sull'inno cretese a Zeus Dicteo." *Antichità Cretesi: Studi in onore di Doro Levi*, 36–38. Catania.

Haft, A. 1984. "Odysseus, Idomeneus and Meriones: The Cretan Lies of *Odyssey* 13–19." *Classical Journal* 79:289–306.

———. 1996. "The Mercurial Significance of Raiding: Baby Hermes and Animal Theft in Contemporary Crete." *Arion* 4:27-48.

Hägg, R., Marinatos, N. and Nordquist, G., eds. 1988. *Early Greek Cult Practice: proceedings of the fifth international symposium at the Swedish Institute at Athens, 26-29 June 1986.* Stockholm.

Hainsworth, B. 1993. *The Iliad: A Commentary.* Vol. 3, Books 9–12. Cambridge.

Halverson, J. 1986. "The Succession Issue in the *Odyssey*." *Greece and Rome* 33:119–128.

Hampe, R. 1951. "'Idäische Grotte' in Olympia?" In Mylonas 1951:336–350.

Harder, A. and Cuypers, M., eds. 2005. *Beginning from Apollo: Studies in Apollonius Rhodius and the Argonautic Tradition.* Leuven.

Harrison, J. E. 1912. *Themis: A Study of the Social Origins of Greek Religion.* Cambridge.

Harsh, P. W. 1950. "Penelope and Odysseus in *Odyssey* XIX." *American Journal of Philology* 71:1–21.

Hatto, A. T. 1946. "Venus and Adonis and the Boar." *Modern Language Review* 41:353–361.

———.1980a. *Essays on Medieval German and Other Poetry.* Cambridge.

———., ed. 1980b. *Traditions of Heroic and Epic Poetry.* Vol. 1, *The Traditions.* London.

Head, B. V. 1967. *Historia Numorum: A Manual of Greek Numismatics.* Chicago.

Heath, J. 1992. *Actaeon, the Unmannerly Intruder: The Myth and its Meaning in Classical Literature.* New York.

———. 2001. "Telemachus PEPNUMENOS: Growing into an Epithet." *Mnemosyne* 54:129–157.

Heitman, R. 2005. *Taking Her Seriously: Penelope & the Plot of Homer's Odyssey.* Ann Arbor.

Henrichs, A. 1978. "Greek Maenadism from Olympias to Messalina." *Harvard Studies in Classical Philology* 82:121–160.

———. 1991. "Namenlosigkeit und Euphemismus: Zur Ambivalenz der chthonischen Mächte im attischen Drama." In Hofmann, ed. 1991:161–201.

Heubeck, A. 1972, "Etymologische Vermutungen zu Eleusis und Eileithyia." *Kadmos* 11:87–95.

———. 1992. *Books XXIII-XXIV.* In Russo, Fernández-Galiano, and Heubeck 1992:313-418.

Heubeck, A. and Hoekstra, A. 1990. A Commentary on Homer's Odyssey. Vol.2, Books IX-XVI. Oxford.

Heubeck, A. West, S., and Hainsworth, J. B. 1988. *A Commentary on Homer's Odyssey.* Vol. 1, *Introduction and Books i–viii.* Oxford.

Herzfeld, M. 1985. *The Poetics of Manhood: Contest and Identity in a Cretan Mountain Village.* Princeton.

———. 1993. "In Defiance of Destiny: The Management of Time and Gender at a Cretan Funeral." *American Ethnologist* 20:241–255.

Hiller, S. 1982. "Amnisos in den mykenischen Texten." *Kadmos* 21:33–63.

Hoekstra, A. 1990. *Books XIII–XVI.* In Heubeck and Hoekstra 1990:147-287.

Hoffman, H. 1967. "Eine Neue Amphora des Eucharidesmalers." *Jahrbuch der Hamburger Kunstsammlungen* 12:9–34.

Hoffman, H., ed. 1991. *Fragmenta dramatica: Beiträge zur Interpretation der griechischen Tragikerfragmente und ihrer Wirkungsgeschichte.* Göttingen.

Hollis, A. S. 1970. *Ovid. Metamorphoses Book VIII.* Oxford.

Hollmann, A. Forthcoming. *The Master of Signs. Signs and the Interpretation of Signs in Herodotus' Histories.* Hellenic Studies 48. Washington, D.C.

Holmberg, I. E. 1995. "The *Odyssey* and Female Subjectivity." *Helios* 22:103–122.

Holtsmark, E. B. 1966. "Spiritual Rebirth of the Hero, *Odyssey* 5." *Classical Journal* 61:206–210.

Honea, S. M. 1991. The Myth of Meleager. PhD diss., State University of New York at Buffalo.

Hopkinson, N. 1984. *Callimachus. Hymn to Demeter.* Cambridge.

Ingalls, W. B. 2000. "Nausikaa, Penelope, and Initiation." *Echos du monde classique* 19:1–18.

Irwin, E. 1974. *Colour Terms in Greek Poetry.* Toronto.

Isler-Kerényi, C. 2001. *Dionysos nella Grecia arcaica: il contributo delle immagini.* Pisa.

Isebaert, L. and Lebrun, R., eds. 1998. *Quaestiones Homericae: Acta Colloquii Namurcensis.* Louvain-Namur.

Jacobson, H. 1999. "Homer, *Odyssey* 17.221 ὃς πολλῆς φλιῇσι παραστὰς θλίψεται ὤμους." *Classical Quarterly* 49:315.

Jamison, S. 1999. "Penelope and the Pigs: Indic Perspectives on the *Odyssey.*" *Classical Antiquity* 18:227–272.

Janko, R. 1984. "P.Oxy. 2509: Hesiod's *Catalogue* on the Death of Actaeon." *Phoenix* 38:229–307.

Jeanmaire, H. 1939/1975. *Couroi et courètes: essai sur l'éducation spartiate et sur les rites d'adolescence dans l'antiquité hellénique.* Lille.

———. 1951. *Dionysos; histoire du culte de Bacchus: l'orgiasme dans l'antiquité et les temps modernes, origine du théâtre en Grèce, orphisme et mystique dionysiaque, évolution du dionysisme après Alexandre.* Paris.

Johnston, S. I. 1994. "Penelope and the Erinyes: *Odyssey* 20.61–82." *Helios* 21:137–159.

———. 2002. "Myth, Festival, and Poet: The 'Homeric Hymn to Hermes' and Its Performative Context." *Classical Philology* 97:109–132.

Kaczyńska, E. 2000. "Równina Omfalijska w Kallimachowym *Hymnie na Dzeusa* (w.42–45)." *Eos* 87:101–111.

Kadletz, E. 1984. "The Sacrifice of Eumaios the Pig Herder." *Greek, Roman and Byzantine Studies* 25:99–105.

Kakridis, J. T. 1987. *Homeric Researches*. New York.

Kamptz, H. von. 1982. *Homerische Personennamen: sprachwissenschaftliche und historische Klassifikation*. Göttingen.

Karetsou, A., ed. 2000. *Krete-Aigyptos. Politismikoi desmoi trion chilietion. Meletes*. Athens.

Katz, M. A. 1991. *Penelope's Renown: Meaning and Indeterminacy in the Odyssey*. Princeton.

Kazazis, J. N. and Rengakos, A. 1999. *Euphrosyne: Studies in Ancient Epic and its Legacy in Honor of Dimitris N. Maronitis*. Stuttgart.

Kelly, A. 2007. *A Referential Commentary and Lexicon to Iliad VIII*. Oxford.

King, B. 1999. "The Rhetoric of the Victim: Odysseus in the Swineherd's Hut." *Classical Antiquity* 18:74–93.

Kirk, Geoffrey S. 1971. *Myth: Its Meaning and Functions in Ancient and Other Cultures*. Cambridge.

———. 1974. *The Nature of Greek Myths*. Harmondsworth.

———. 1985. *The Iliad: A Commentary*. Vol.1. Cambridge.

Koller, H. 1973. "Λυκάβας." *Glotta* 51:29–34.

Kretschmer, P. 1896. *Einleitung in die Geschichte der griechischen Sprache*. Göttingen.

———. 1945. "Penelope." *Anzeiger der Akademie der Wissenshaften in Wien* 82:80–93.

Kurke, L. 1991. *The Traffic in Praise: Pindar and the Poetics of Social Economy*. Ithaca.

Lang, M. L. 1983. "Reverberation and Mythology in the *Iliad*." In Rubino and Shelmerdine, eds. 1983:140–164.

Lebessi, A. 1981. "*Synecheia tes Kretomykenaikes threskeias. Anabioseis kai Epibioseis*." *Archaiologike Ephemeris* 1981:1–24.

———. 1985. *To iero tou Erme kai tes Aphrodites sten Syme Viannou I.1: Khalkina Kretika Toreumata*. Athens.

———. 2000. "*Antifegismata kai Diathlaseis apo Aigypto sto Iero tes Symes*." In Karetsou 2000:174–183.

Leitao, D. D. 1995. "The Perils of Leukippos: Initiatory Transvestism and Male Ideology in the Ekdusia." *Classical Antiquity* 14:130–163.

Leumann, M. 1950. *Homerische Wörter*. Basel.

Levaniouk, O. A. 1999. "Penelope and the *Pênelops*." In Carlisle and Levaniouk 1999:95–136.

———. 2000a. "Aithôn, Aithon, and Odysseus." *Harvard Studies in Classical Philology* 100:25–51.

———. 2000b. Odyssean Usages of Local Traditions. PhD diss., Harvard University.

———. 2007. "The Toys of Dionysos" *HSCP* 103:165-202

Lobel, E. 1964. *The Oxyrhynchus Papyri*, Part XXX. London.

Lonsdale, S H. 1995. "A Dancing Floor for Ariadne (*Iliad* 18.590–592): Aspects of Ritual Movement in Homer and Minoan Religion." In Carter and Morris 1995:273–284.

Loraux, N. 1987. *Tragic Ways of Killing a Woman.* Cambridge, MA.

Lord, A B. 1960. *The Singer of Tales.* Cambridge, MA. 2ⁿᵈ edition 2000.

Lorimer, H L. 1950. *Homer and the Monuments.* London.

Lowenstam, S. 1981. *The Death of Patroklos: A Study in Typology.* Königstein im Taunus.

———. 1993. *The Scepter and the Spear. Studies on Forms of Repetition in the Homeric Poems.* Lanham.

———. 2000. "The shroud of Laertes and Penelope's guile." *CJ* 95: 333-348.

Malkin, I. 1998. *The Returns of Odysseus: Colonization and Ethnicity.* Berkeley.

Marinatos, N. 1993. *Minoan Religion: Ritual, Image, and Symbol.* Columbia.

———. 2003. "Striding across Boundaries: Hermes and Aphrodite as Gods of Initiation." In Dodd and Faraone 2003:130–151.

Marinatos, S. 1929. Ἀνασκαφαὶ ἐν Κρήτῃ. *Praktika tes en Athenais Archaiologikes Hetaireias* 94-104.

———. 1930. Ἀνασκαφαὶ ἐν Κρήτῃ. *Praktika tes en Athenais Archaiologikes Hetaireias* 91-99.

Marquardt, P. 1985. "Penelope 'Πολύτροπος'." *American Journal of Philology* 106:32–48.

Martin, R. P. 1984. "Hesiod, Odysseus, and the Instruction of Princes." *Transactions of the American Philological Association* 114:29–48.

———. 1989. *The Language of Heroes: Speech and Performance in the Iliad.* Ithaca.

Massé, H. 1959. *Le Roman de Wîs et Râmîn.* Paris.

McDonald, W. E. 1997. "On Hearing the Silent Voice: Penelope and the Daughters of Pandareus." *Helios* 24:3–22.

McKay, K. J. 1959. "Studies in Aithon." *Mnemosyne* 12:12–13.

———. 1962. *Erysichthon: A Callimachean Comedy.* Leiden.

Merkelbach, R. and West, M. L. 1967. *Fragmenta Hesiodea.* Oxford.

Meuli, K. 1921. *Odyssee und Argonautika; Untersuchungen zur griechischen Sagengeschichte und zum Epos.* Berlin.

———. 1946. "Griechische Opferbräuche." In Gigon et al. 1946:185–288.

———. 1968 (1926). *Der griechische Agon: Kampf und Kampfspiel im Totenbrauch, Totentanz, Totenklage, und Totenlob.* Cologne.

Mihailov, G. 1955. *La légende de Térée. Annuaire de l'Université de Sofia* 50 (2):77–197.

Minchin, E. 2007. *Homeric Voices: Discourse, Memory, Gender.* Oxford.

Mondi, R. J. 1980. "ΣΚΗΠΤΟΥΧΟΙ ΒΑΣΙΛΕΙΣ: An Argument for Divine Kingship in Early Greece." *Arethusa* 13:203–216.

Montanari, F. and Ascheri, P., eds. 2002. *Omero tremila anni dopo.* Rome.

Morrison, G. 1972. *Vis and Ramin. Translated from the Persian of Fakhr ud-Dîn Gurgânî.* New York.

Most, G. W. 1983. "Of Motifemes and Megatexts: Comment on Rubin/Sale and Segal." *Arethusa* 16:199–218.

Müller, F. M. 1897. *Contributions to the Science of Mythology.* London.

Muellner, L. 1976. *The Meaning of Homeric EYXOMAI though its Formulas.* Innsbruck.

———. 1990. "The Simile of the Cranes and Pygmies. A Study of Homeric Metaphor." *Harvard Studies in Classical Philology* 93:59–101.

———. 1996. *The Anger of Achilles: Menis in Greek Epic.* Ithaca.

———. 1998. "Glaucus Redivivus." *Harvard Studies in Classical Philology* 98:1–30.

Murnaghan, S. 1986. "Penelope's *Agnoia*: Knowledge, Power, and Gender in the *Odyssey*." *Helios* 13:103–115.

———. 1987. *Disguise and Recognition in the Odyssey.* Princeton.

Murray, G. 1908–1909. "The Hymn of the Kouretes." *Annual of the British School at Athens* 15:357–365.

Murray, J. 2005. "The Constructions of the Argo in Apollonius' *Argonautica*." In Harder and Cuypers, eds. 2005:88–106.

Murray, R. 1965. "Theognis 341-50." *Transactions of the American Philological Association* 96:277–281.

Mylonas, G. E., ed. 1951. *Studies Presented to David Moore Robinson on his Seventieth Birthday.* Vol. 1, *Prehistoric Greece, Egypt and the Far East, Architecture and Topography, Sculpture, Paintings and Mosaics.* Saint Louis.

Naiden, F. 1999. "Homer's Leopard Simile." In Carlisle and Levaniouk 1999:177–206.

Nagler, M. N. 1974. *Spontaneity and Tradition: A Study in the Oral Art of Homer.* Berkeley.

———. 1990. "Ethical Anxiety and Artistic Inconsistency: The Case of Oral Epic." In Griffith and Mastronarde, eds. 1990:225–239.

Nagy, G. 1969. Review of John Chadwick, *The Decipherment of Linear B* (2nd ed. Cambridge 1967). *General Linguistics* 9:123–132.

———. 1979. *The Best of the Achaeans: Concepts of the Hero in Archaic Greek Poetry.* Baltimore. Revised edition, 1999.

———. 1983. "*Sêma* and *Noesis*: Some Illustrations." *Arethusa* 16:35–55.

———. 1985. "Theognis and Megara: A Poet's Vision of his City." In Figueira and Nagy 1985:22–81.

——. 1990a. *Pindar's Homer: The Lyric Possession of an Epic Past.* Baltimore.

——. 1990b. *Greek Mythology and Poetics.* Ithaca.

——. 1996a. *Poetry as Performance: Homer and beyond.* Cambridge.

——. 1996b. *Homeric Questions.* Austin.

——. 1999. "Irreversible Mistakes and Homeric Poetry." In Kazazis and Rengakos 1999:259–274.

——. 2000. Review of M.L. West 1998–2000. *Bryn Mawr Classical Review* 2000.09.12 http://bmcr.brynmawr.edu/2000/2000-09-12.html. Reprinted in Nagy 2004a:75–109.

——. 2002. "The Language of Heroes as Mantic Poetry. *Hypokrisis* in Homer." In Reichel and Rengakos 2002:141–149.

——. 2004. *Homer's Text and Language.* Urbana.

——. 2005. "The Epic Hero." In Foley 2005.71-89.

——. 2007a. "Homer and Greek Myth." In Woodard 2007:52-82.

——. 2007b. "Lyric and Greek Myth." In Woodard 2007:19-51.

——. 2009. *Homer the Classic.* Hellenic Studies 36. Washington, D.C.

——. Forthcoming. *Homer the Preclassic.* Berkeley.

Newton, R. M. 1984. "The Rebirth of Odysseus." *Greek, Roman and Byzantine Studies* 25:5–20.

——. 1998. "Cloak and Shield in *Odyssey* 14." *Classical Journal* 93:143–156.

Ní Shéaghdha, N., ed. 1967. *Tóruigheacht Dhiarmuda agus Ghráinne.* Irish Texts Society, Series 48. Dublin.

Nieto Hernández, P. 2008. "Penelope's Absent Song." *Phoenix* 62:39-62.

Nilsson, Martin P. 1906. *Griechische Feste von religiöser Bedeutung mit Ausschluss der attischen.* Leipzig.

——. 1933. *Homer and Mycenae.* London.

——. 1950. *The Minoan-Mycenaean Religion and its Survival in Greek Religion.* Lund.

——. 1955. *Geschichte der griechischen Religion.* Vol. 1, *Die Religion Griechenlands bis auf die griechische Weltherrschaft.* München.

van Nortwick, T. 1979. "Penelope and Nausicaa." *Transactions of the American Philological Association* 109:269–276.

Notopoulos, J. A. 1949. "Parataxis in Homer: A New Approach to Homeric Literary Criticism." *Transactions of the American Philological Association* 80:1–23.

Olson, Douglas S. 1989. "*Odyssey* 8: Guile, Force and the Subversive Poetics of Desire." *Arethusa* 22:135–145.

Ong, Walter J. 1981. *Fighting for Life: Contest, Sexuality, and Consciousness.* Ithaca.

Otto, W. F. 1981. *Les dieux de la Grèce: La figure du divin au miroir de l'esprit grec.* Paris.

Padilla, M. W., ed. 1999. *Rites of Passage in Ancient Greece: Literature, Religion, Society.* London.

Page, D. 1937. "A New Fragment of a Greek Tragedy." *Classical Quarterly* 31:178–181.

Papadopoulou-Belmehdi, I. 1992. *L'art de Pandora: La mythologie du tissage en Grèce ancienne.* EHESS. Lille.

———. 1994. *Le chant de Pénélope: Poétique du tissage féminin dans l'Odyssée.* Paris.

Parker, R. 1988. "Demeter, Dionysus and the Spartan Pantheon." In Hägg, Marinatos and Nordquist 1988:99-103.

Pélékidis, C. 1962. *Histoire de l'Éphébie attique des origines à 31 avant Jésus-Christ.* Paris.

Penkovsky, L. M. 1982. *Alpamysh: Uzbekskii narodnyi epos.* Translated from Uzbek. Leningrad.

Peradotto, J. 1990. *Man in the Middle Voice: Name and Narration in the Odyssey.* Princeton.

———. 2002. "Prophecy and Persons: Reading Character in the *Odyssey.*" *Arethusa* 35:3–15.

Perlman, P. J. 1995. "Invocation and Imprecation: The Hymn to the Greatest Kouros from Palaikastro and the Oath in Ancient Crete." *Journal of Hellenic Studies* 115:161–167.

Petropoulou, A. 1987. "The Sacrifice of Eumaeus Reconsidered." *Greek, Roman and Byzantine Studies* 28:135–149.

Pettersson, M. 1992. *Cults of Apollo at Sparta: The Hyakinthia, the Gymnopaidiai and the Karneia.* Stockholm.

Polinskaya, I. 2003. "Liminality as Metaphor: Initiation and the Frontiers of Ancient Athens." In Dodds and Faraone 2003:85–106.

Powell, J. U. 1925/1970. *Collectanea Alexandrina.* Oxford.

Pozzi, D. C. and Wickersham, J. M., eds. 1991. *Myth and the Polis.* Ithaca.

Pratt, L. H. 1994. "*Odyssey* 19.535–50: On the Interpretation of Dreams and Signs in Homer." *Classical Philology* 89:147–152.

Pretagostini, R., ed. 1993. *Tradizione e innovazione nella cultura greca da Omero all'età ellenistica: Scritti in onore di Bruno Gentili.* Rome.

Propp, V. 1928. Morfologia Skazki. Leningrad.

———. 1958. *Morphology of the Folktale.* Translated by Laurence Scott. Bloomington.

Pucci, P. 1987. *Odysseus Polutropos: Intertextual Readings in the Odyssey and the Iliad.* Ithaca.

Rankin, A. V. 1962. "Penelope's Dreams in Books XIX and XX of the *Odyssey.*" *Helikon* 2:617–24.

Redfield, J. M. 1975. *Nature and Culture in the Iliad: The Tragedy of Hector.* Chicago.

———. 1983. "The Economic Man." In Rubino and Shelmerdine 1983:218–247.

Reichel, M. and Rengakos, A. 2002. *Epea pteroenta: Beiträge zur Homerforschung: Festschrift für Wolfgang Kullmann zum 75. Geburtstag.* Stuttgart.

Reichl, K. 2001. *Das usbekische Heldenepos Alpomish: Einführung, Text, Übersetzung.* Wiesbaden.

Reinhardt, K. 1961. *Die Ilias und ihr Dichter.* Ed. U. Hölscher. Göttingen.

Renner, T. 1978. "Four Michigan Papyri of Classical Greek Authors." *Zeitschrift für Papyrologie und Epigraphik* 29:5–28.

Richardson, N. J. 1974. *The Homeric Hymn to Demeter.* Oxford.

Richter, G. M. A. 1950. *The Sculpture and Sculptors of the Greeks.* New Haven.

Risch, E. 1977. *Wortbildung der homerischen Sprache.* Berlin.

Robert, C. 1892. *Die Nekyia des Polygnot.* Hallisches Winckelmannsprogramm 16. Halle.

Robertson, N. 1991. "The Betrothal Symposium in Early Greece." In Slater 1991:25–57.

Roes, A. 1951. "Une fibule étrusque du Musée de Dijon." *Mnemosyne* 4:216–222.

Roessel, D. 1989. "The Stag on Circe's Island: An Exegesis of a Homeric Digression." *Transactions of the American Philological Association* 119:31–36.

Rohde, E. 1925. *Psyche: The Cult of Souls and Belief in Immortality among the Greeks.* London.

Roisman, H. M. 1987. "Penelope's Indignation." *Transactions of the American Philological Association* 117:59–68.

——. 1990. "Eumaeus and Odysseus—Covert Recognition and Self-Revelation?" *Illinois Classical Studies* 15:215–238.

——. 1994. "Like Father Like Son: Telemachus' *Kerdea.*" *Rheinisches Museum für Philologie* 137:1–22.

——. 2002. "Alice and Penelope: Female Indignation in *Eyes Wide Shut* and the *Odyssey.*" *Mouseion* 36:341–364.

Roscher, W. H. 1886–1903. *Ausführliches Lexikon der griechischen und römischen Mythologie.* Leipzig.

Rose, G. P. 1979. "Odysseus' Barking Heart." *Transactions of the American Philological Association* 109:215–230.

Rozokoki, A. 2001. "Penelope's Dream in Book 19 of the *Odyssey.*" *Classical Quarterly* 51:1–6.

Rubino, C. A. and Shelmerdine, C. W., eds. 1983. *Approaches to Homer.* Austin.

Ruijgh, C. J. 1957. *L'élément achéen dans la langue épique.* Assen.

——. 1967. *Études sur la grammaire et le vocabulaire du grec mycénien.* Amsterdam.

Russo, J. 1974. "The Inner Man in Archilochus and the *Odyssey.*" *Greek, Roman and Byzantine Studies* 15:139–52.

——. 1982. "Interview and Aftermath: Dream, Fantasy, and Intuition in *Odyssey* 19 and 20." *American Journal of Philology* 103:4–18.

——. 1985. *Omero, Odissea*. Vol.5, *Libri XVII–XX. Introduzione, testo e commento.* Rome.

——. 1992. *Books XVII–XX*. In Russo, Fernandez-Galiano and Heubeck 1192:3–127 .

——. 1993. "*Odyssey* 19.440–443, the Boar in the Bush: Formulaic Repetition and Narrative Innovation." In Pretagostini 1993:51–59.

——. 2004. "Odysseus' Trial of the Bow as Symbolic Performance" In Bierl et al. 2004:95–102.

Russo, J., Fernandez-Galiano, M. and Heubeck, A. 1992. *A Commentary on Homer's Odyssey*. Vol. 3, *Books XVII–XXIV*. Oxford.

Rutherford, R. B. 1992. *Homer: Odyssey Books XIX and XX*. Cambridge, MA.

Rutkowski, B. 1986. *The Cult Places of the Aegean*. New Haven.

Rutkowski, B. and Nowicki, K. 1996. *The Psychro Cave and Other Sacred Grottoes in Crete*. Warsaw.

Sansone, D. 1988. *Greek Athletics and the Genesis of Sport*. Berkeley.

Saunier, G. 1983. *Τό Δημοτικό Τραγούδι τῆς Ξενιτιᾶς*. Athens.

Schachter, A. 1981. *Cults of Boiotia*. Vol. 1, *Acheloos to Hera*. London.

——. 1986. *Cults of Boiotia*. Vol. 2, *Herakles to Poseidon*. London.

Schäfer, J., ed. 1992. *Amnisos: Nach den archäologischen, topographischen, historischen und epigraphischen Zeugnissen des Altertums und der Neuzeit.* Berlin.

Schein, S. 1995. "Female Representations and Interpreting the *Odyssey*." In Cohen 1995:17–28.

——., ed. 1996. *Reading the Odyssey: Selected Interpretive Essays*. Princeton.

Schelmerdine, S. 1986. "Odyssean Allusions in the Fourth Homeric Hymn." *Transactions of the American Philological Association* 116:49–63.

Schmitt, R. 1967. *Dichtung und Dichtersprache in indogermanischer Zeit.* Wiesbaden.

Schnapp-Gourbeillon, A. 1981. *Lions, héros, masques: Les représentations de l'animal chez Homère*. Paris.

Schwartz, E. 1924. *Die Odyssee*. Munich.

Schultze, W. 1933. *Kleine Schriften*. Göttingen.

Scodel, R. 2001. "The Suitors' Games." *American Journal of Philology* 122:307–327.

——. 2002. *Listening to Homer: Tradition, Narrative, and Audience*. Ann Arbor.

Séchan, L. 1967. *Études sur la tragédie grecque dans ses rapports avec la céramique*. Paris.

Segal, C. P. 1962. "The Phaeacians and the Symbolism of Odysseus' return." *Arion* 1:17–64.

——. 1967. "Transition and Ritual in Odysseus' Return." *La Parola del Passato* 116:321–342.

——. 1971. *The Theme of the Mutilation of the Corpse in the Iliad*. Leiden.

———. 1994. *Singers, Heroes, and Gods in the Odyssey*. Ithaca.

Slater, W J., ed. 1991. *Dining in a Classical Context*. Ann Arbor.

Slatkin, L. M. 1986. "The Wrath of Thetis." *Transactions of the American Philological Association* 116:1–24.

———. 1991. *The Power of Thetis: Allusion and Interpretation in the Iliad*. Berkeley.

———. 1996. "Composition by Theme and the *Metis* of the *Odyssey*." In Schein 1996:223–237.

Snell, B. 1931. "Joachim Böhme: Die Seele und das Ich im homerischen Epos." *Gnomon* 7:74–86.

Snowden, F. M. 1970. *Blacks in Antiquity: Ethiopians in the Greco-Roman Experience*. Cambridge, MA.

Snyder, J. M. 1980–1981. "The Web of Song: Weaving Imagery in Homer and the Lyric Poets." *Classical Journal* 76:193–196.

Sotiriadis, G. 1903. "Anaskaphai en Thermo." *Archaiologike Ephemeris* 71–96.

Sourvinou-Inwood, C. 1991. *"Reading" Greek Culture: Texts and Images, Rituals and Myths*. Oxford, London.

Sporn, K. 2002. *Heiligtümer und Kulte Kretas in klassischer und hellenistischer Zeit*. Heidelberg.

Stanford, W. B. 1952. "The Homeric Etymology of the Name Odysseus." *Classical Philology* 47:209–213.

———. 1965. *The Odyssey of Homer*. London.

Sulzberger M., 1926. "Ὄνομα ἐπώνυμων. Les noms propres chez Homère et dans la mythologie grecque." *Revue des études grecques* 39: 381–447.

Suter, A. 2002. *The Narcissus and the Pomegranate: An Archaeology of the Homeric Hymn to Demeter*. Ann Arbor.

Sutton, D. F. 1984. *The Lost Sophocles*. Lanham.

Svenbro, J. 1976. *La parole et le marbre: Aux origins de la poétique grecque*. Lund.

Szemerenyi, O. 1974. "The Origins of the Greek Lexicon: *Ex oriente lux*." *Journal of Hellenic Studies* 94:144–57.

Taylor, C. H., ed. 1963. *Essays on the Odyssey, Selected Modern Criticism*. Bloomington.

Thompson, D. W. 1936. *A Glossary of Greek Birds*. London.

Toepffer, J. 1889. *Attische Genealogie*. Berlin.

Trahman, C. 1952. "Odysseus' Lies (*Odyssey*, Books 13–19)." *Phoenix* 34:285–297.

Van der Valk, M. H. A. L. H. 1949. *Textual Criticism of the Odyssey*. Leiden.

Van Gennep, A. 1909. *Les rites de passage*. Paris.

———. 1977. *The Rites of Passage*. Translated by Monika B. Vizedom and Gabrielle L. Caffee. London.

Vermeule, E. 1979. *Aspects of Death in Early Greek Art and Poetry*. Berkeley.

Versnel, H. S. 1985. "Apollo and Mars One Hundred Years after Roscher." *Visible Religion* 4–5:134–172.

———. 1993. *Transition and Reversal in Myth and Ritual*. Leiden.

Vian, F. 1960. "La triade des rois d'Orchomene: Etéoclès, Phlégyas, Minyas." *Hommages à Georges Dumézil.* Collection Latomus 45:215–224. Brussels.

Vidal-Naquet, P. 1983. *The Black Hunter.* Baltimore.

Waldner, K. 2000. *Geburt und Hochzeit des Kriegers: Geschlechterdifferenz und Initiation in Mythos und Ritual der griechischen Polis.* Berlin.

Watkins, C. 1979. "*Is tre fír flathemon*: Marginalia on Audacht Morainn." *Ériu* 30:181–198.

———. 1994. "NAM.RA GUD UDU in Hittite: Indo-European Poetic Language and the Folk Taxonomy of Wealth." In Watkins 1994a:644–662.

———. 1994a. *Selected Writings.* Innsbrucker Beitrage zur Sprachwissenschaft 80. Innsbruck.

———. 1995. *How to Kill a Dragon: Aspects of Indo-European Poetics.* New York.

Webster, T. and Green, J. 1960. *Monuments Illustrating Old and Middle Comedy.* Bulletin de correspondance hellénique, Supplement 9. London.

West, M. 1965. "The Dictaean Hymn to the Kouros." *Journal of Hellenic Studies* 85:149–159.

———, ed. 1966. *Hesiod: Theogony.* Oxford.

———. 1985. *The Hesiodic Catalogue of Women: Its Nature, Structure, and Origins.* Oxford.

———. 1998–2000. *Homeri Ilias,* 2 vols. Leipzig.

———. 2001a. *Studies in the Text and Transmission of the Iliad.* Stuttgart.

———. 2001b. Reply to Nagy 2000. *Bryn Mawr Classical Review* 2001.01.03, http://bmcr.brynmawr.edu/2001/2001-01-03.html/.

———. 2003. "*Iliad* and *Aethiopis.*" *Classical Quarterly* 53:1–14.

———. 2007. *Indo-European Poetry and Myth.* Oxford.

West, S. 1988. "The Transmission of the Text." In Heubeck, West, and Hainsworth 1988:33–48.

Whitman, C. H. 1958. *Homer and the Heroic Tradition.* Cambridge, MA.

Wilamowitz-Moellendorff, U. von. 1884. *Homerische Untersuchungen.* Berlin.

———. 1927. *Die Heimkehr des Odysseus.* Berlin.

———. 1931. *Der Glaube der Hellenen.* Berlin.

Wilcock, M. 1964. "Mythological *Paradeigma* in the *Iliad.*" *Classical Quarterly* 14:141–154.

———. 1977. "Ad Hoc Invention in the *Iliad.*" *Harvard Studies in Classical Philology* 81:41–53.

Willetts, R. F. 1962. *Cretan Cults and Festivals.* London.

Winkler, J. J. 1990. *The Constraints of Desire: The Anthropology of Sex and Gender in Ancient Greece.* New York.

Wohl, V. 1993. "Standing by the *Stathmos*: The Creation of Sexual Ideology in the *Odyssey.*" *Arethusa* 26:19–50.

Wolters, P. and Bruns, G., 1940. *Das Kabirenheiligtum bei Theben.* Das Kabirenheiligtum bei Theben 1. Berlin.

Woodard, R., ed. 2007. *The Cambridge Companion to Greek Mythology*. Cambridge.
Woodhouse, W. 1930. *The Composition of Homer's Odyssey*. Oxford.
Zeitlin, F. 1995. "Figuring Fidelity in Homer's *Odyssey*." In Cohen 1995:117-152.
Zhirmunsky, V. 1967. "The Epic of Alpamysh and the Return of Odysseus."
    Proceedings of the British Academy 52:267–86 London.

INDEX LOCORUM

INDEX OF SUBJECTS

games: at the Hermaia in Pellene, 121, 126; Eleusinian, 102; funeral, for Patroklos, 71, 76, 78, 134; of Lemnos, 134; of Phaeacians, at Skheria, 133; of the Argonauts on Lemnos, 133; on Lemnos, 123; Phaeacian, on Skheria, 69-72, 76, 119; Pythian, 82, 89

gaster (γαστήρ), 39, 48

geese, 229-233, 236, 237, 289, 291, 295; twenty, in Penelope's dream, 231, 232

geranos (γέρανος), 87, 88, 92

geron (γέρων), 77

gift exchange, 40

Glaukos, son of Minos, 103

Greatest Kouros, Hymn to, 104

gualon (γύαλον), 106

guros (γυρός): of shoulders, 155

halcyon, 291, 292, 297, 302, 303, 305, 306, 309, 318; and lament, 292; and *penelops*, 296, 298; compared to nightingale, 293; voice of, 293

halcyon days, 302

haliporphuris (ἁλιπορφυρίς), 291

haliporphuros (ἁλιπόρφυρος), 291

hebe (ἥβη), 70, 72, 75, 166, 180

Hecuba, 45, 47, 255

Hektor, 46, 47, 54, 55, 85, 86, 88, 91, 117, 139

Helen, 130, 226, 237, 238, 240, 255

Helios, 300, 301, 305, 306, 315

Hephaestus, 68, 72-74, 126-29, 132, 133

Hephaistia, city on Lemnos, 127, 128

Hera, 83, 94, 127, 151, 157, 275, 276, 296, 297

Hermaia, 64, 121, 126, 163

Hermes, 62, 63-66, 70-75, 126, 131, 149, 150, 162, 164, 301, 322

hero, 16, 41, 49, 62, 68, 79, 81, 120, 156, 162, 165, 173, 178, 183, 242, 306, 309, 310, 324

hero cult, 56, 309

Hesperos, 308

Hippolytus, 145, 299

Homeric Hymn 19 (to Pan), 17.18, 295n25

homophrosune (ὁμοφροσύνη), 211, 260

honey, 93, 96, 276, 297

honorific portion (of meat), 170, 171

hunt: and Aktaion's death, 146; and Atys, son of Croesus, 182; and coming of age, 103, 161, 180, 181, 188, 323; and grandsons of Cadmus, 151; and Learchus, 151; and Odysseus' pin, 142; and Pentheus, 150; and reversal, 146, 152; and sexuality, 183-185; and the festival of Apollo, 323; and young men, 141; at Kato Syme, 149; Calydonian, 181, 184, 187; deer and boar, 182; on Circe's island, 148; with maternal uncles, 180, 181, 185; *see also* boar hunt

hunter: Aktaion as, 145; and Artemis, 145; Atalanta as, 187; black, 161; Odysseus as, 139, 141, 146, 148, 161, 162, 180, 182; Orion as, 145; Telemachus as, 140, 141

hupar (ὕπαρ), 244-246

huphainein (ὑφαίνειν), 267

I